TSUBASA

20

CLAMP

TRANSLATED AND ADAPTED BY
William Flanagan

LETTERED BY
Dana Hayward

WITHDRAWN

BALLANTINE BOOKS • NEW YORK

Tsubasa, volume 20 is a work of fiction. Names, characters, places, and incidents are the products of the author's imagination or are used fictitiously. Any resemblance to actual events, locales, or persons, living or dead, is entirely coincidental.

A Del Rey Manga/Kodansha Trade Paperback Original

Published in the United States by Del Rey Books, an imprint of The Random House Publishing Group, a division of Random House, Inc., New York.

Publication rights arranged through Kodansha Ltd.

First published in Japan in 2007 by Kodansha Ltd., Tokyo

ISBN 978-0-345-50580-4

Printed in the United States of America

www.delreymanga.com

9 8 7 6 5 4 3 2 1

Translator/Adapter—William Flanagan
Lettering—Dana Hayward

Contents

Tsubasa crosses over with *xxxHOLiC*. Although it isn't necessary to read *xxxHOLiC* to understand the events in *Tsubasa*, you'll get to see the same events from different perspectives if you read both series!

Honorifics Explained

Throughout the Del Rey Manga books, you will find Japanese honorifics left intact in the translations. For those not familiar with how the Japanese use honorifics and, more important, how they differ from American honorifics, we present this brief overview.

Politeness has always been a critical facet of Japanese culture. Ever since the feudal era, when Japan was a highly stratified society, use of honorifics—which can be defined as polite speech that indicates relationship or status—has played an essential role in the Japanese language. When you address someone in Japanese, an honorific usually takes the form of a suffix attached to one's name (example: "Asuna-san"), is used as a title at the end of one's name, or appears in place of the name itself (example: "Negi-sensei," or simply "Sensei!").

Honorifics can be expressions of respect or endearment. In the context of manga and anime, honorifics give insight into the nature of the relationship between characters. Many English translations leave out these important honorifics and therefore distort the feel of the original Japanese. Because Japanese honorifics contain nuances that English honorifics lack, it is our policy at Del Rey not to translate them. Here, instead, is a guide to some of the honorifics you may encounter in Del Rey Manga.

-san: This is the most common honorific and is equivalent to Mr., Miss, Ms., or Mrs. It is the all-purpose honorific and can be used in any situation where politeness is required.

-sama: This is one level higher than "-san" and is used to confer great respect.

-dono: This comes from the word "tono," which means "lord." It is an even higher level than "-sama" and confers utmost respect.

-kun: This suffix is used at the end of boys' names to express familiarity or endearment. It is also sometimes used by men among friends, or when addressing someone younger or of a lower station.

-chan: This is used to express endearment, mostly toward girls. It is also used for little boys, pets, and even among lovers. It gives a sense of childish cuteness.

Bozu: This is an informal way to refer to a boy, similar to the English terms "kid" and "squirt."

Sempai/Senpai: This title suggests that the addressee is one's senior in a group or organization. It is most often used in a school setting, where underclassmen refer to their upperclassmen as "sempai." It can also be used in the workplace, such as when a newer employee addresses an employee who has seniority in the company.

Kohai: This is the opposite of "sempai" and is used toward underclassmen in school or newcomers in the workplace. It connotes that the addressee is of a lower station.

Sensei: Literally meaning "one who has come before," this title is used for teachers, doctors, or masters of any profession or art.

-[blank]: This is usually forgotten in these lists, but it is perhaps the most significant difference between Japanese and English. The lack of honorific means that the speaker has permission to address the person in a very intimate way. Usually, only family, spouses, or very close friends have this kind of permission. Known as *yobisute*, it can be gratifying when someone who has earned the intimacy starts to call one by one's name without an honorific. But when that intimacy hasn't been earned, it can be very insulting.

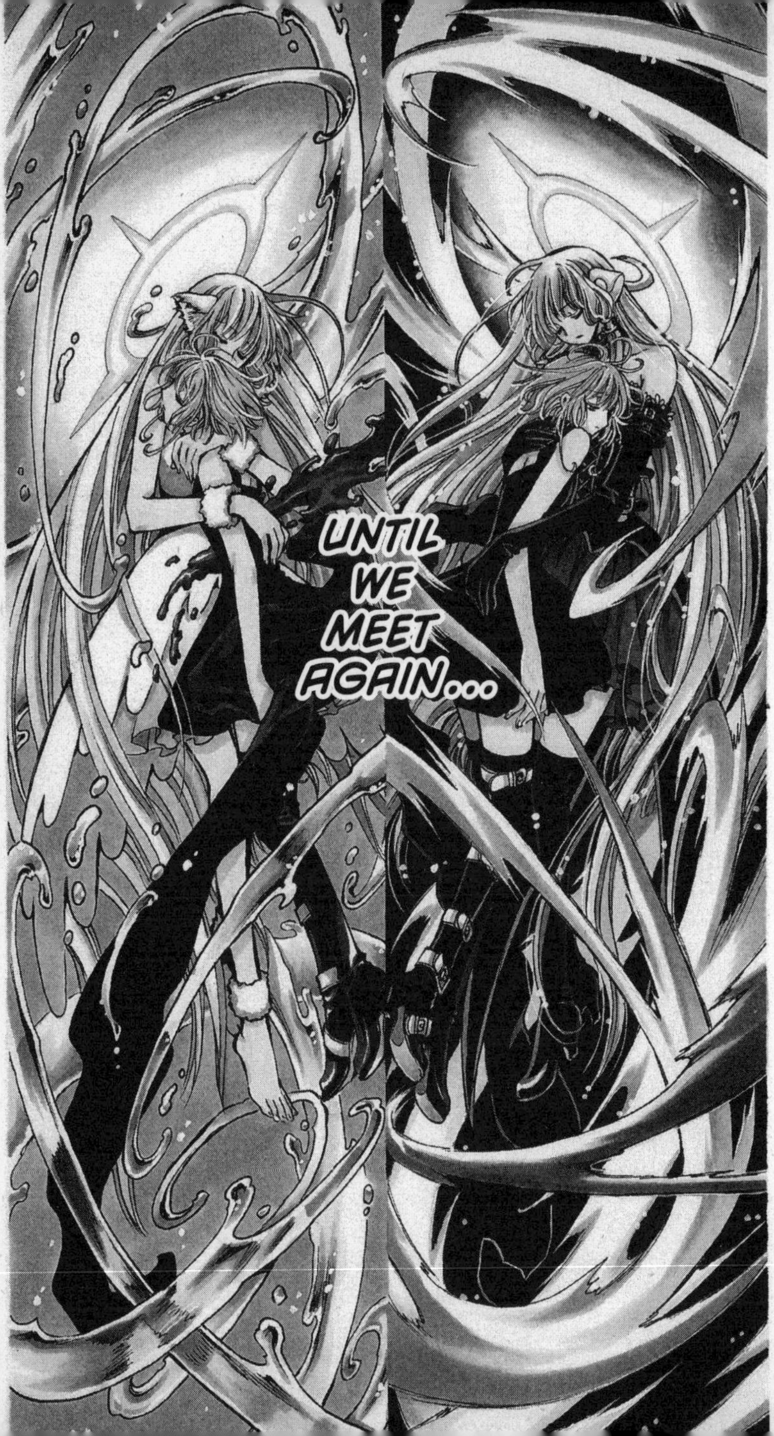
UNTIL WE MEET AGAIN...

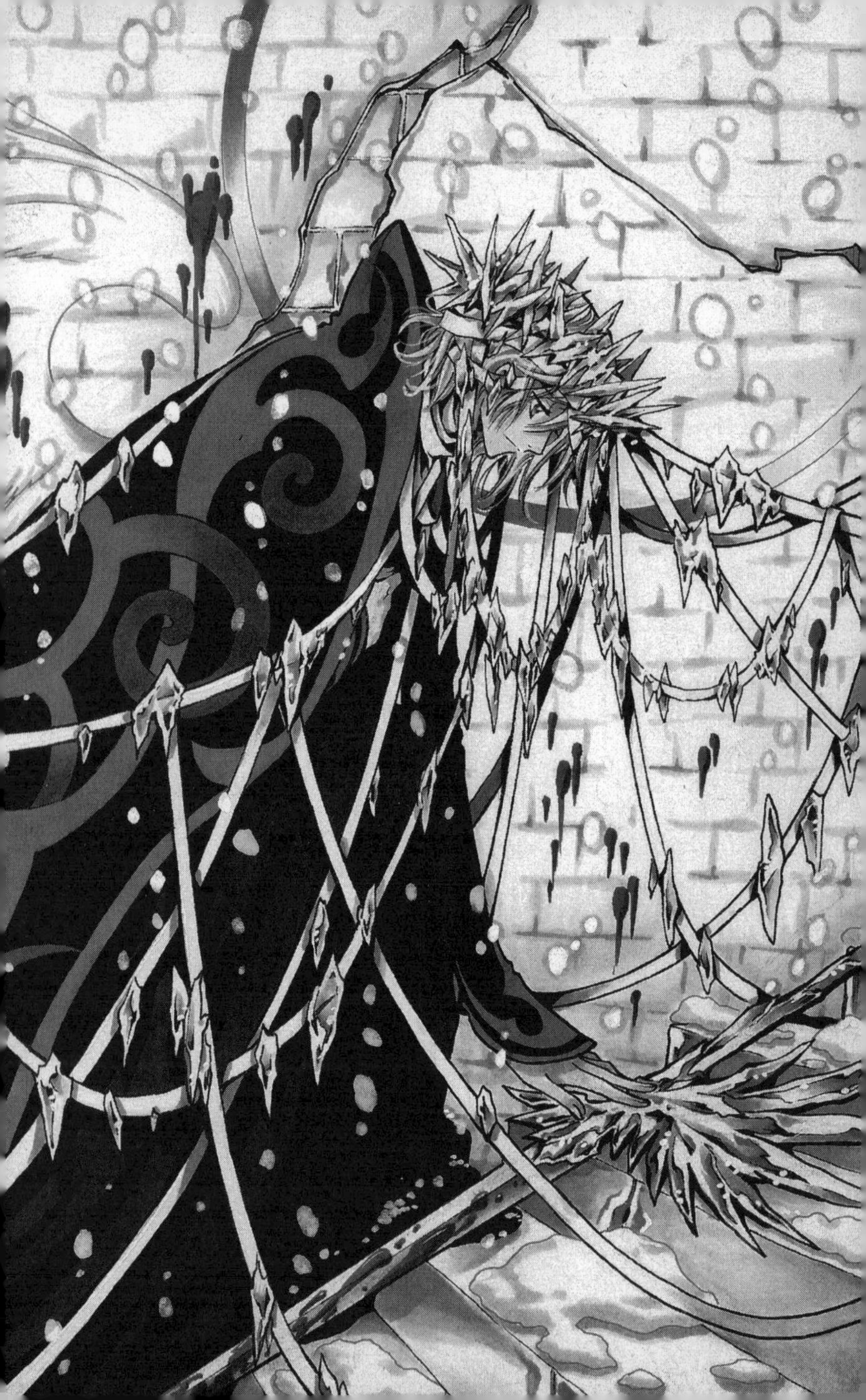

Chapitre. 150
Those Left Behind

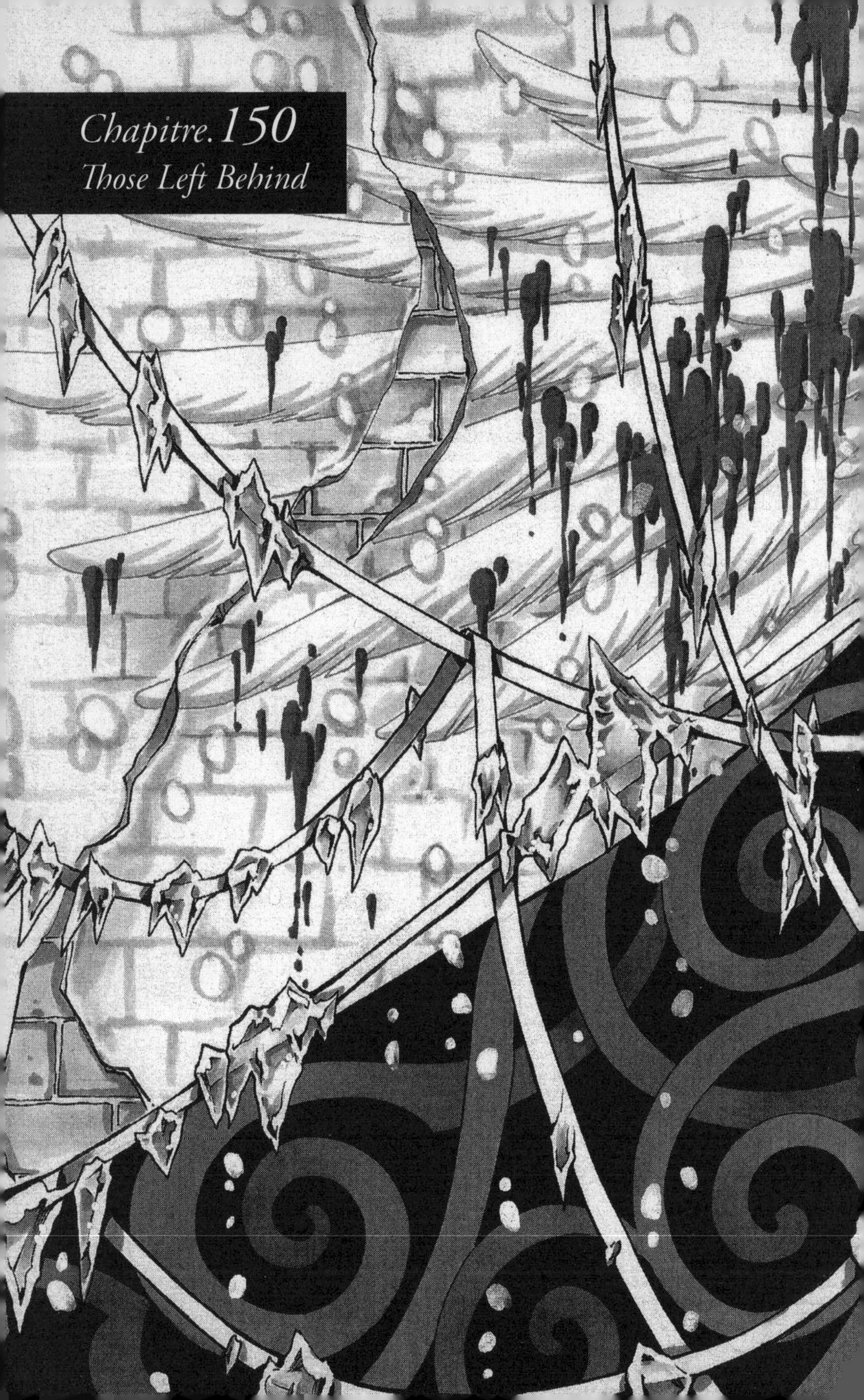

ツバサ

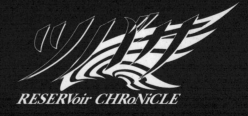

RESERVoir CHRoNiCLE

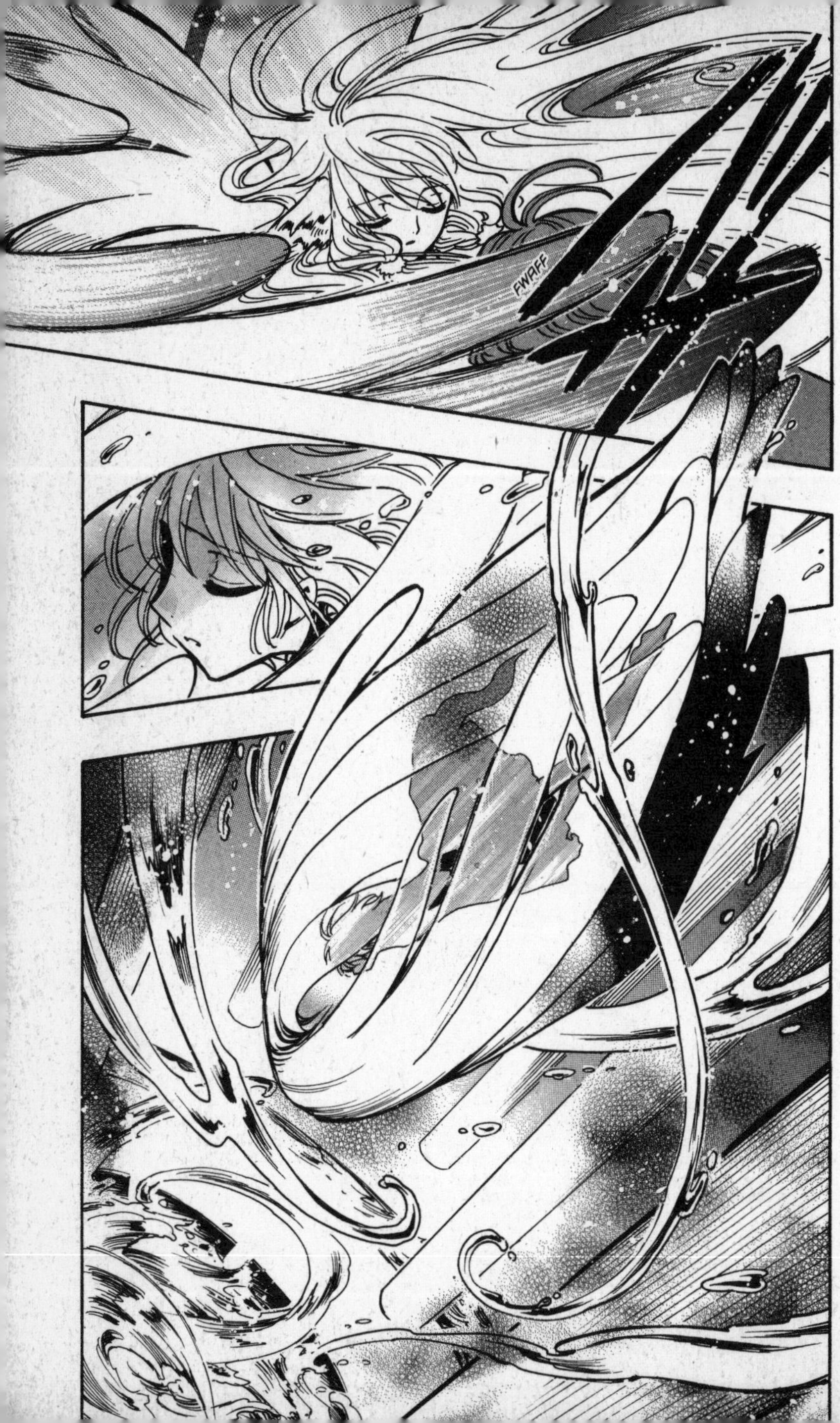
FWAFF

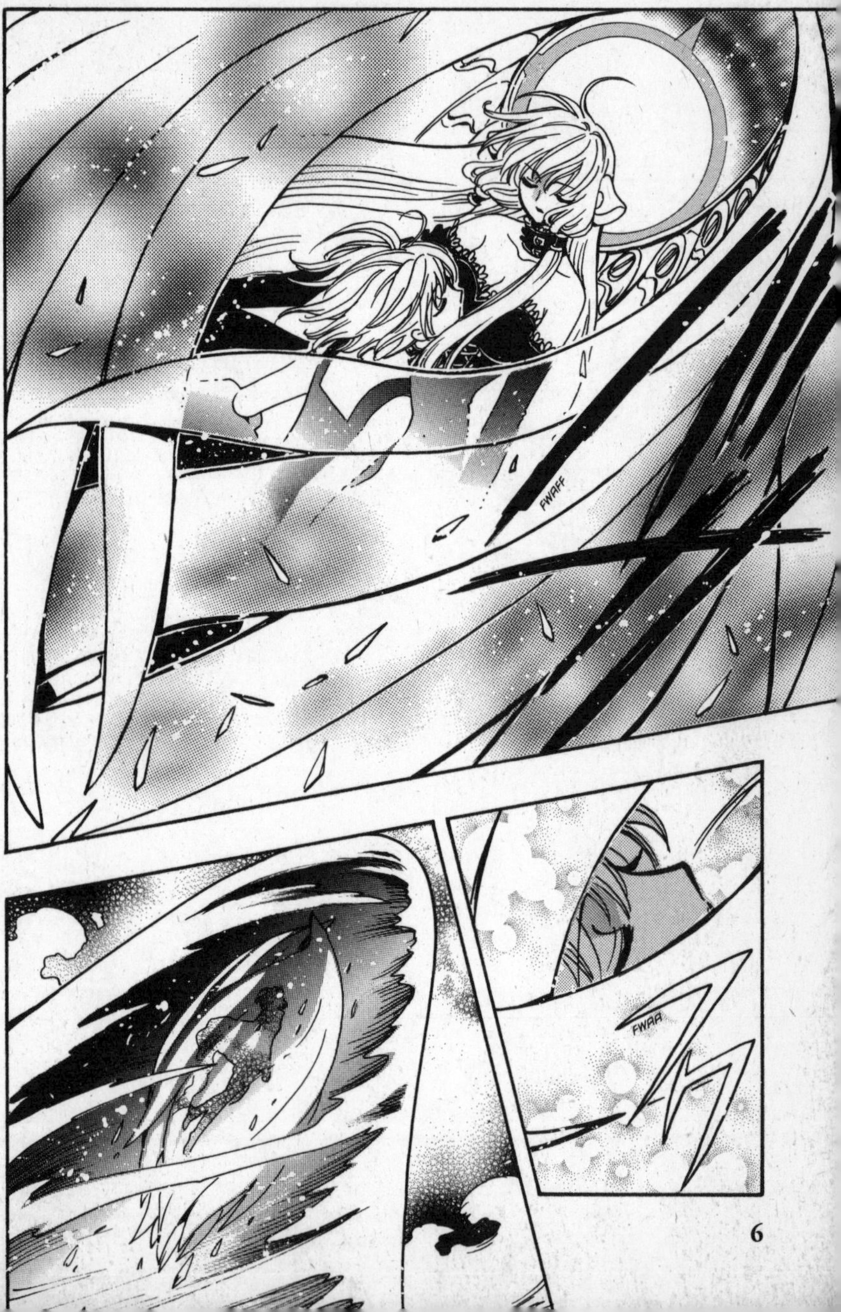
FWAFF
FWAA

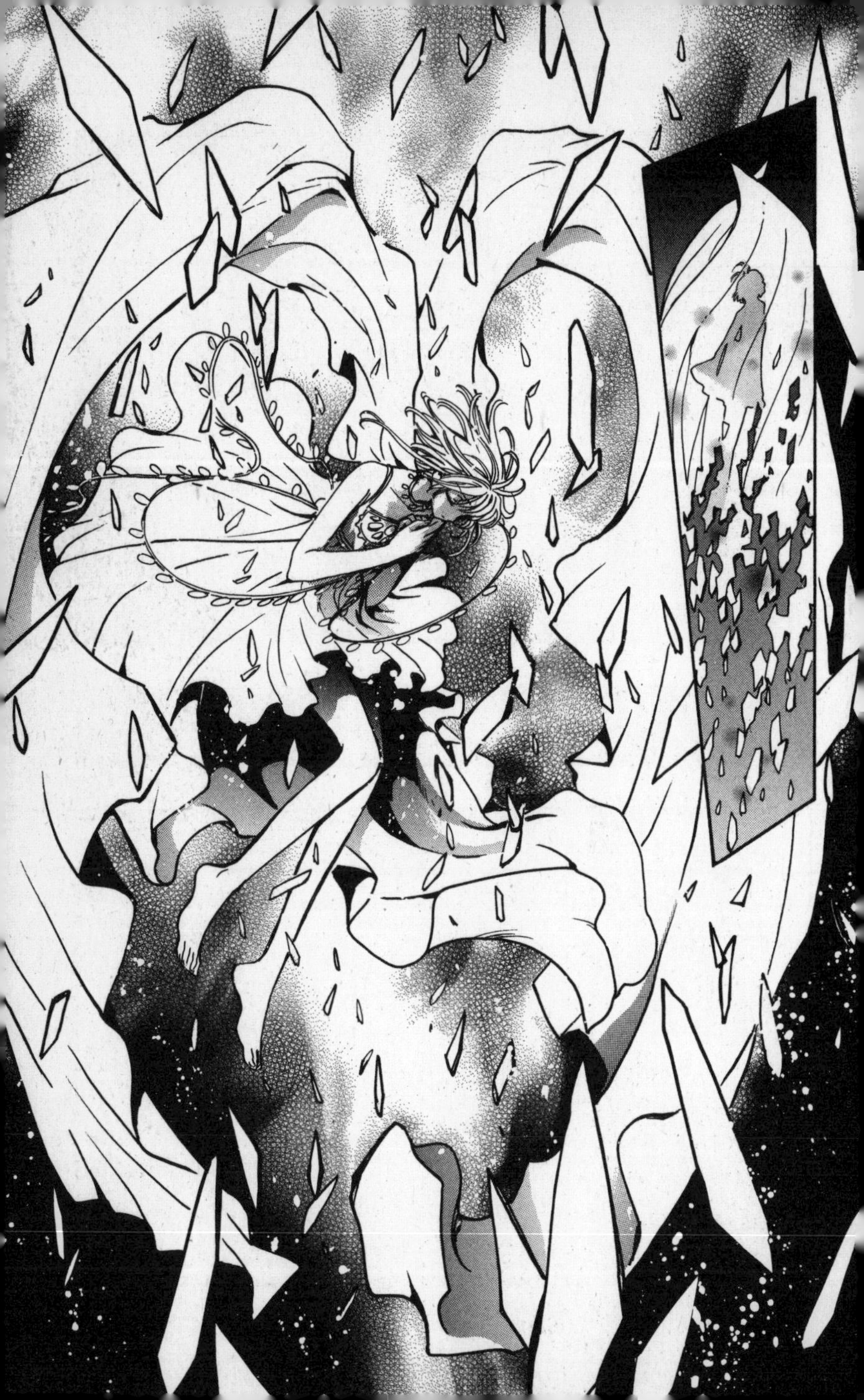

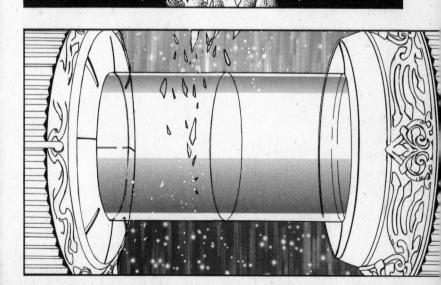

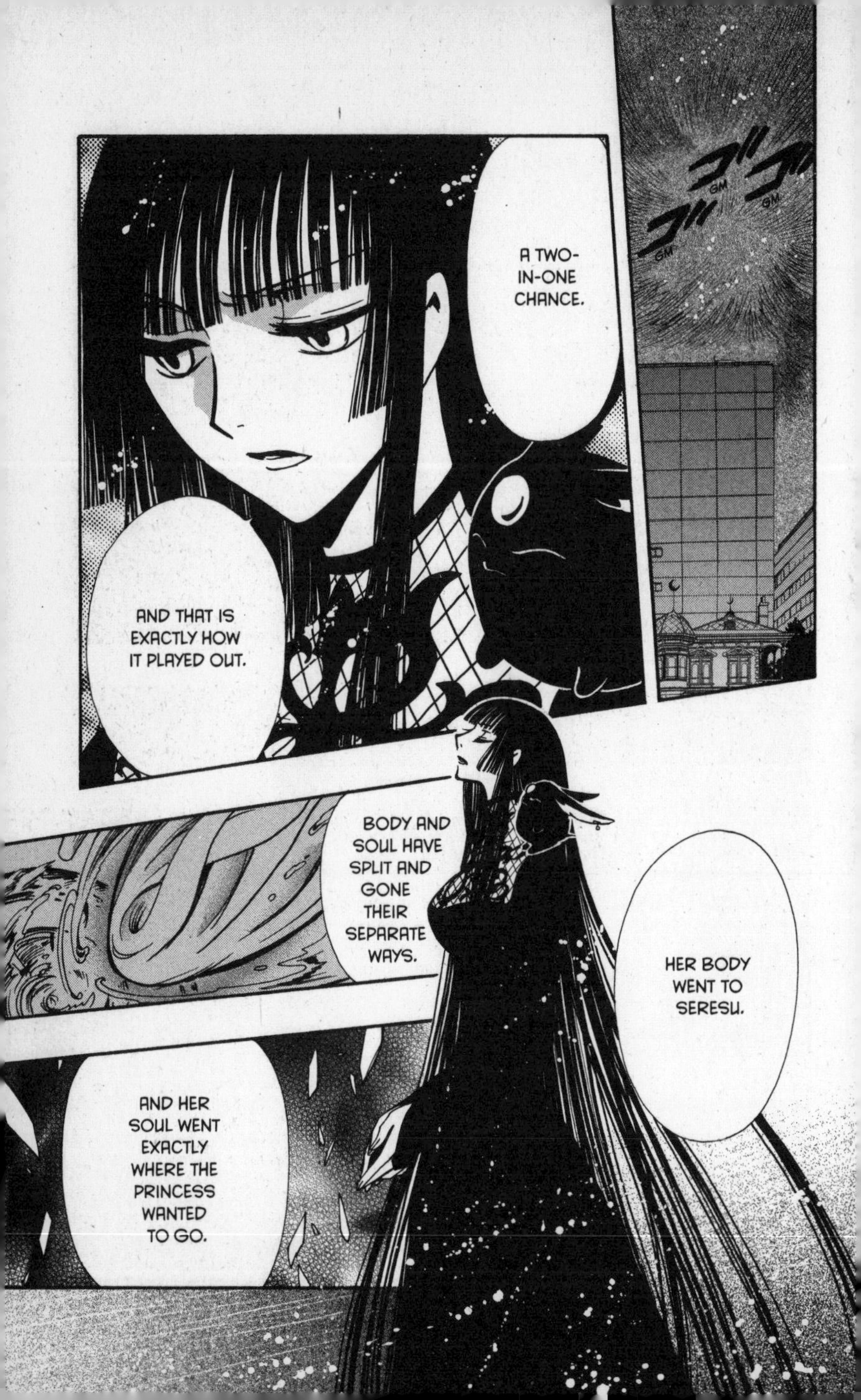
GM
GM
GM
A TWO-IN-ONE CHANCE.
AND THAT IS EXACTLY HOW IT PLAYED OUT.
BODY AND SOUL HAVE SPLIT AND GONE THEIR SEPARATE WAYS.
HER BODY WENT TO SERESU.
AND HER SOUL WENT EXACTLY WHERE THE PRINCESS WANTED TO GO.

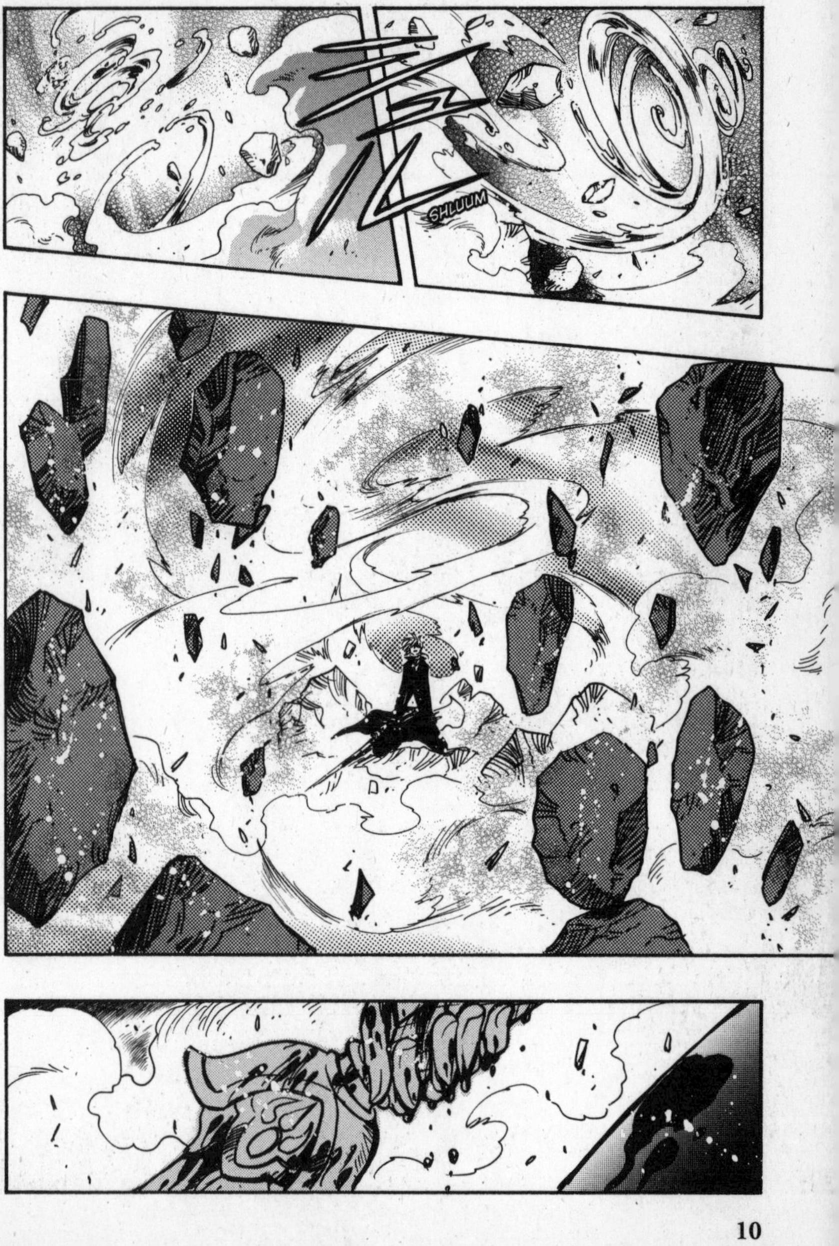
SHLUUM

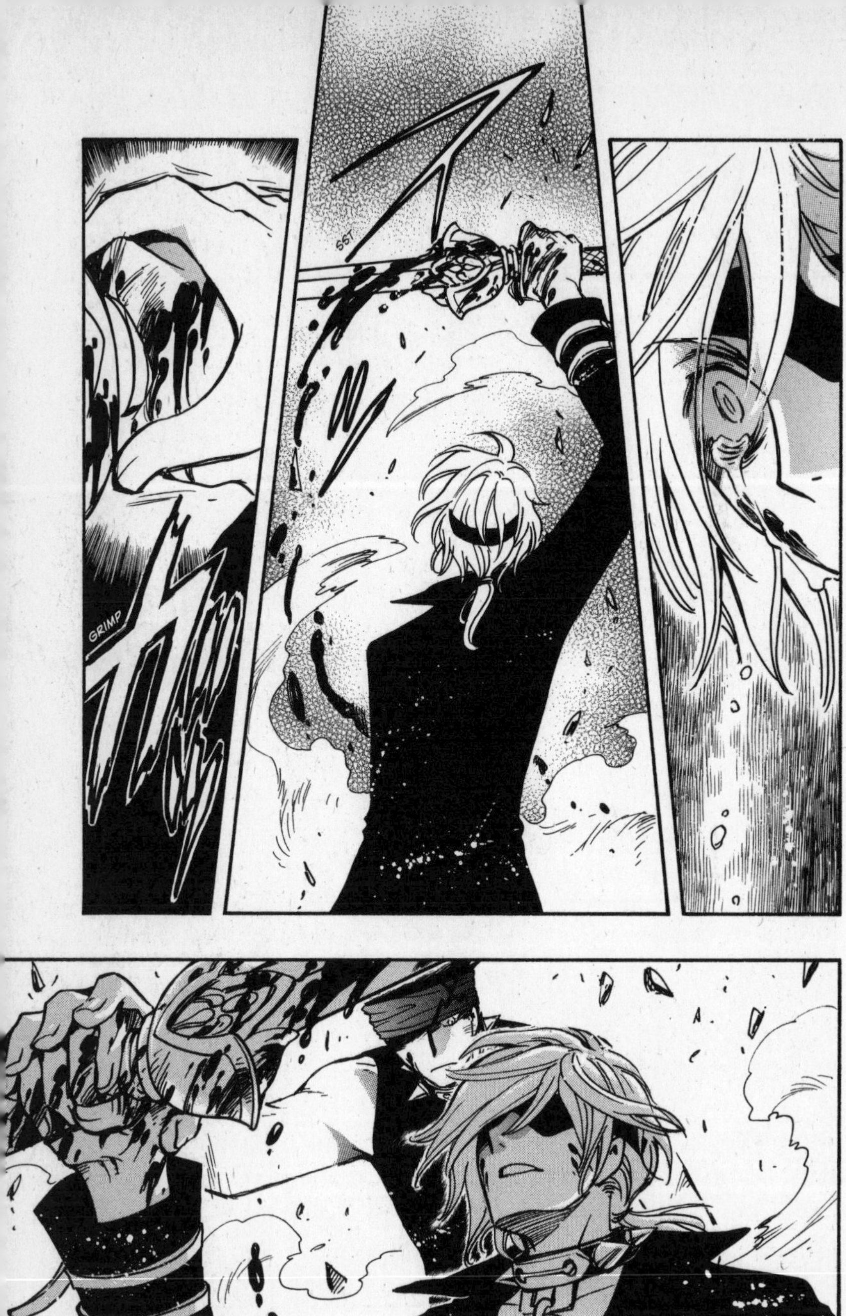
SST
GRIMP

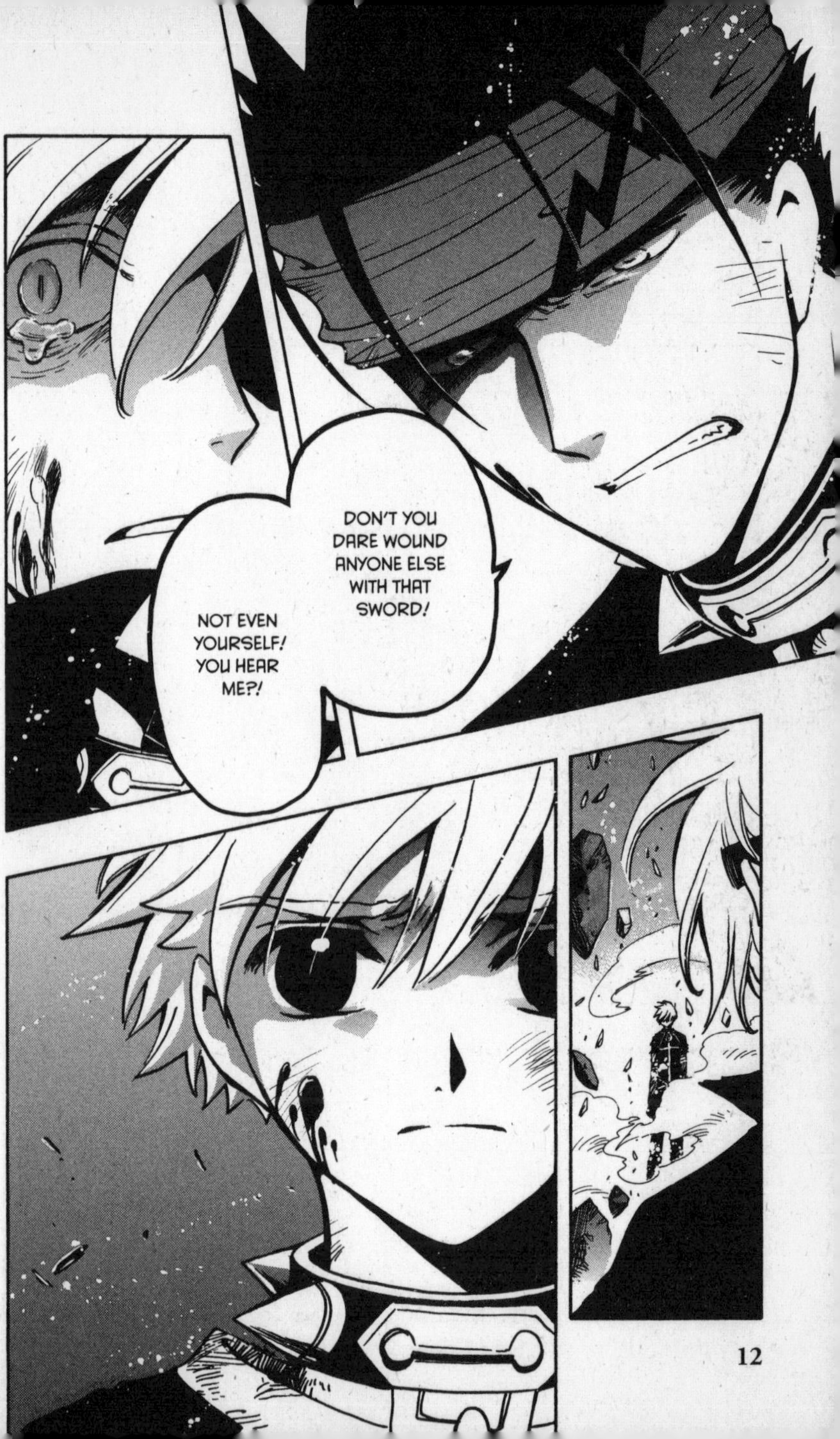
DON'T YOU DARE WOUND ANYONE ELSE WITH THAT SWORD!
NOT EVEN YOURSELF! YOU HEAR ME?!

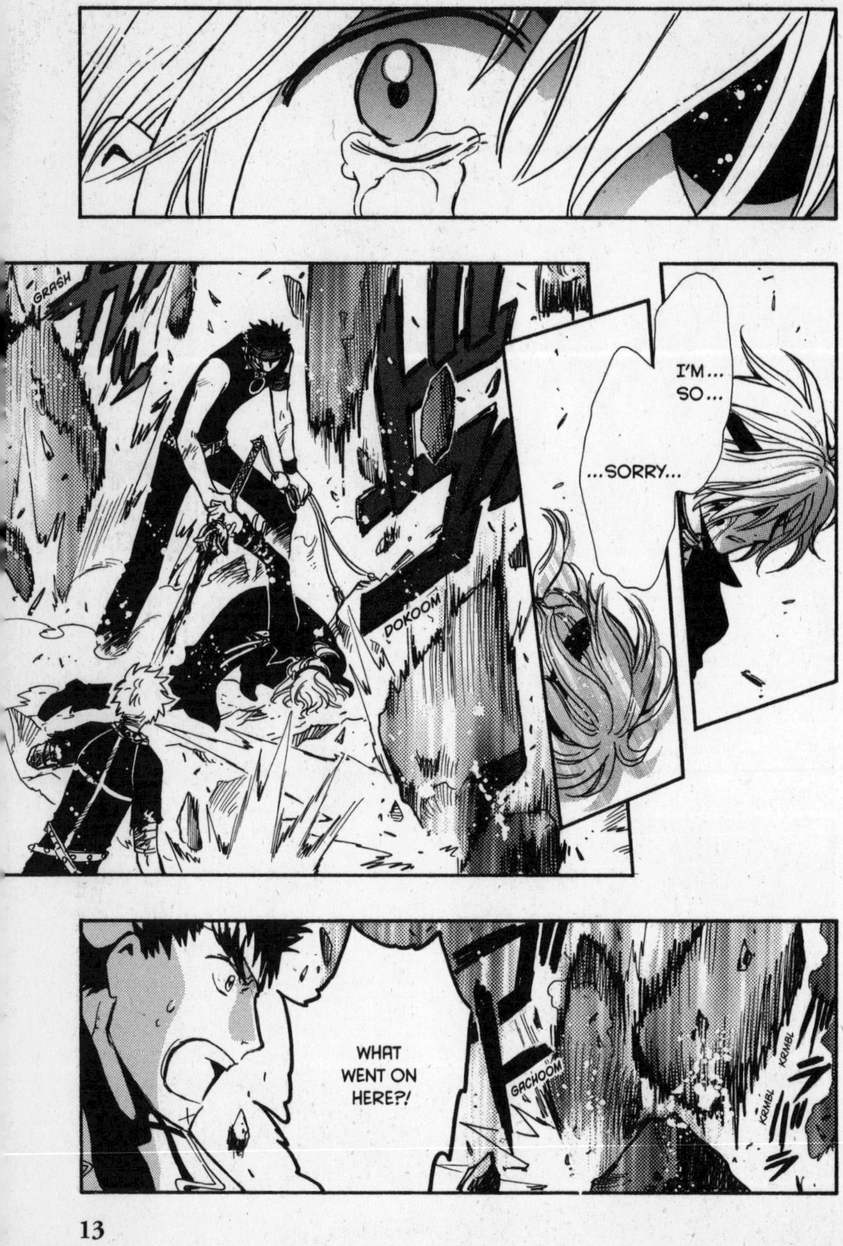
I'M... SO...
...SORRY...
GRASH
DOKOOM
KRMBL KRMBL
GACHOOM
WHAT WENT ON HERE?!

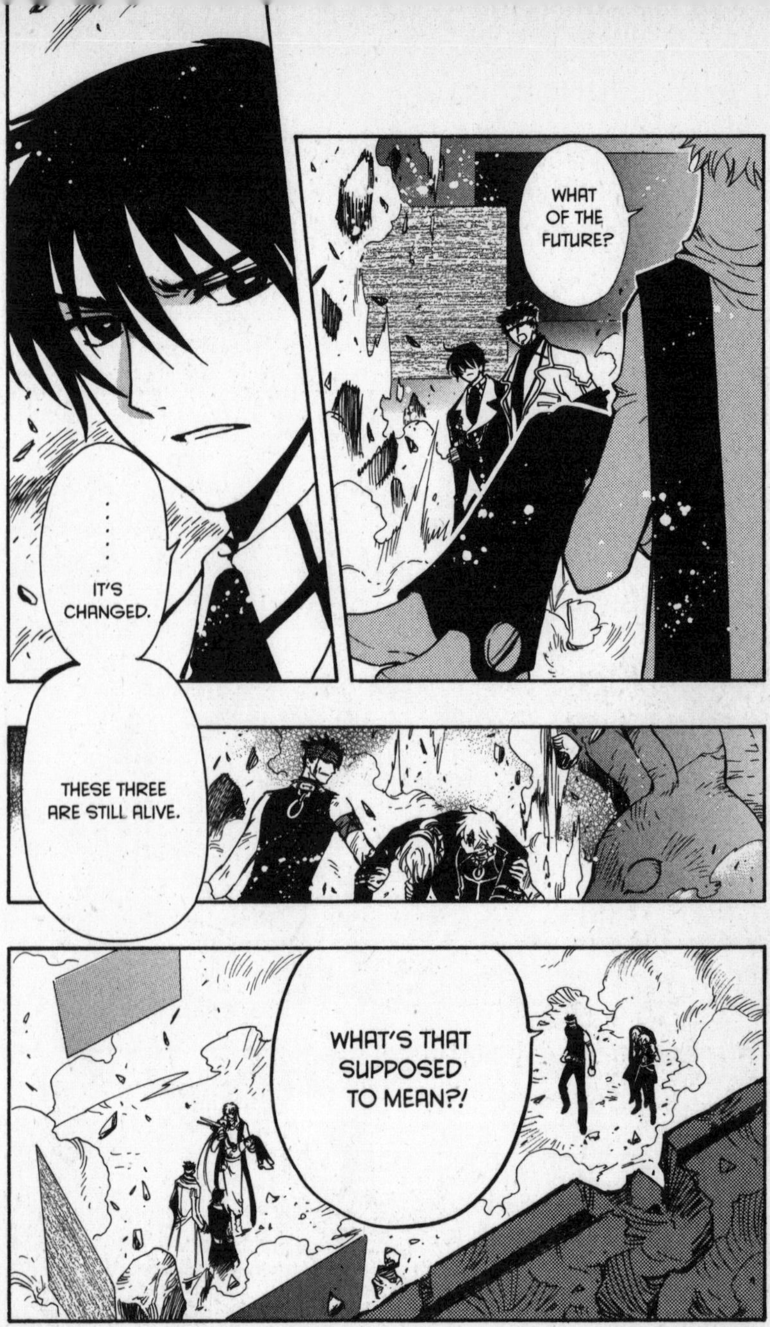
WHAT OF THE FUTURE?
... IT'S CHANGED.
THESE THREE ARE STILL ALIVE.
WHAT'S THAT SUPPOSED TO MEAN?!

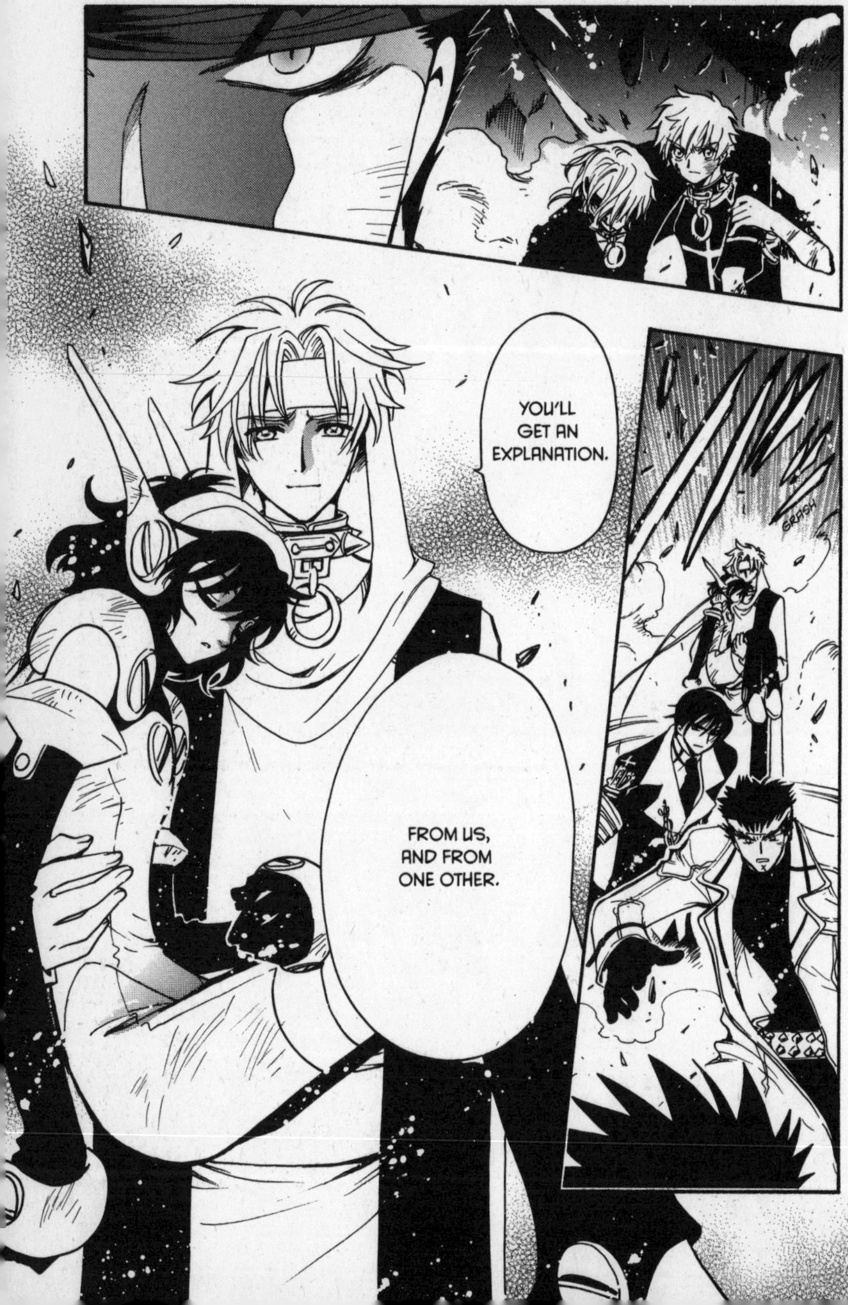
GRASH
YOU'LL GET AN EXPLANATION.
FROM US, AND FROM ONE OTHER.

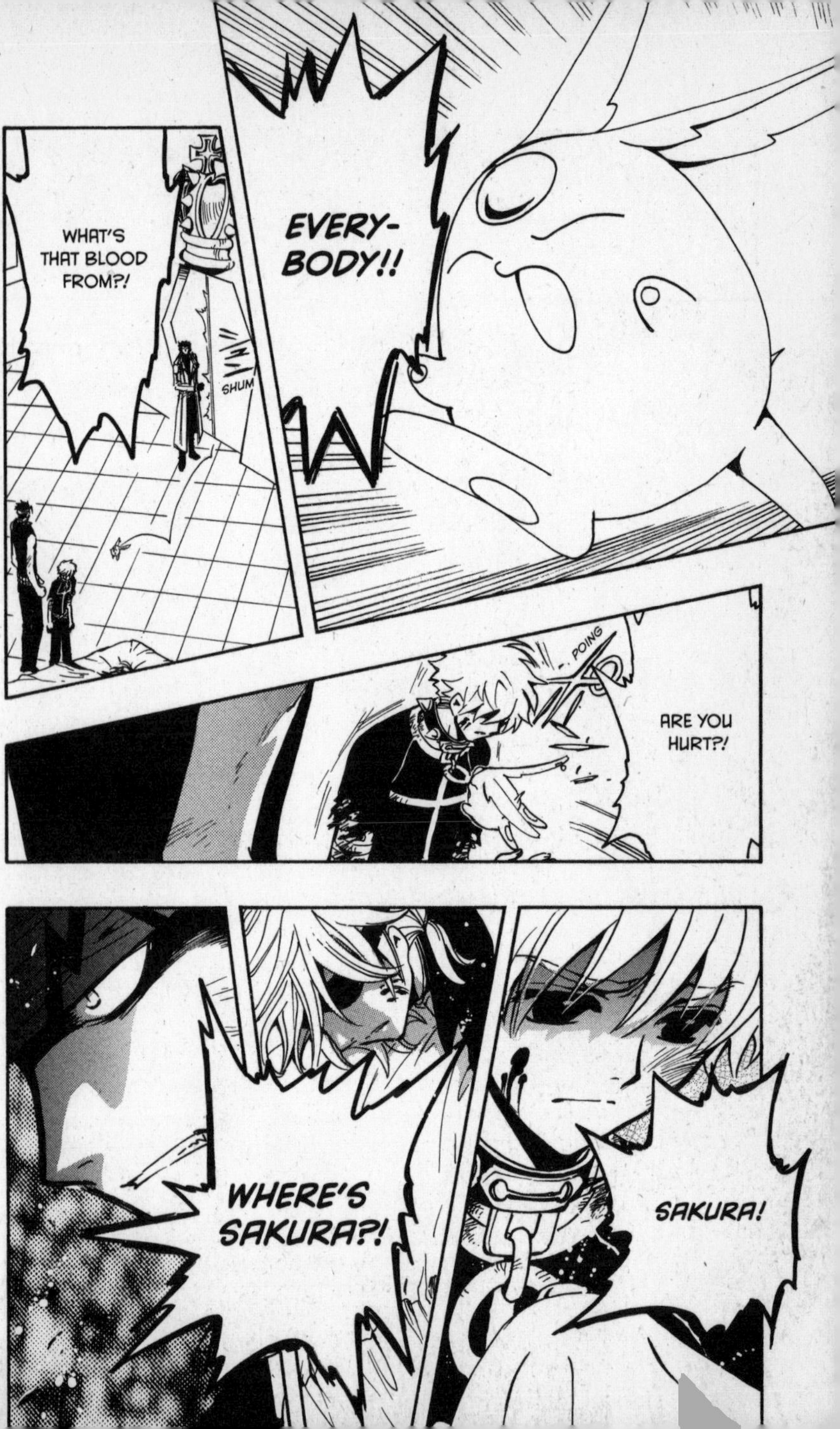
EVERY-
BODY!!
WHAT'S
THAT BLOOD
FROM?!
SHUM
POING
ARE YOU
HURT?!
SAKURA!
WHERE'S
SAKURA?!

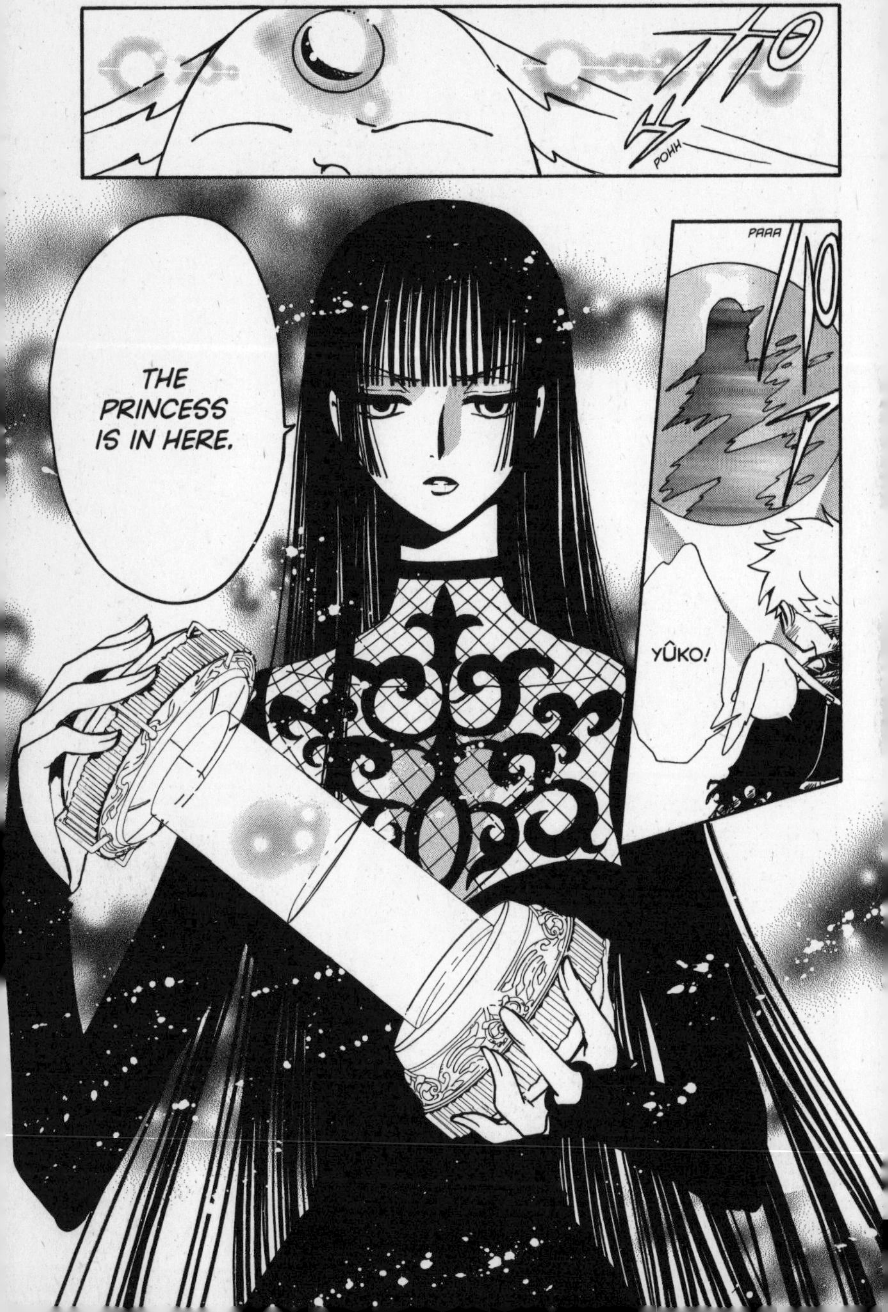
POHH
PAAA
YÛKO!
THE PRINCESS IS IN HERE.

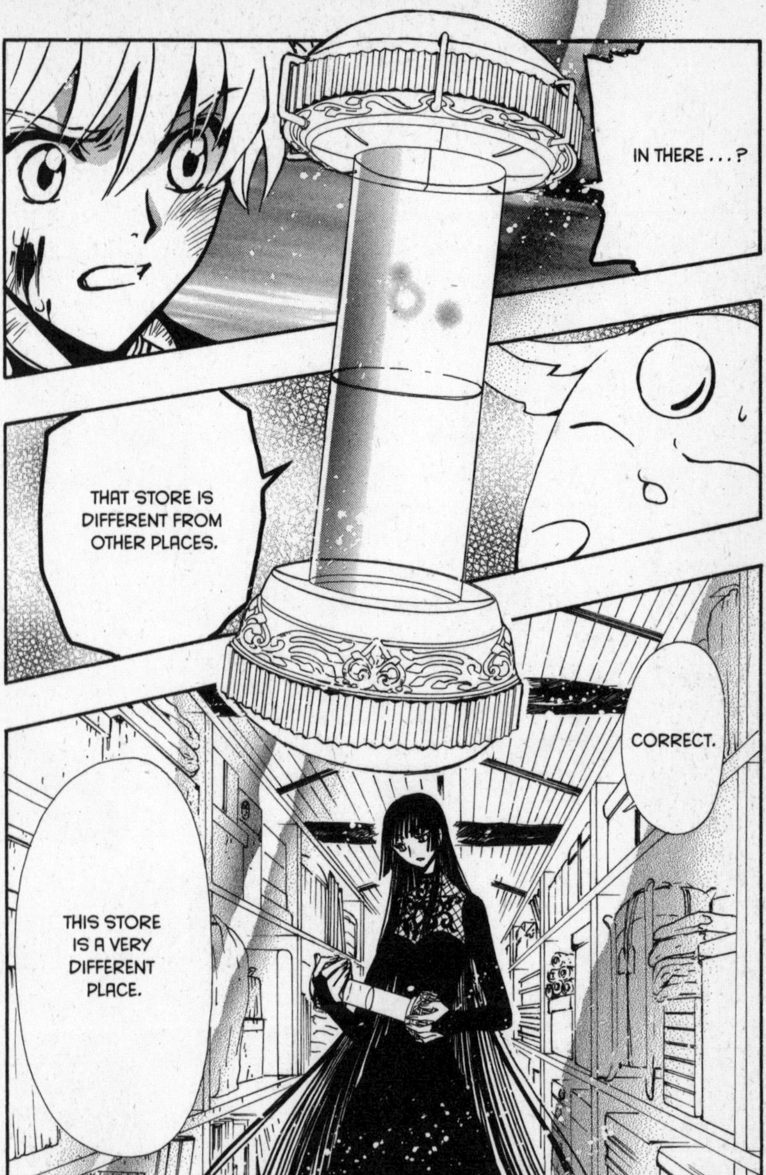
IN THERE . . . ?
THAT STORE IS DIFFERENT FROM OTHER PLACES.
CORRECT.
THIS STORE IS A VERY DIFFERENT PLACE.

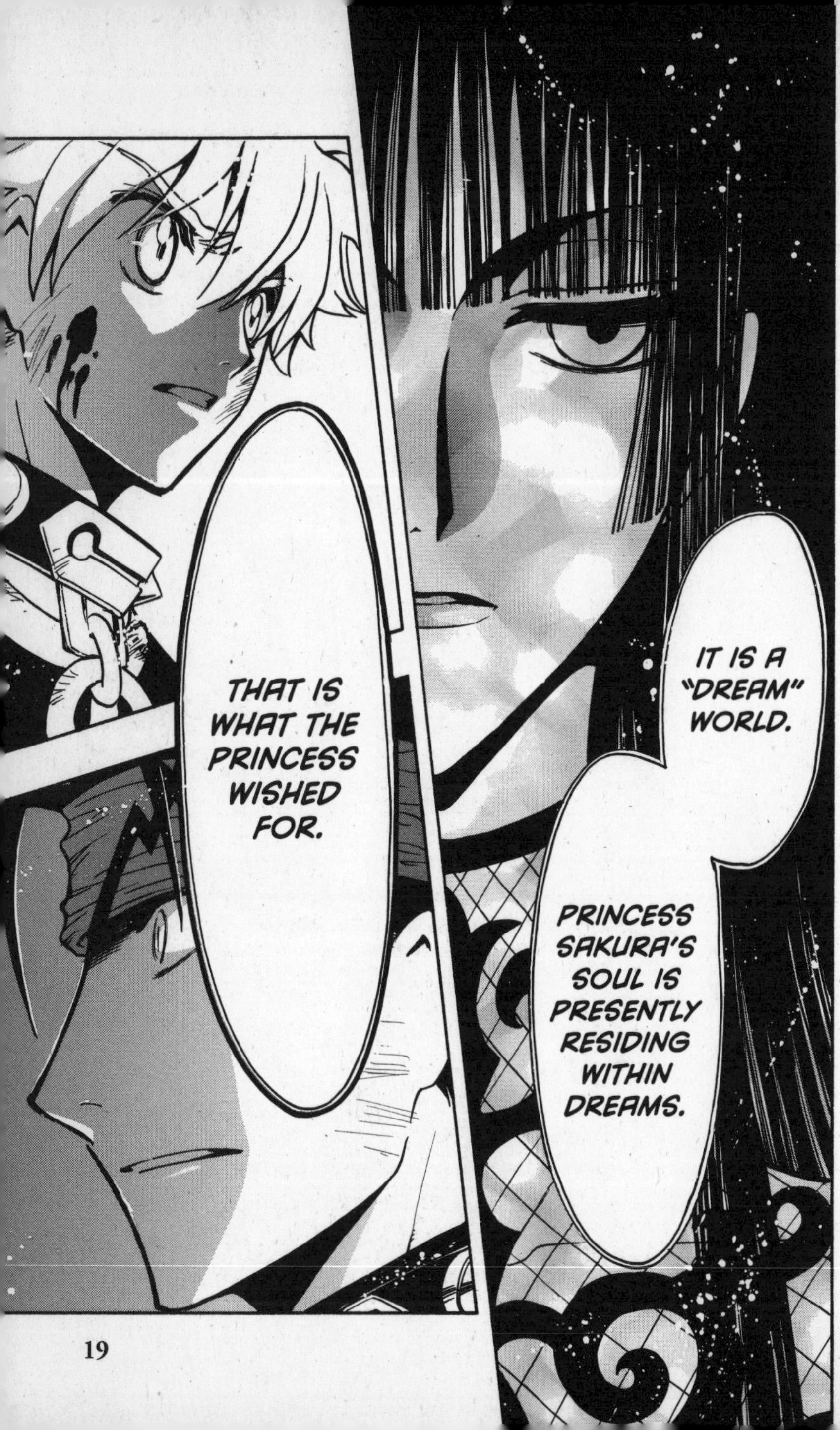
IT IS A "DREAM" WORLD.
PRINCESS SAKURA'S SOUL IS PRESENTLY RESIDING WITHIN DREAMS.
THAT IS WHAT THE PRINCESS WISHED FOR.

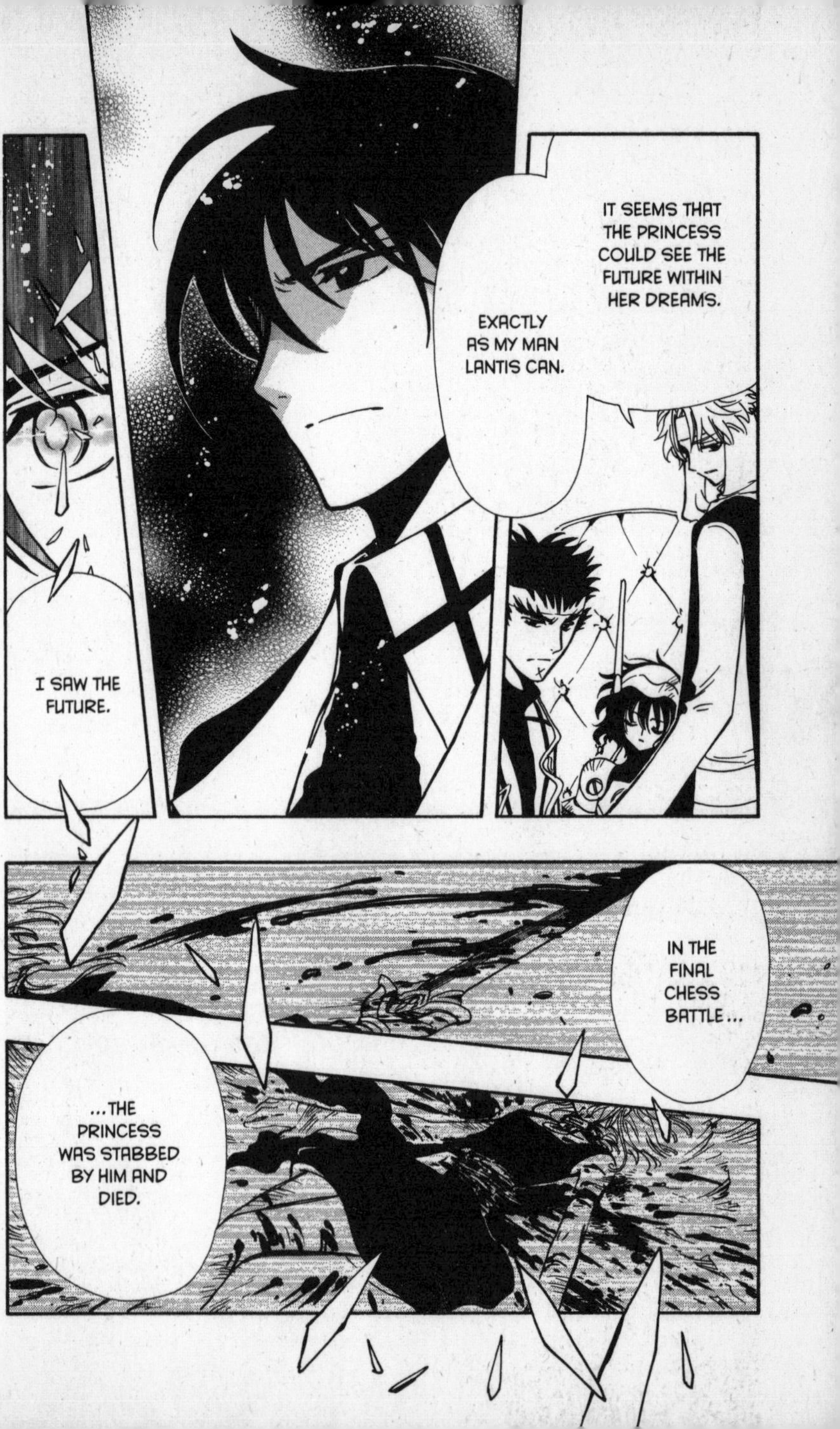
IT SEEMS THAT THE PRINCESS COULD SEE THE FUTURE WITHIN HER DREAMS.
EXACTLY AS MY MAN LANTIS CAN.
I SAW THE FUTURE.
IN THE FINAL CHESS BATTLE...
...THE PRINCESS WAS STABBED BY HIM AND DIED.

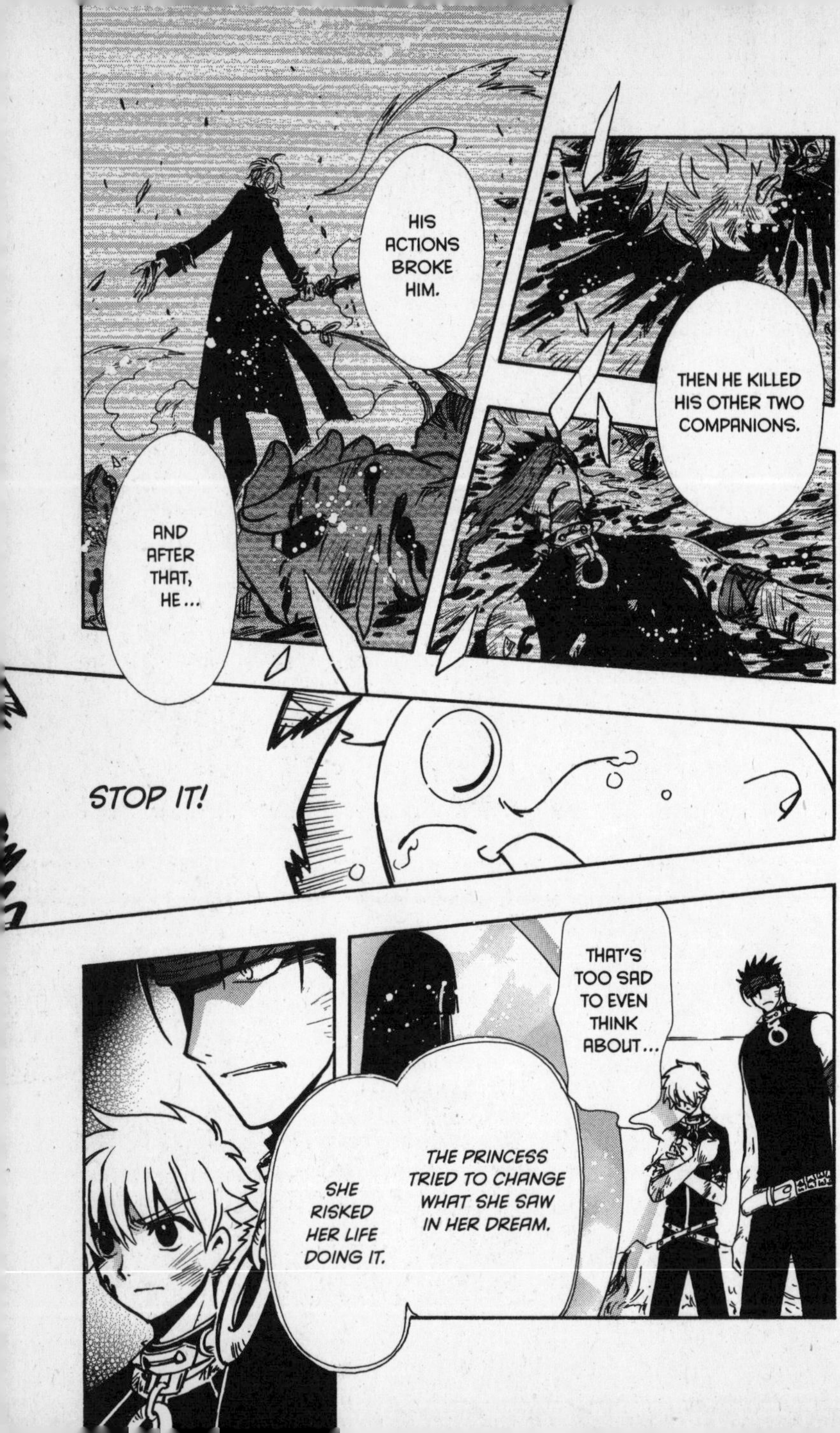
HIS ACTIONS BROKE HIM.
THEN HE KILLED HIS OTHER TWO COMPANIONS.
AND AFTER THAT, HE...
STOP IT!
THAT'S TOO SAD TO EVEN THINK ABOUT...
THE PRINCESS TRIED TO CHANGE WHAT SHE SAW IN HER DREAM.
SHE RISKED HER LIFE DOING IT.

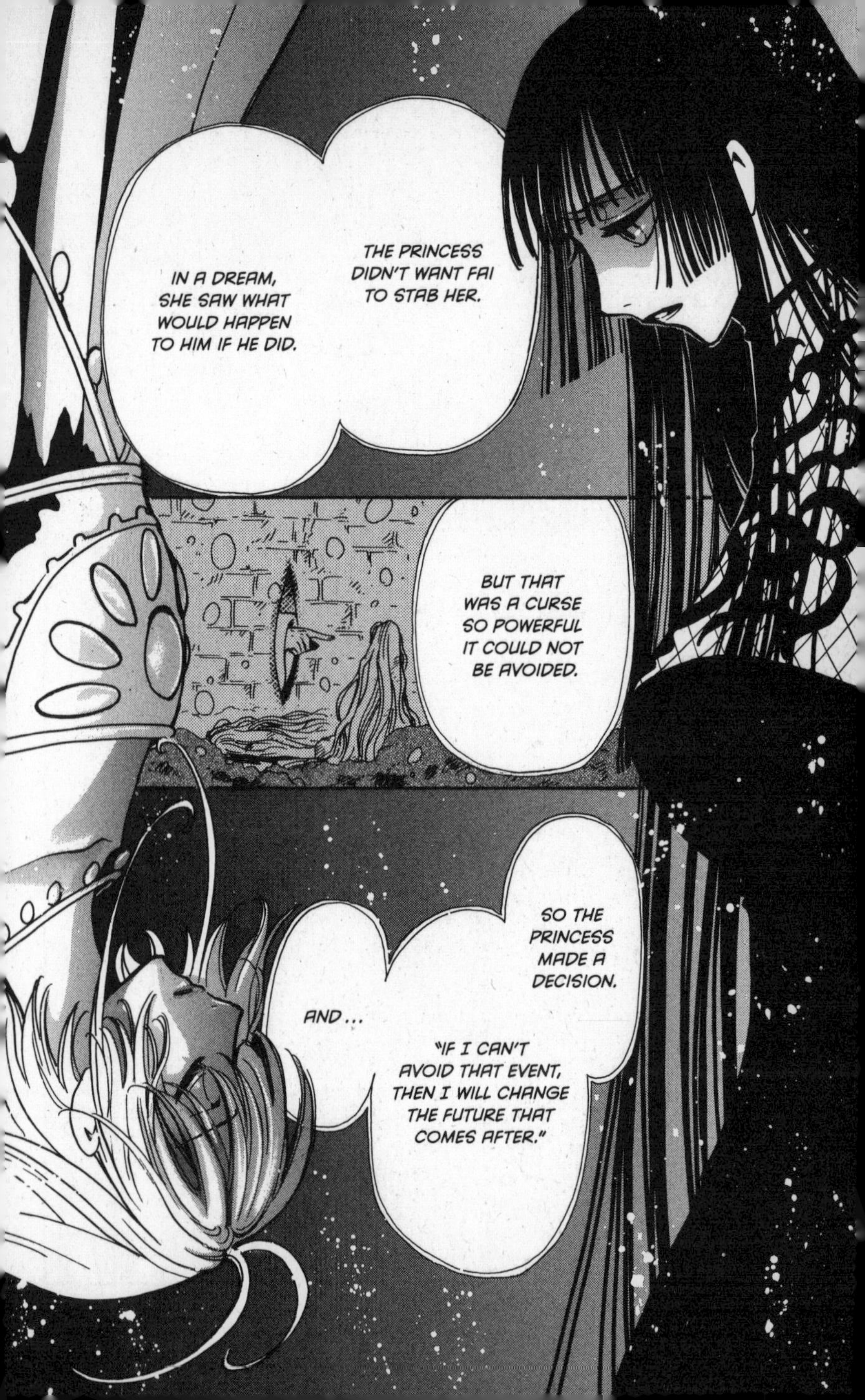
THE PRINCESS DIDN'T WANT FAI TO STAB HER.
IN A DREAM, SHE SAW WHAT WOULD HAPPEN TO HIM IF HE DID.
BUT THAT WAS A CURSE SO POWERFUL IT COULD NOT BE AVOIDED.
SO THE PRINCESS MADE A DECISION.
AND...
"IF I CAN'T AVOID THAT EVENT, THEN I WILL CHANGE THE FUTURE THAT COMES AFTER."

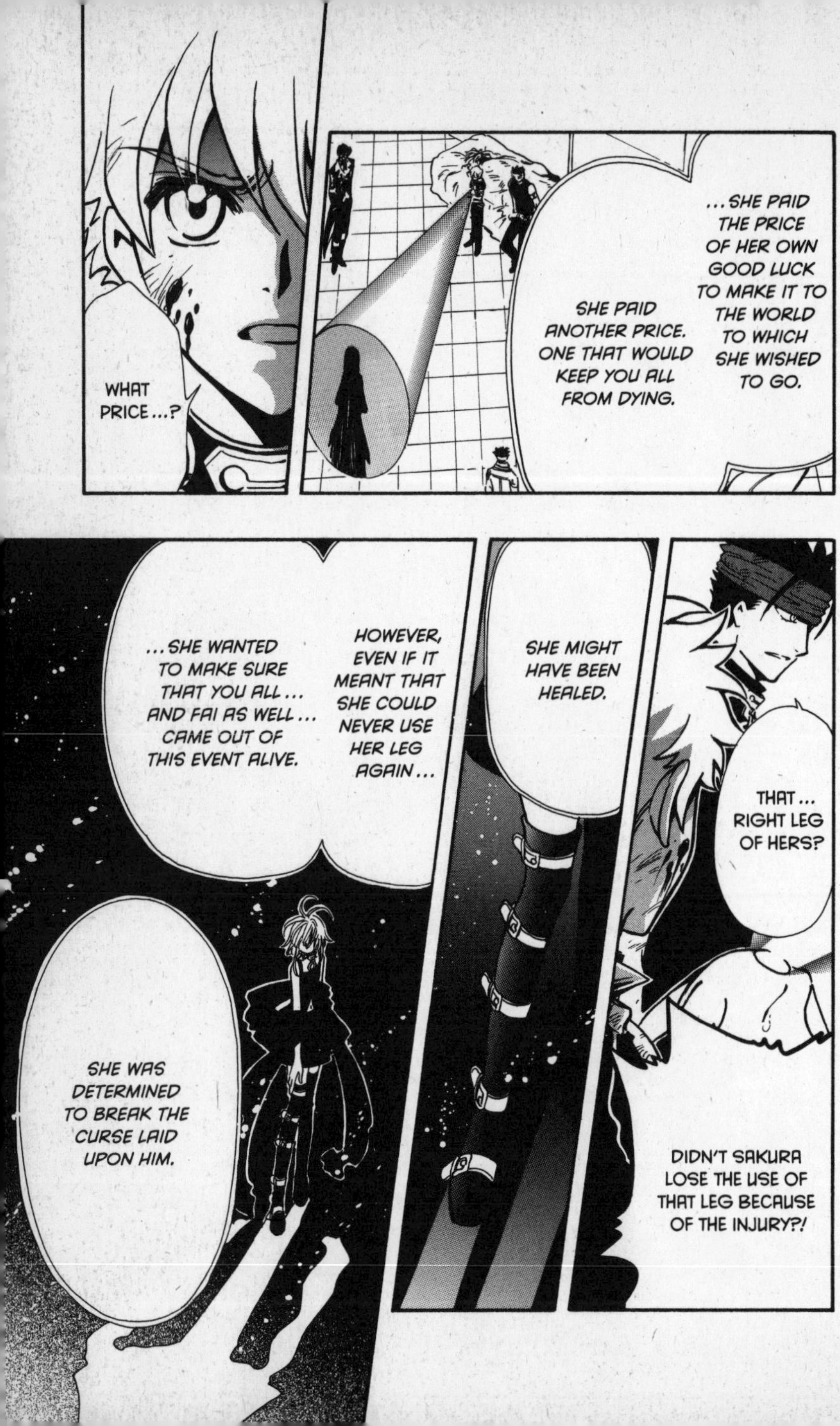
...SHE PAID THE PRICE OF HER OWN GOOD LUCK TO MAKE IT TO THE WORLD TO WHICH SHE WISHED TO GO.
SHE PAID ANOTHER PRICE. ONE THAT WOULD KEEP YOU ALL FROM DYING.
WHAT PRICE...?
THAT... RIGHT LEG OF HERS?
DIDN'T SAKURA LOSE THE USE OF THAT LEG BECAUSE OF THE INJURY?!
SHE MIGHT HAVE BEEN HEALED.
HOWEVER, EVEN IF IT MEANT THAT SHE COULD NEVER USE HER LEG AGAIN...
...SHE WANTED TO MAKE SURE THAT YOU ALL... AND FAI AS WELL... CAME OUT OF THIS EVENT ALIVE.
SHE WAS DETERMINED TO BREAK THE CURSE LAID UPON HIM.

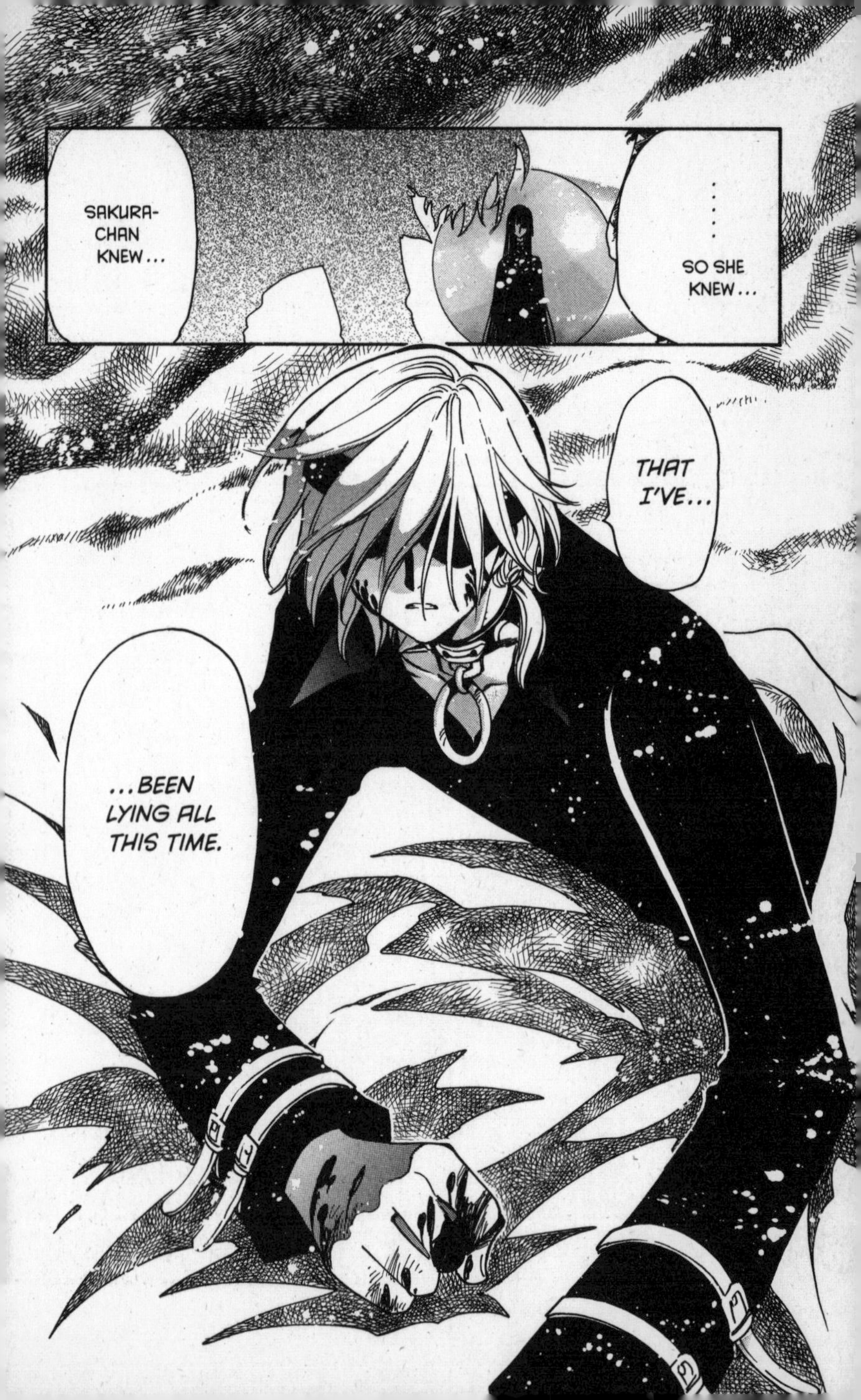
. . . .
SO SHE KNEW…
SAKURA-CHAN KNEW…
THAT I'VE…
…BEEN LYING ALL THIS TIME.

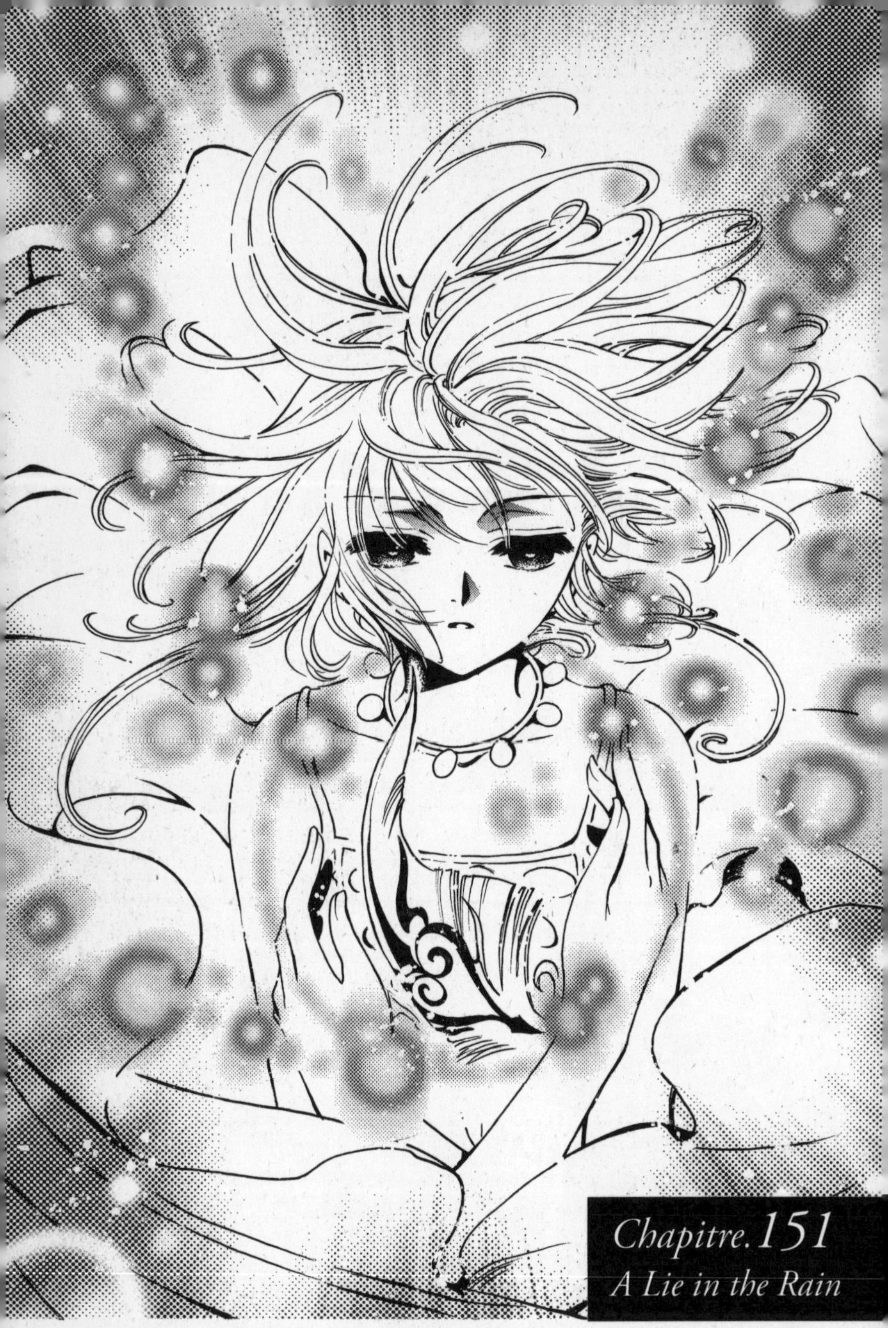

Chapitre. 151
A Lie in the Rain

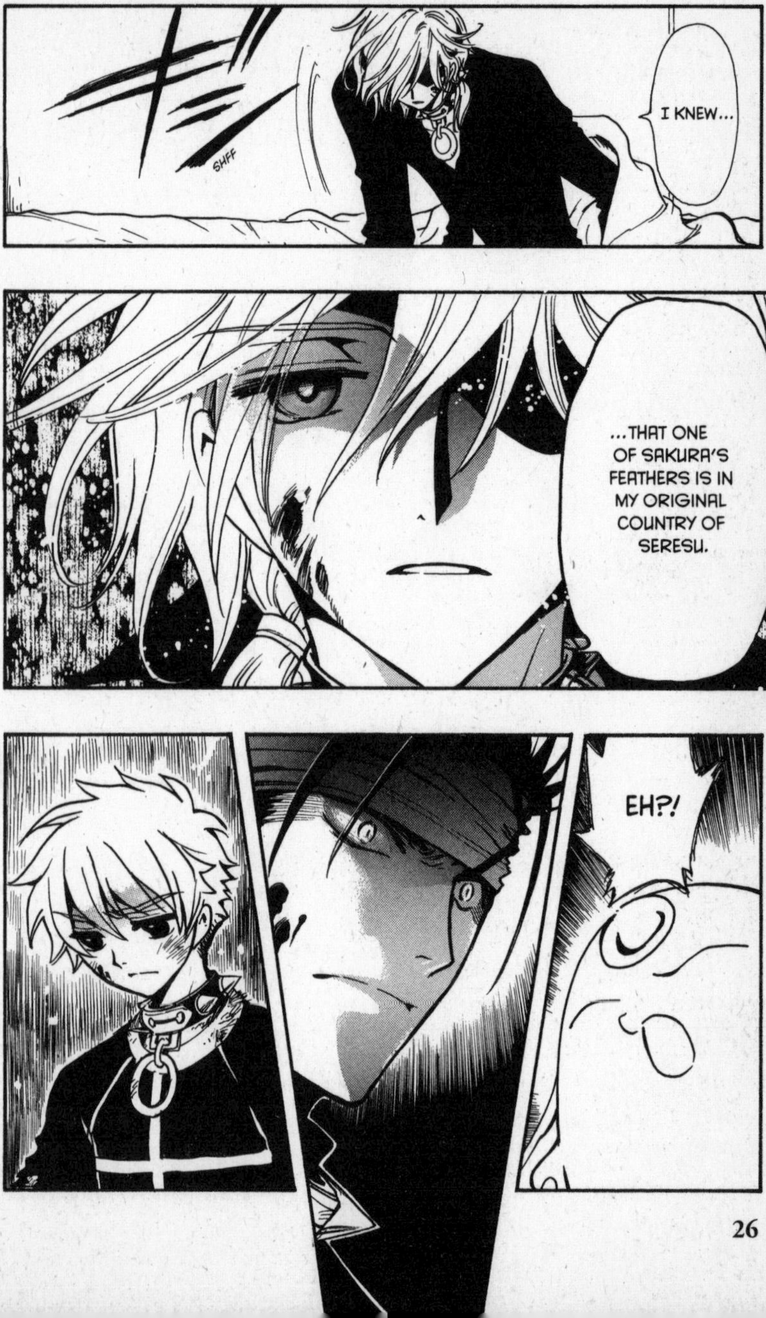
I KNEW...
SHFF
...THAT ONE OF SAKURA'S FEATHERS IS IN MY ORIGINAL COUNTRY OF SERESU.
EH?!

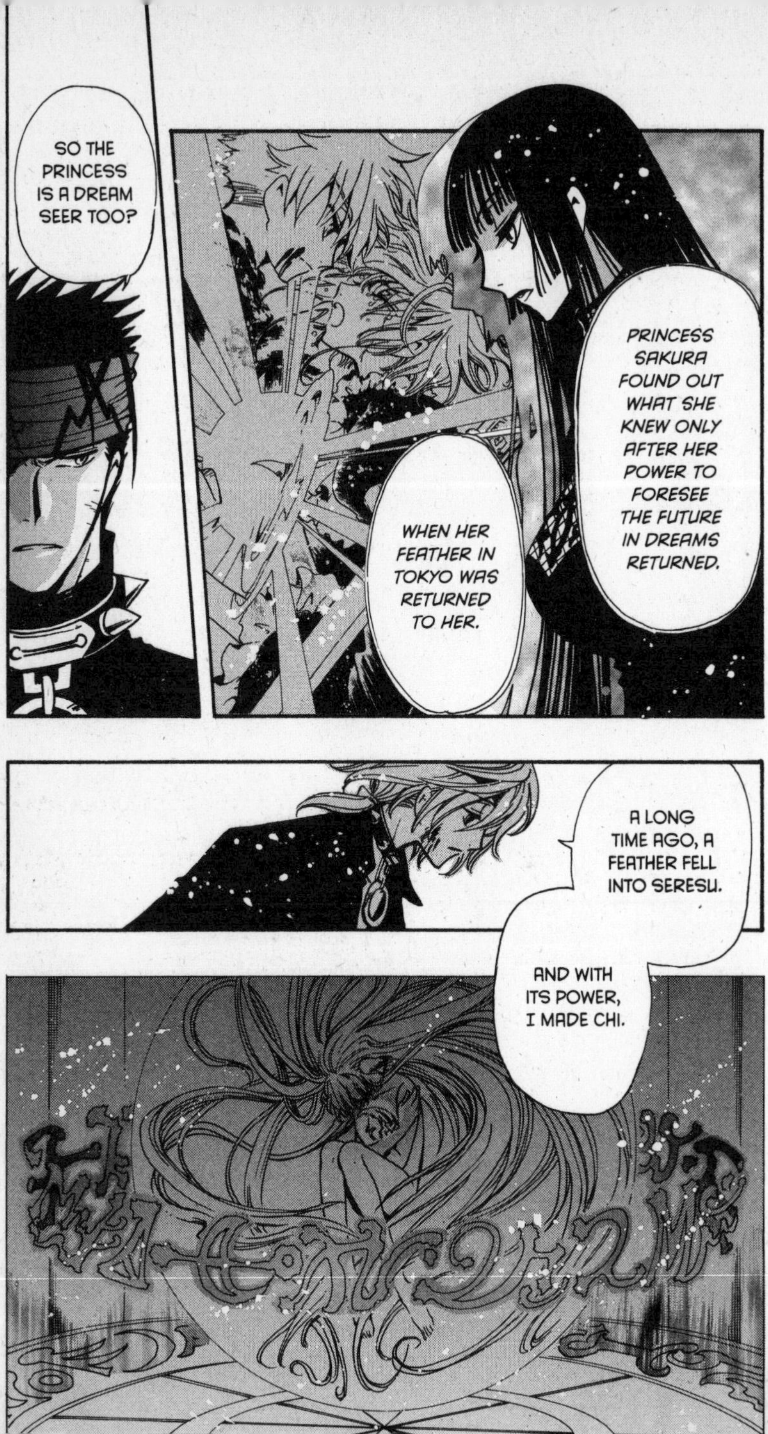
PRINCESS SAKURA FOUND OUT WHAT SHE KNEW ONLY AFTER HER POWER TO FORESEE THE FUTURE IN DREAMS RETURNED.
WHEN HER FEATHER IN TOKYO WAS RETURNED TO HER.
SO THE PRINCESS IS A DREAM SEER TOO?
A LONG TIME AGO, A FEATHER FELL INTO SERESU.
AND WITH ITS POWER, I MADE CHI.

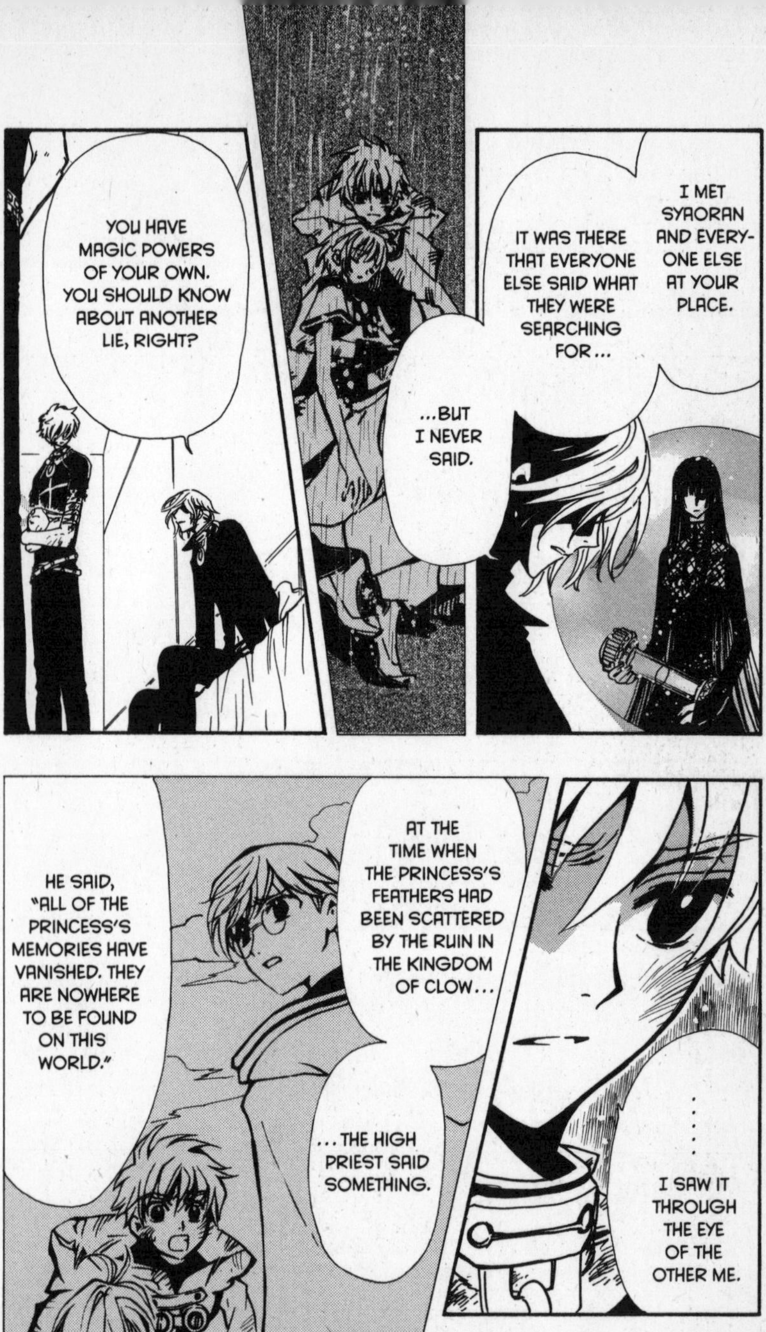
I MET SYAORAN AND EVERY-ONE ELSE AT YOUR PLACE.
IT WAS THERE THAT EVERYONE ELSE SAID WHAT THEY WERE SEARCHING FOR...
...BUT I NEVER SAID.
YOU HAVE MAGIC POWERS OF YOUR OWN. YOU SHOULD KNOW ABOUT ANOTHER LIE, RIGHT?
....
I SAW IT THROUGH THE EYE OF THE OTHER ME.
AT THE TIME WHEN THE PRINCESS'S FEATHERS HAD BEEN SCATTERED BY THE RUIN IN THE KINGDOM OF CLOW...
...THE HIGH PRIEST SAID SOMETHING.
HE SAID, "ALL OF THE PRINCESS'S MEMORIES HAVE VANISHED. THEY ARE NOWHERE TO BE FOUND ON THIS WORLD."

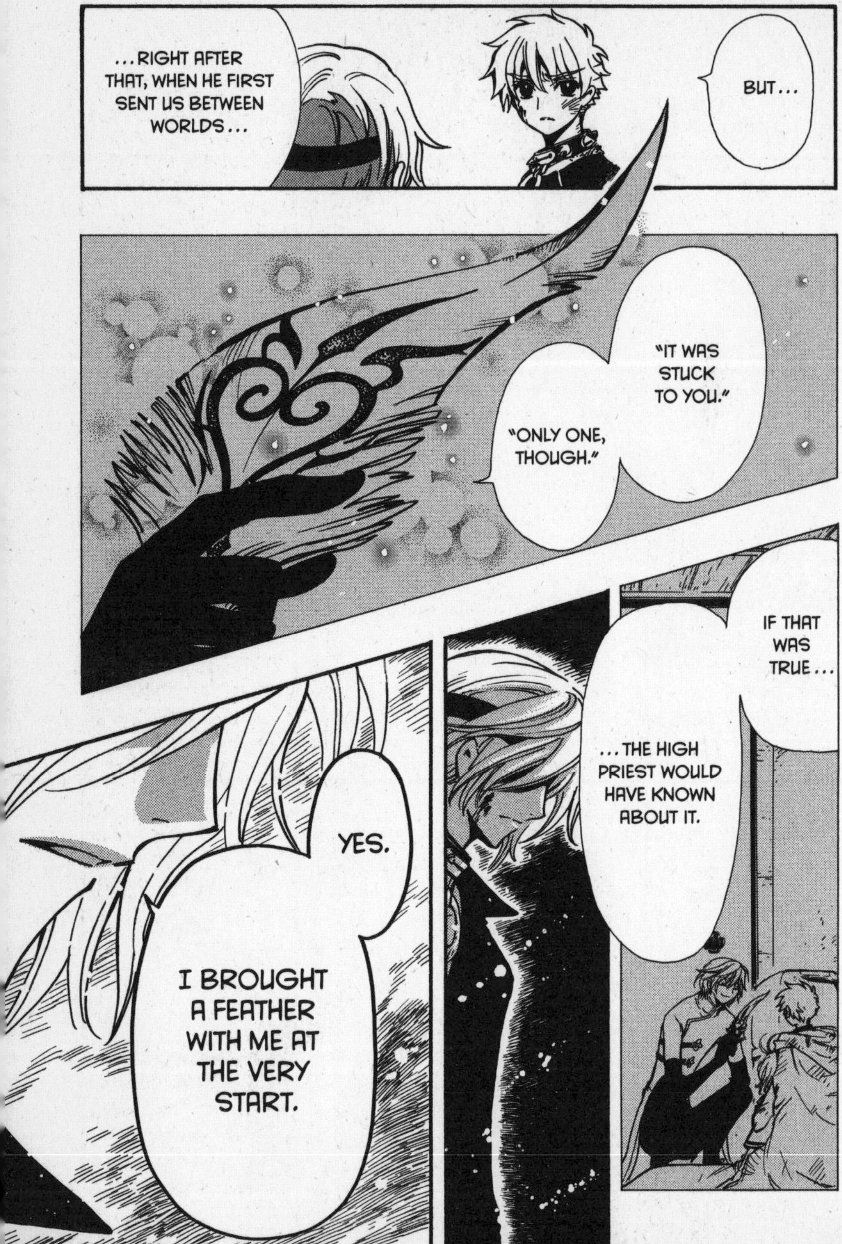
BUT...
...RIGHT AFTER THAT, WHEN HE FIRST SENT US BETWEEN WORLDS...
"IT WAS STUCK TO YOU."
"ONLY ONE, THOUGH."
IF THAT WAS TRUE...
...THE HIGH PRIEST WOULD HAVE KNOWN ABOUT IT.
YES.
I BROUGHT A FEATHER WITH ME AT THE VERY START.

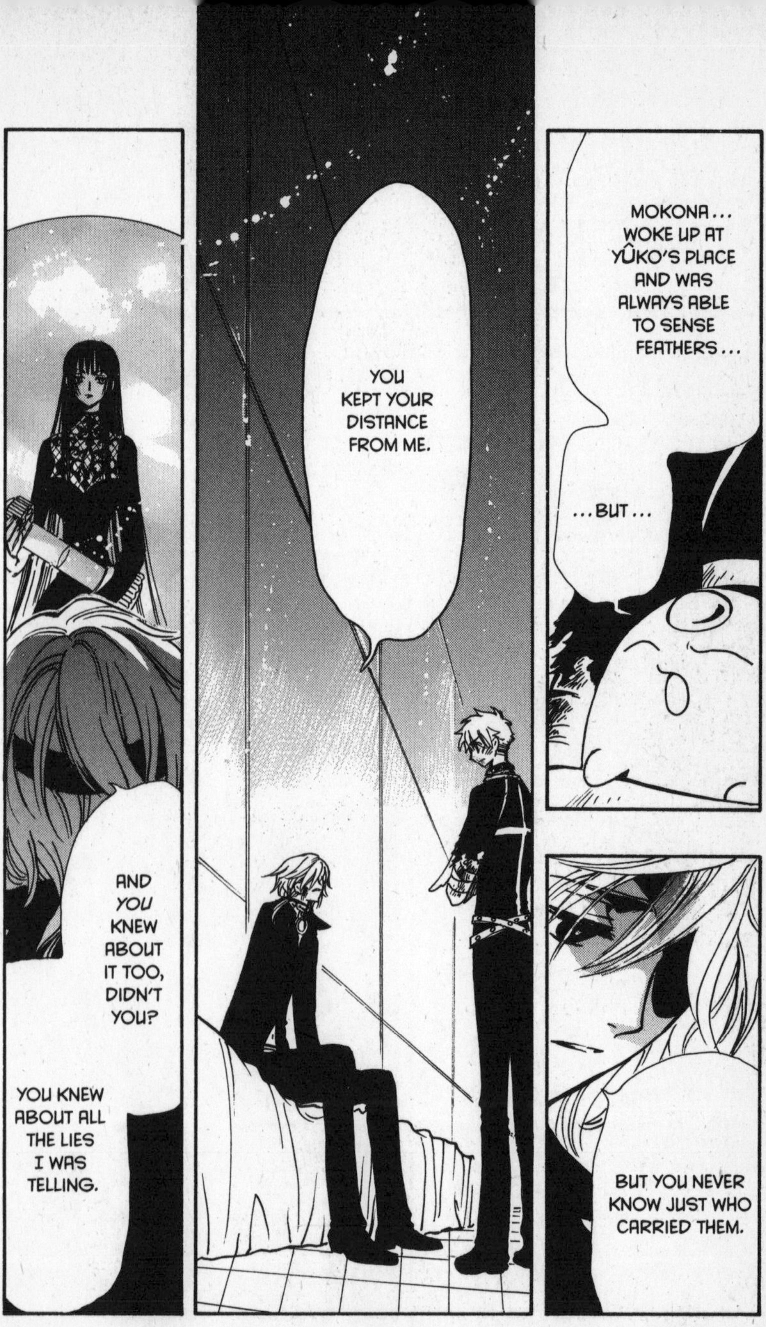
MOKONA... WOKE UP AT YÛKO'S PLACE AND WAS ALWAYS ABLE TO SENSE FEATHERS...
...BUT...
BUT YOU NEVER KNOW JUST WHO CARRIED THEM.
YOU KEPT YOUR DISTANCE FROM ME.
AND *YOU* KNEW ABOUT IT TOO, DIDN'T YOU?
YOU KNEW ABOUT ALL THE LIES I WAS TELLING.

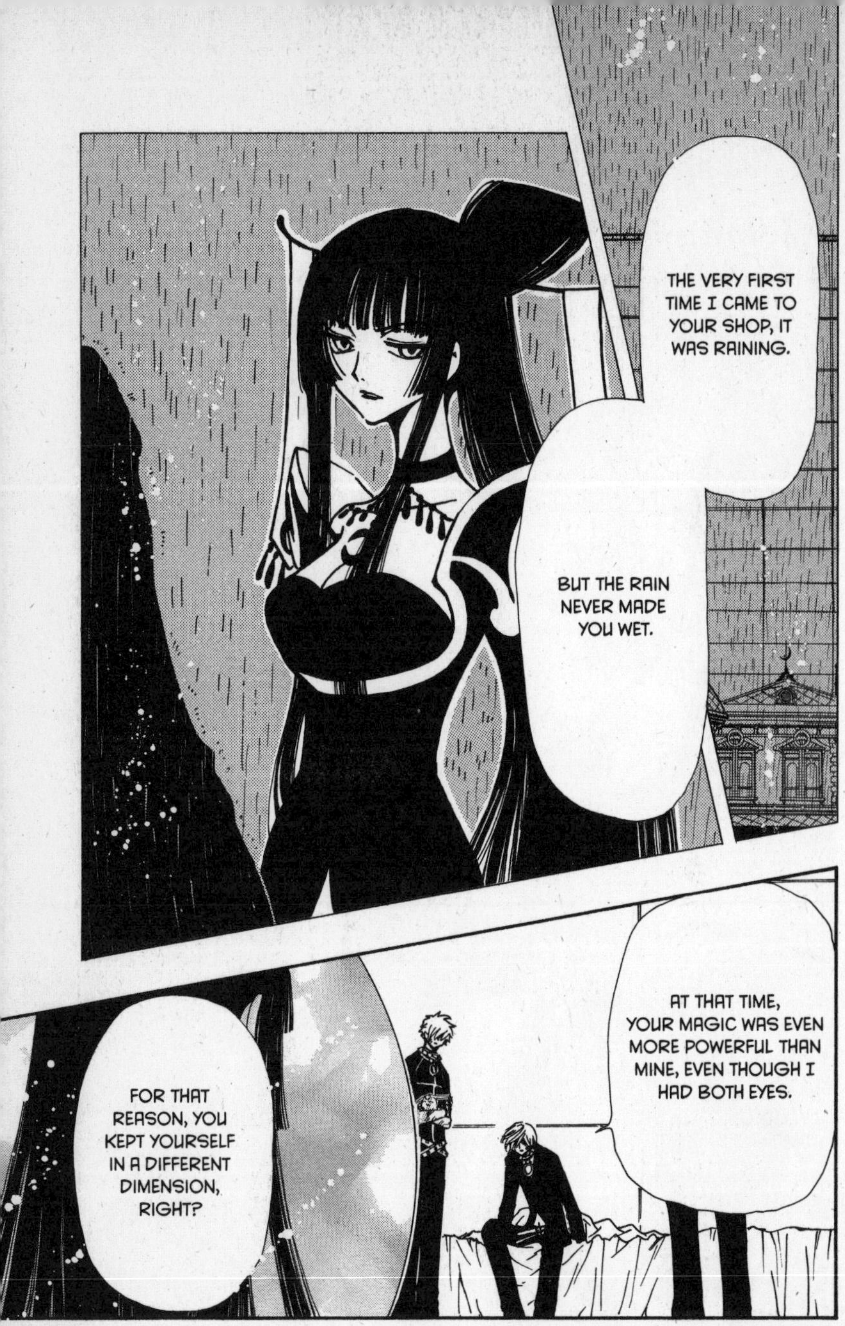
THE VERY FIRST TIME I CAME TO YOUR SHOP, IT WAS RAINING.
BUT THE RAIN NEVER MADE YOU WET.
AT THAT TIME, YOUR MAGIC WAS EVEN MORE POWERFUL THAN MINE, EVEN THOUGH I HAD BOTH EYES.
FOR THAT REASON, YOU KEPT YOURSELF IN A DIFFERENT DIMENSION, RIGHT?

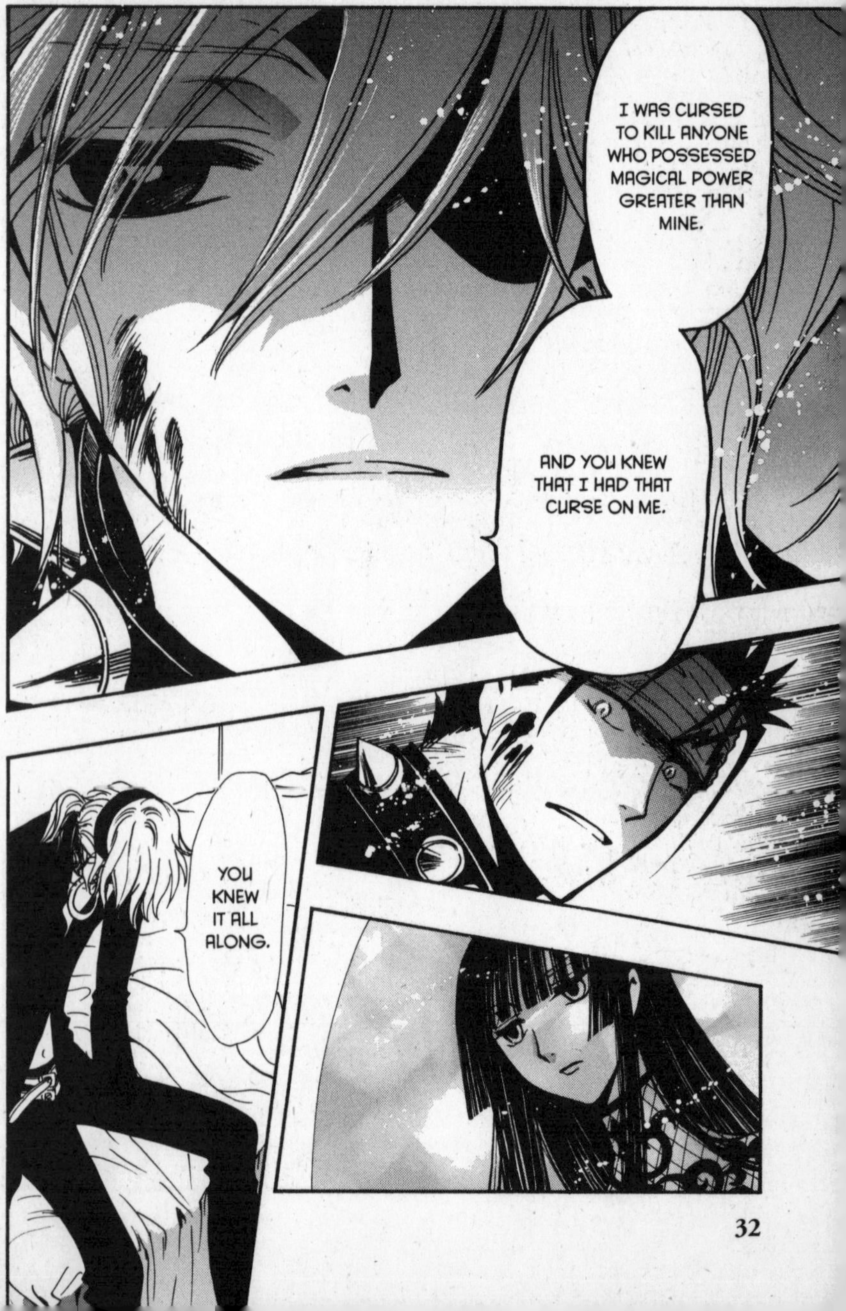
I WAS CURSED TO KILL ANYONE WHO POSSESSED MAGICAL POWER GREATER THAN MINE.
AND YOU KNEW THAT I HAD THAT CURSE ON ME.
YOU KNEW IT ALL ALONG.

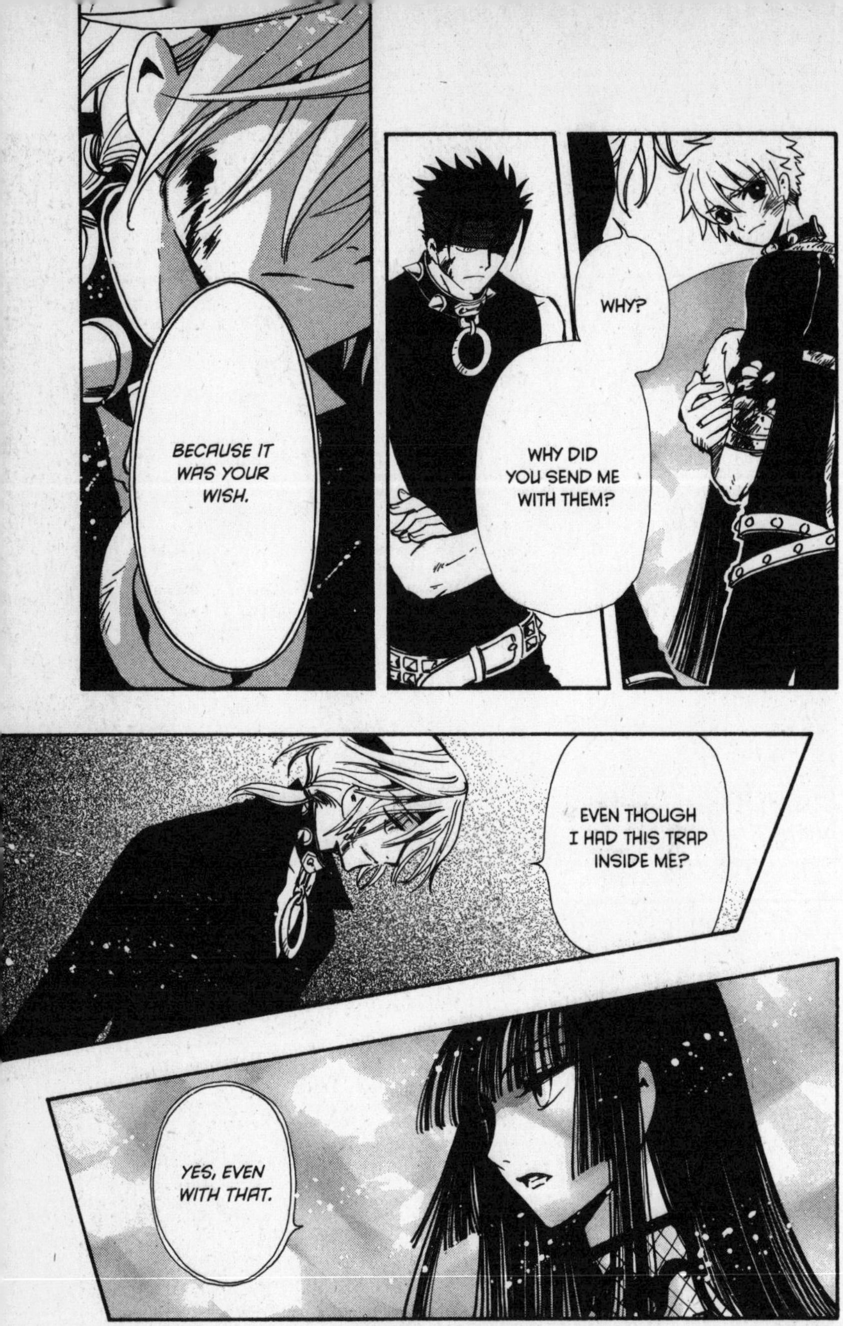
WHY?
WHY DID YOU SEND ME WITH THEM?
BECAUSE IT WAS YOUR WISH.
EVEN THOUGH I HAD THIS TRAP INSIDE ME?
YES, EVEN WITH THAT.

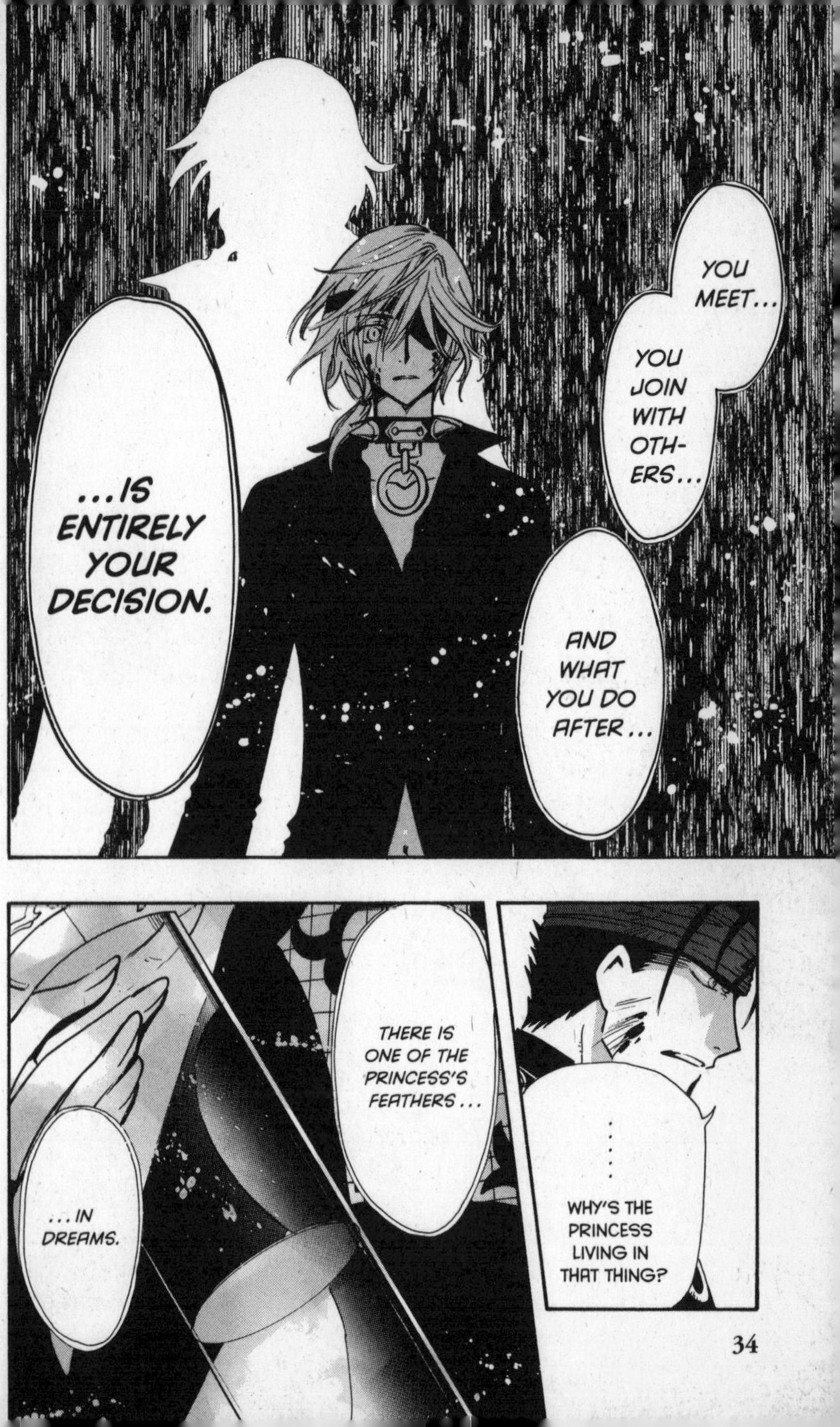
YOU MEET...
YOU JOIN WITH OTH-ERS...
AND WHAT YOU DO AFTER...
...IS ENTIRELY YOUR DECISION.
......
WHY'S THE PRINCESS LIVING IN THAT THING?
THERE IS ONE OF THE PRINCESS'S FEATHERS...
...IN DREAMS.

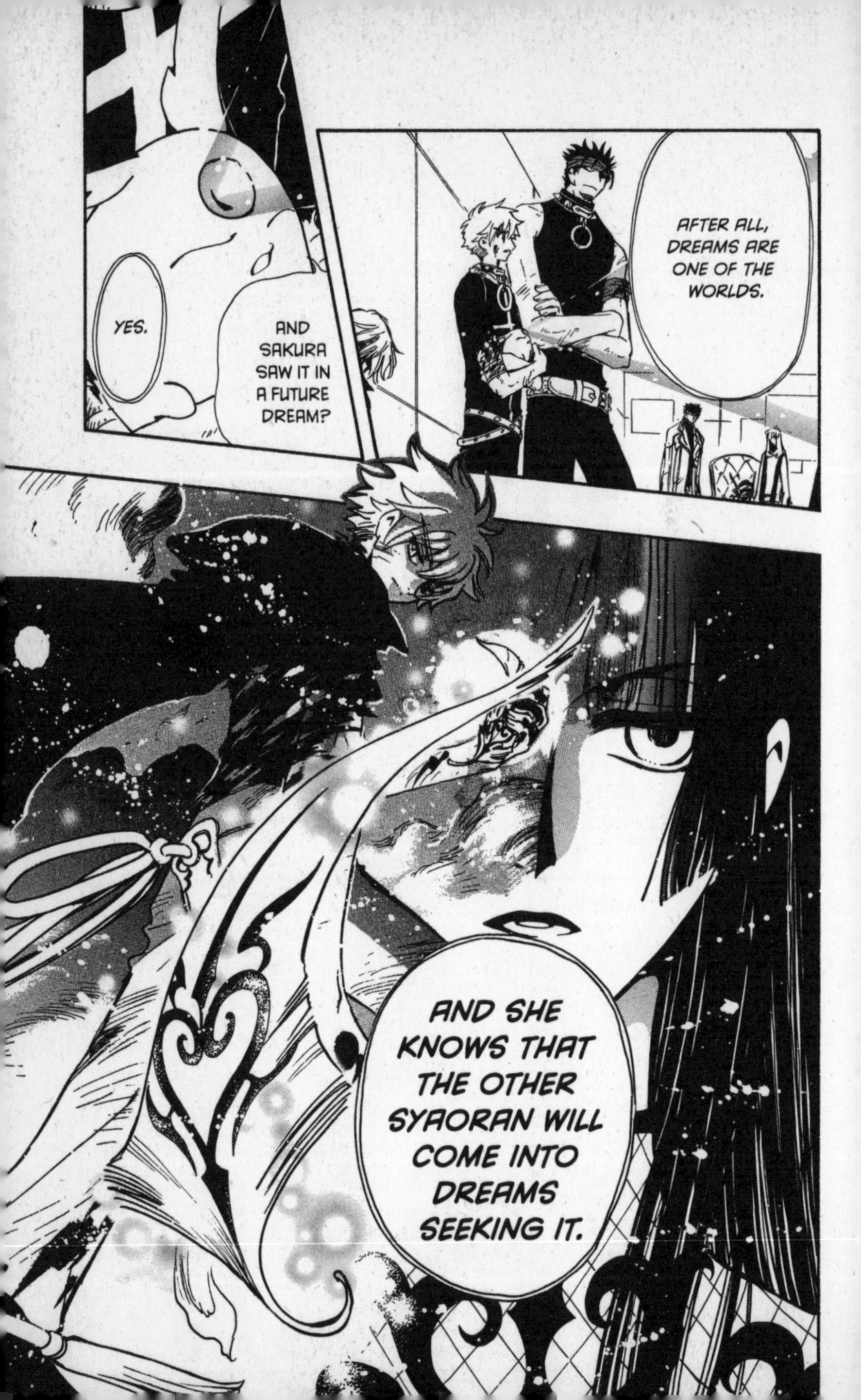
AFTER ALL, DREAMS ARE ONE OF THE WORLDS.
AND SAKURA SAW IT IN A FUTURE DREAM?
YES.
AND SHE KNOWS THAT THE OTHER SYAORAN WILL COME INTO DREAMS SEEKING IT.

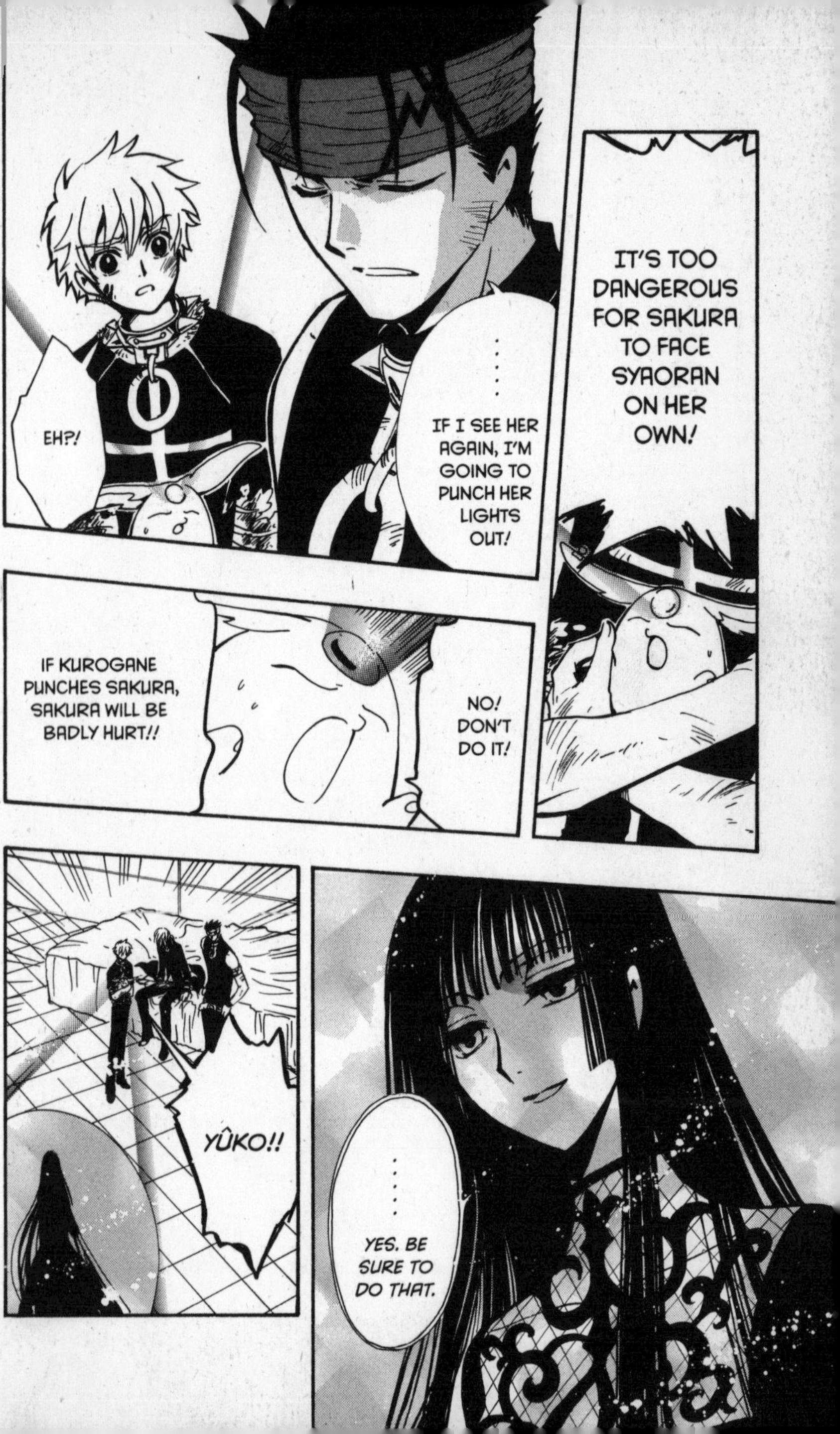
IT'S TOO DANGEROUS FOR SAKURA TO FACE SYAORAN ON HER OWN!
.....
IF I SEE HER AGAIN, I'M GOING TO PUNCH HER LIGHTS OUT!
EH?!
NO! DON'T DO IT!
IF KUROGANE PUNCHES SAKURA, SAKURA WILL BE BADLY HURT!!
.....
YES. BE SURE TO DO THAT.
YÛKO!!

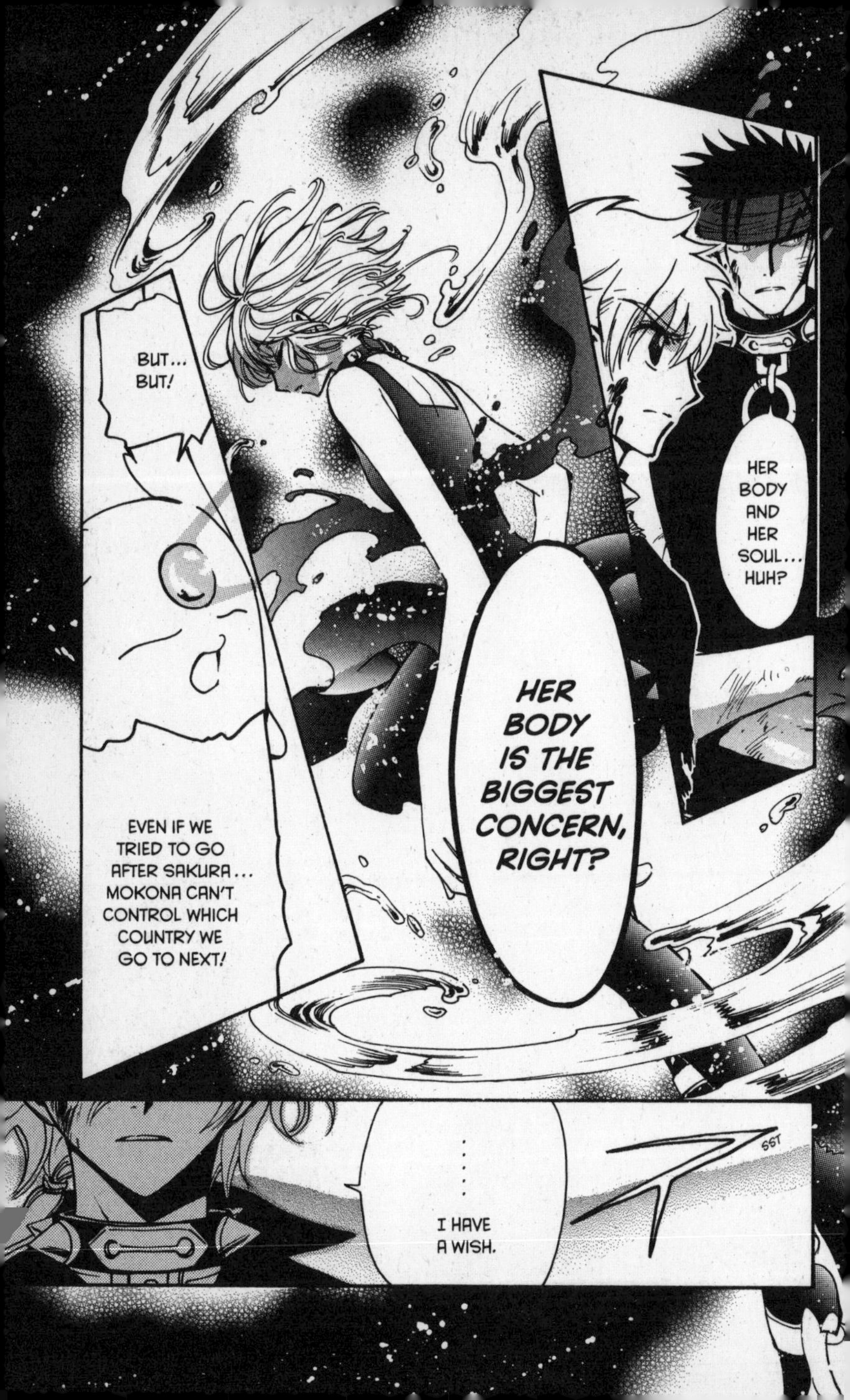
HER BODY AND HER SOUL... HUH?
HER BODY IS THE BIGGEST CONCERN, RIGHT?
BUT... BUT!
EVEN IF WE TRIED TO GO AFTER SAKURA... MOKONA CAN'T CONTROL WHICH COUNTRY WE GO TO NEXT!
SST
....
I HAVE A WISH.

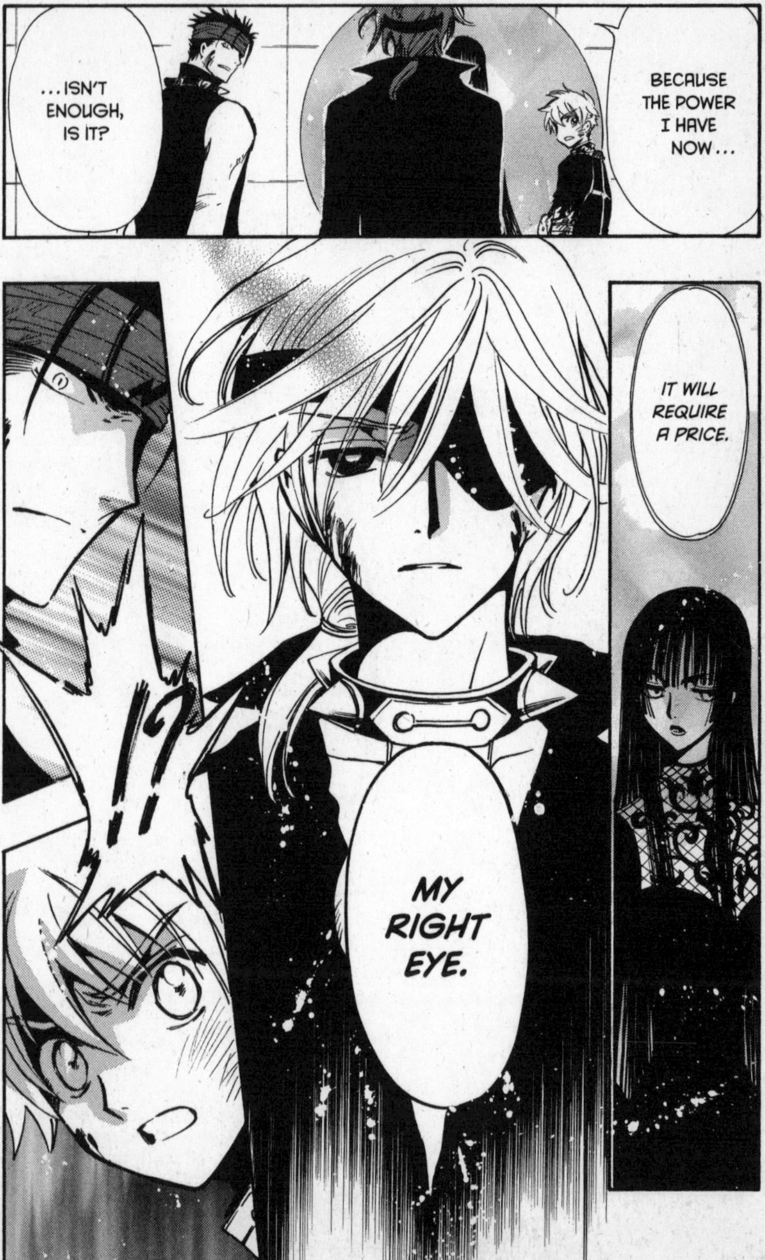
BECAUSE THE POWER I HAVE NOW...
...ISN'T ENOUGH, IS IT?
IT WILL REQUIRE A PRICE.
MY RIGHT EYE.

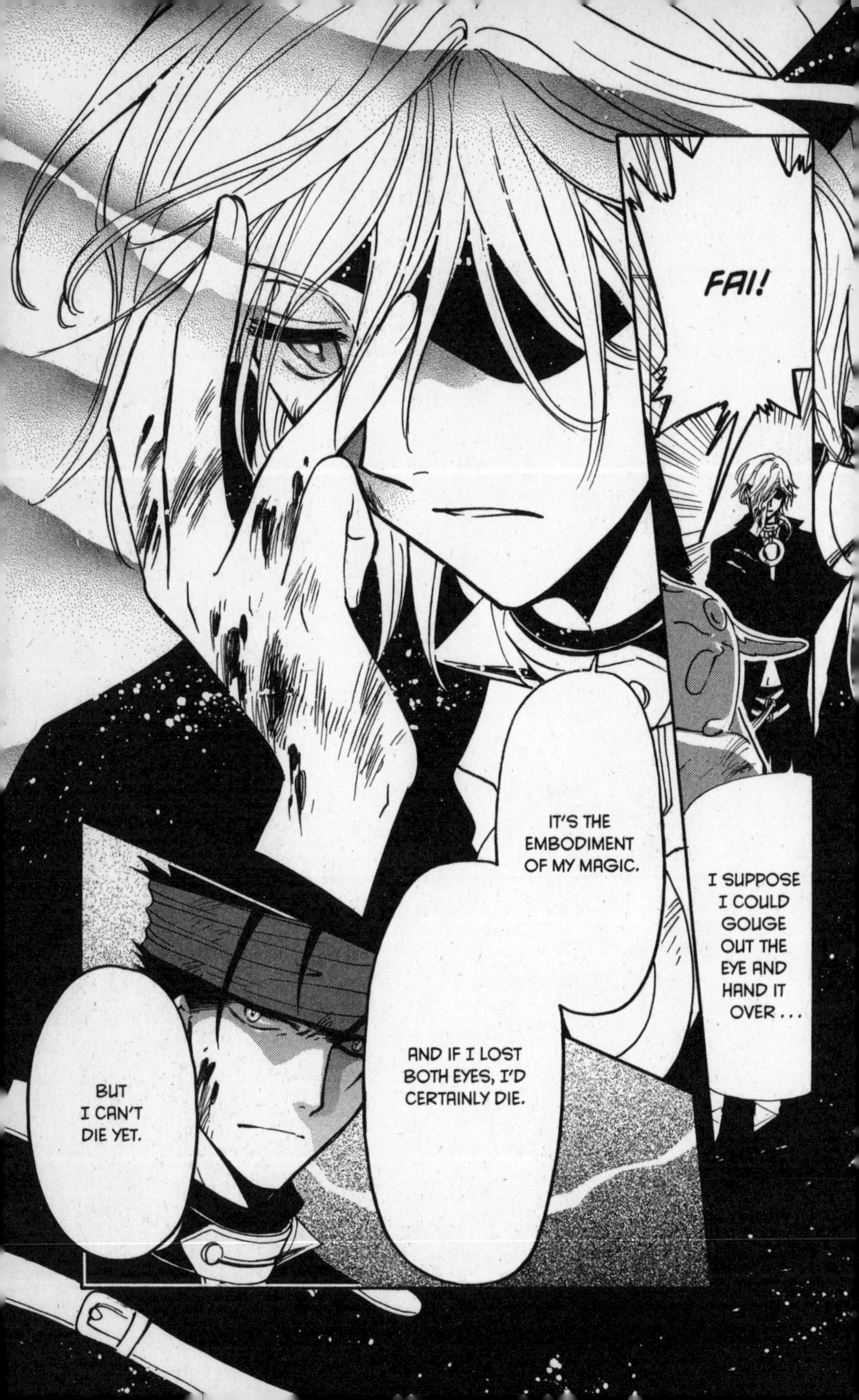
FAI!
I SUPPOSE I COULD GOUGE OUT THE EYE AND HAND IT OVER . . .
IT'S THE EMBODIMENT OF MY MAGIC.
AND IF I LOST BOTH EYES, I'D CERTAINLY DIE.
BUT I CAN'T DIE YET.

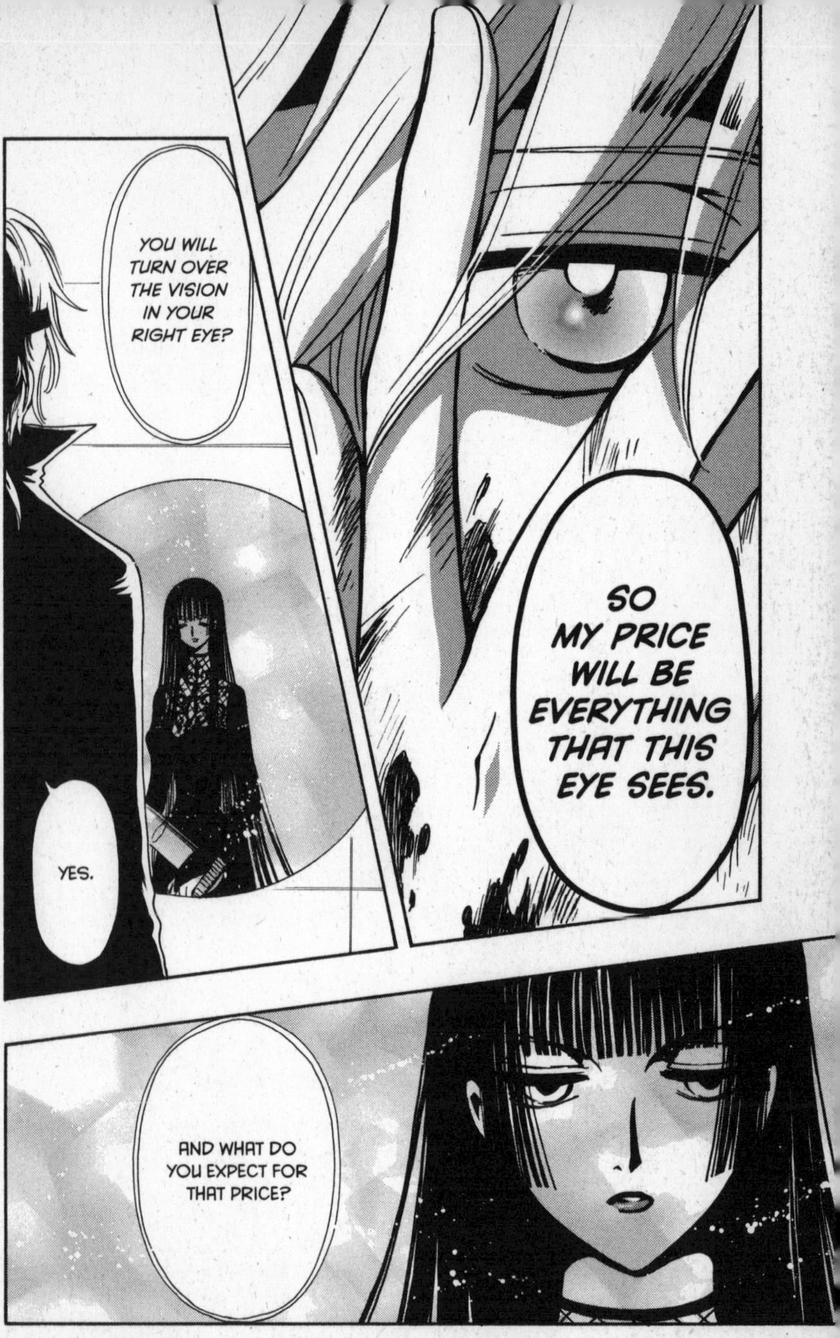
SO MY PRICE WILL BE EVERYTHING THAT THIS EYE SEES.
YOU WILL TURN OVER THE VISION IN YOUR RIGHT EYE?
YES.
AND WHAT DO YOU EXPECT FOR THAT PRICE?

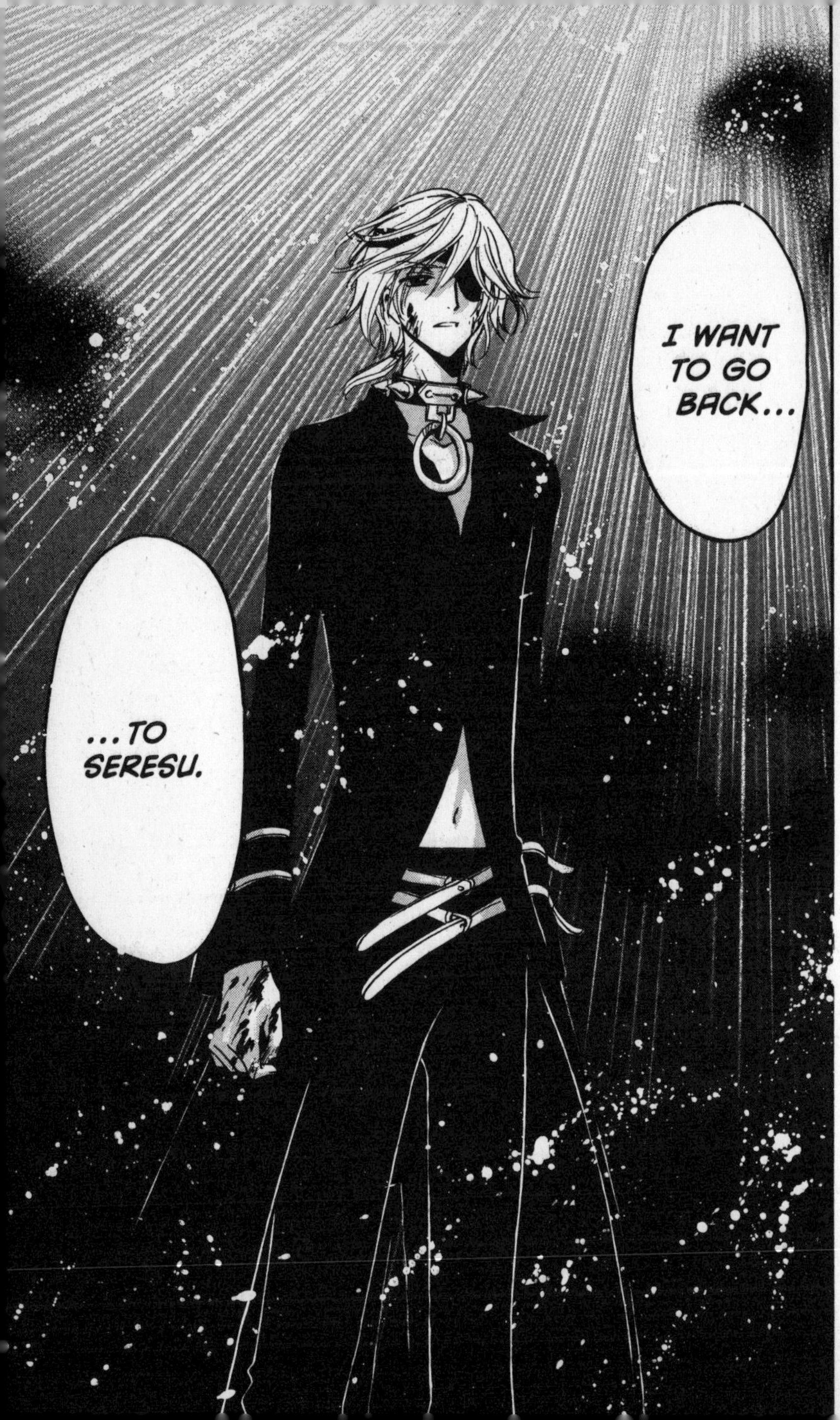
I WANT TO GO BACK...
...TO SERESU.

ツバサ
RESERVoir CHRoNiCLE

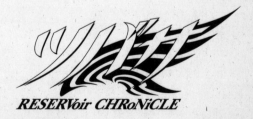

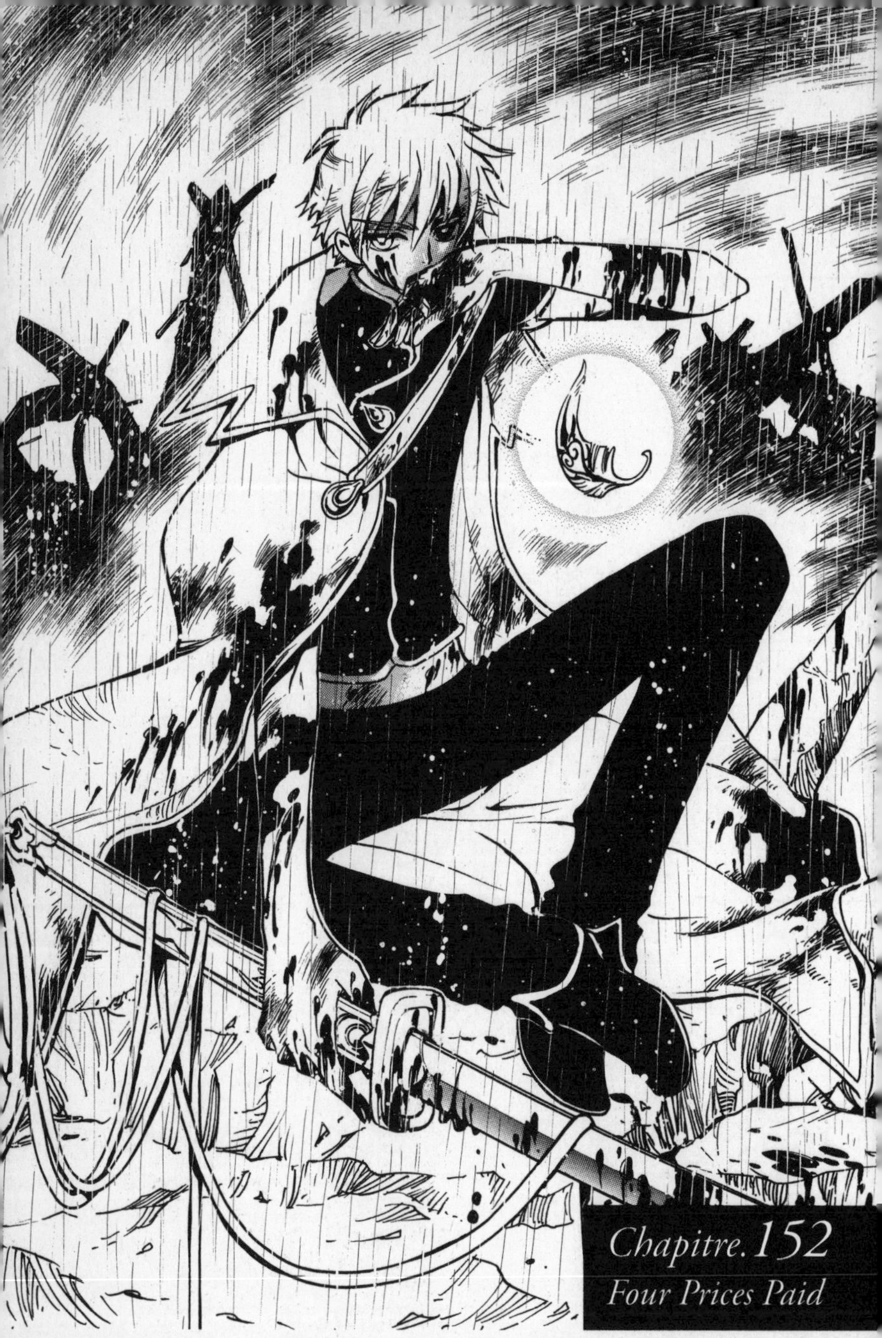

Chapitre. 152
Four Prices Paid

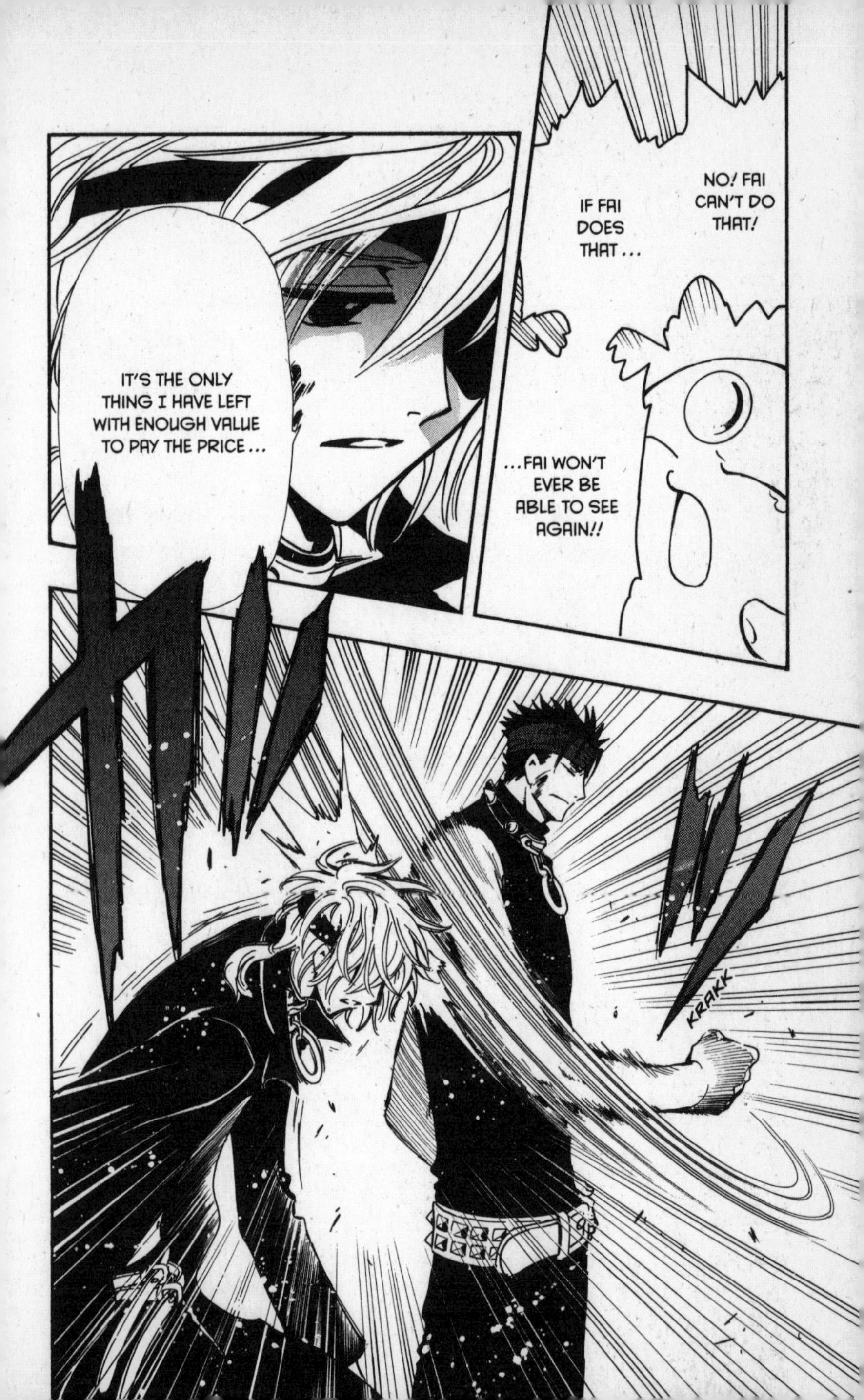
NO! FAI CAN'T DO THAT!
IF FAI DOES THAT...
...FAI WON'T EVER BE ABLE TO SEE AGAIN!!
IT'S THE ONLY THING I HAVE LEFT WITH ENOUGH VALUE TO PAY THE PRICE...
KRAKK

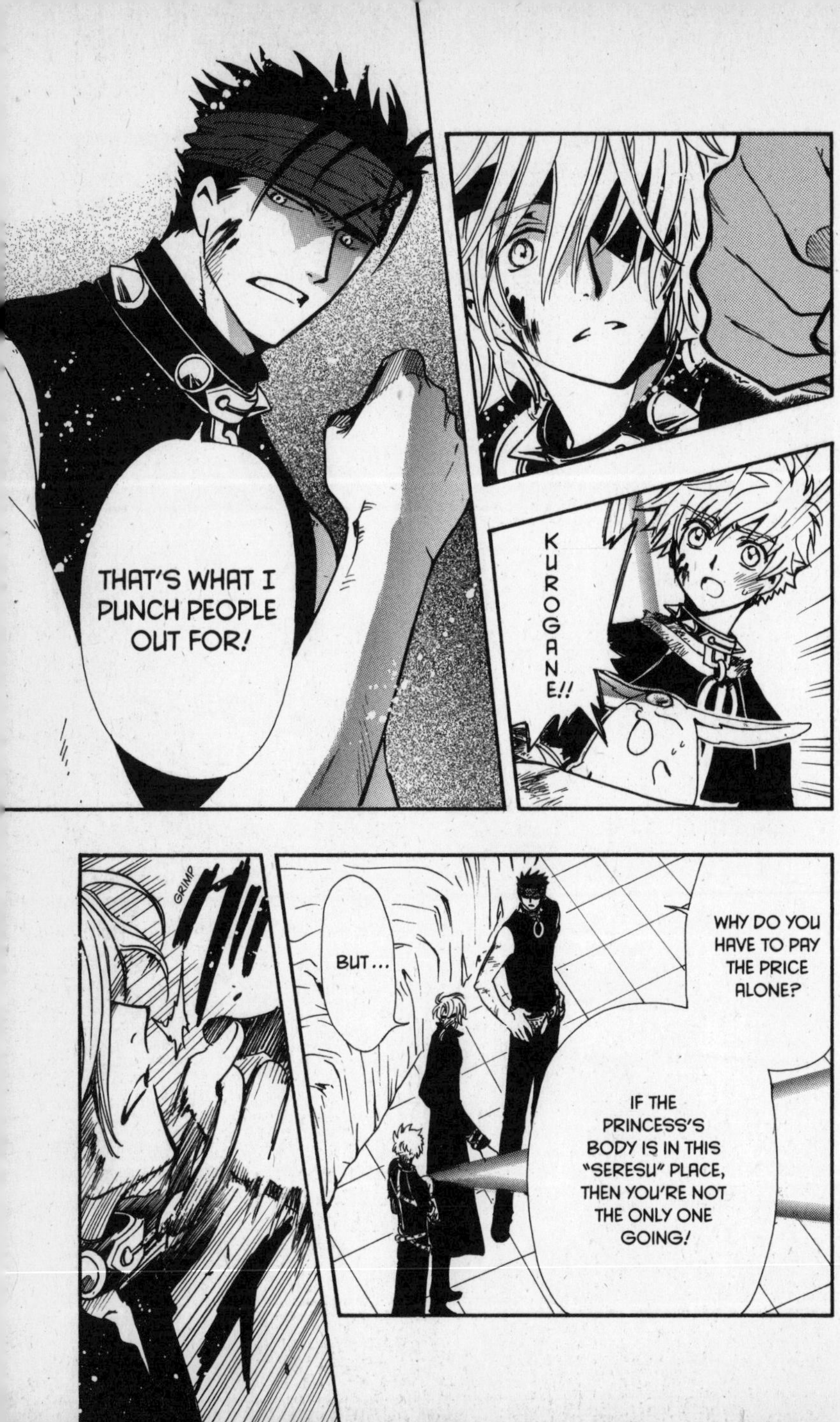
KUROGANE!!
THAT'S WHAT I PUNCH PEOPLE OUT FOR!
WHY DO YOU HAVE TO PAY THE PRICE ALONE?
IF THE PRINCESS'S BODY IS IN THIS "SERESU" PLACE, THEN YOU'RE NOT THE ONLY ONE GOING!
BUT...
GRIMP

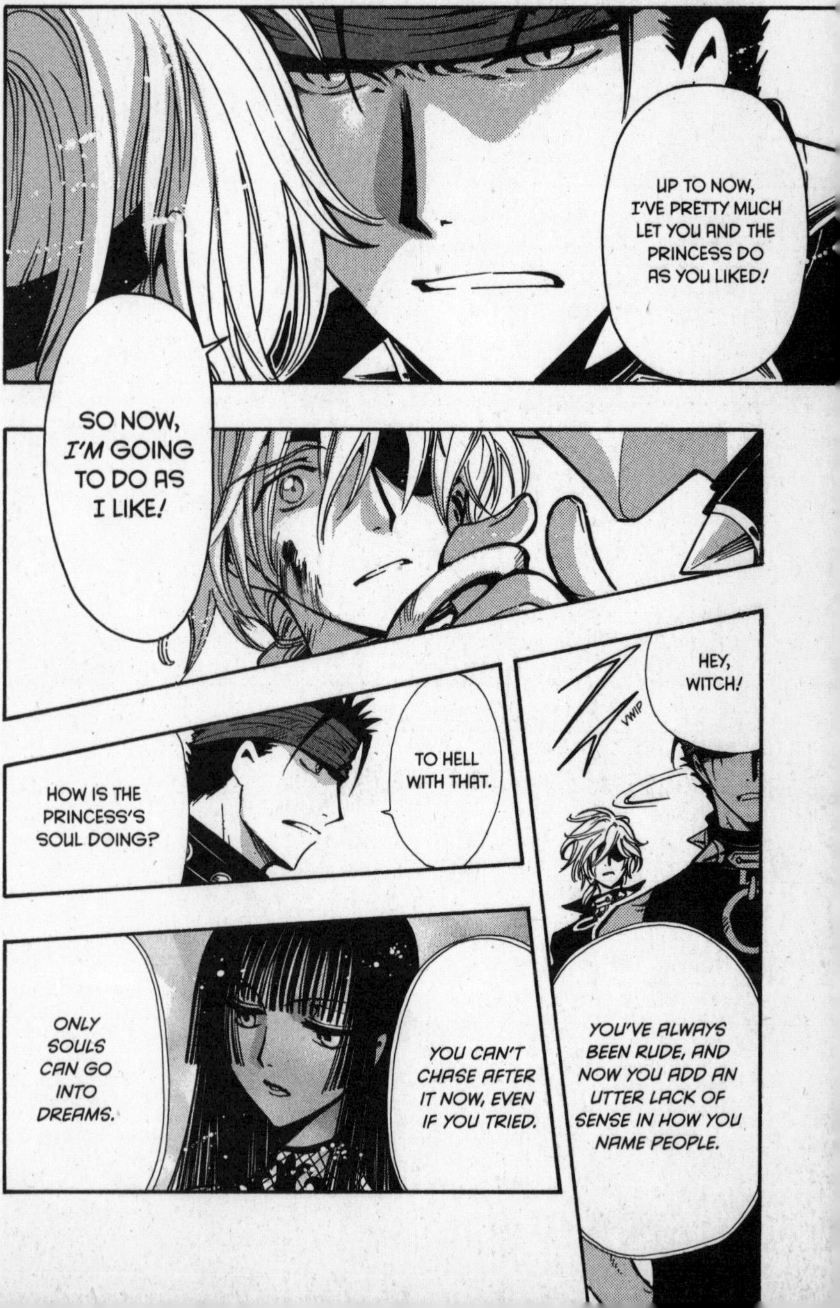
UP TO NOW, I'VE PRETTY MUCH LET YOU AND THE PRINCESS DO AS YOU LIKED!
SO NOW, *I'M* GOING TO DO AS I LIKE!
HEY, WITCH!
VWIP
YOU'VE ALWAYS BEEN RUDE, AND NOW YOU ADD AN UTTER LACK OF SENSE IN HOW YOU NAME PEOPLE.
TO HELL WITH THAT.
HOW IS THE PRINCESS'S SOUL DOING?
YOU CAN'T CHASE AFTER IT NOW, EVEN IF YOU TRIED.
ONLY SOULS CAN GO INTO DREAMS.

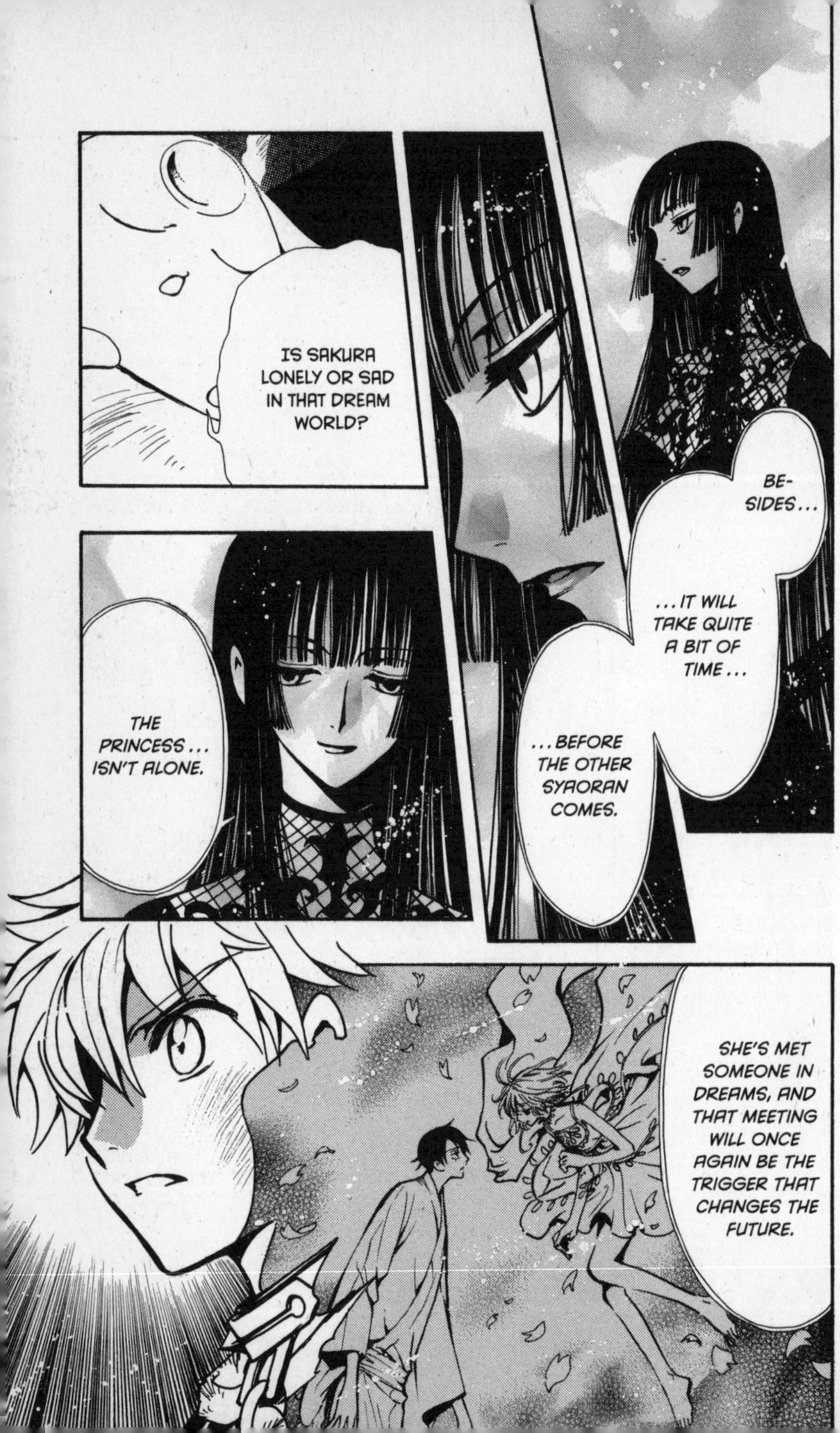
BE-SIDES...
...IT WILL TAKE QUITE A BIT OF TIME...
...BEFORE THE OTHER SYAORAN COMES.
IS SAKURA LONELY OR SAD IN THAT DREAM WORLD?
THE PRINCESS... ISN'T ALONE.
SHE'S MET SOMEONE IN DREAMS, AND THAT MEETING WILL ONCE AGAIN BE THE TRIGGER THAT CHANGES THE FUTURE.

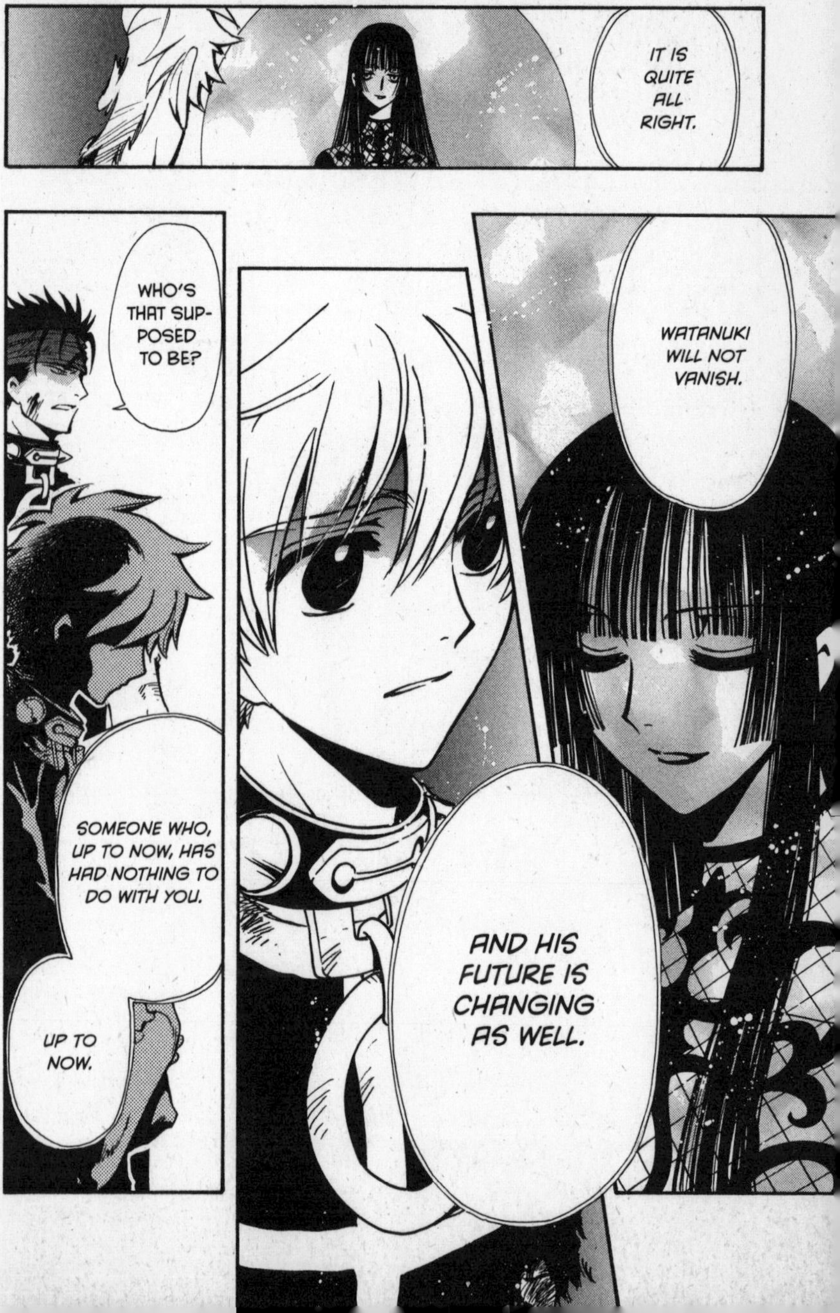
IT IS QUITE ALL RIGHT.
WATANUKI WILL NOT VANISH.
AND HIS FUTURE IS CHANGING AS WELL.
WHO'S THAT SUP-POSED TO BE?
SOMEONE WHO, UP TO NOW, HAS HAD NOTHING TO DO WITH YOU.
UP TO NOW.

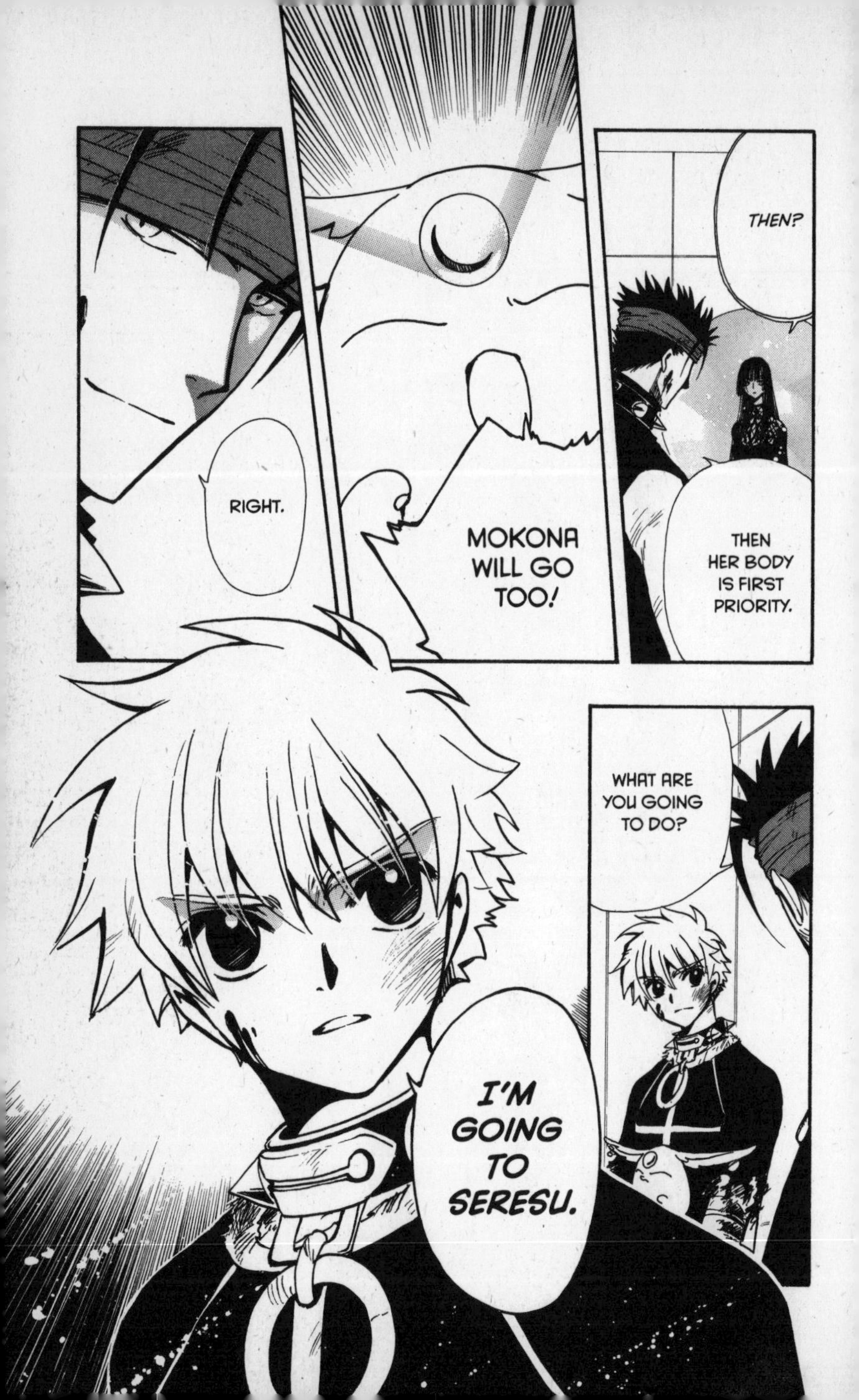
THEN?
THEN HER BODY IS FIRST PRIORITY.
MOKONA WILL GO TOO!
RIGHT.
WHAT ARE YOU GOING TO DO?
I'M GOING TO SERESU.

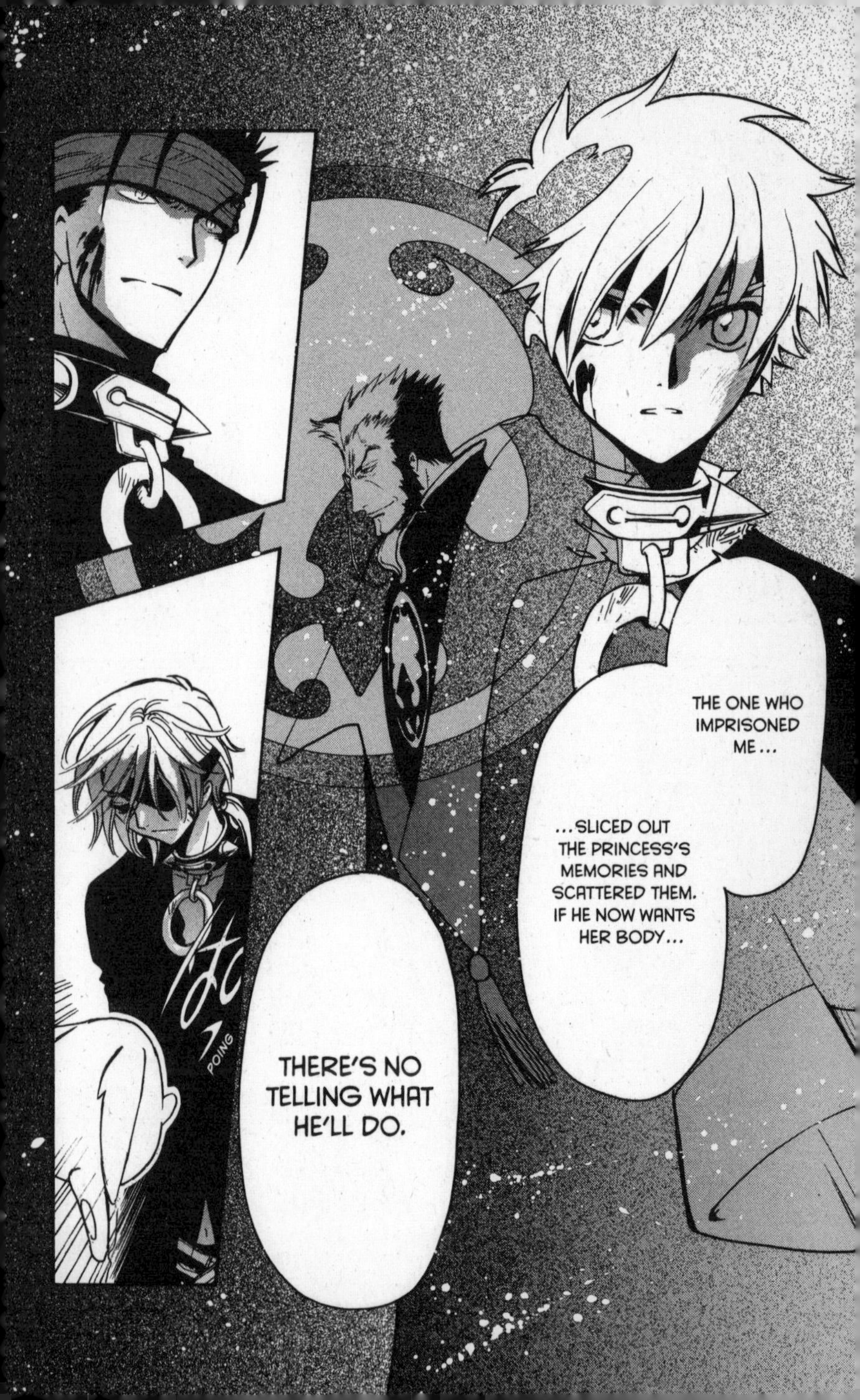
THE ONE WHO IMPRISONED ME...
...SLICED OUT THE PRINCESS'S MEMORIES AND SCATTERED THEM. IF HE NOW WANTS HER BODY...
THERE'S NO TELLING WHAT HE'LL DO.
POING

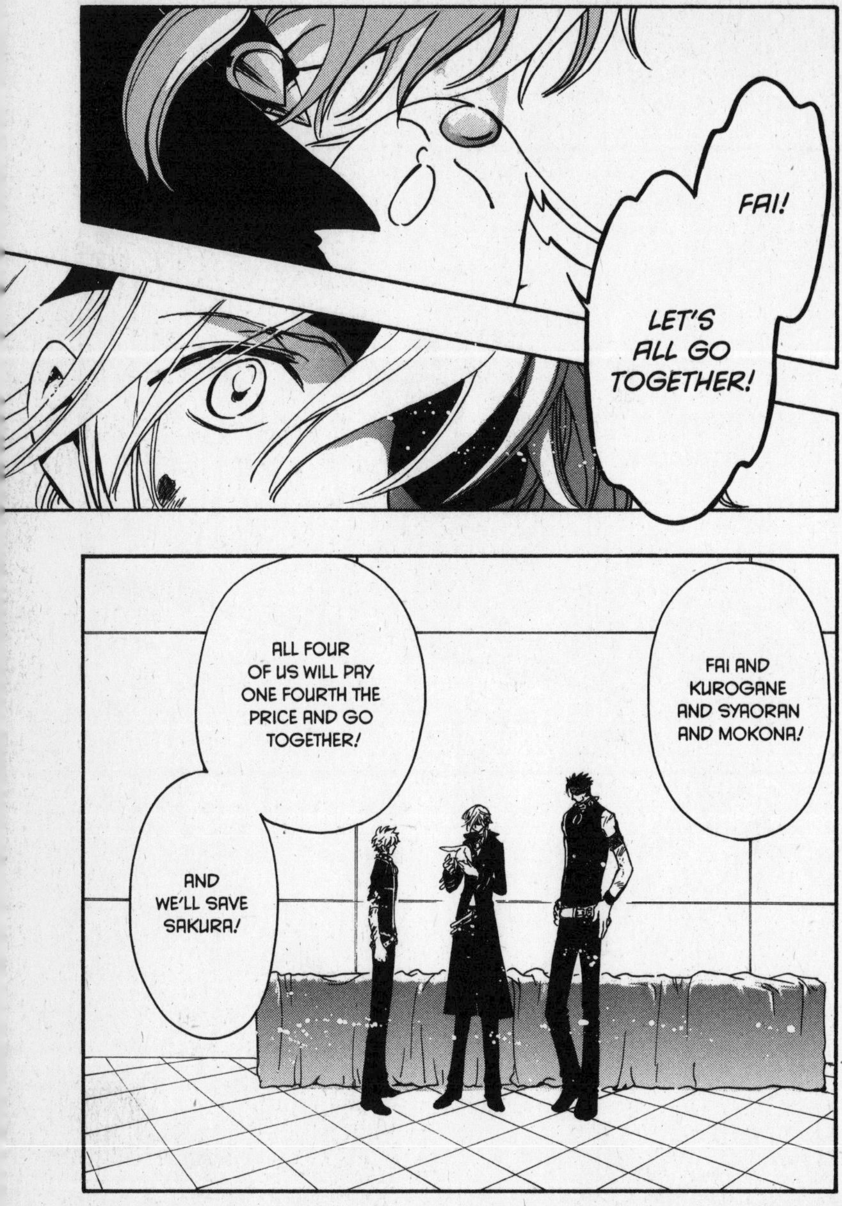
FAI! LET'S ALL GO TOGETHER!
FAI AND KUROGANE AND SYAORAN AND MOKONA!
ALL FOUR OF US WILL PAY ONE FOURTH THE PRICE AND GO TOGETHER!
AND WE'LL SAVE SAKURA!

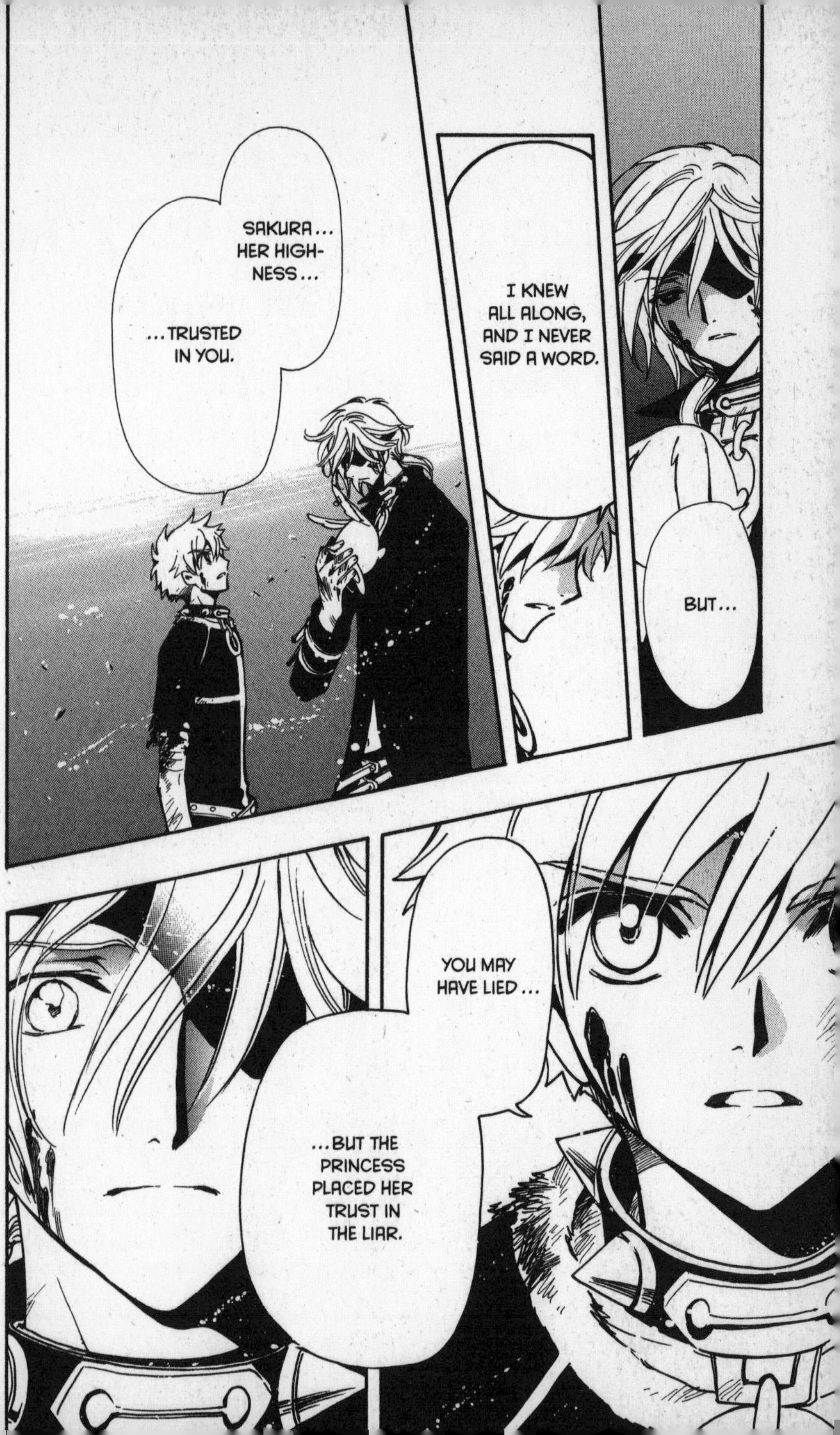
BUT...
I KNEW ALL ALONG, AND I NEVER SAID A WORD.
SAKURA... HER HIGHNESS...
...TRUSTED IN YOU.
YOU MAY HAVE LIED...
...BUT THE PRINCESS PLACED HER TRUST IN THE LIAR.

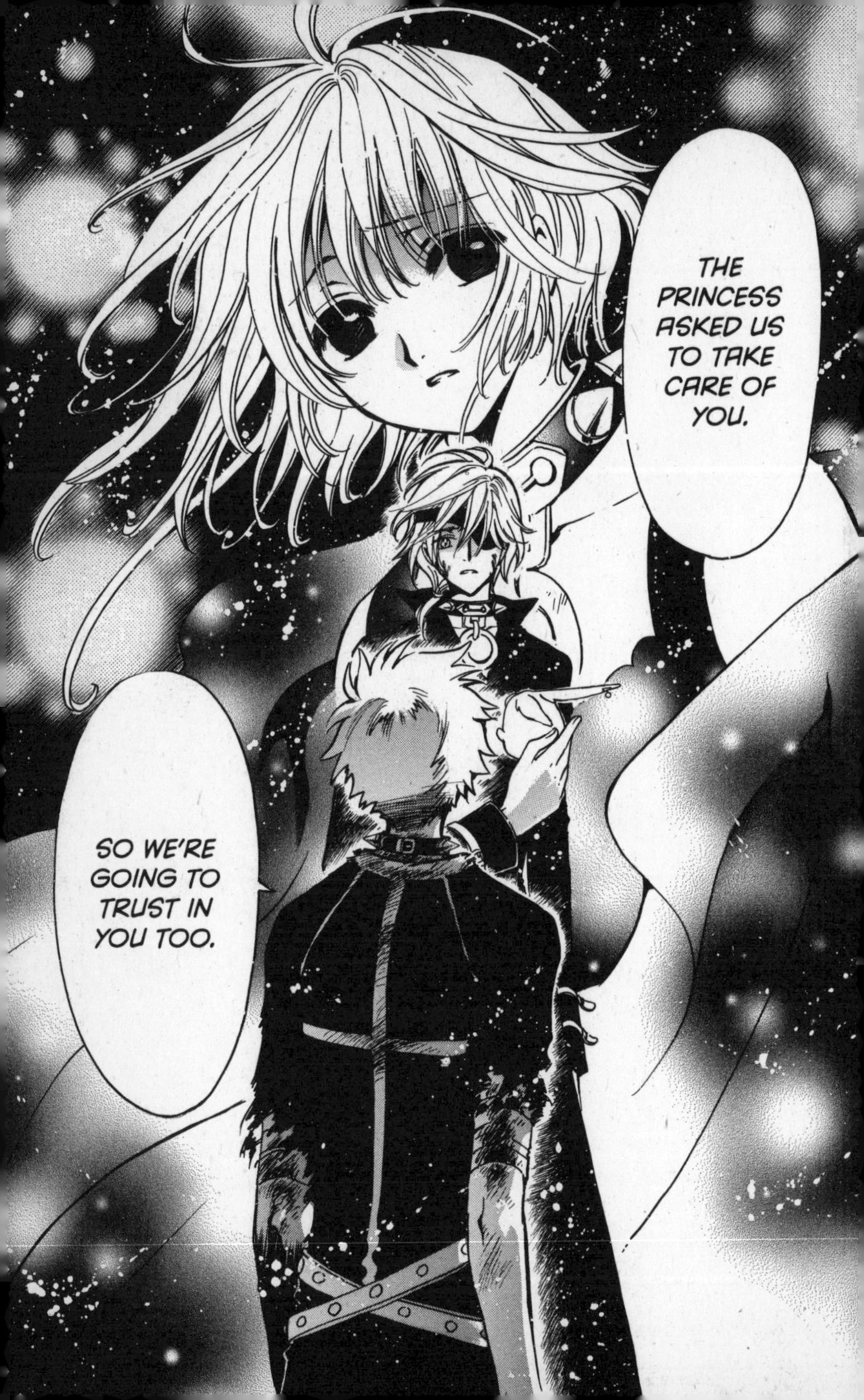
THE PRINCESS ASKED US TO TAKE CARE OF YOU.
SO WE'RE GOING TO TRUST IN YOU TOO.

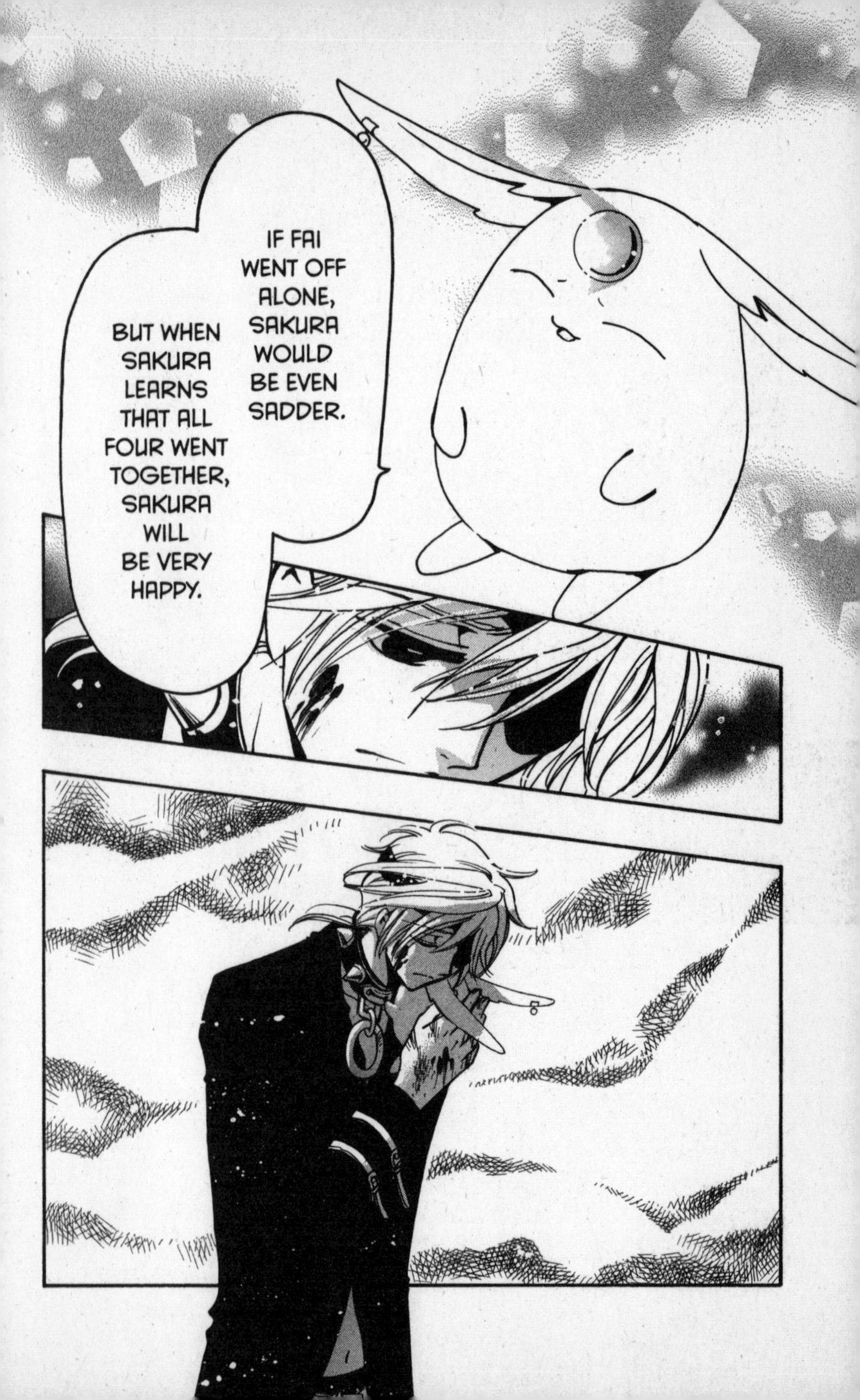
IF FAI WENT OFF ALONE, SAKURA WOULD BE EVEN SADDER.
BUT WHEN SAKURA LEARNS THAT ALL FOUR WENT TOGETHER, SAKURA WILL BE VERY HAPPY.

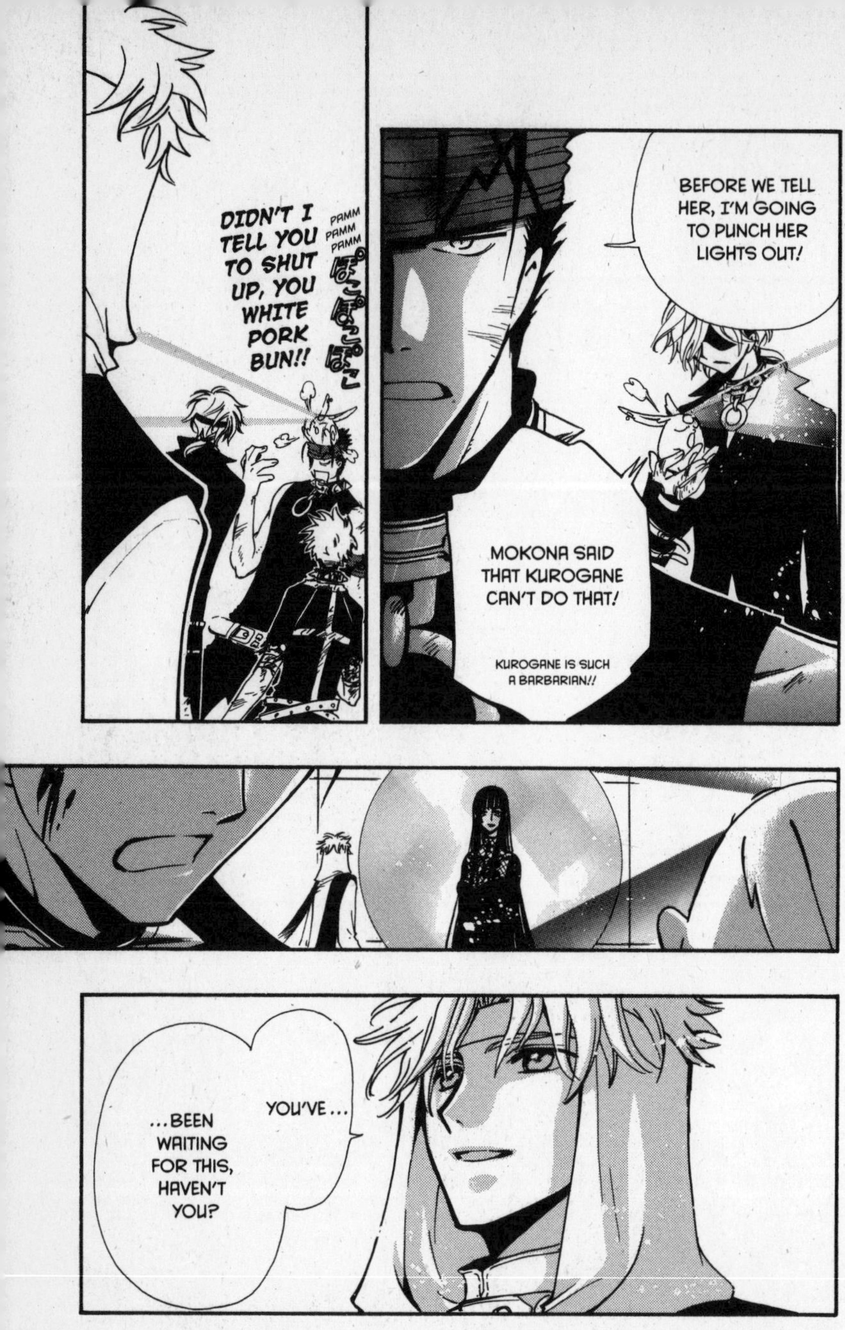
BEFORE WE TELL HER, I'M GOING TO PUNCH HER LIGHTS OUT!
MOKONA SAID THAT KUROGANE CAN'T DO THAT!
KUROGANE IS SUCH A BARBARIAN!!
DIDN'T I TELL YOU TO SHUT UP, YOU WHITE PORK BUN!!
PAMM PAMM PAMM
YOU'VE...
...BEEN WAITING FOR THIS, HAVEN'T YOU?

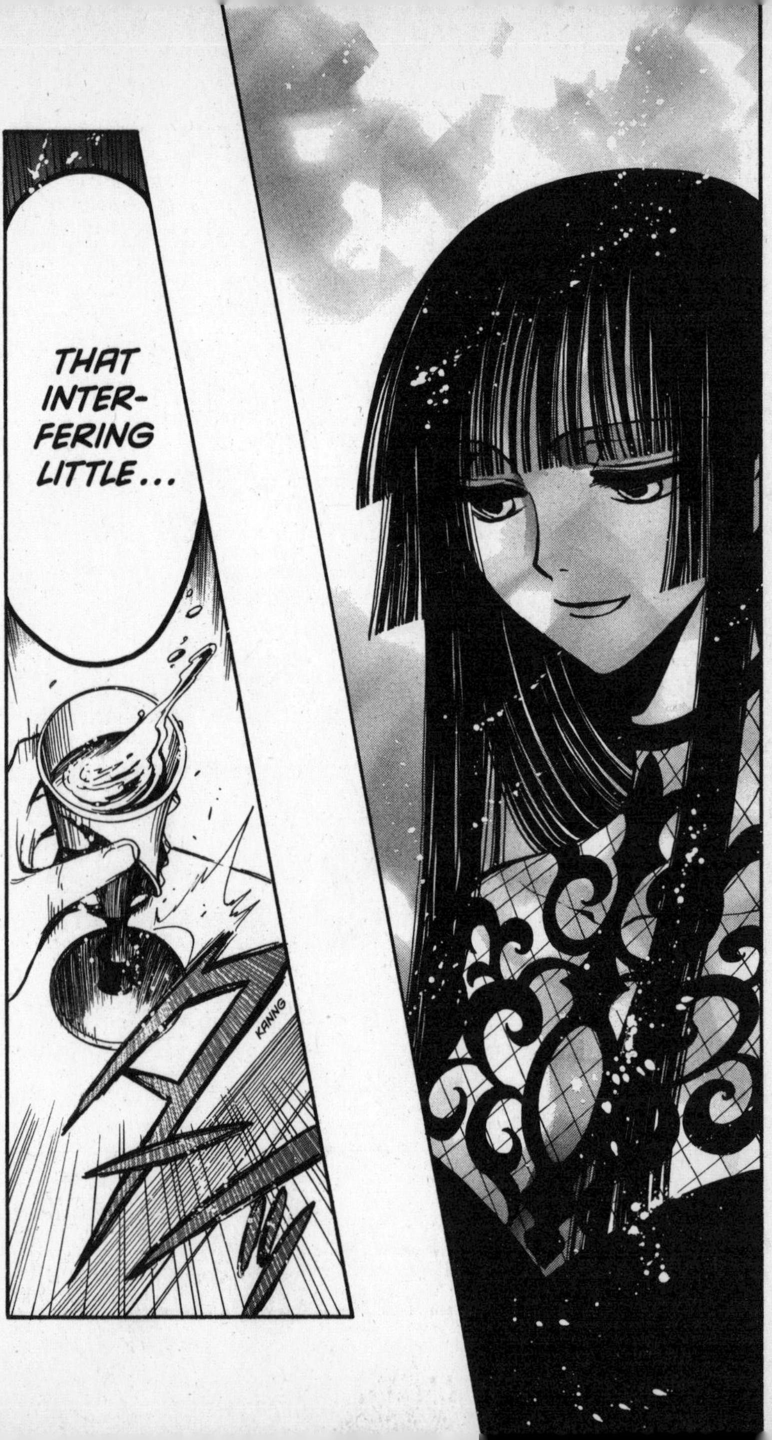
THAT INTER-FERING LITTLE...
KANNG

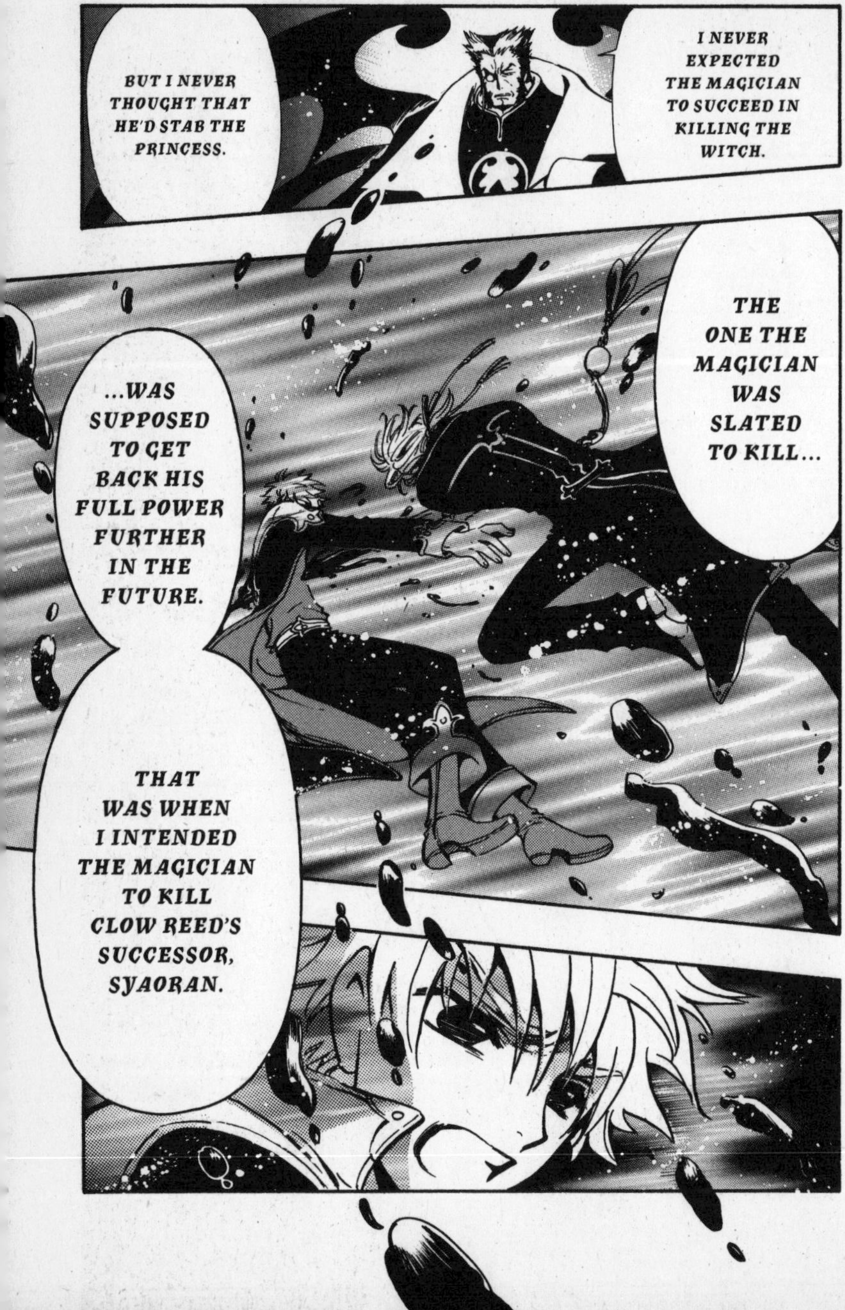
I NEVER EXPECTED THE MAGICIAN TO SUCCEED IN KILLING THE WITCH.
BUT I NEVER THOUGHT THAT HE'D STAB THE PRINCESS.
THE ONE THE MAGICIAN WAS SLATED TO KILL...
...WAS SUPPOSED TO GET BACK HIS FULL POWER FURTHER IN THE FUTURE.
THAT WAS WHEN I INTENDED THE MAGICIAN TO KILL CLOW REED'S SUCCESSOR, SYAORAN.

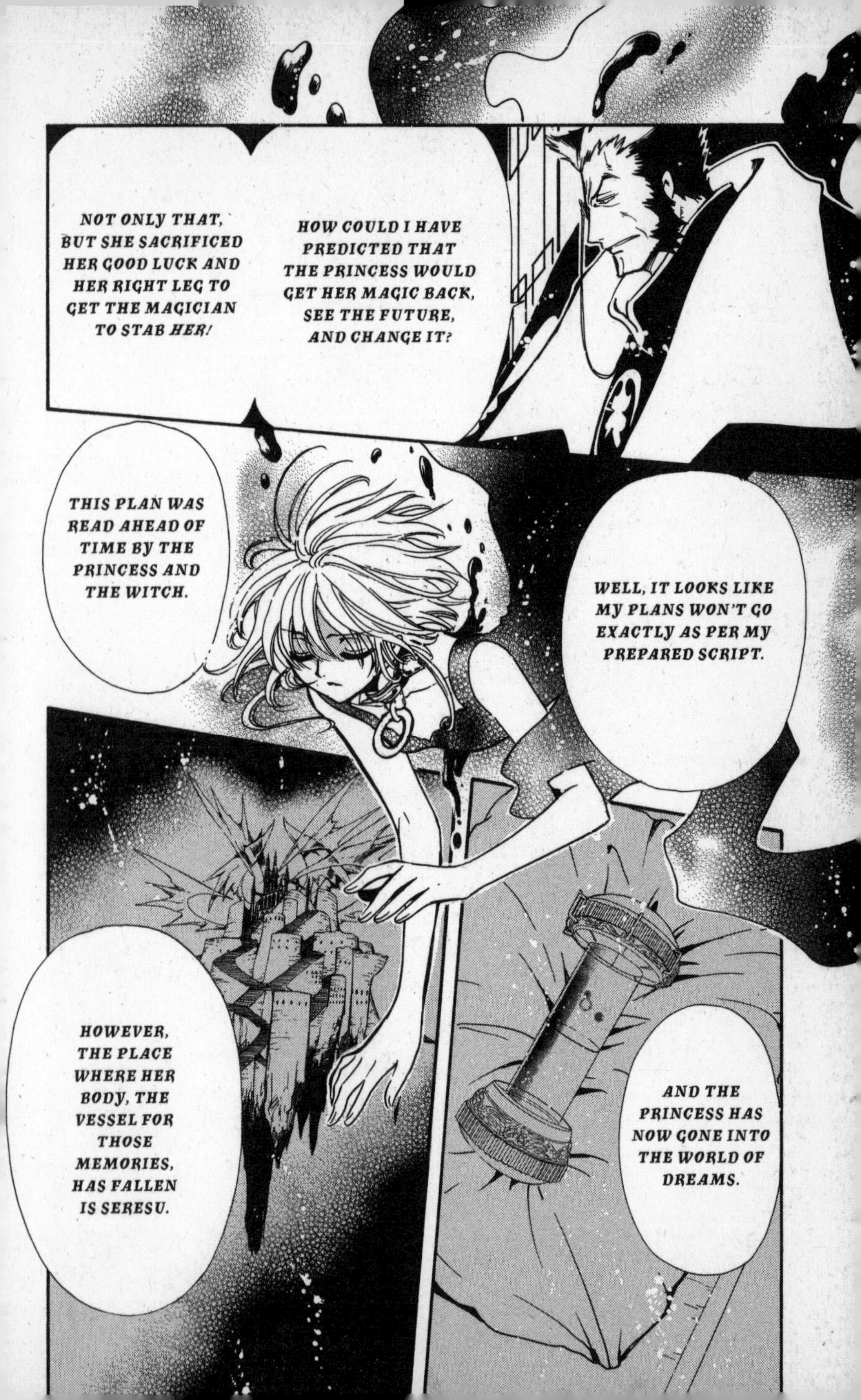
HOW COULD I HAVE PREDICTED THAT THE PRINCESS WOULD GET HER MAGIC BACK, SEE THE FUTURE, AND CHANGE IT?
NOT ONLY THAT, BUT SHE SACRIFICED HER GOOD LUCK AND HER RIGHT LEG TO GET THE MAGICIAN TO STAB HER!
WELL, IT LOOKS LIKE MY PLANS WON'T GO EXACTLY AS PER MY PREPARED SCRIPT.
THIS PLAN WAS READ AHEAD OF TIME BY THE PRINCESS AND THE WITCH.
AND THE PRINCESS HAS NOW GONE INTO THE WORLD OF DREAMS.
HOWEVER, THE PLACE WHERE HER BODY, THE VESSEL FOR THOSE MEMORIES, HAS FALLEN IS SERESU.

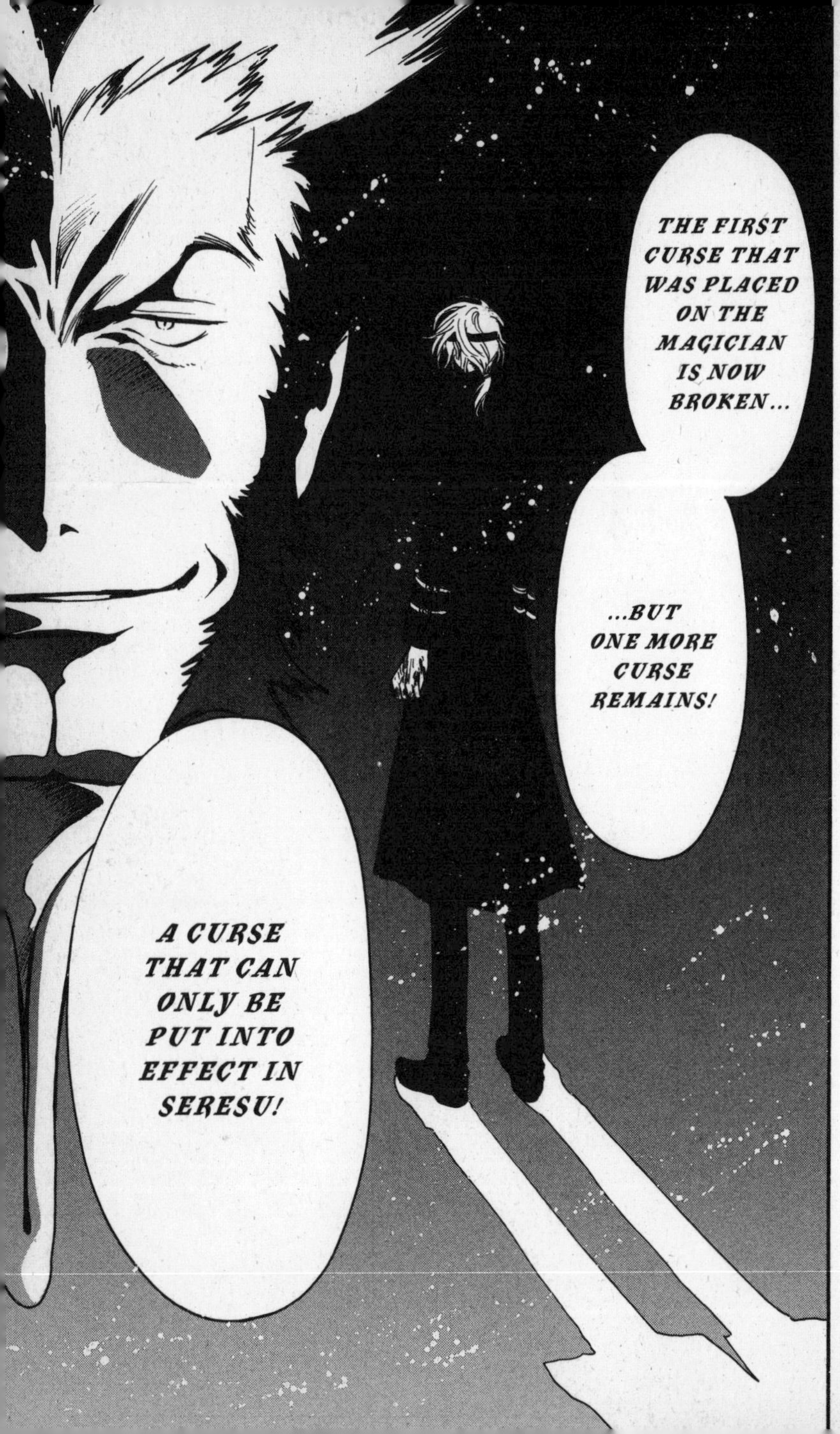
THE FIRST CURSE THAT WAS PLACED ON THE MAGICIAN IS NOW BROKEN...
...BUT ONE MORE CURSE REMAINS!
A CURSE THAT CAN ONLY BE PUT INTO EFFECT IN SERESU!

RESERVoir CHRoNiCLE

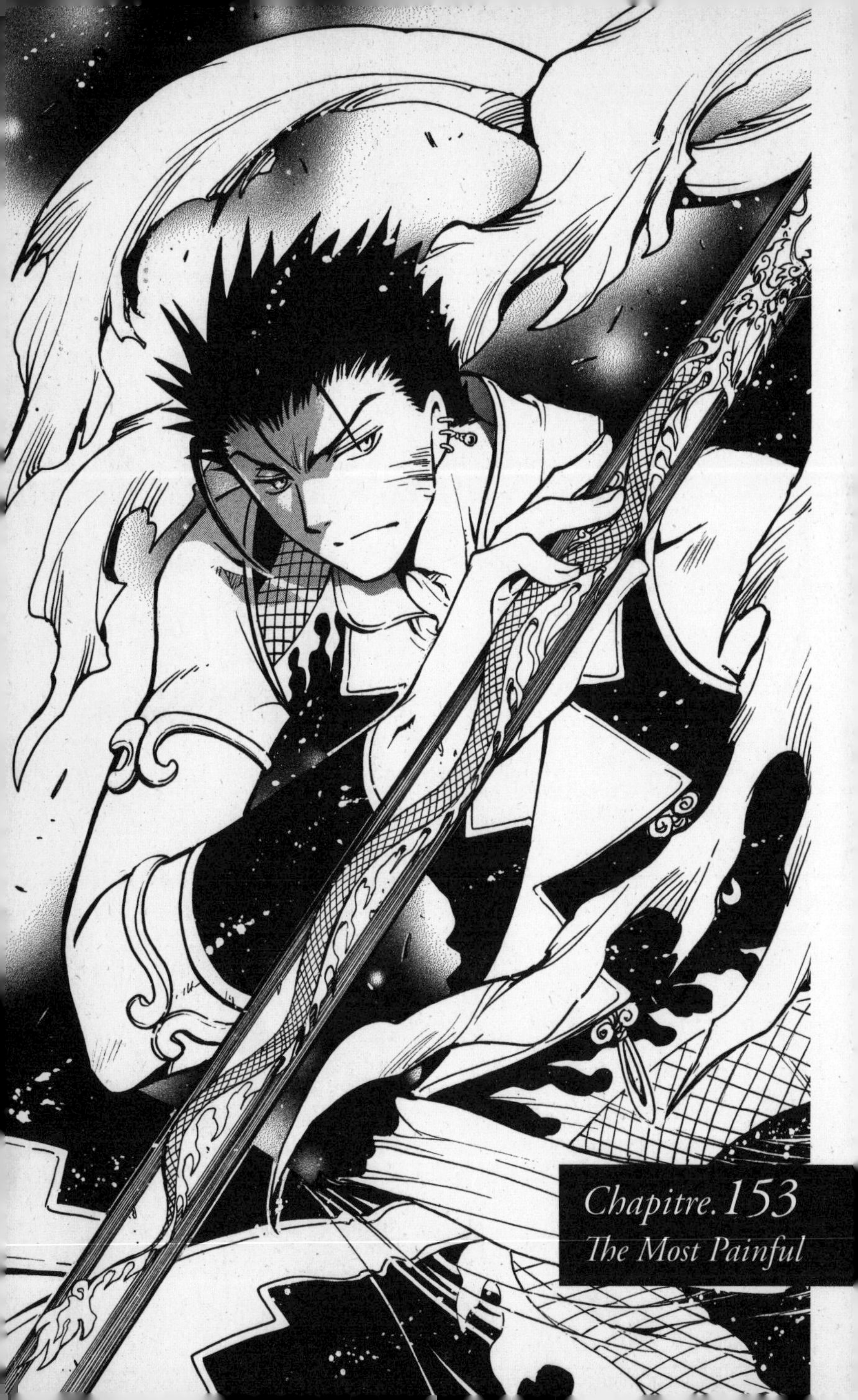
Chapitre. 153
The Most Painful

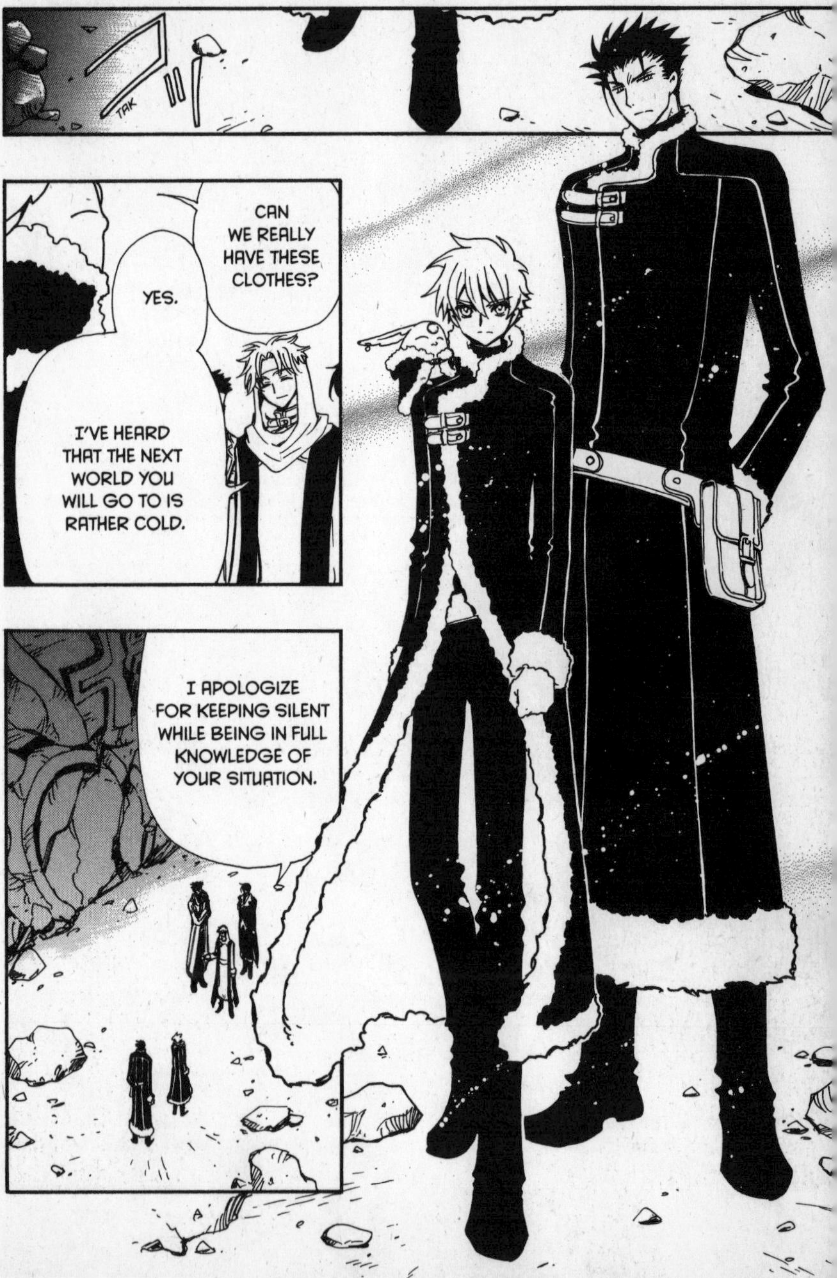
TAK
CAN WE REALLY HAVE THESE CLOTHES?
YES.
I'VE HEARD THAT THE NEXT WORLD YOU WILL GO TO IS RATHER COLD.
I APOLOGIZE FOR KEEPING SILENT WHILE BEING IN FULL KNOWLEDGE OF YOUR SITUATION.

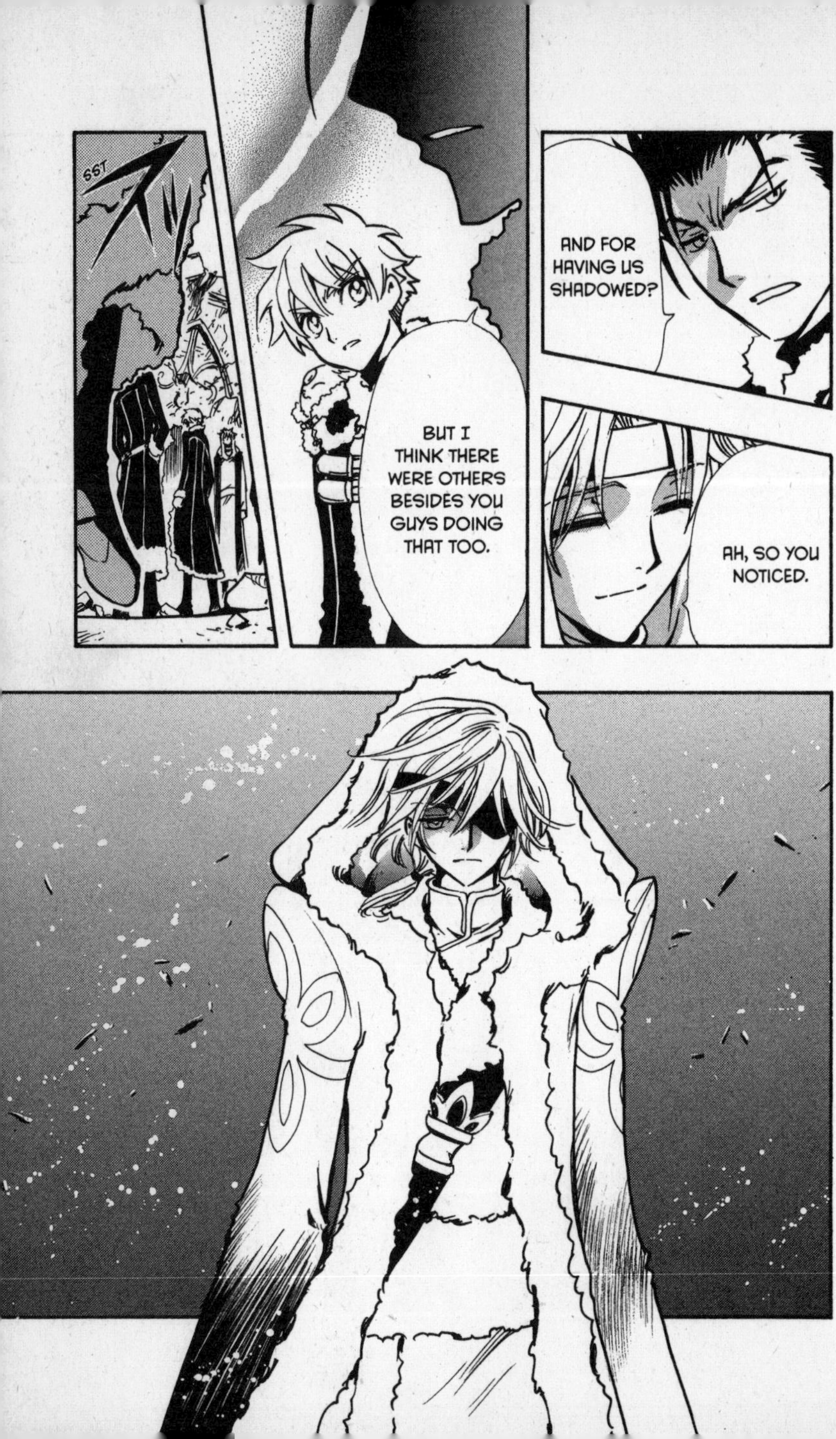
AND FOR HAVING US SHADOWED?
AH, SO YOU NOTICED.
BUT I THINK THERE WERE OTHERS BESIDES YOU GUYS DOING THAT TOO.
SST

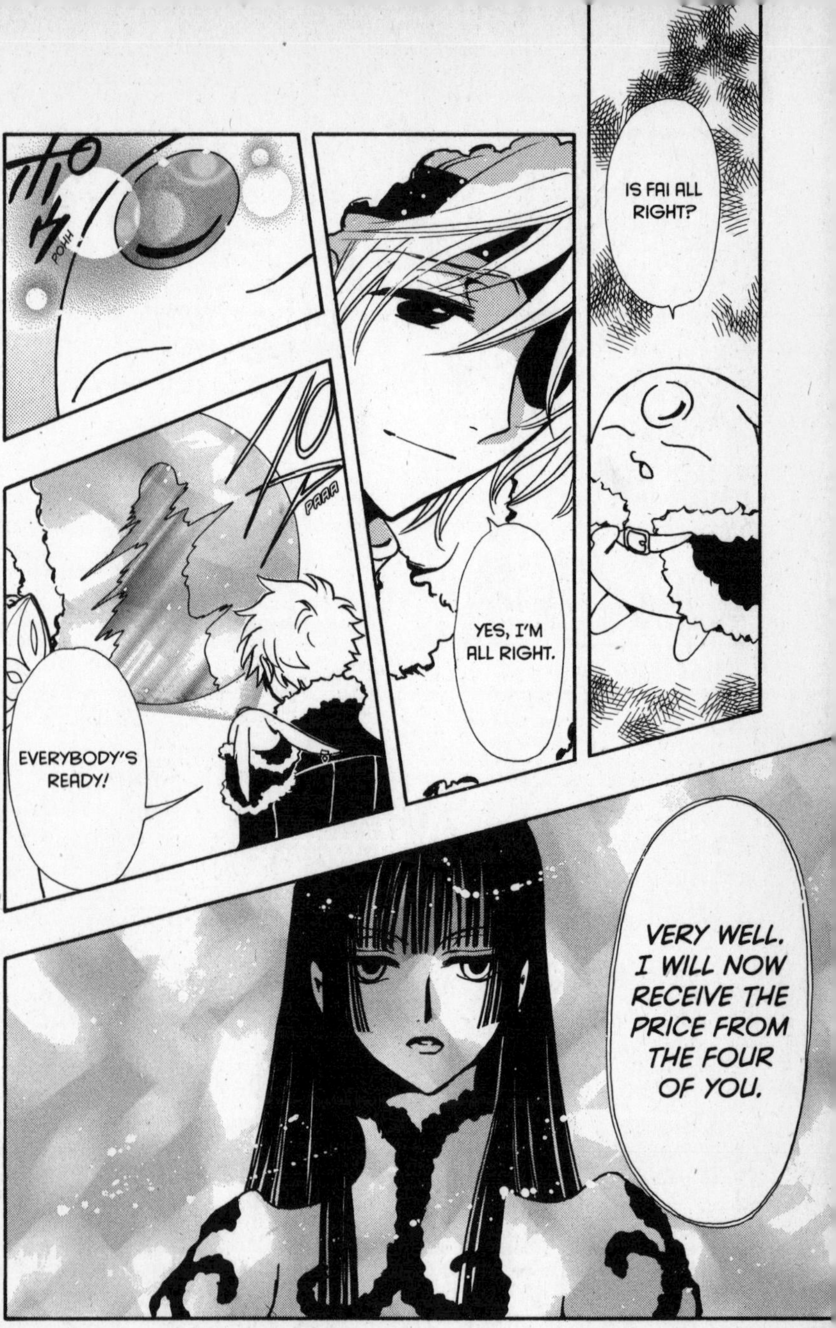
IS FAI ALL RIGHT?
YES, I'M ALL RIGHT.
POHH
PAAA
EVERYBODY'S READY!
VERY WELL. I WILL NOW RECEIVE THE PRICE FROM THE FOUR OF YOU.

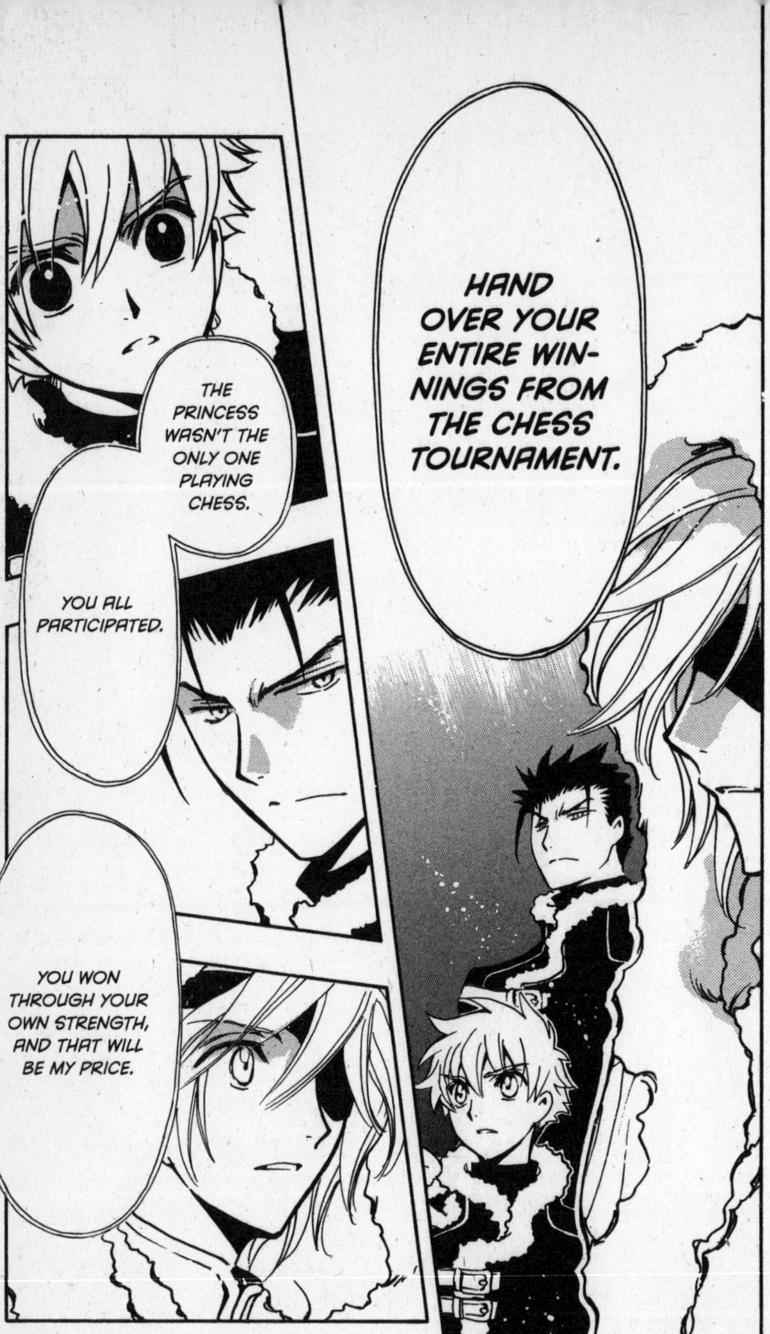
HAND OVER YOUR ENTIRE WIN- NINGS FROM THE CHESS TOURNAMENT.
THE PRINCESS WASN'T THE ONLY ONE PLAYING CHESS.
YOU ALL PARTICIPATED.
YOU WON THROUGH YOUR OWN STRENGTH, AND THAT WILL BE MY PRICE.

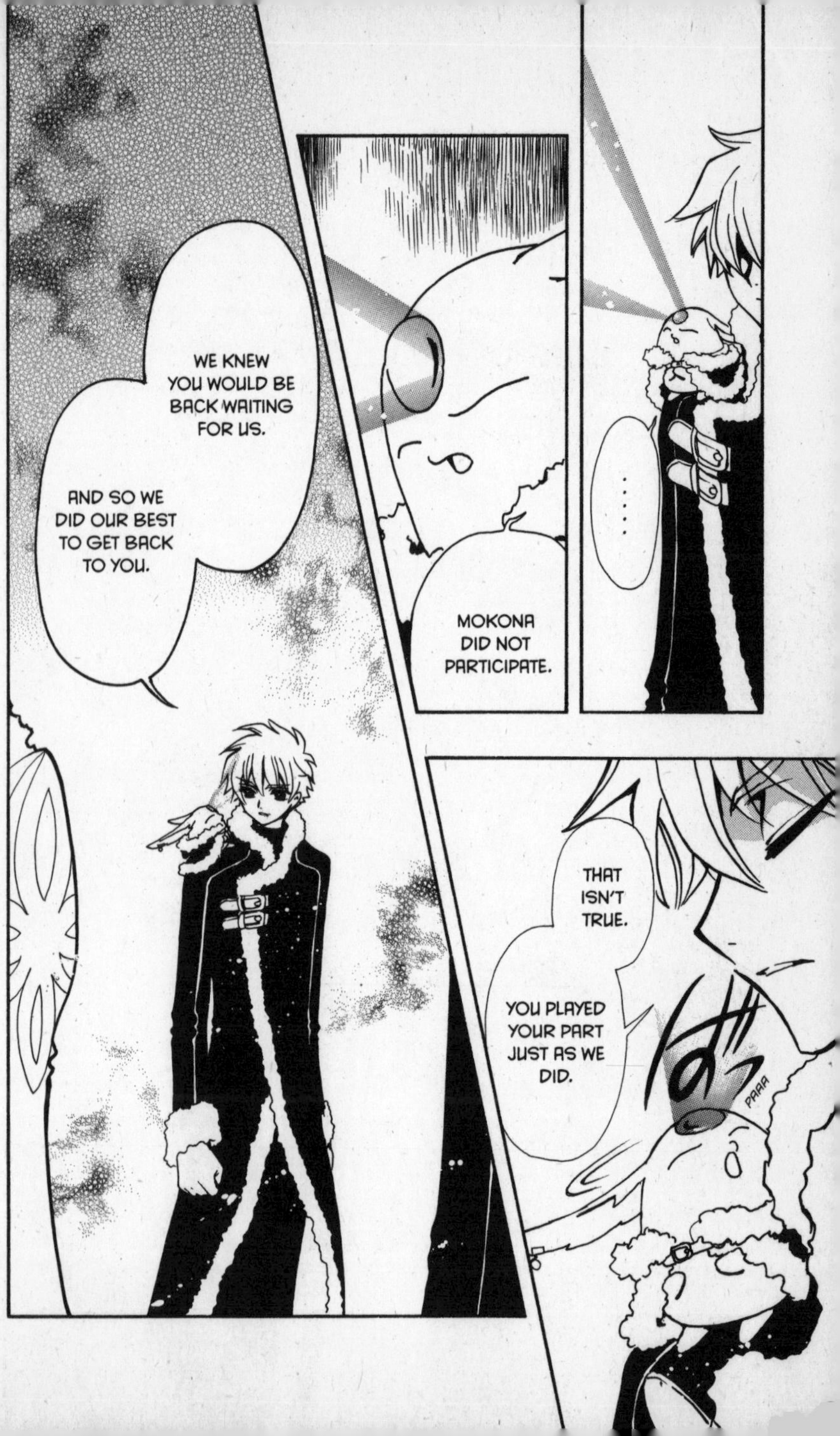
......
MOKONA DID NOT PARTICIPATE.
THAT ISN'T TRUE.
YOU PLAYED YOUR PART JUST AS WE DID.
PAAA
WE KNEW YOU WOULD BE BACK WAITING FOR US.
AND SO WE DID OUR BEST TO GET BACK TO YOU.

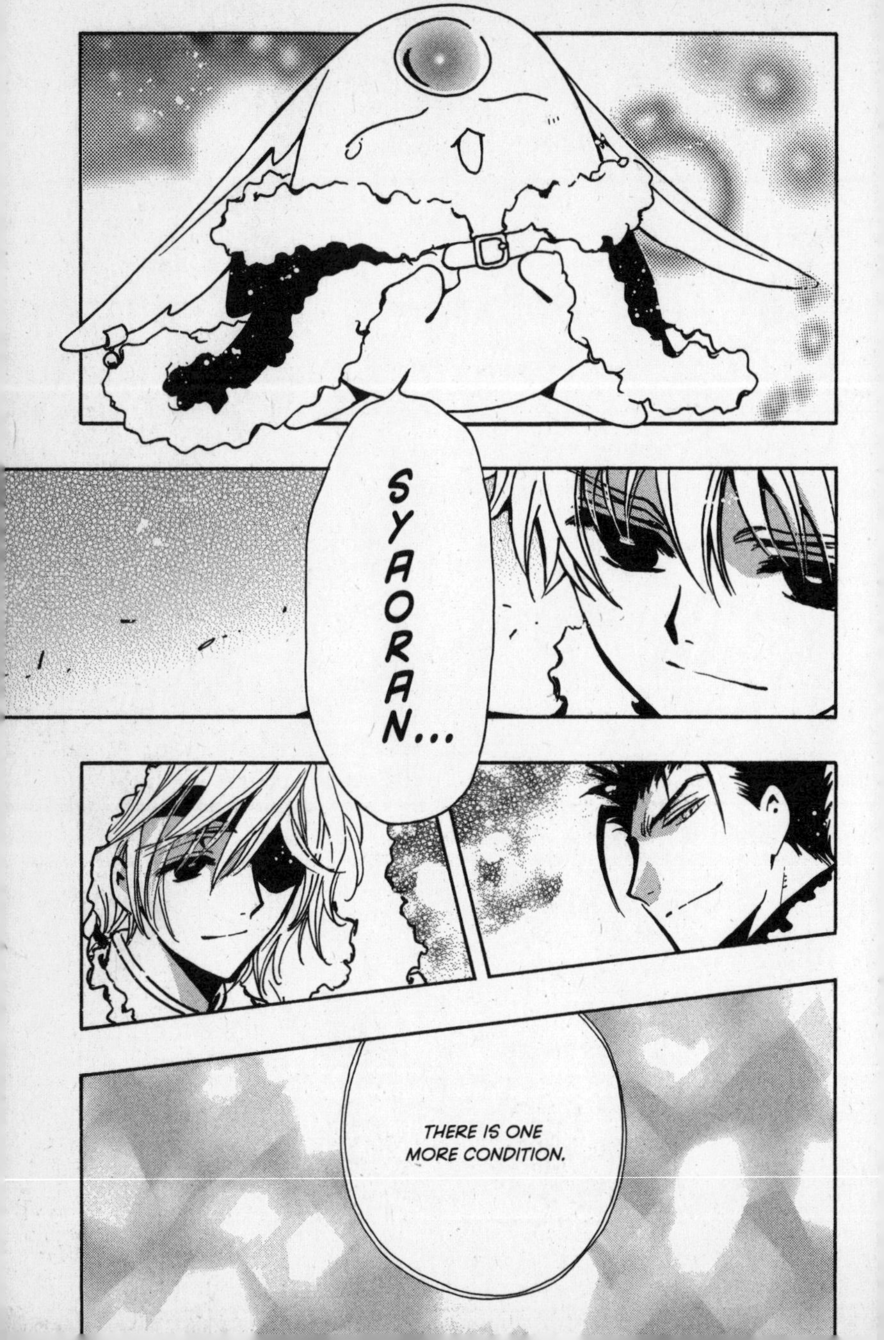
SYAORAN...
THERE IS ONE MORE CONDITION.

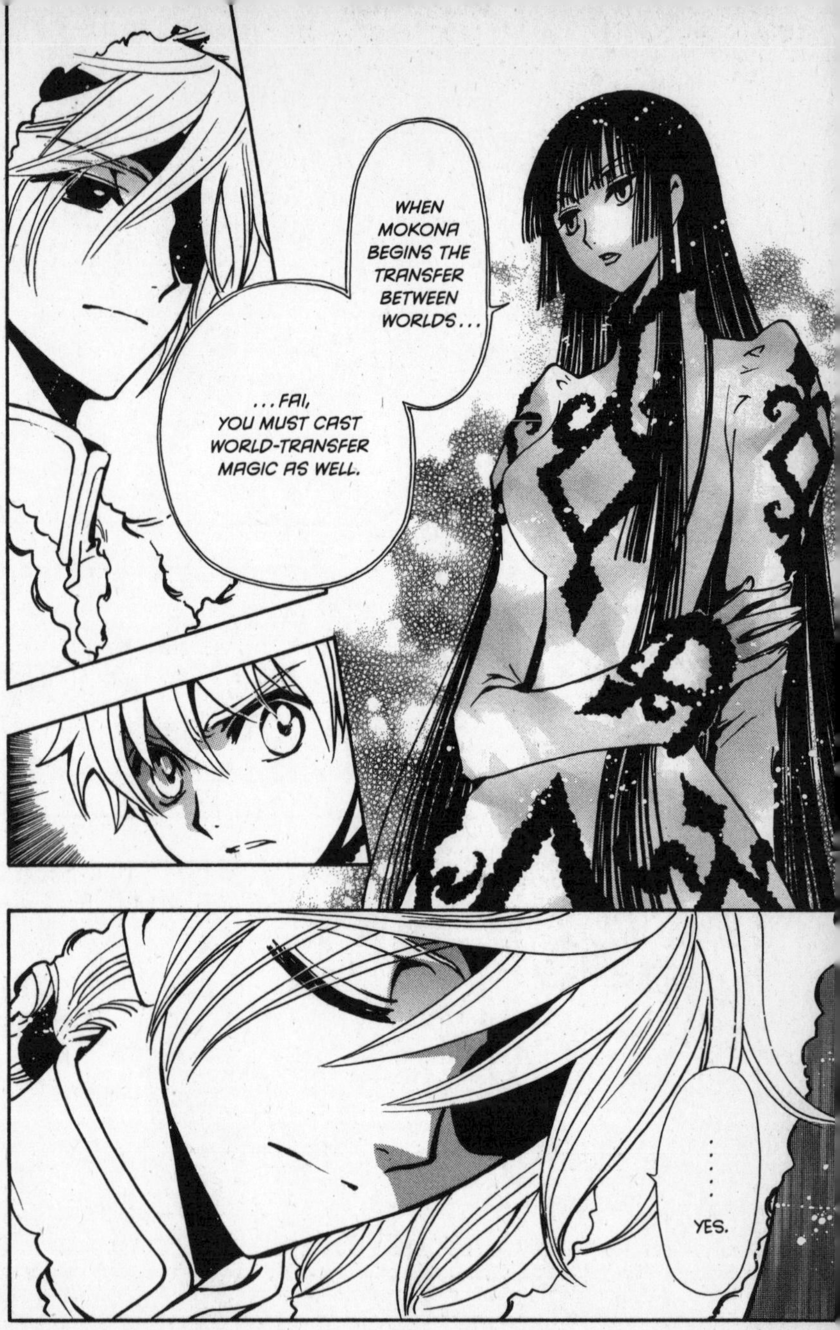
WHEN MOKONA BEGINS THE TRANSFER BETWEEN WORLDS...
...FAI, YOU MUST CAST WORLD-TRANSFER MAGIC AS WELL.
.....
YES.

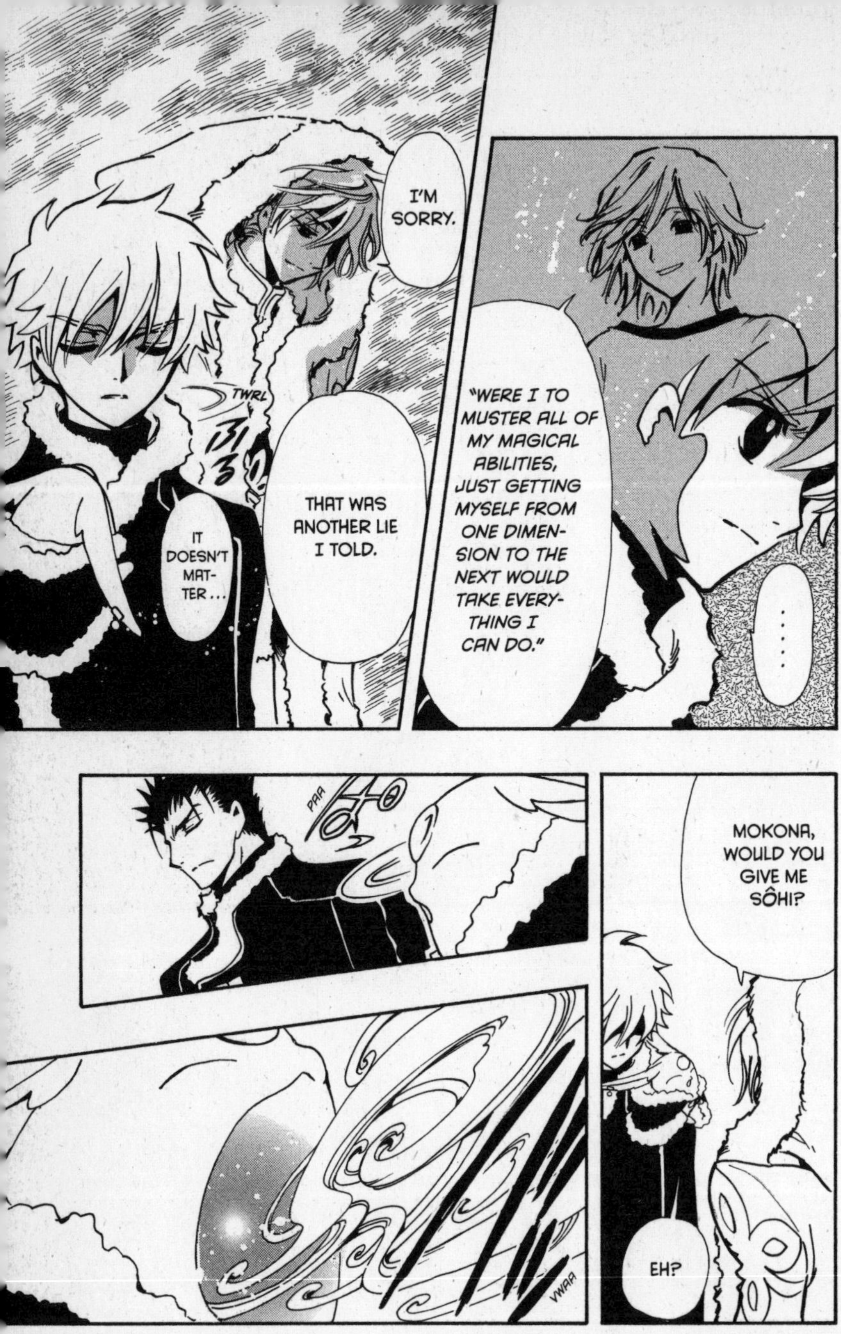
"WERE I TO MUSTER ALL OF MY MAGICAL ABILITIES, JUST GETTING MYSELF FROM ONE DIMENSION TO THE NEXT WOULD TAKE EVERYTHING I CAN DO."
......
I'M SORRY.
THAT WAS ANOTHER LIE I TOLD.
TWRL
IT DOESN'T MATTER...
MOKONA, WOULD YOU GIVE ME SÔHI?
EH?
PAA
VWAA

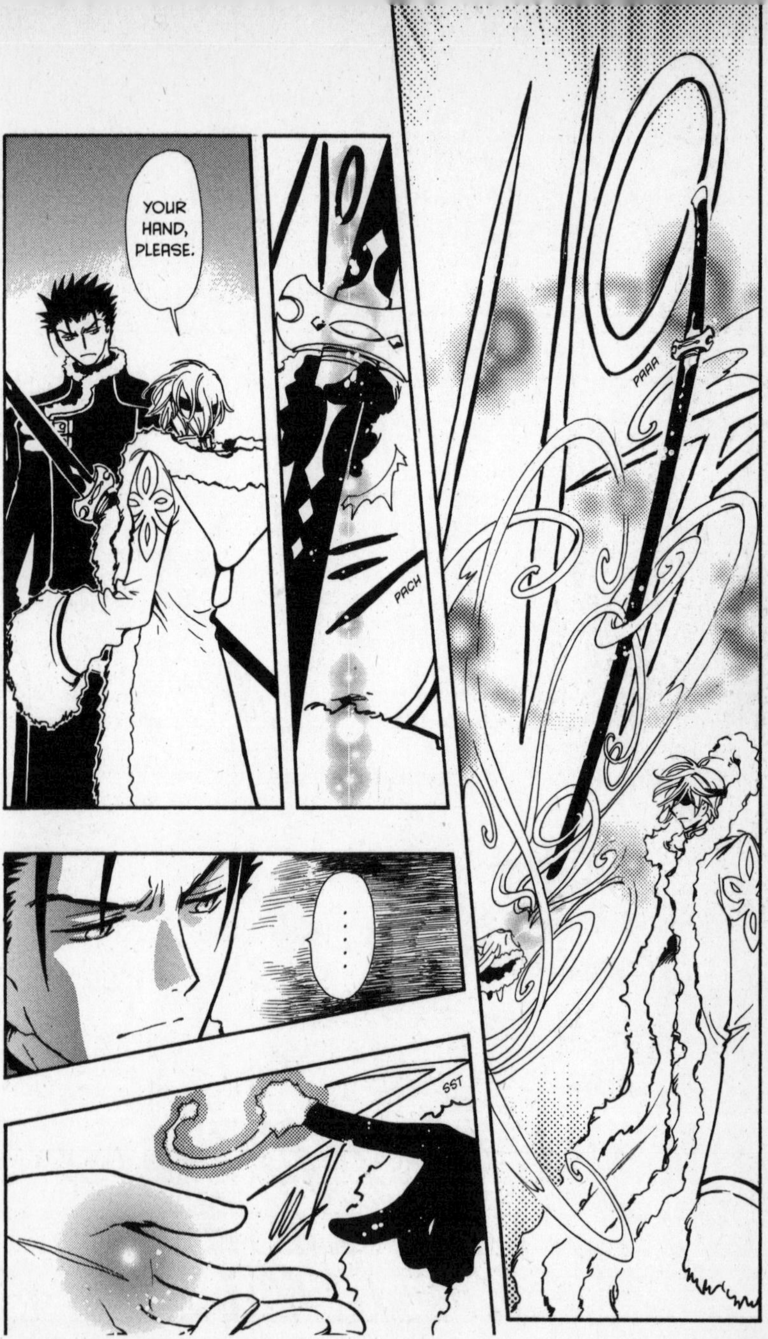
PAAA
PACH
YOUR HAND, PLEASE.
SST
.....

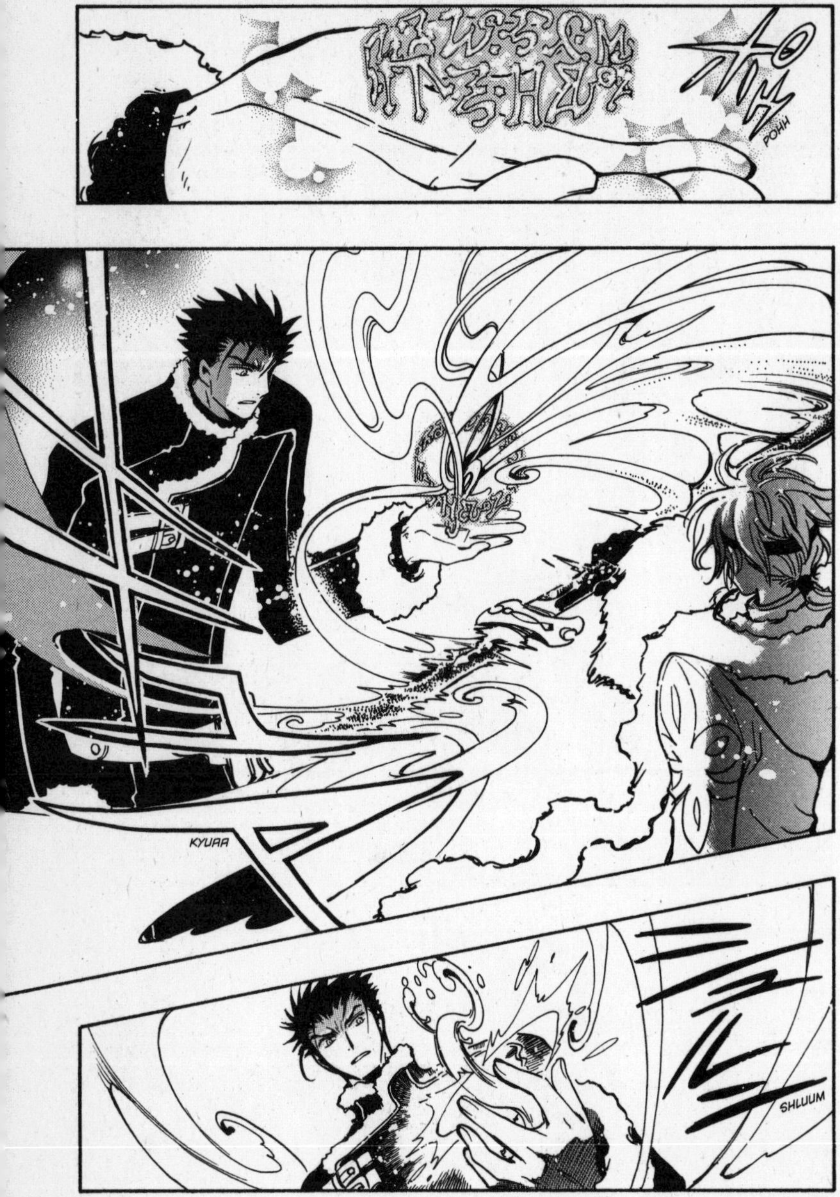
POHH
KYUAA
SHLUUM

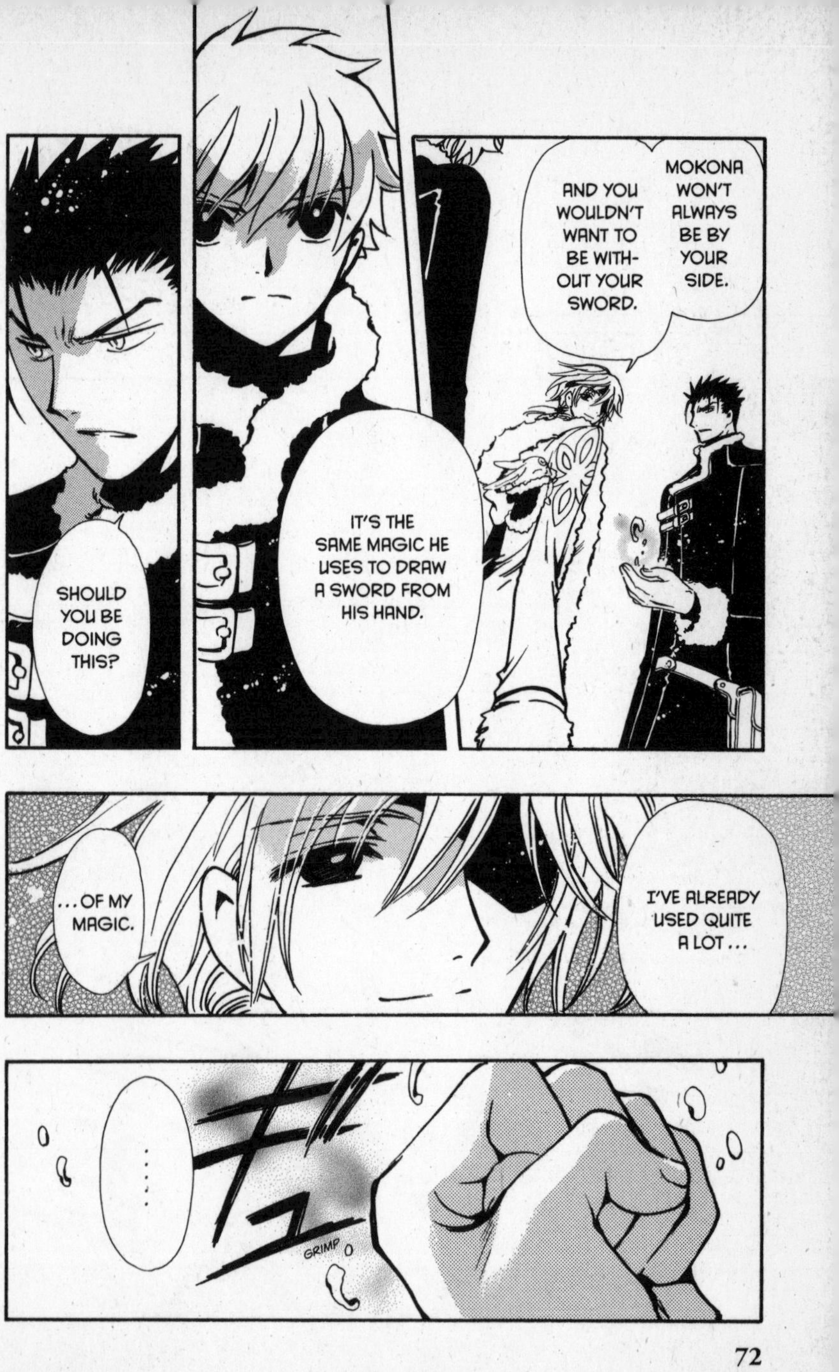
MOKONA WON'T ALWAYS BE BY YOUR SIDE.
AND YOU WOULDN'T WANT TO BE WITH-OUT YOUR SWORD.
IT'S THE SAME MAGIC HE USES TO DRAW A SWORD FROM HIS HAND.
SHOULD YOU BE DOING THIS?
I'VE ALREADY USED QUITE A LOT...
...OF MY MAGIC.
GRIMP
......

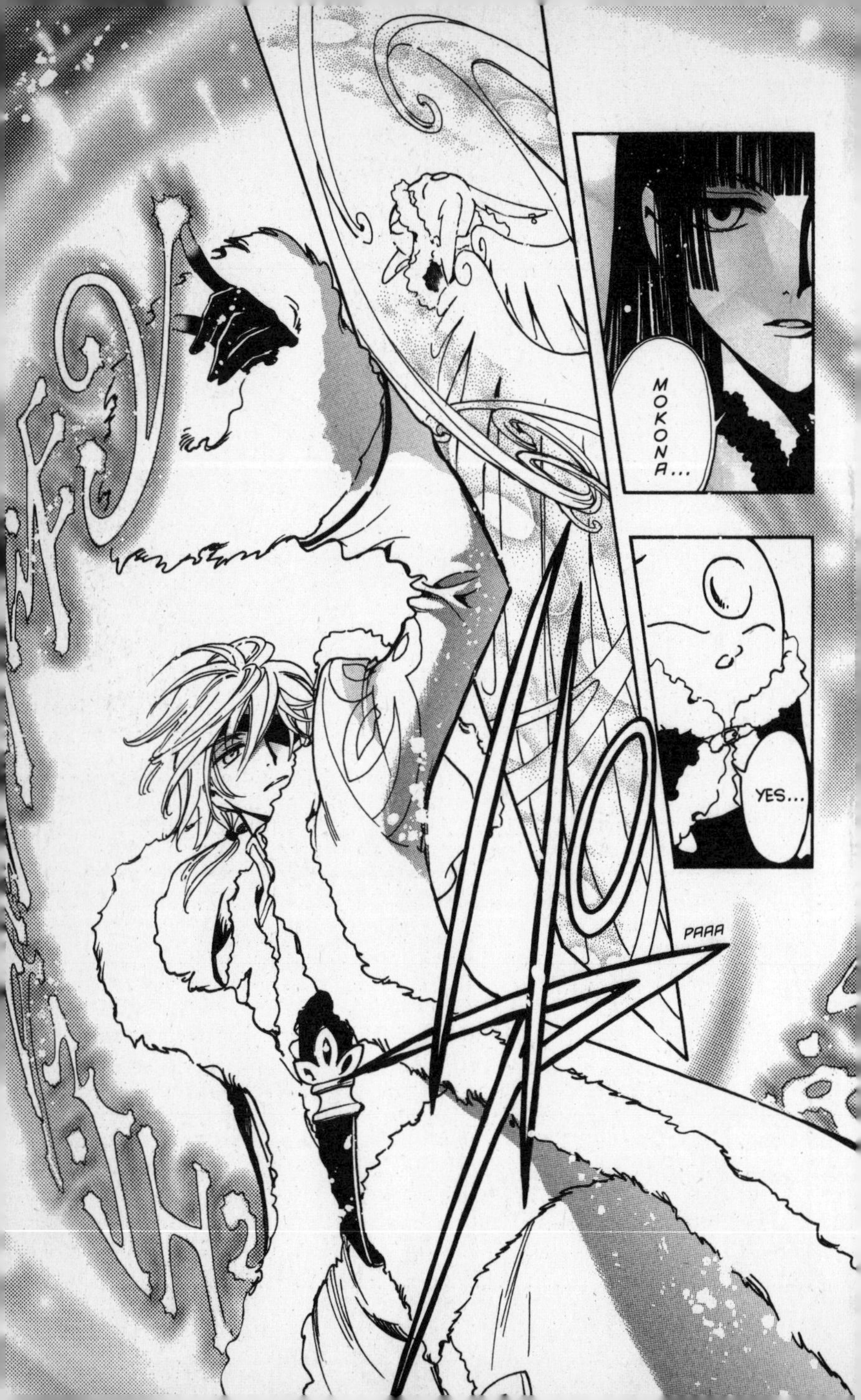
MOKONA...
YES...
PAAA

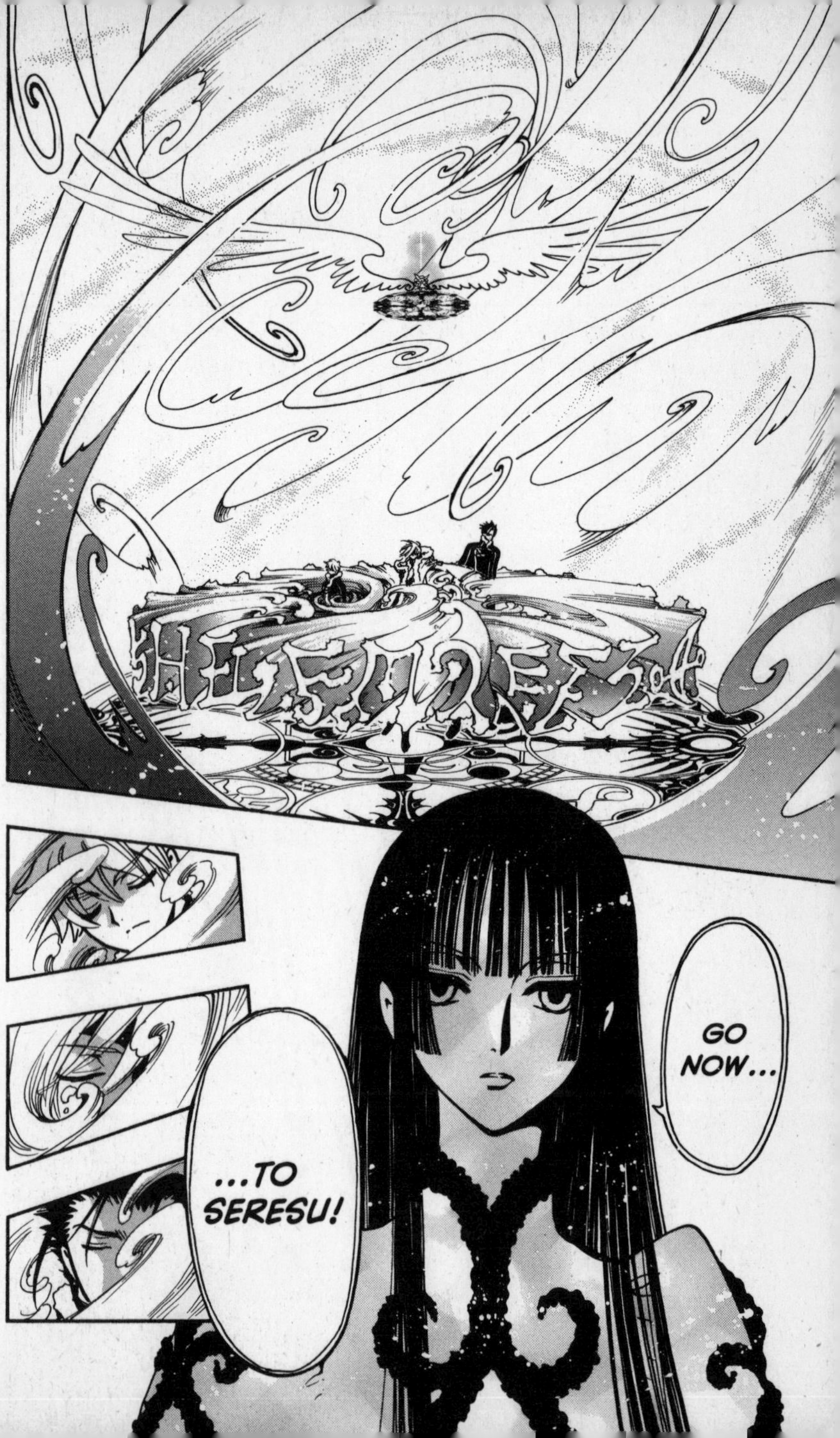
GO NOW...
...TO SERESU!

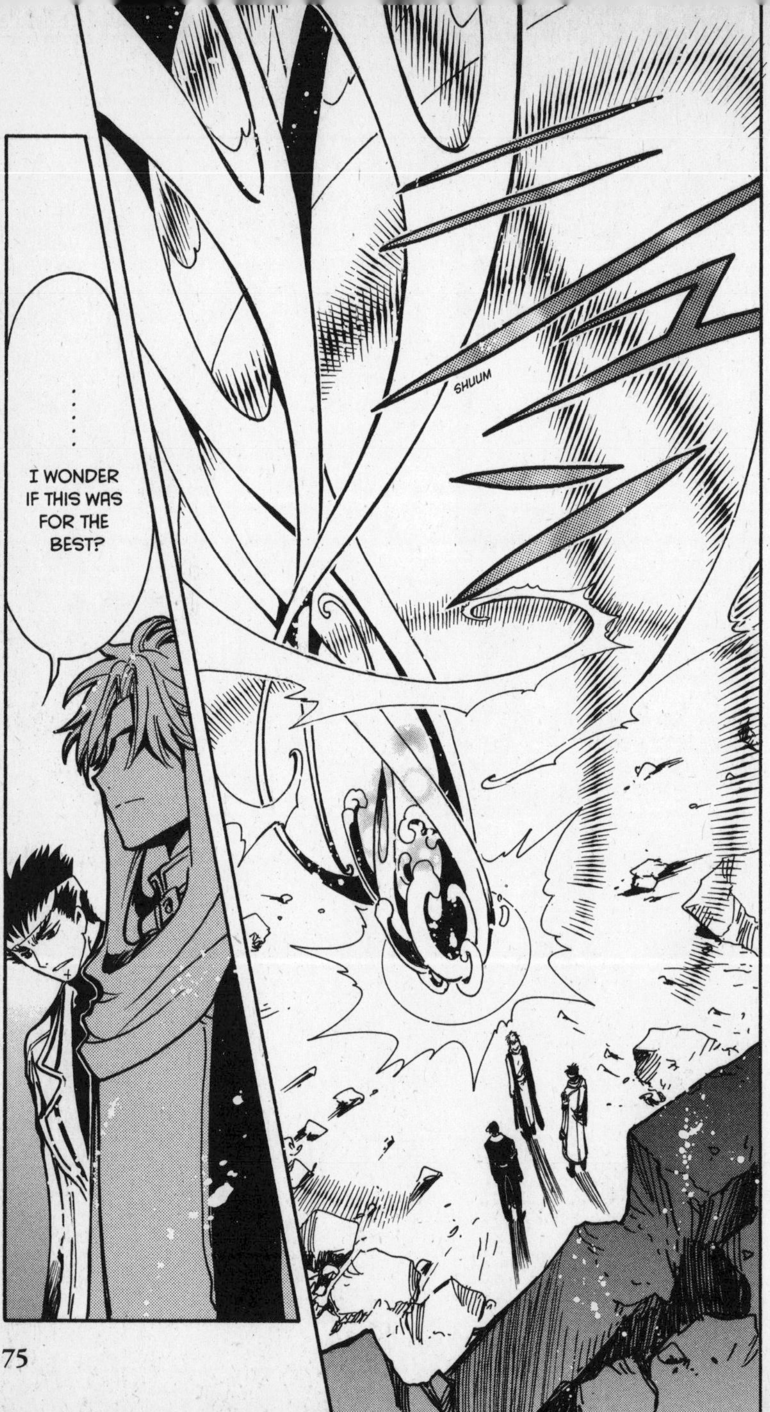
SHUUM
.....
I WONDER IF THIS WAS FOR THE BEST?

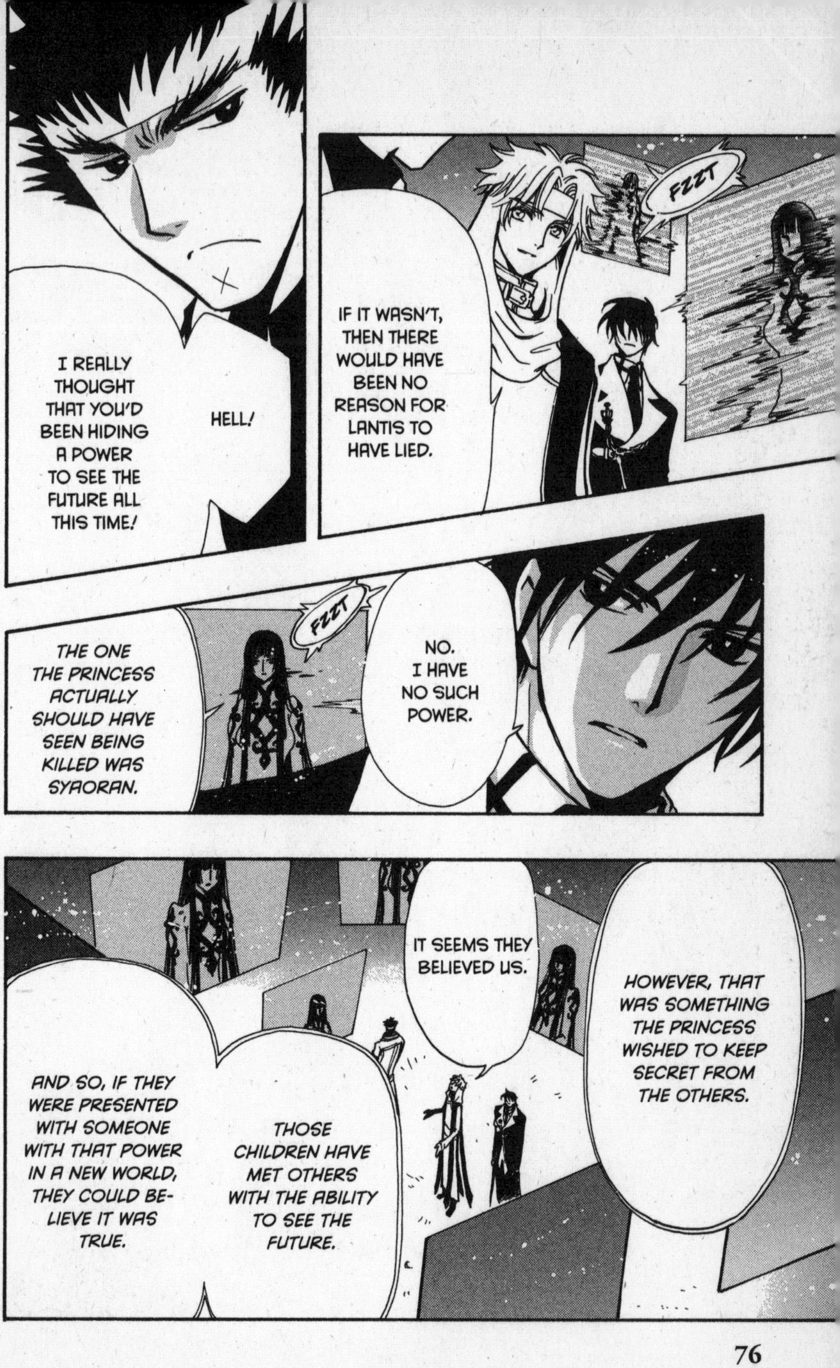
FZZT
IF IT WASN'T, THEN THERE WOULD HAVE BEEN NO REASON FOR LANTIS TO HAVE LIED.
HELL!
I REALLY THOUGHT THAT YOU'D BEEN HIDING A POWER TO SEE THE FUTURE ALL THIS TIME!
FZZT
NO. I HAVE NO SUCH POWER.
THE ONE THE PRINCESS ACTUALLY SHOULD HAVE SEEN BEING KILLED WAS SYAORAN.
HOWEVER, THAT WAS SOMETHING THE PRINCESS WISHED TO KEEP SECRET FROM THE OTHERS.
IT SEEMS THEY BELIEVED US.
THOSE CHILDREN HAVE MET OTHERS WITH THE ABILITY TO SEE THE FUTURE.
AND SO, IF THEY WERE PRESENTED WITH SOMEONE WITH THAT POWER IN A NEW WORLD, THEY COULD BE-LIEVE IT WAS TRUE.

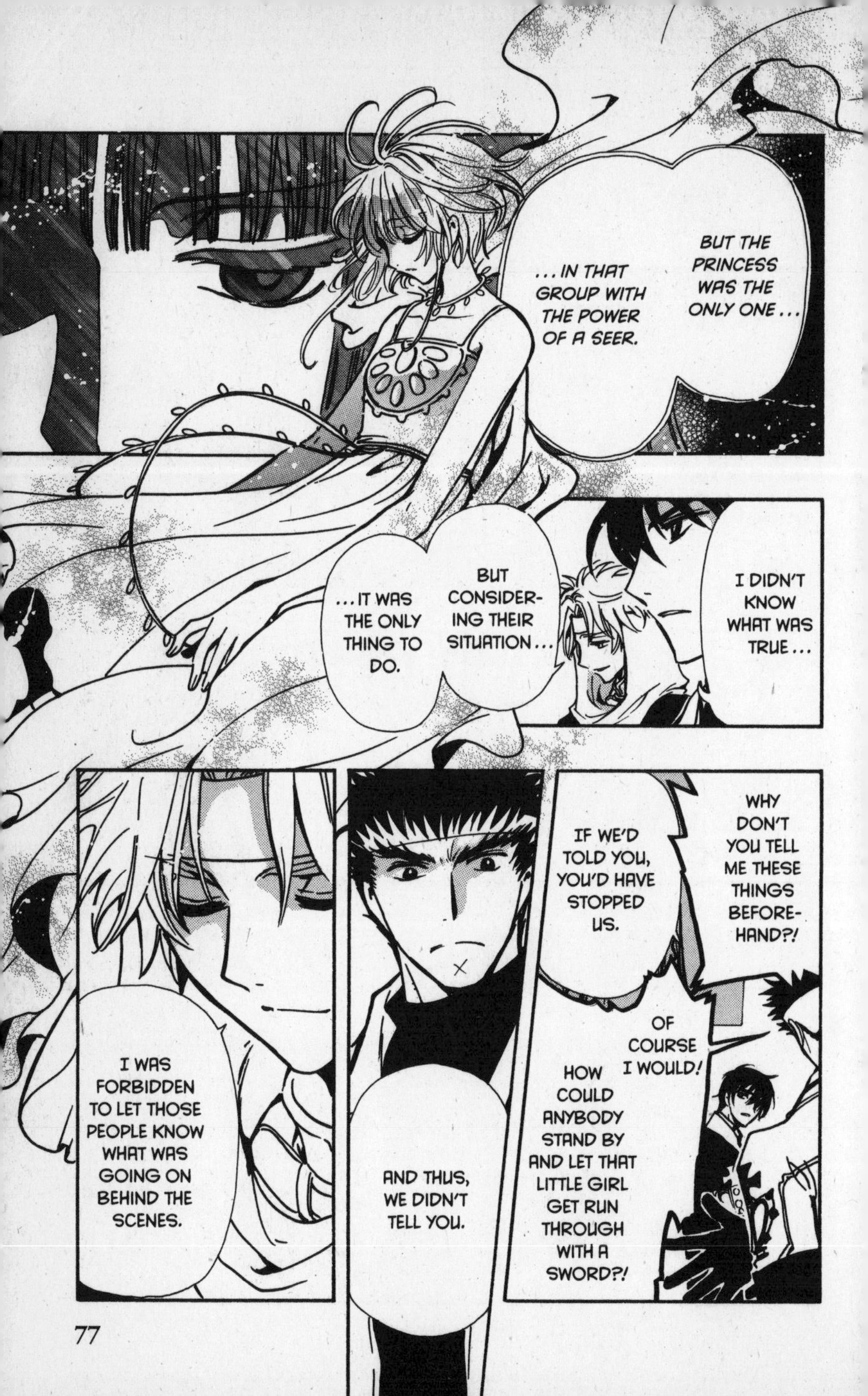
BUT THE PRINCESS WAS THE ONLY ONE...
...IN THAT GROUP WITH THE POWER OF A SEER.
I DIDN'T KNOW WHAT WAS TRUE...
BUT CONSIDER-ING THEIR SITUATION...
...IT WAS THE ONLY THING TO DO.
WHY DON'T YOU TELL ME THESE THINGS BEFORE-HAND?!
IF WE'D TOLD YOU, YOU'D HAVE STOPPED US.
OF COURSE I WOULD!
HOW COULD ANYBODY STAND BY AND LET THAT LITTLE GIRL GET RUN THROUGH WITH A SWORD?!
AND THUS, WE DIDN'T TELL YOU.
I WAS FORBIDDEN TO LET THOSE PEOPLE KNOW WHAT WAS GOING ON BEHIND THE SCENES.

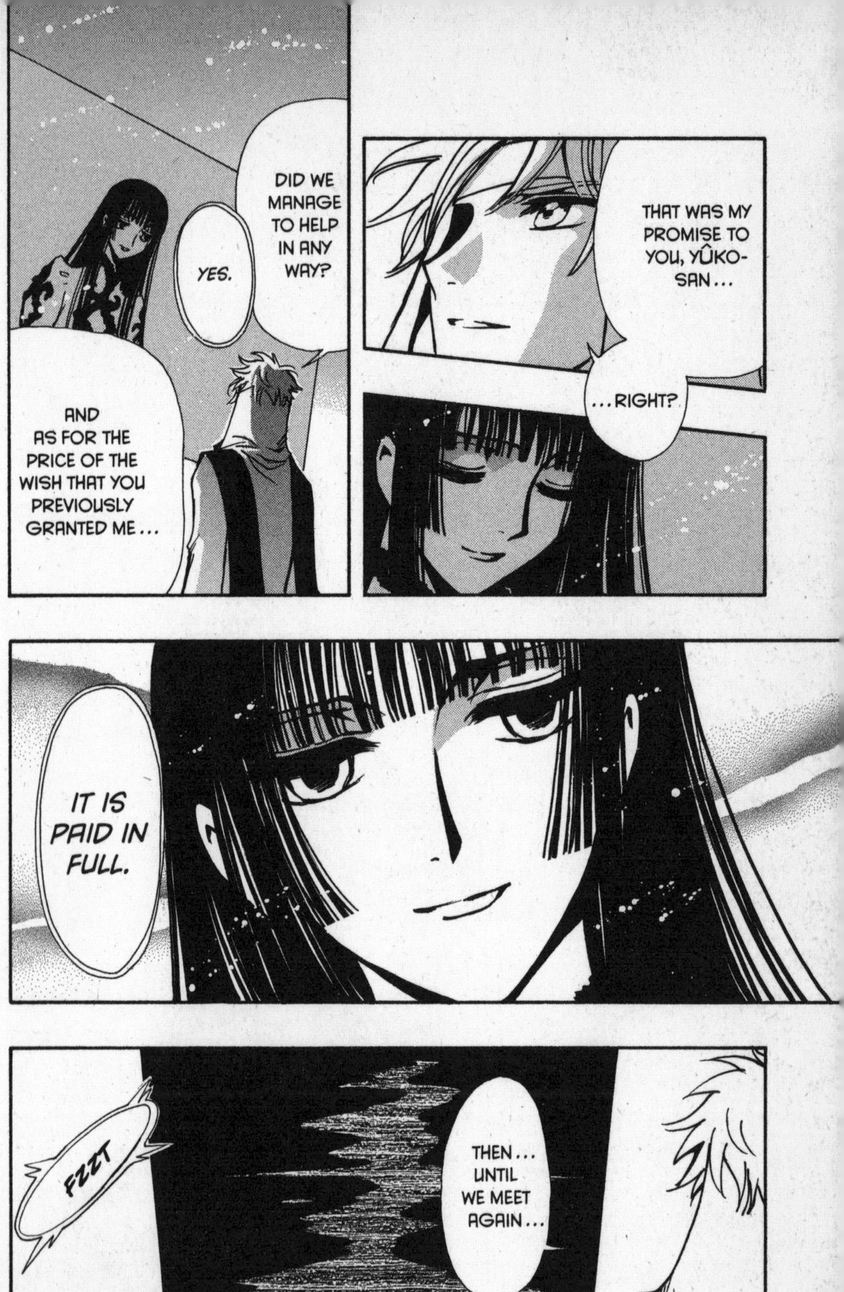
THAT WAS MY PROMISE TO YOU, YÛKO-SAN...
...RIGHT?
DID WE MANAGE TO HELP IN ANY WAY?
YES.
AND AS FOR THE PRICE OF THE WISH THAT YOU PREVIOUSLY GRANTED ME...
IT IS PAID IN FULL.
THEN... UNTIL WE MEET AGAIN...
FZZT

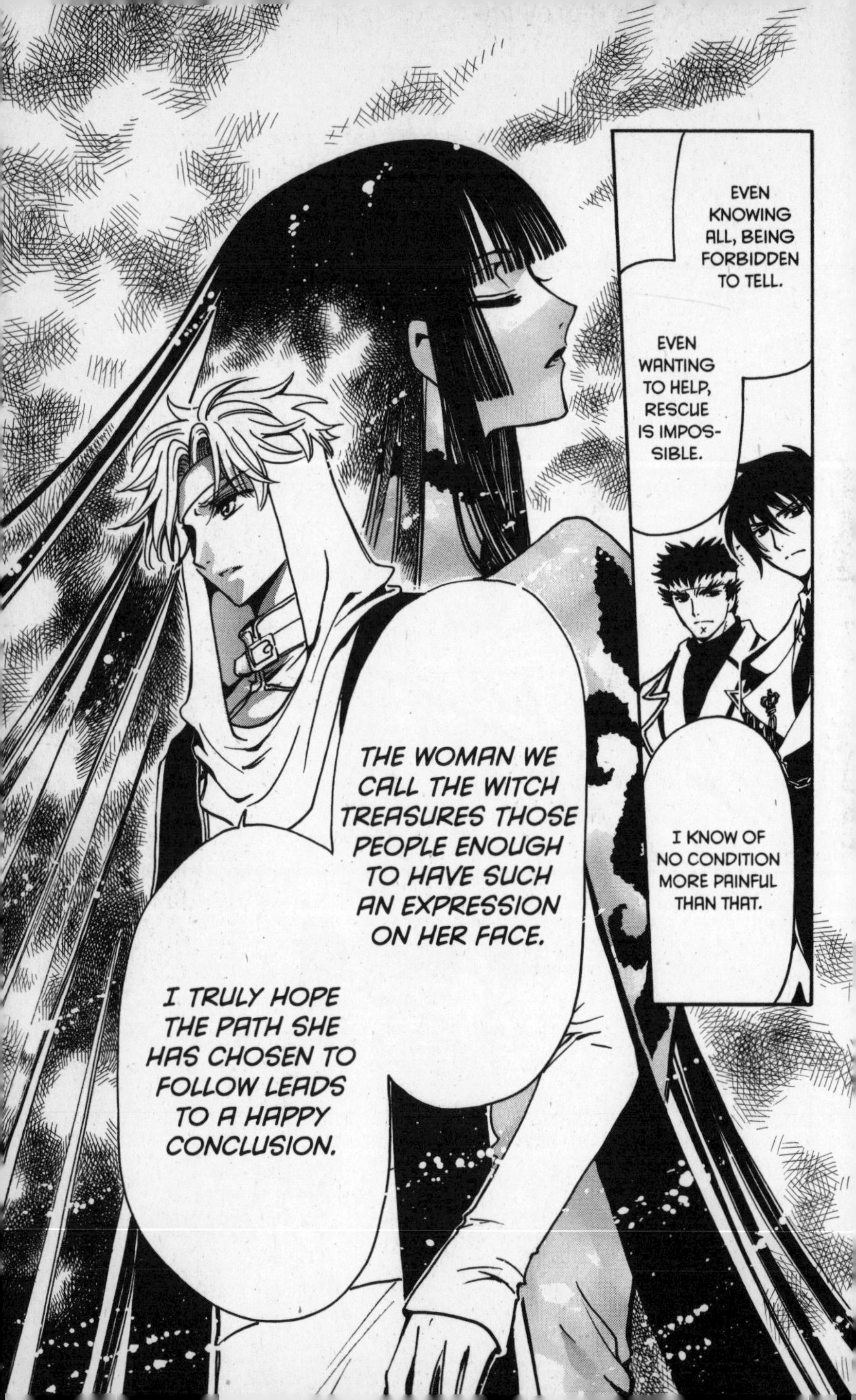
EVEN KNOWING ALL, BEING FORBIDDEN TO TELL.
EVEN WANTING TO HELP, RESCUE IS IMPOSSIBLE.
I KNOW OF NO CONDITION MORE PAINFUL THAN THAT.
THE WOMAN WE CALL THE WITCH TREASURES THOSE PEOPLE ENOUGH TO HAVE SUCH AN EXPRESSION ON HER FACE.
I TRULY HOPE THE PATH SHE HAS CHOSEN TO FOLLOW LEADS TO A HAPPY CONCLUSION.

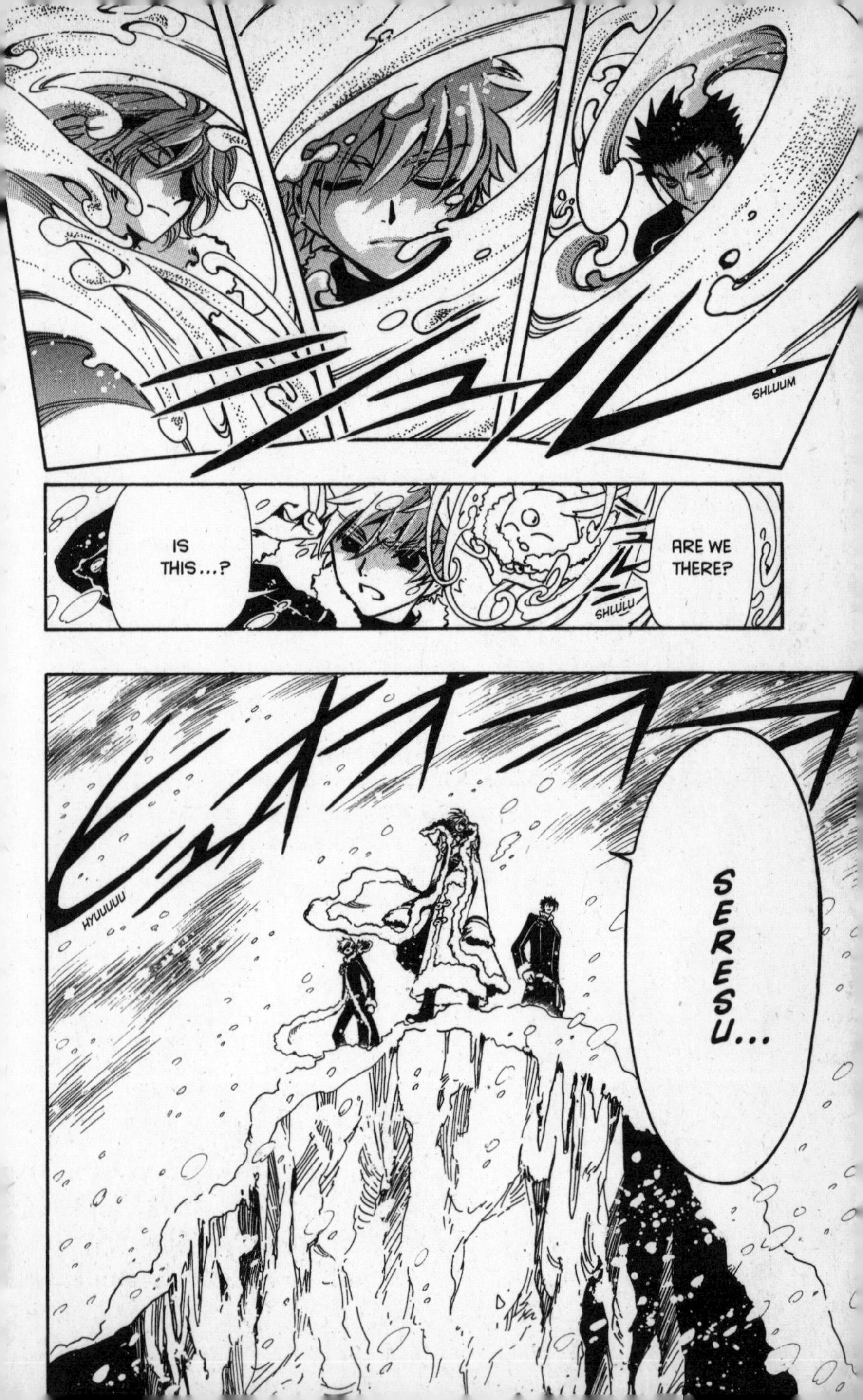
SHLUUM
ARE WE THERE?
SHLULU
IS THIS...?
SERESU...
HYUUUUU

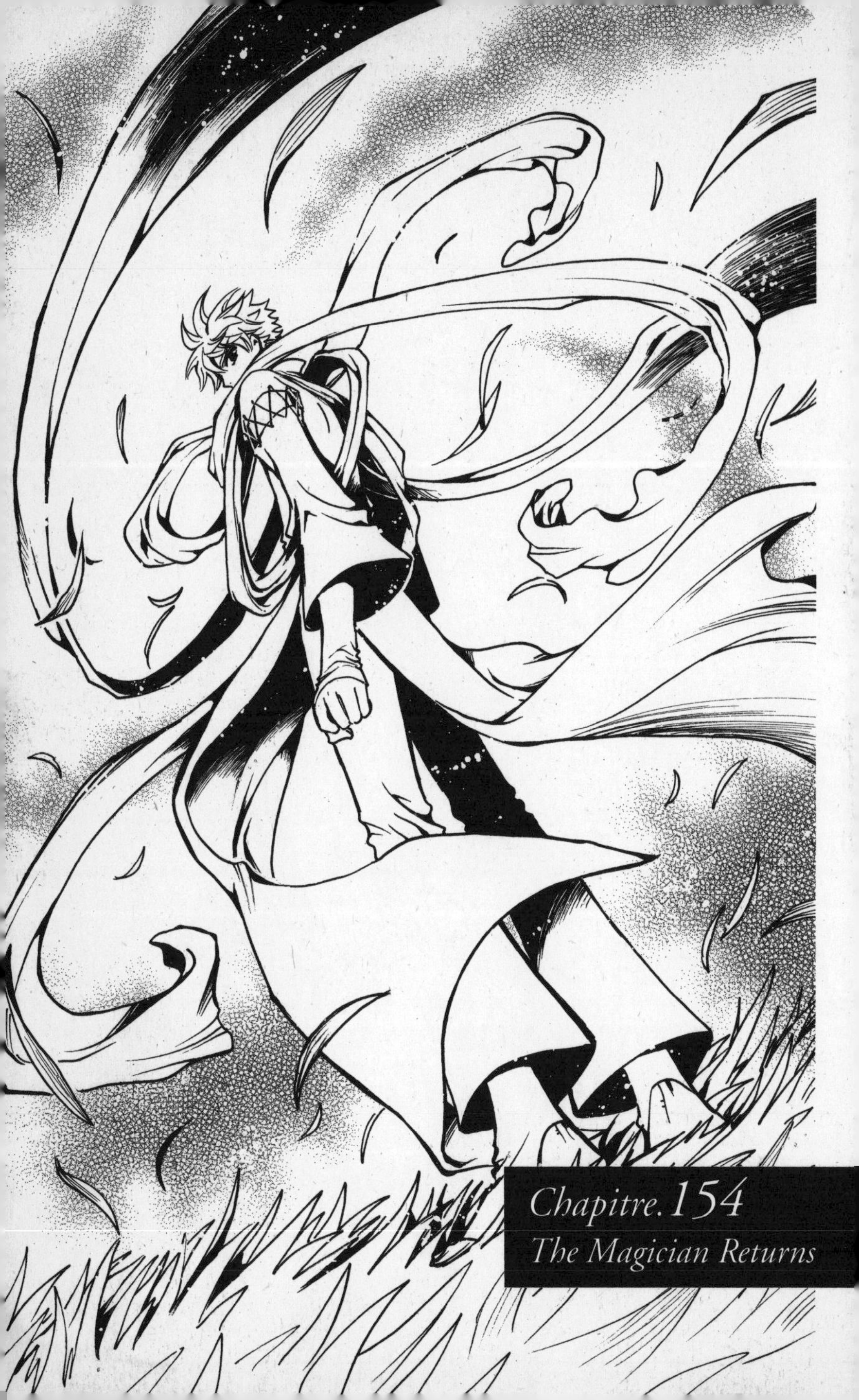
Chapitre.154
The Magician Returns

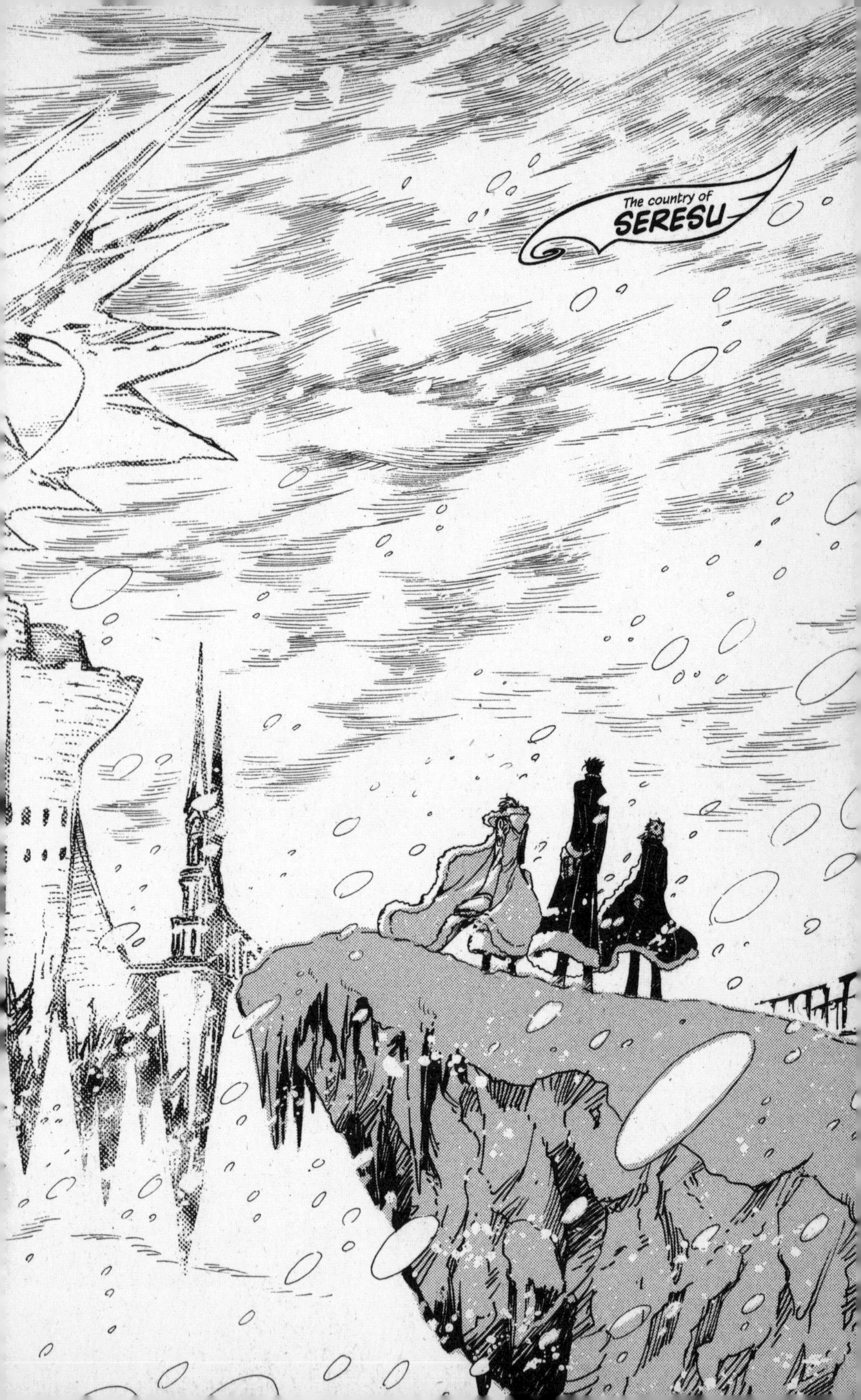
The country of
SERESU

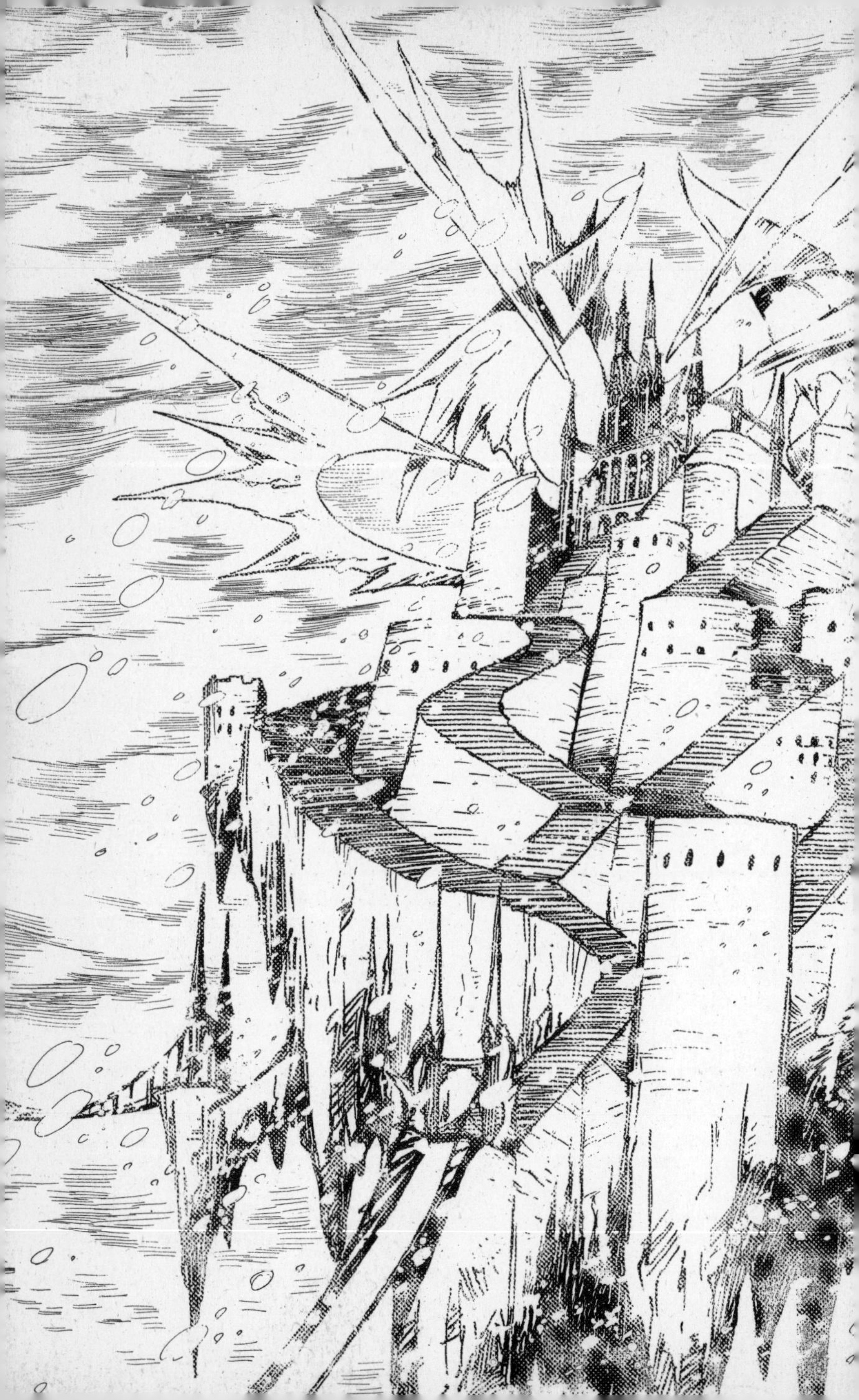

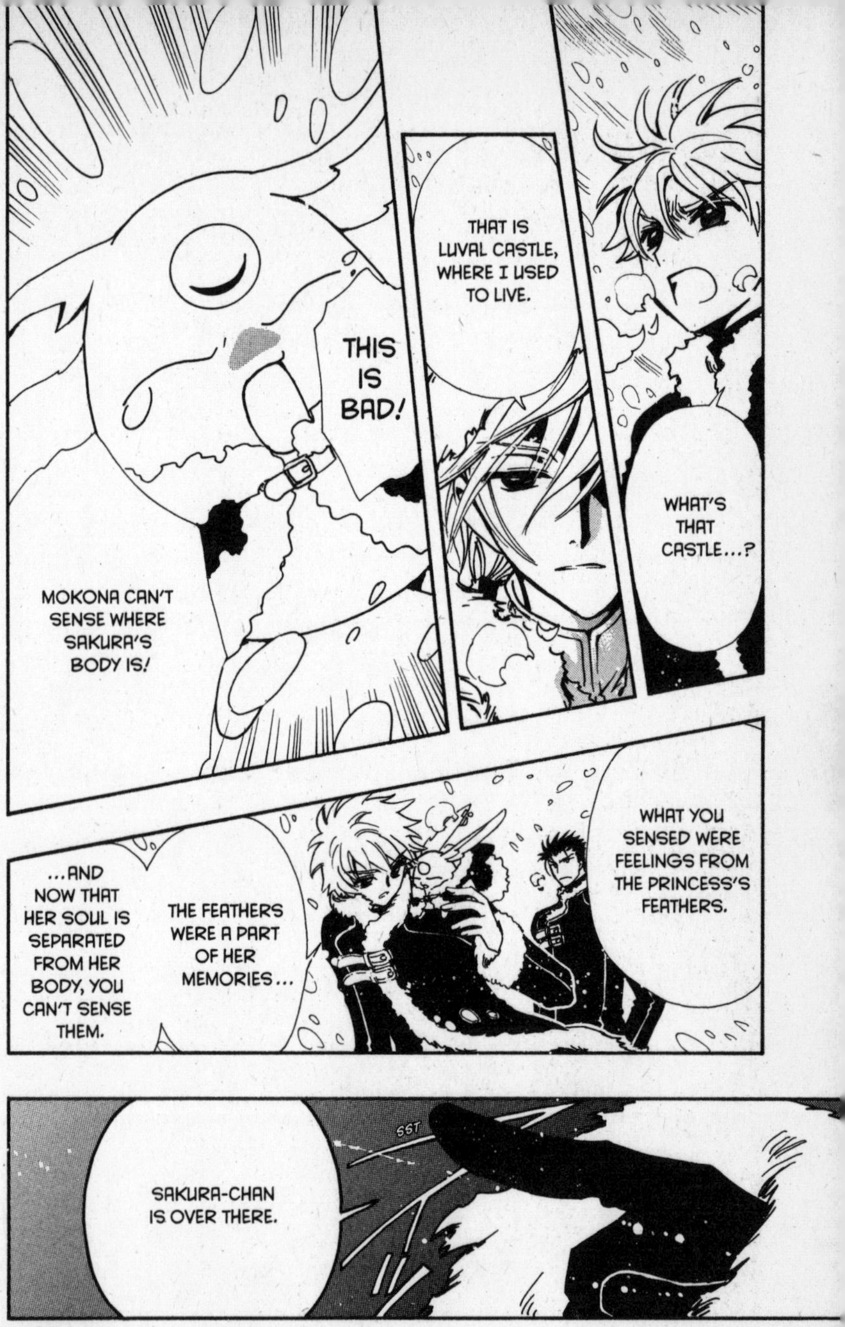
WHAT'S THAT CASTLE...?
THAT IS LUVAL CASTLE, WHERE I USED TO LIVE.
THIS IS BAD!
MOKONA CAN'T SENSE WHERE SAKURA'S BODY IS!
WHAT YOU SENSED WERE FEELINGS FROM THE PRINCESS'S FEATHERS.
THE FEATHERS WERE A PART OF HER MEMORIES...
...AND NOW THAT HER SOUL IS SEPARATED FROM HER BODY, YOU CAN'T SENSE THEM.
SST
SAKURA-CHAN IS OVER THERE.

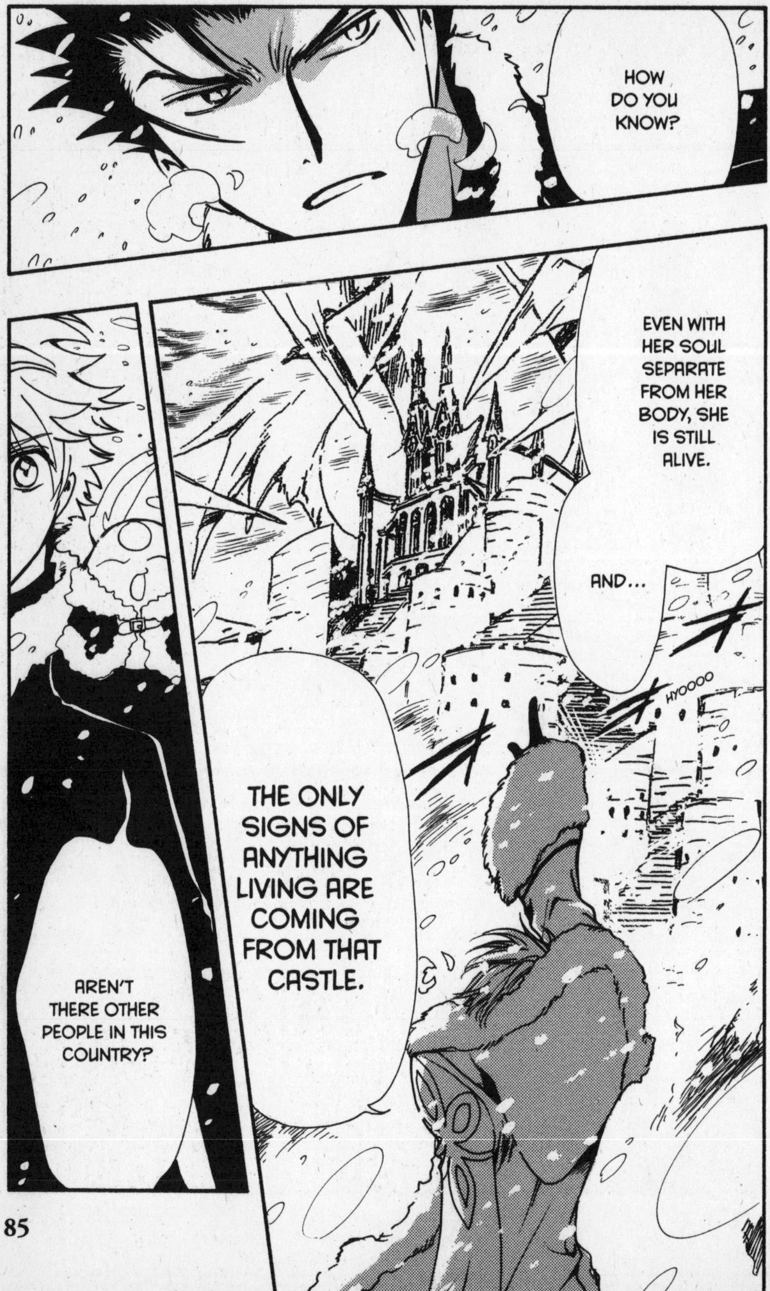
HOW DO YOU KNOW?
EVEN WITH HER SOUL SEPARATE FROM HER BODY, SHE IS STILL ALIVE.
AND...
HYOOOO
THE ONLY SIGNS OF ANYTHING LIVING ARE COMING FROM THAT CASTLE.
AREN'T THERE OTHER PEOPLE IN THIS COUNTRY?

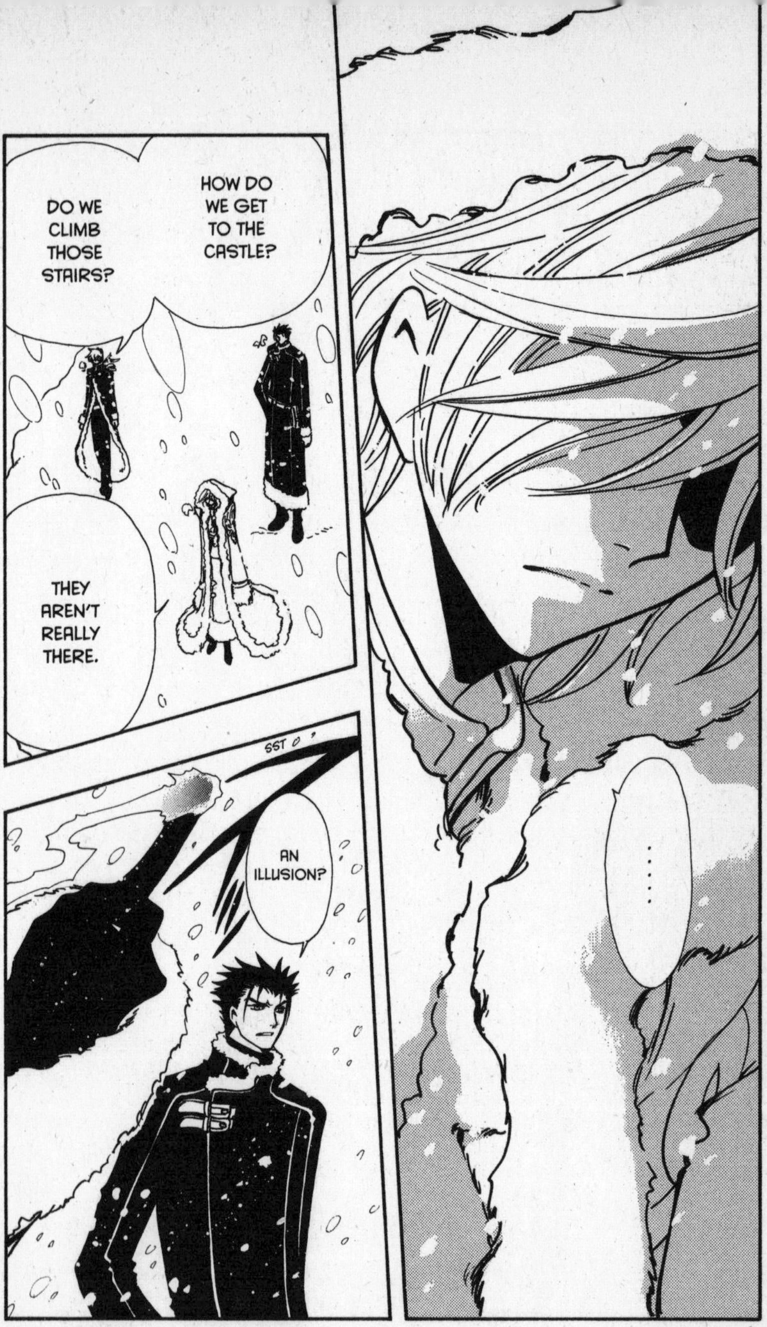

......
HOW DO WE GET TO THE CASTLE?
DO WE CLIMB THOSE STAIRS?
THEY AREN'T REALLY THERE.
SST
AN ILLUSION?

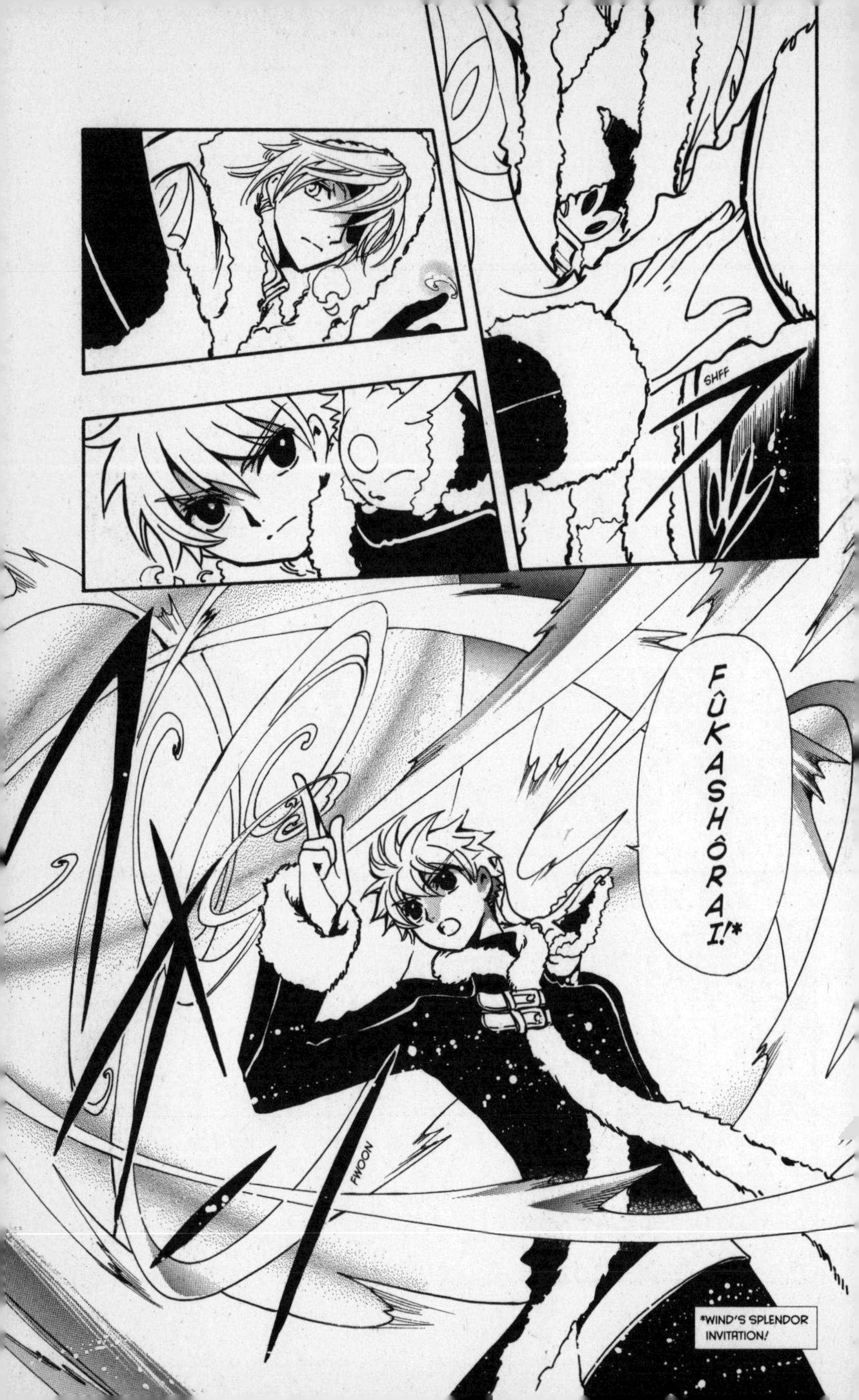
SHFF
FÛKASHÔRAI!*
FWOON
*WIND'S SPLENDOR INVITATION!

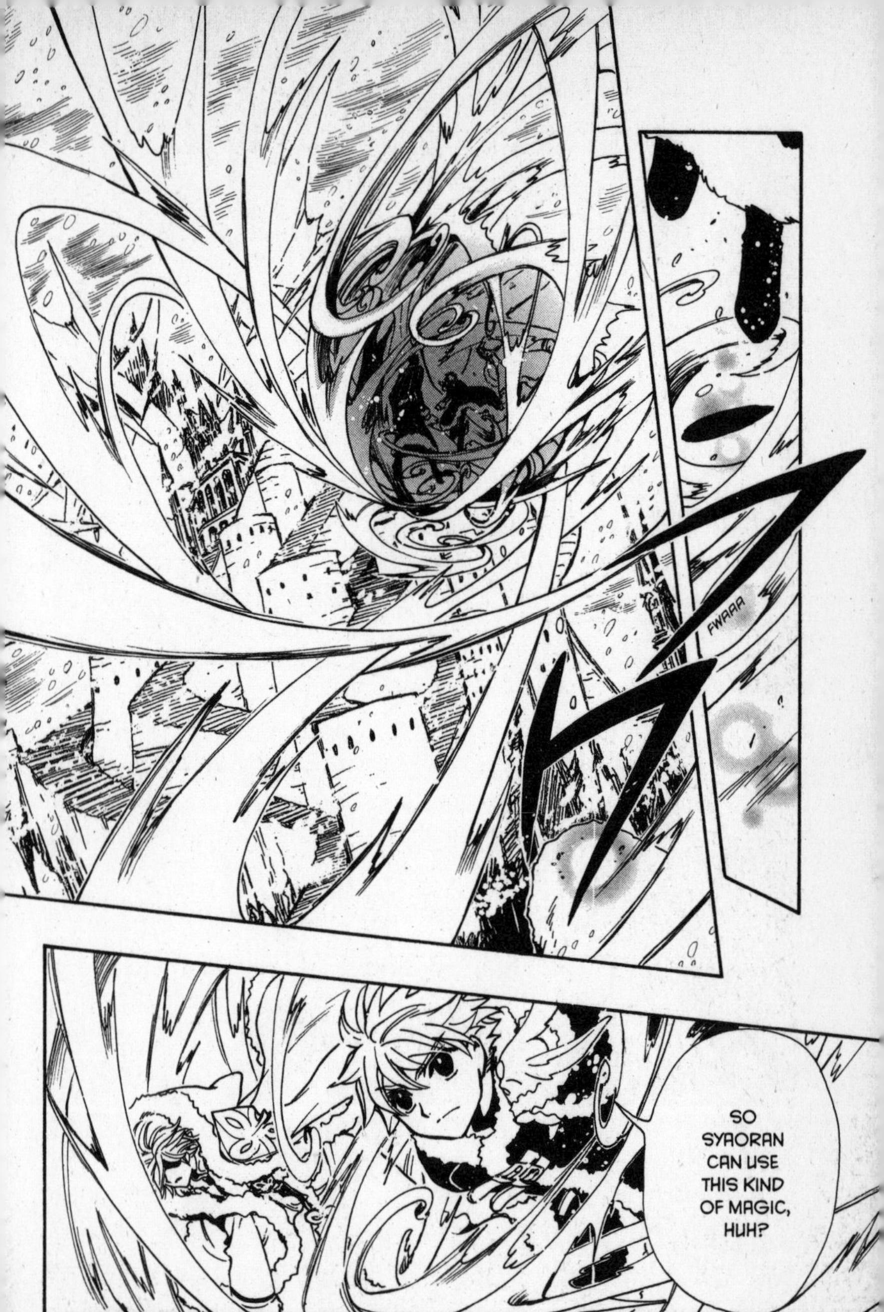
FWAAA
SO SYAORAN CAN USE THIS KIND OF MAGIC, HUH?

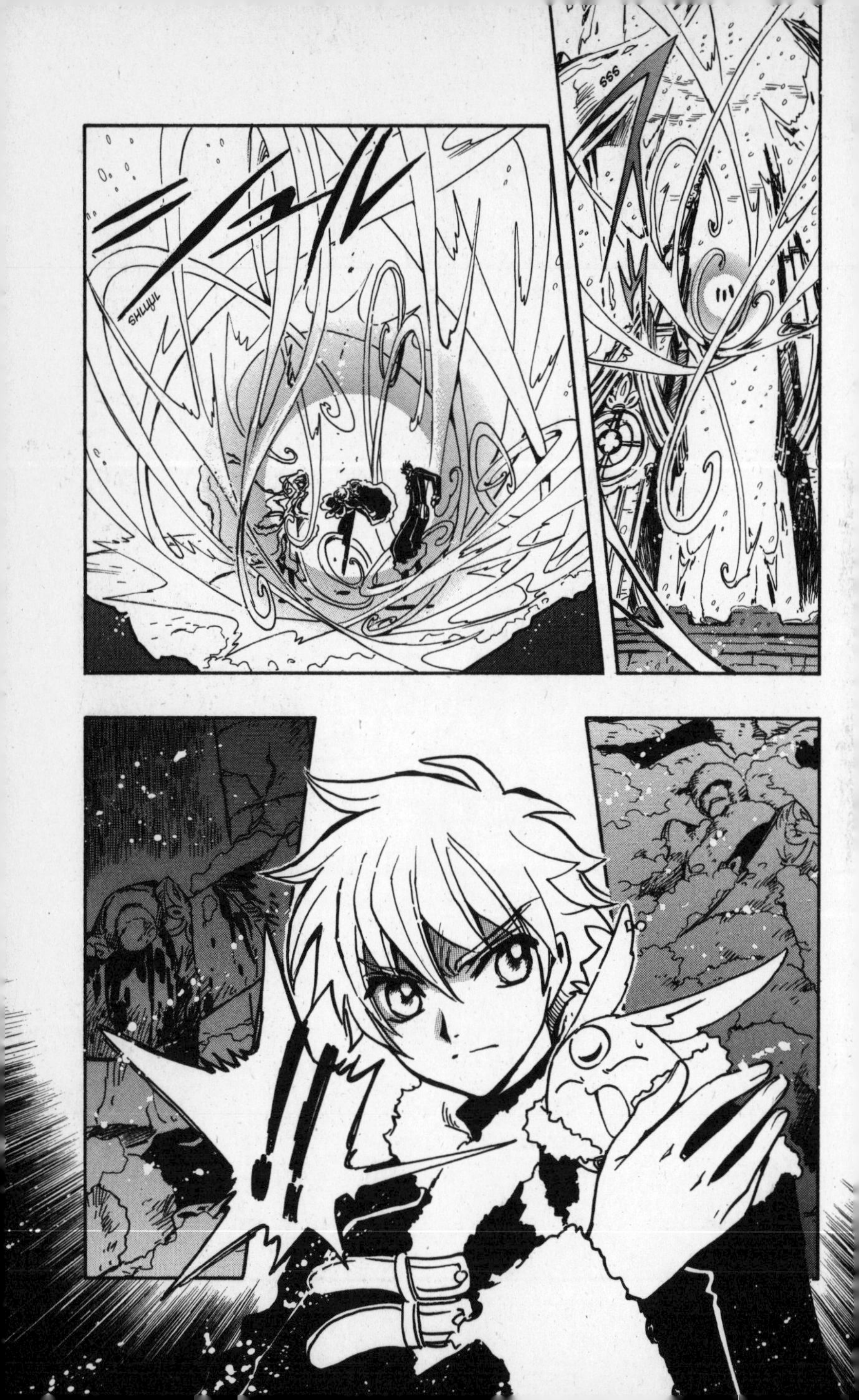
SSS

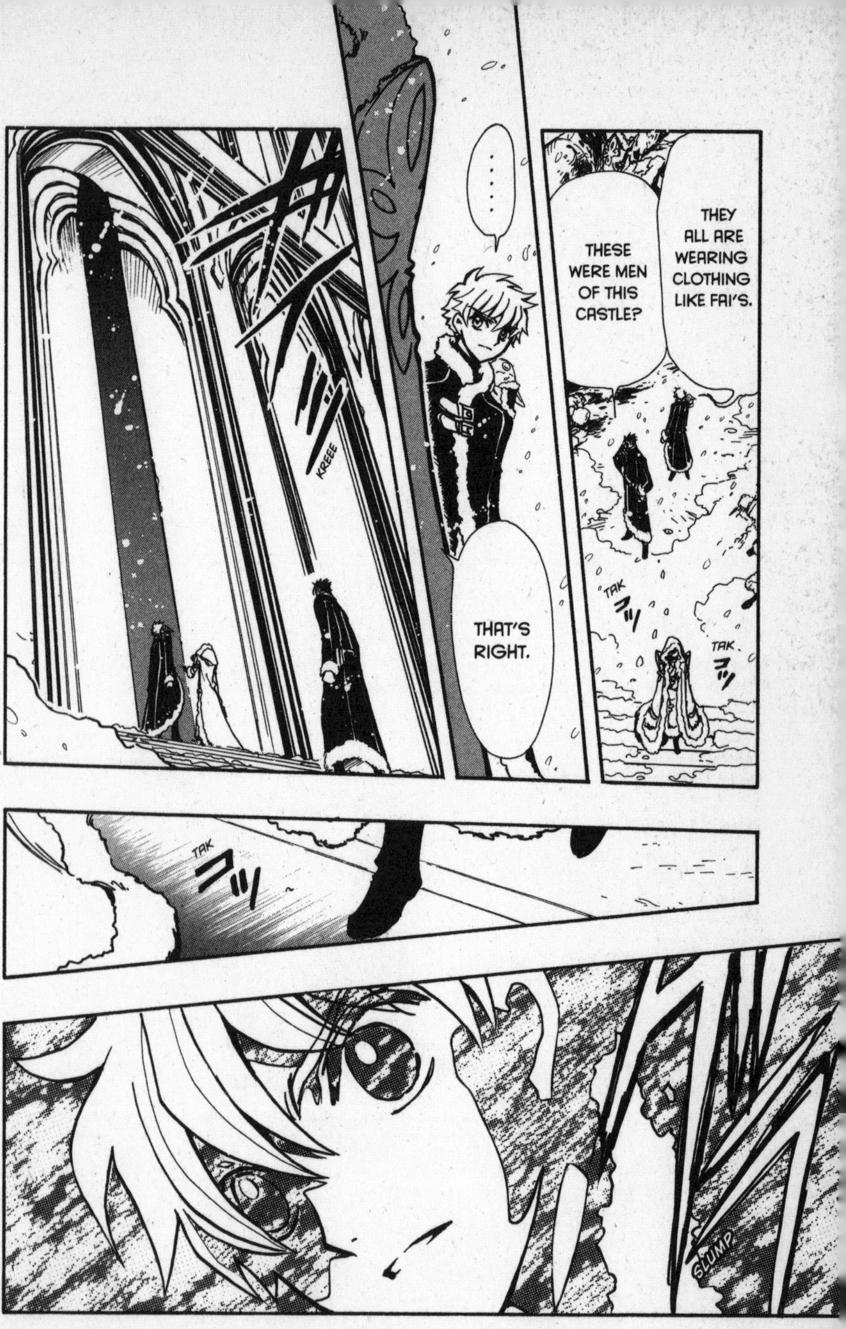
THEY ALL ARE WEARING CLOTHING LIKE FAI'S.
THESE WERE MEN OF THIS CASTLE?
TAK
TAK
.....
THAT'S RIGHT.
KREEE
TAK
SLUMP

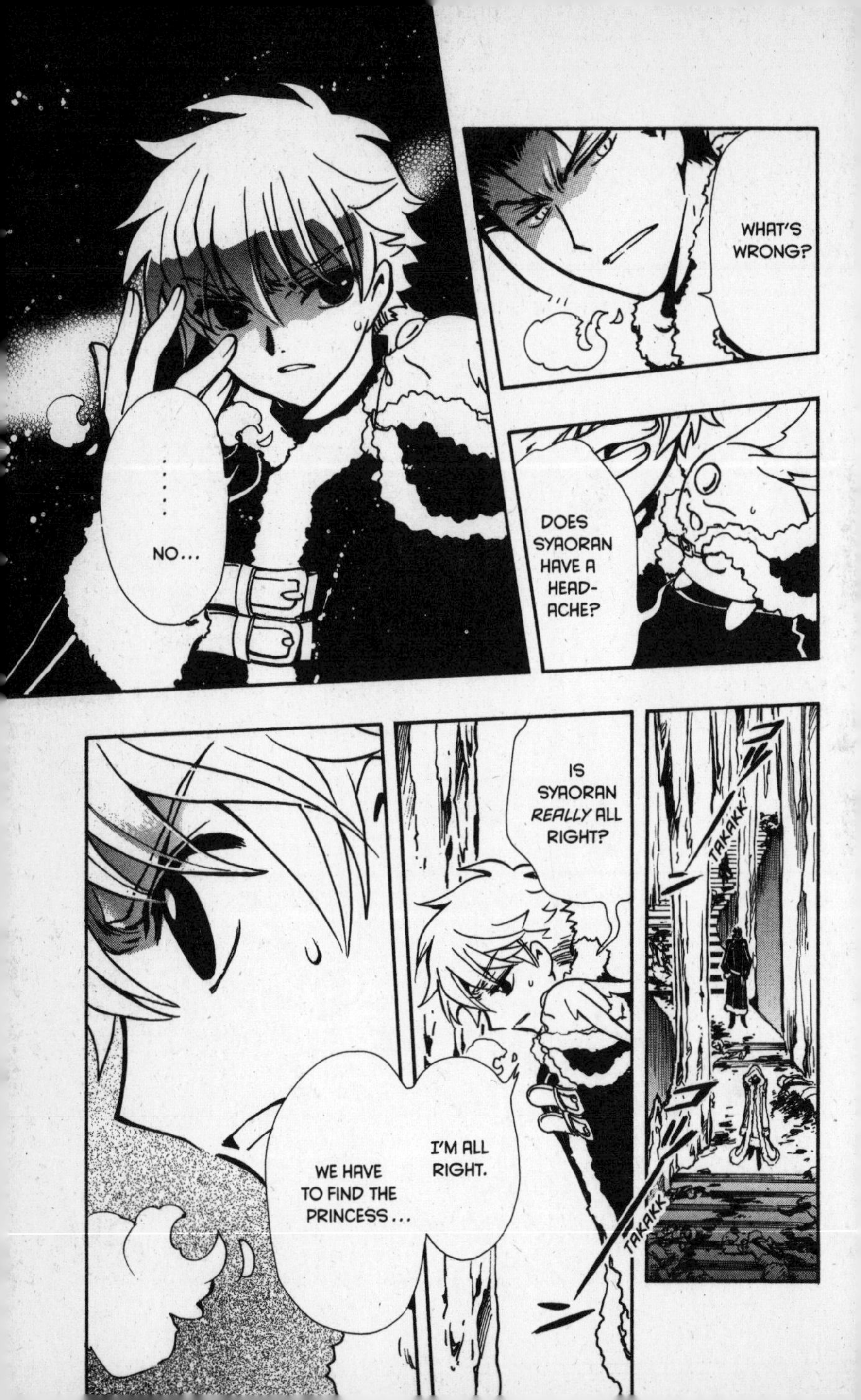
WHAT'S WRONG?
DOES SYAORAN HAVE A HEAD-ACHE?
...... NO...
TAKAKK
TAKAKK
IS SYAORAN *REALLY* ALL RIGHT?
I'M ALL RIGHT.
WE HAVE TO FIND THE PRINCESS...

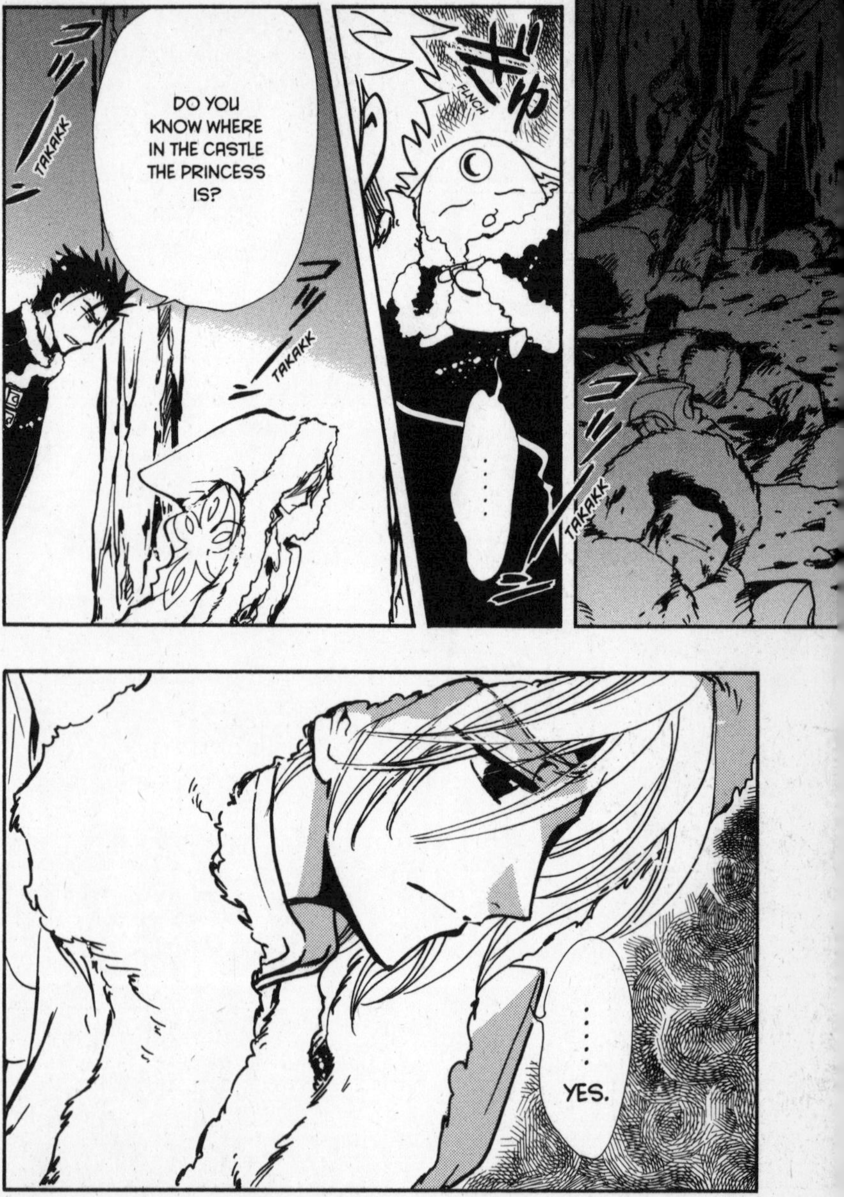
TAKAKK
FLNCH
ぎゅ
.....
TAKAKK
DO YOU KNOW WHERE IN THE CASTLE THE PRINCESS IS?
TAKAKK
.....
YES.

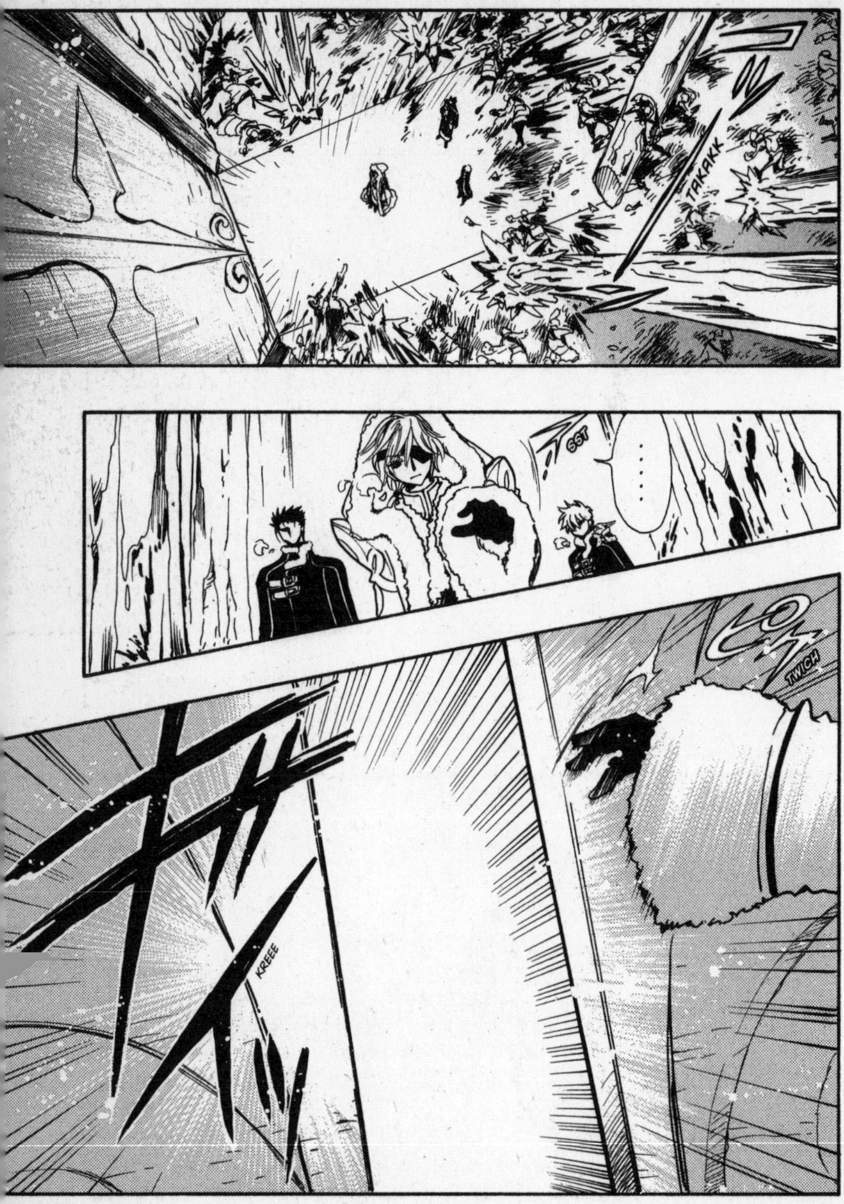
TAKAKK
SST
......
TWICH
KREEE

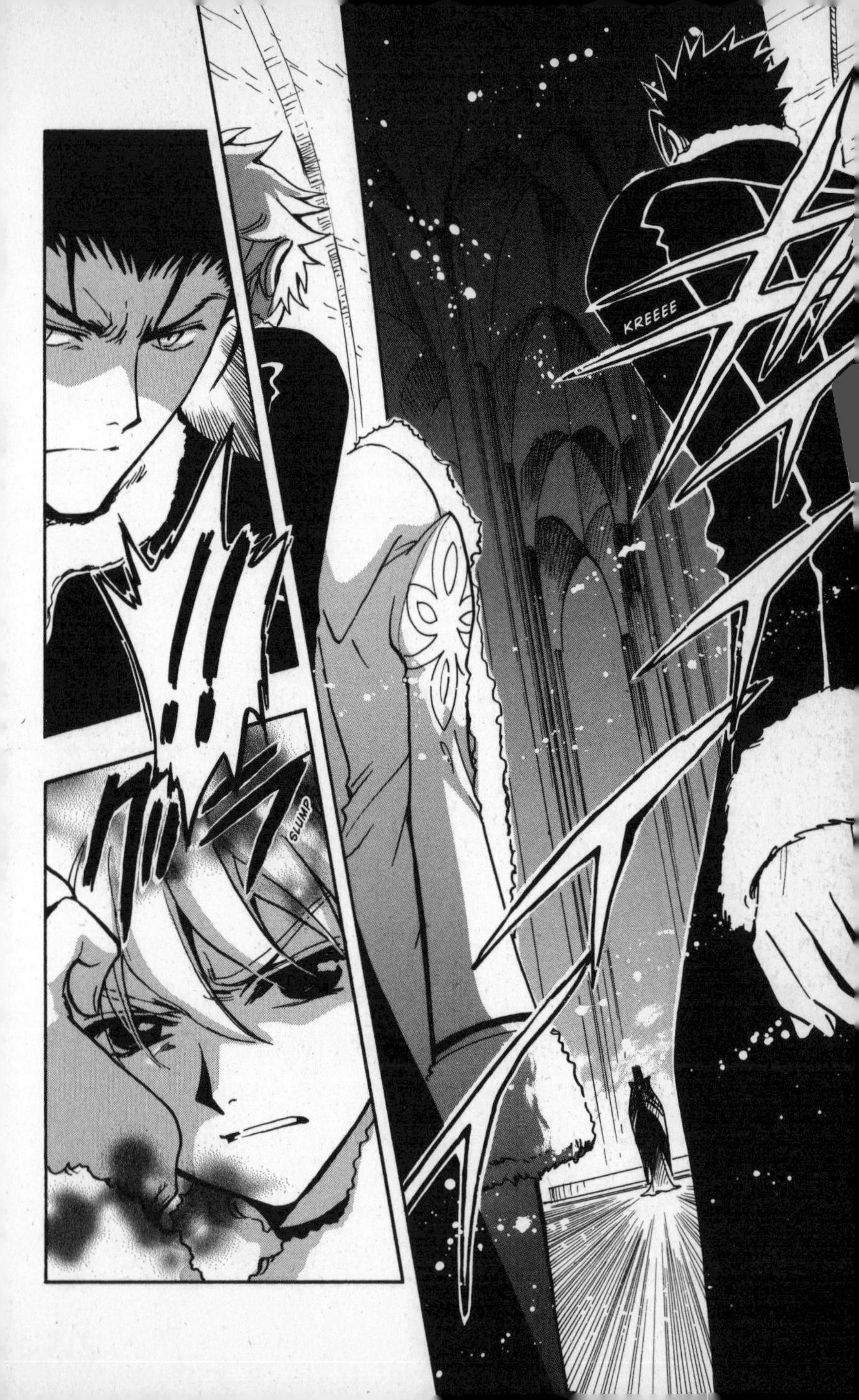
KREEEE
SLUMP

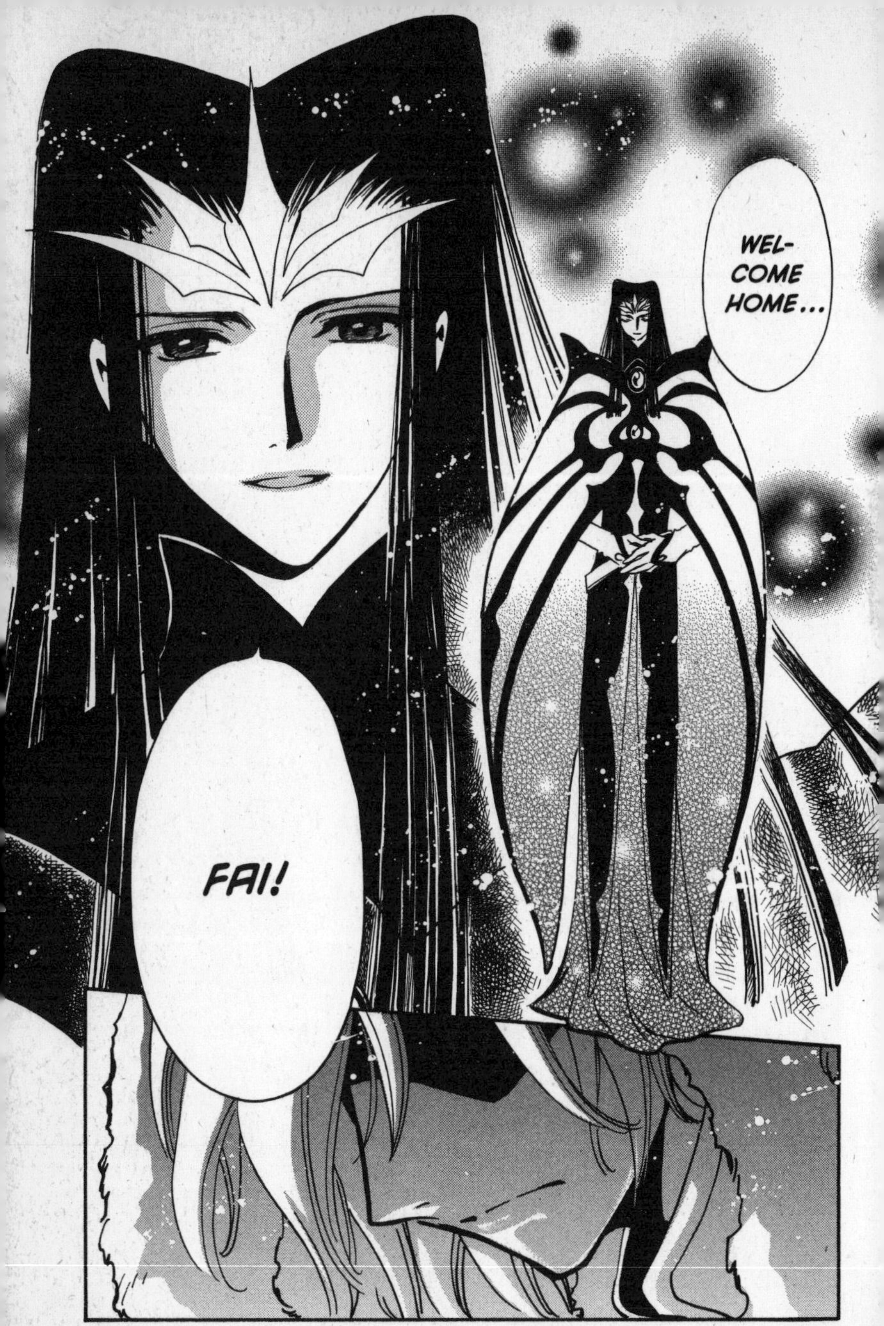
WEL-COME HOME...
FAI!

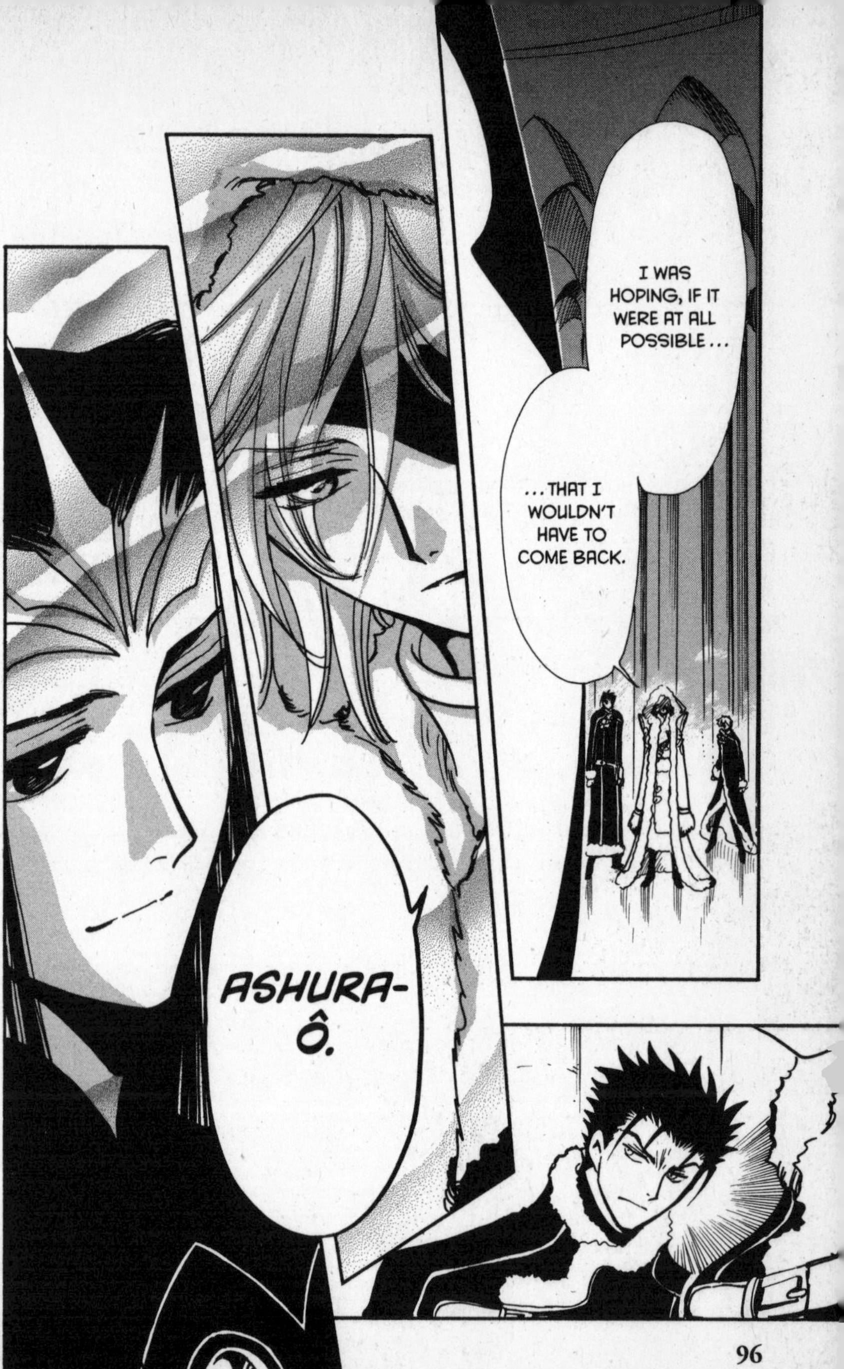
I WAS HOPING, IF IT WERE AT ALL POSSIBLE...
...THAT I WOULDN'T HAVE TO COME BACK.
ASHURA-Ô.

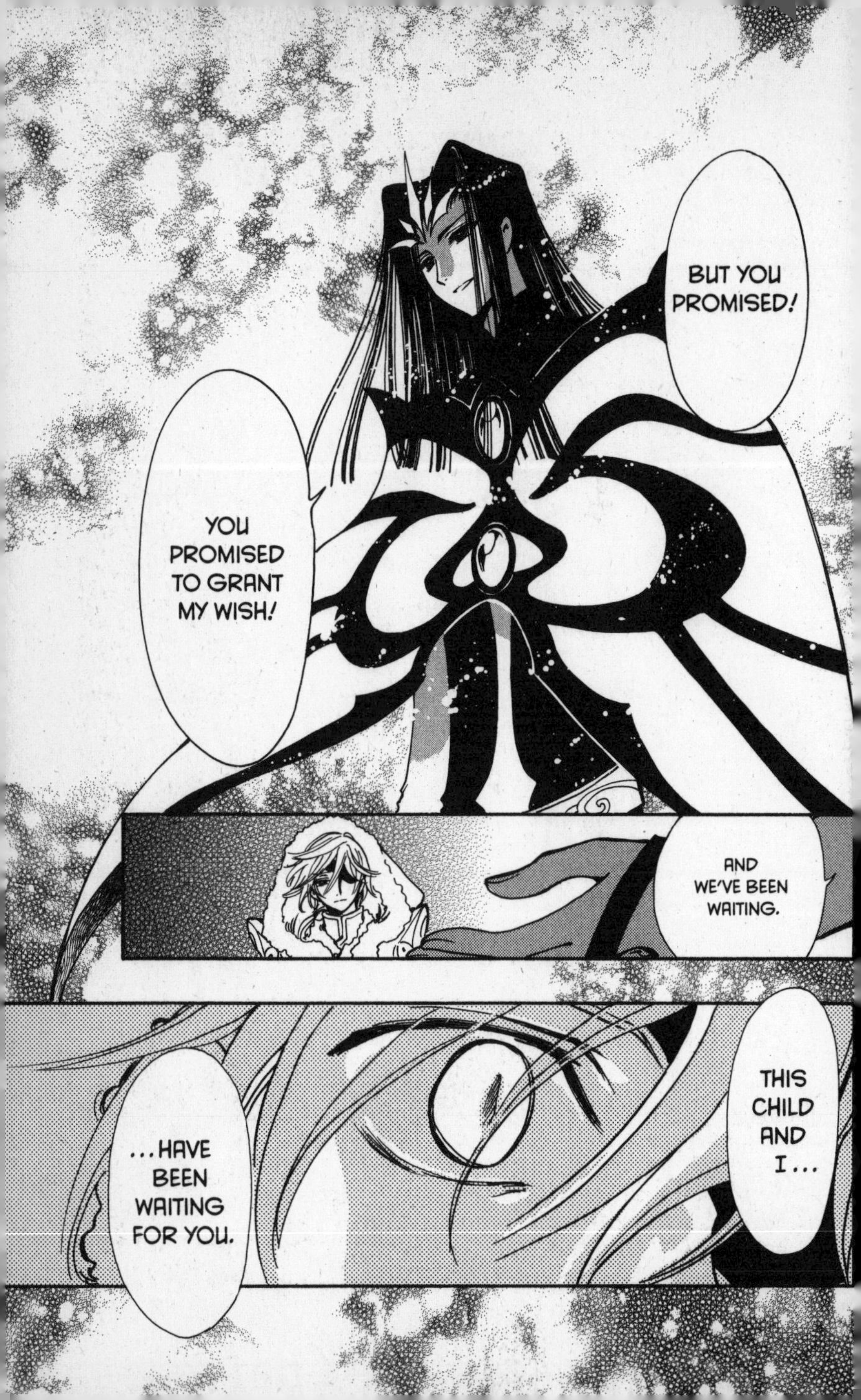
BUT YOU PROMISED!
YOU PROMISED TO GRANT MY WISH!
AND WE'VE BEEN WAITING.
THIS CHILD AND I...
...HAVE BEEN WAITING FOR YOU.

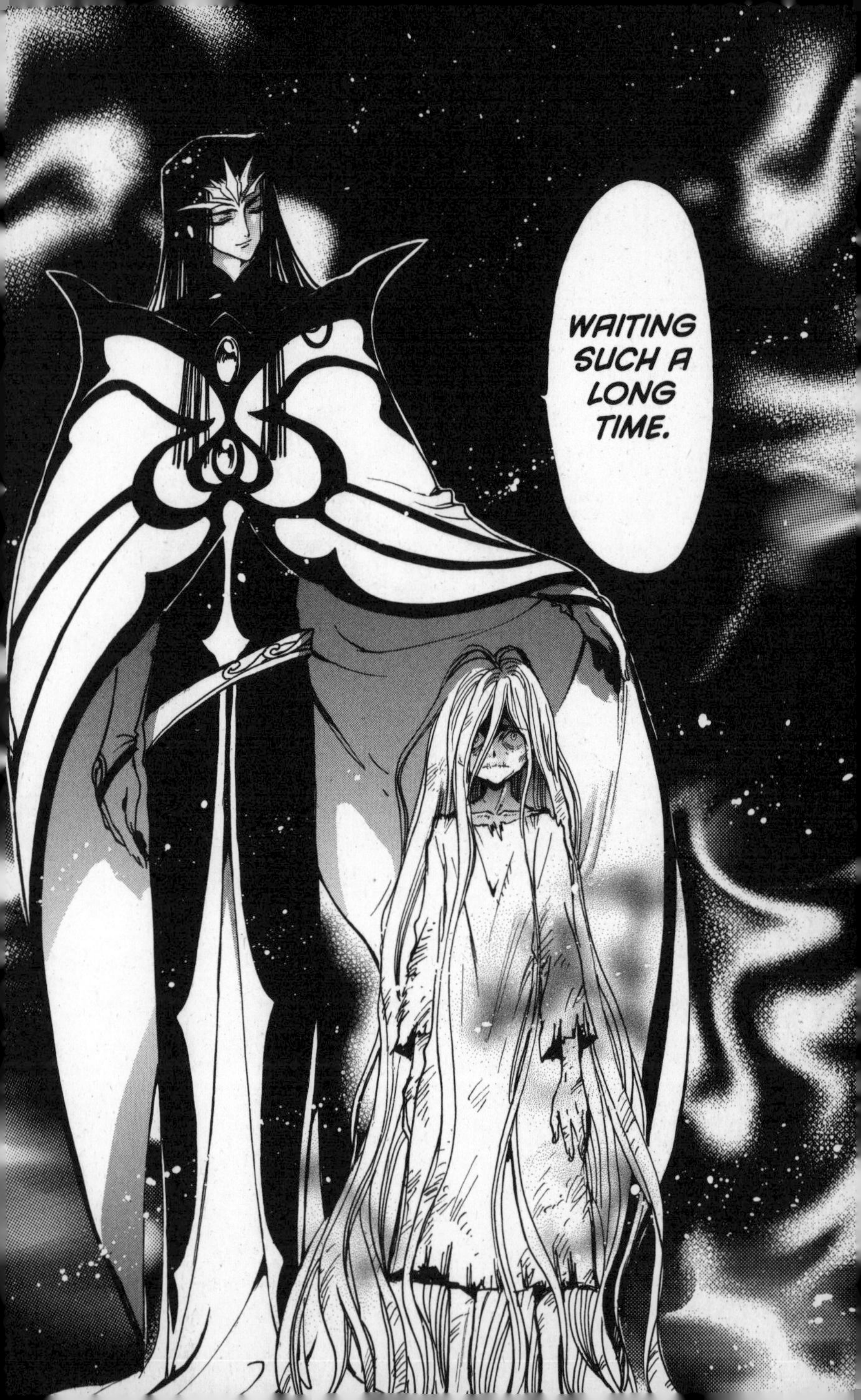
WAITING SUCH A LONG TIME.

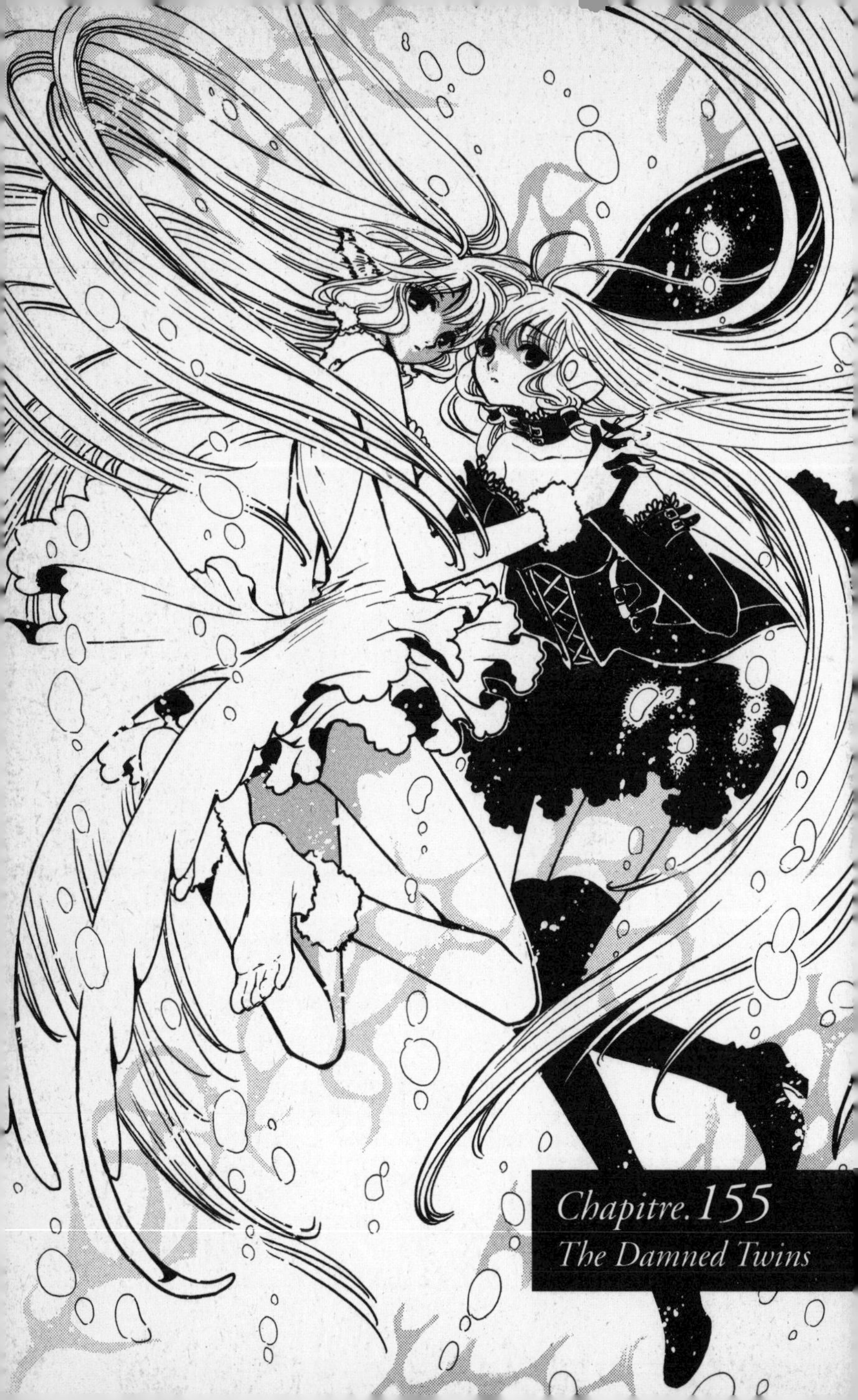
Chapitre. 155
The Damned Twins

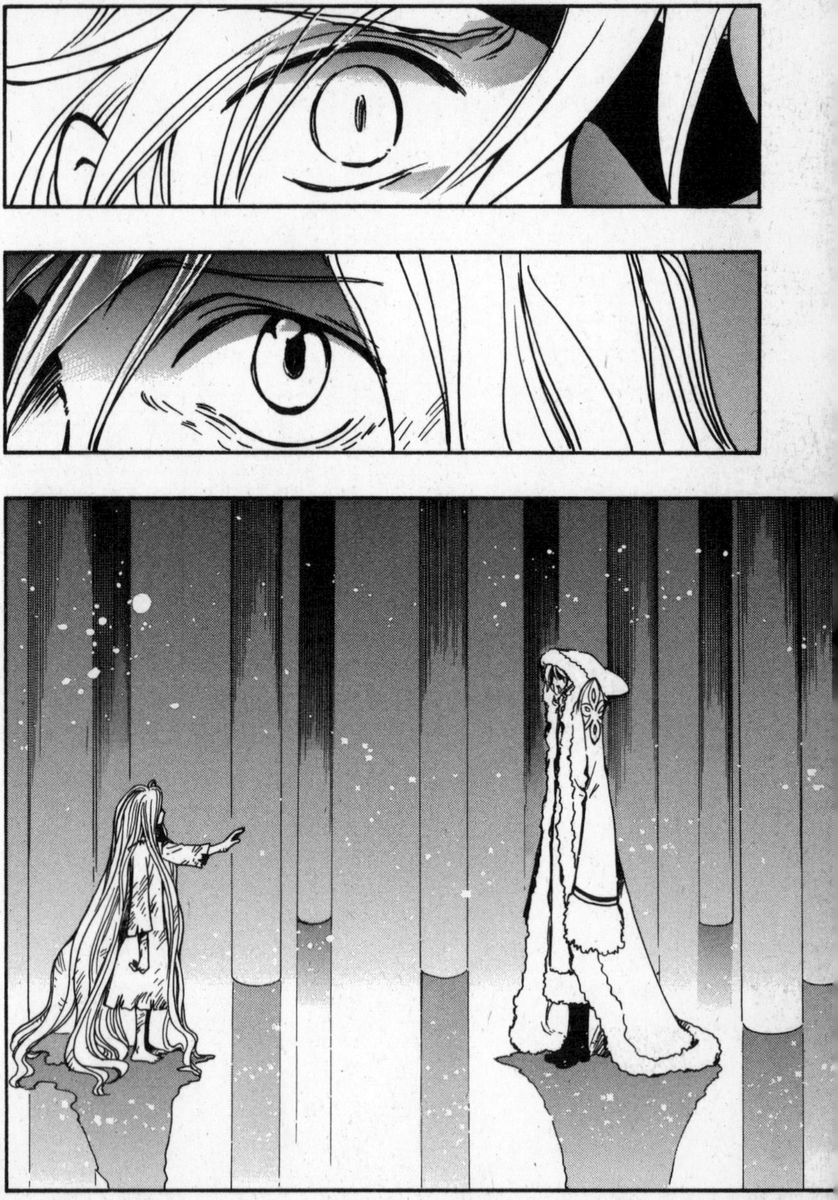

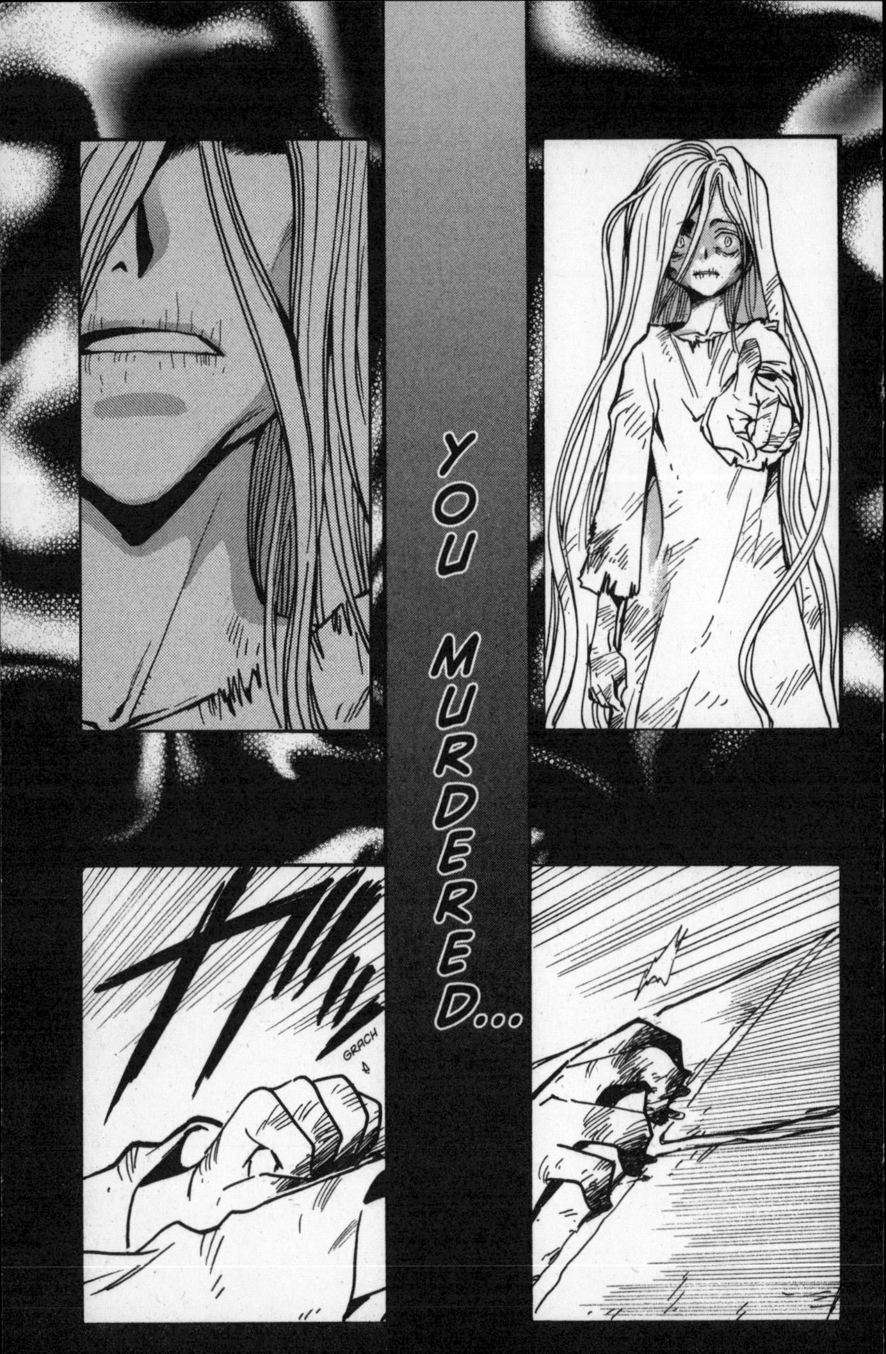
YOU MURDERED...
GRACH

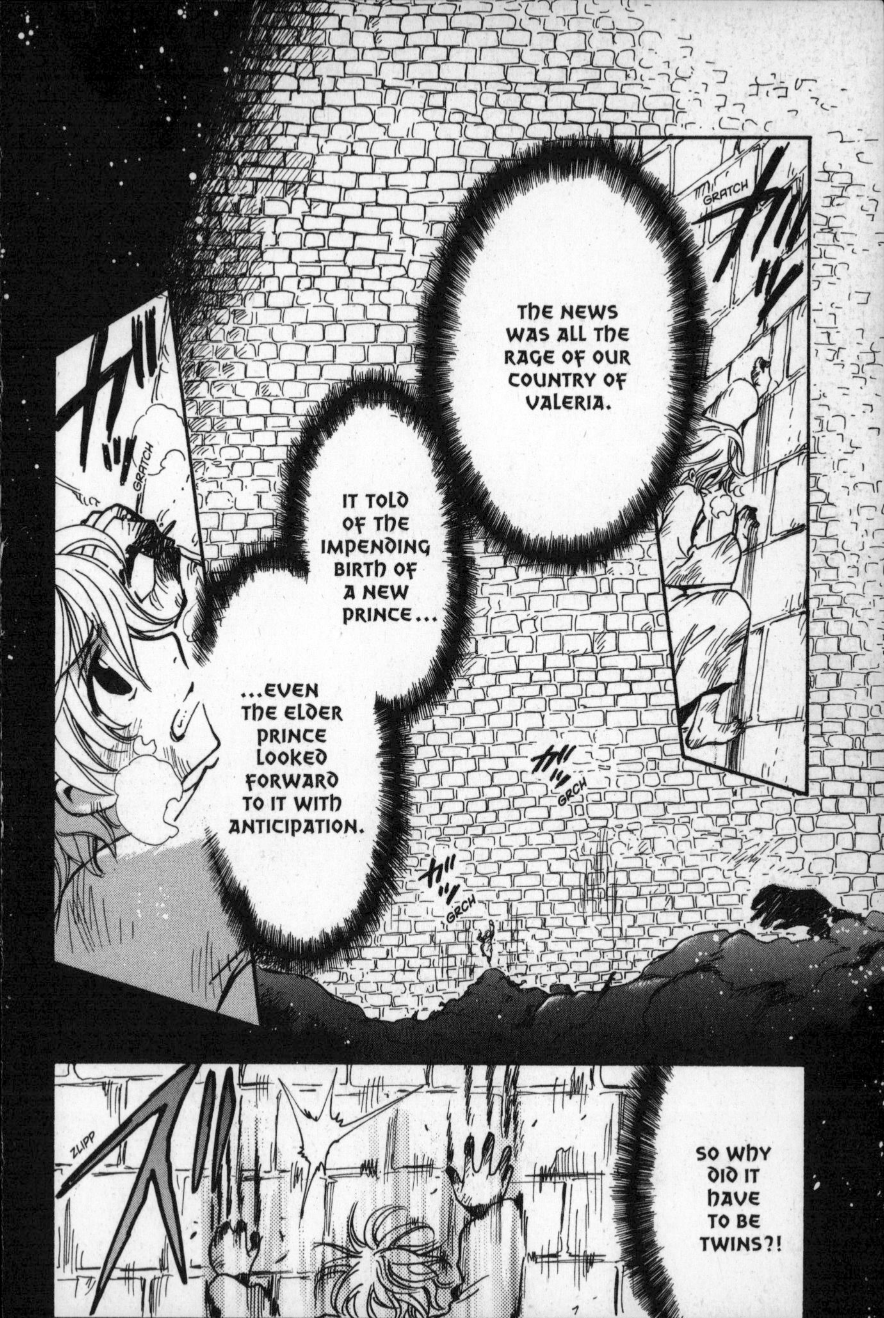
GRATCH
THE NEWS WAS ALL THE RAGE OF OUR COUNTRY OF VALERIA.
IT TOLD OF THE IMPENDING BIRTH OF A NEW PRINCE...
...EVEN THE ELDER PRINCE LOOKED FORWARD TO IT WITH ANTICIPATION.
GRATCH
GRCH
GRCH
SO WHY DID IT HAVE TO BE TWINS?!
ZLIPP

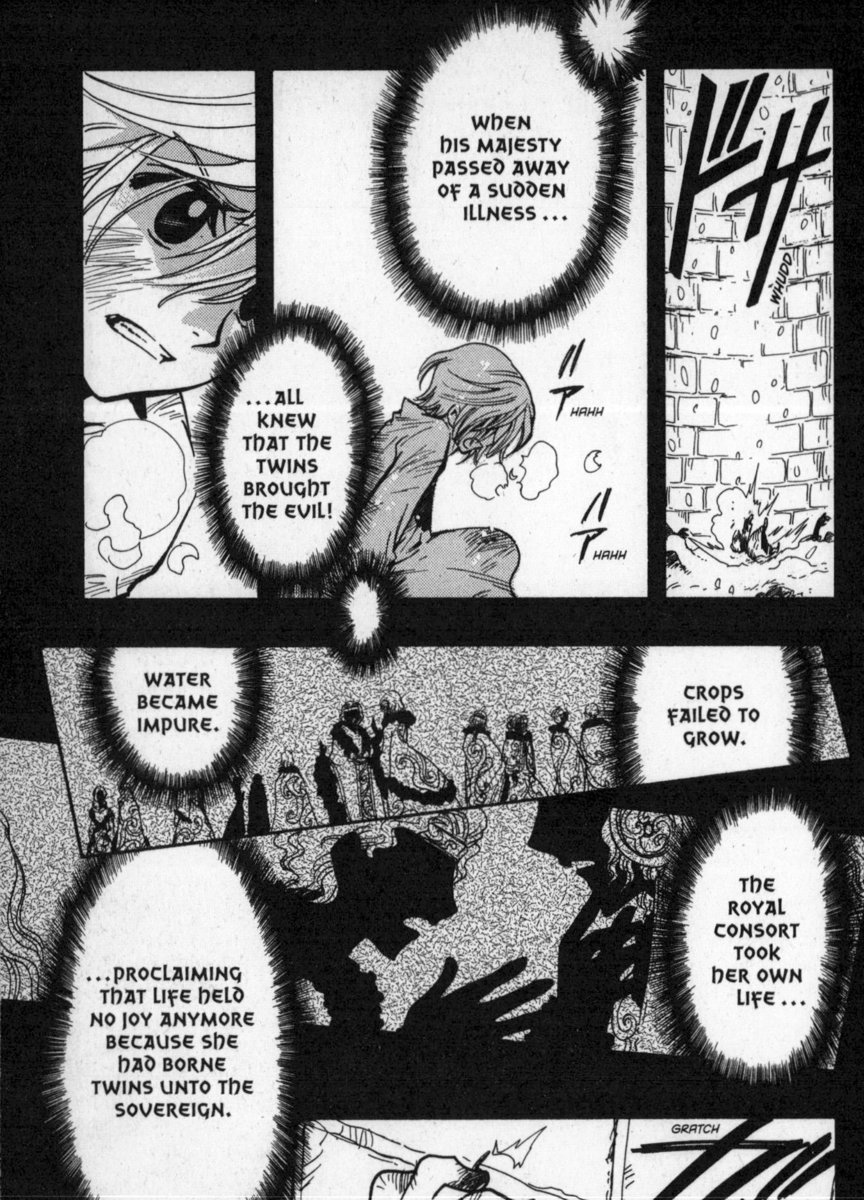
WHUDD
WHEN HIS MAJESTY PASSED AWAY OF A SUDDEN ILLNESS ...
...ALL KNEW THAT THE TWINS BROUGHT THE EVIL!
HAHH
HAHH
CROPS FAILED TO GROW.
WATER BECAME IMPURE.
THE ROYAL CONSORT TOOK HER OWN LIFE ...
...PROCLAIMING THAT LIFE HELD NO JOY ANYMORE BECAUSE SHE HAD BORNE TWINS UNTO THE SOVEREIGN.
GRATCH

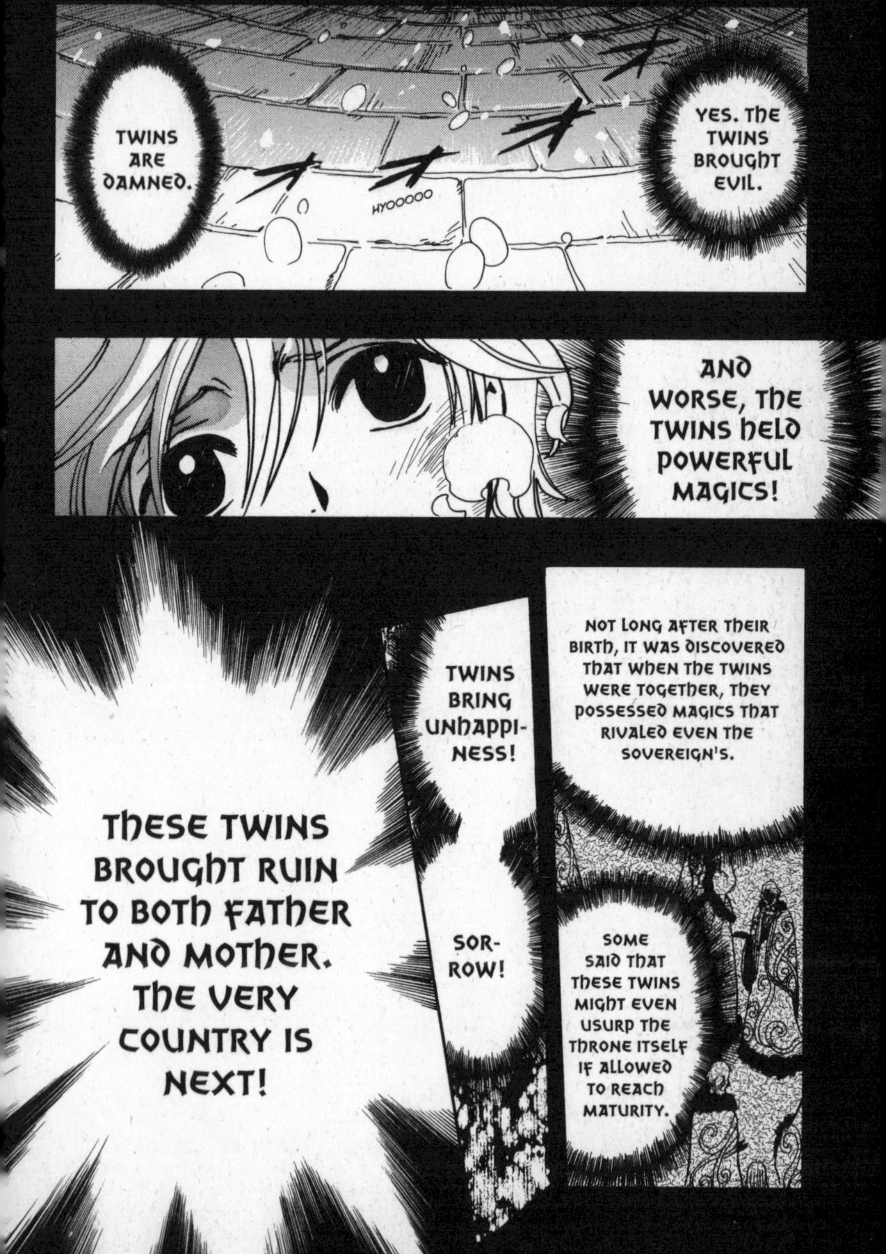
YES. THE TWINS BROUGHT EVIL.
TWINS ARE DAMNED.
HYOOOOO
AND WORSE, THE TWINS HELD POWERFUL MAGICS!
NOT LONG AFTER THEIR BIRTH, IT WAS DISCOVERED THAT WHEN THE TWINS WERE TOGETHER, THEY POSSESSED MAGICS THAT RIVALED EVEN THE SOVEREIGN'S.
SOME SAID THAT THESE TWINS MIGHT EVEN USURP THE THRONE ITSELF IF ALLOWED TO REACH MATURITY.
TWINS BRING UNHAPPI-NESS!
SOR-ROW!
THESE TWINS BROUGHT RUIN TO BOTH FATHER AND MOTHER. THE VERY COUNTRY IS NEXT!

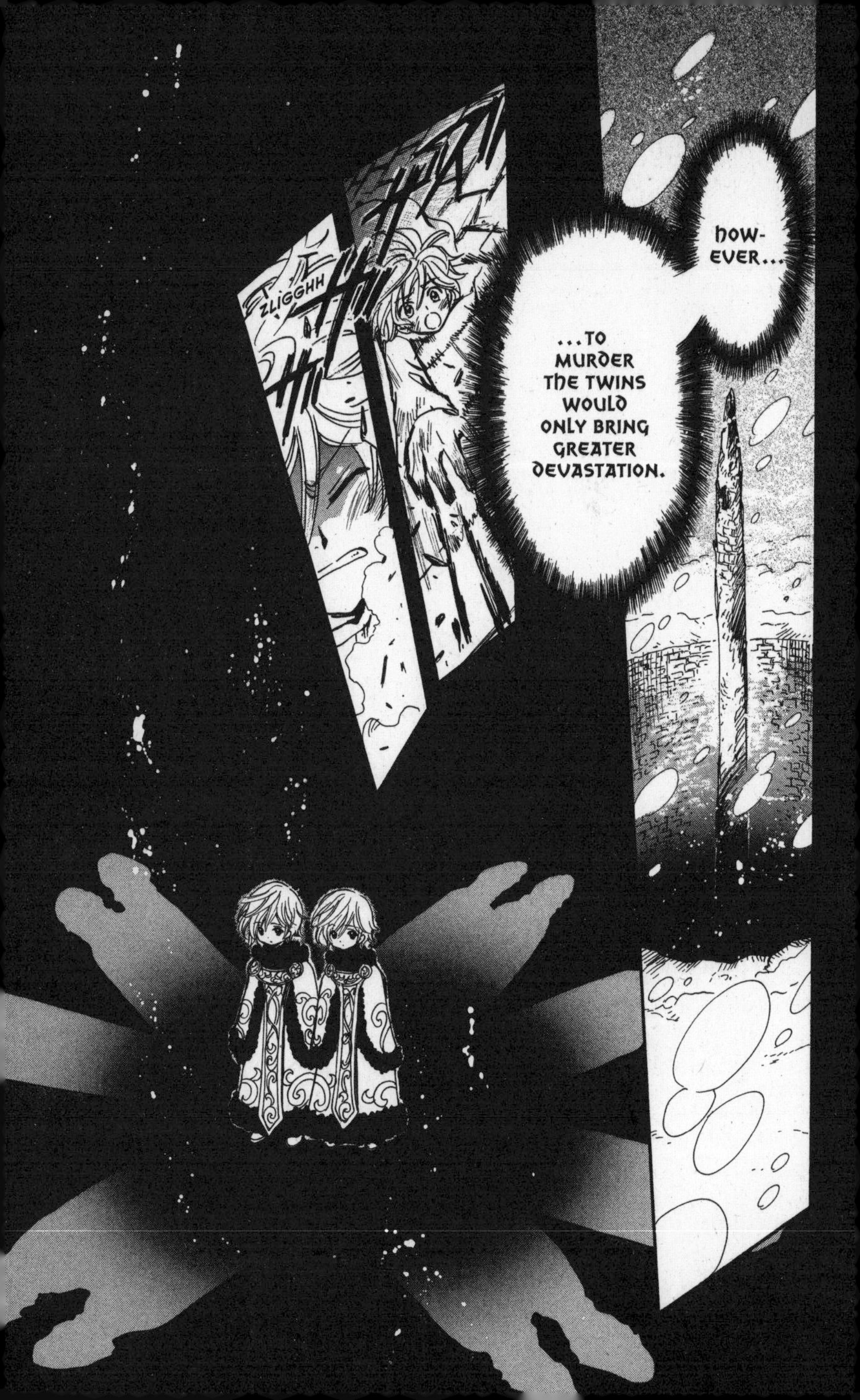
HOW-
EVER...
...TO MURDER THE TWINS WOULD ONLY BRING GREATER DEVASTATION.
ZLIGGHH

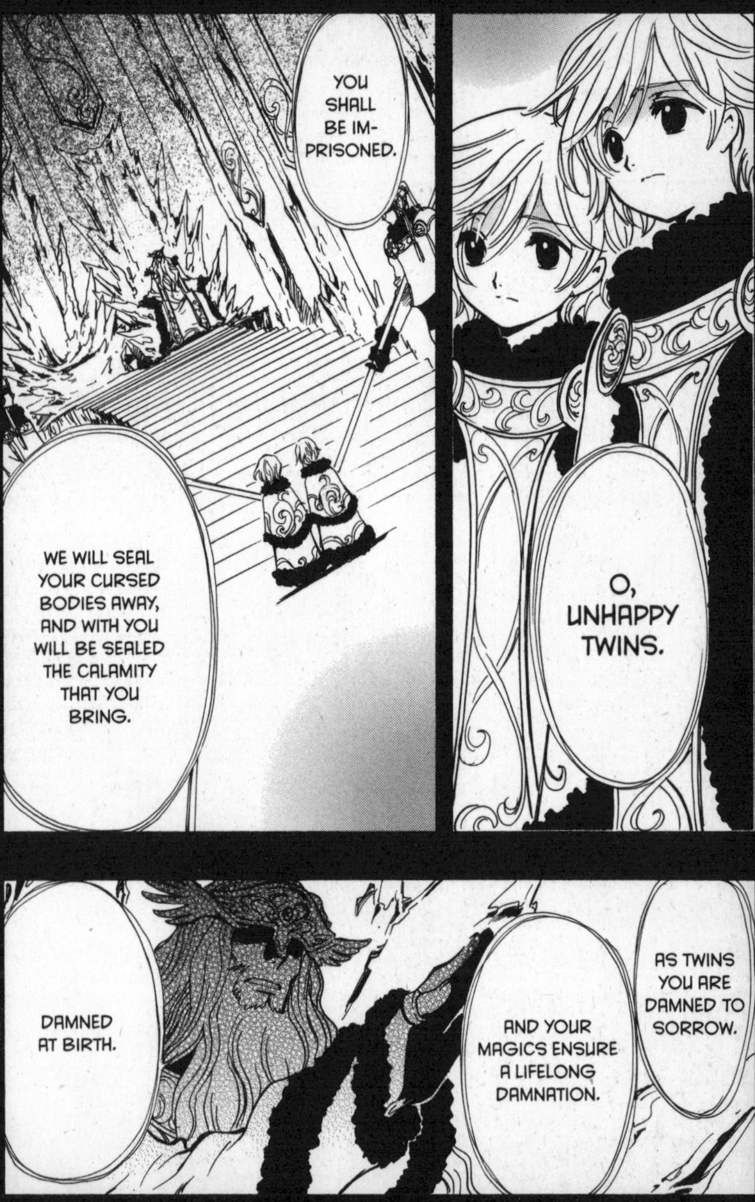
O, UNHAPPY TWINS.
YOU SHALL BE IM-PRISONED.
WE WILL SEAL YOUR CURSED BODIES AWAY, AND WITH YOU WILL BE SEALED THE CALAMITY THAT YOU BRING.
AS TWINS YOU ARE DAMNED TO SORROW.
AND YOUR MAGICS ENSURE A LIFELONG DAMNATION.
DAMNED AT BIRTH.

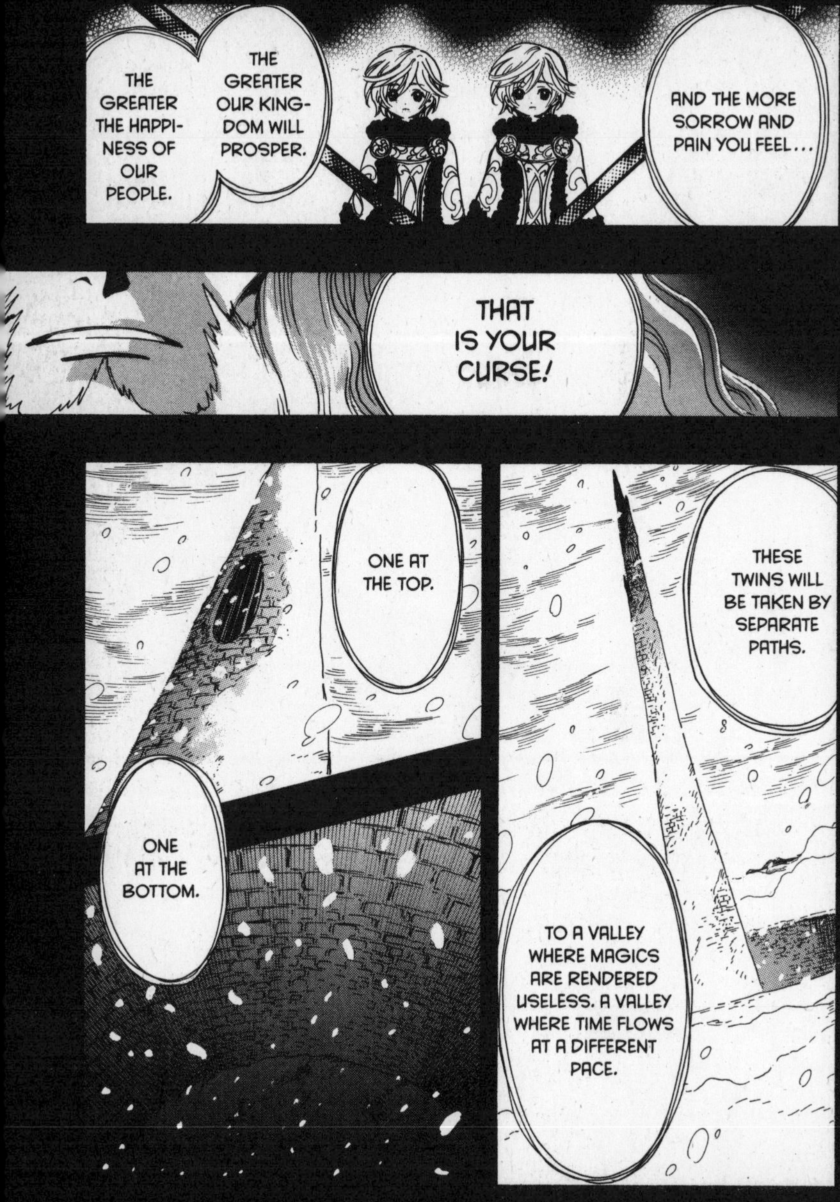
AND THE MORE SORROW AND PAIN YOU FEEL...
THE GREATER OUR KING-DOM WILL PROSPER.
THE GREATER THE HAPPI-NESS OF OUR PEOPLE.
THAT IS YOUR CURSE!
THESE TWINS WILL BE TAKEN BY SEPARATE PATHS.
TO A VALLEY WHERE MAGICS ARE RENDERED USELESS. A VALLEY WHERE TIME FLOWS AT A DIFFERENT PACE.
ONE AT THE TOP.
ONE AT THE BOTTOM.

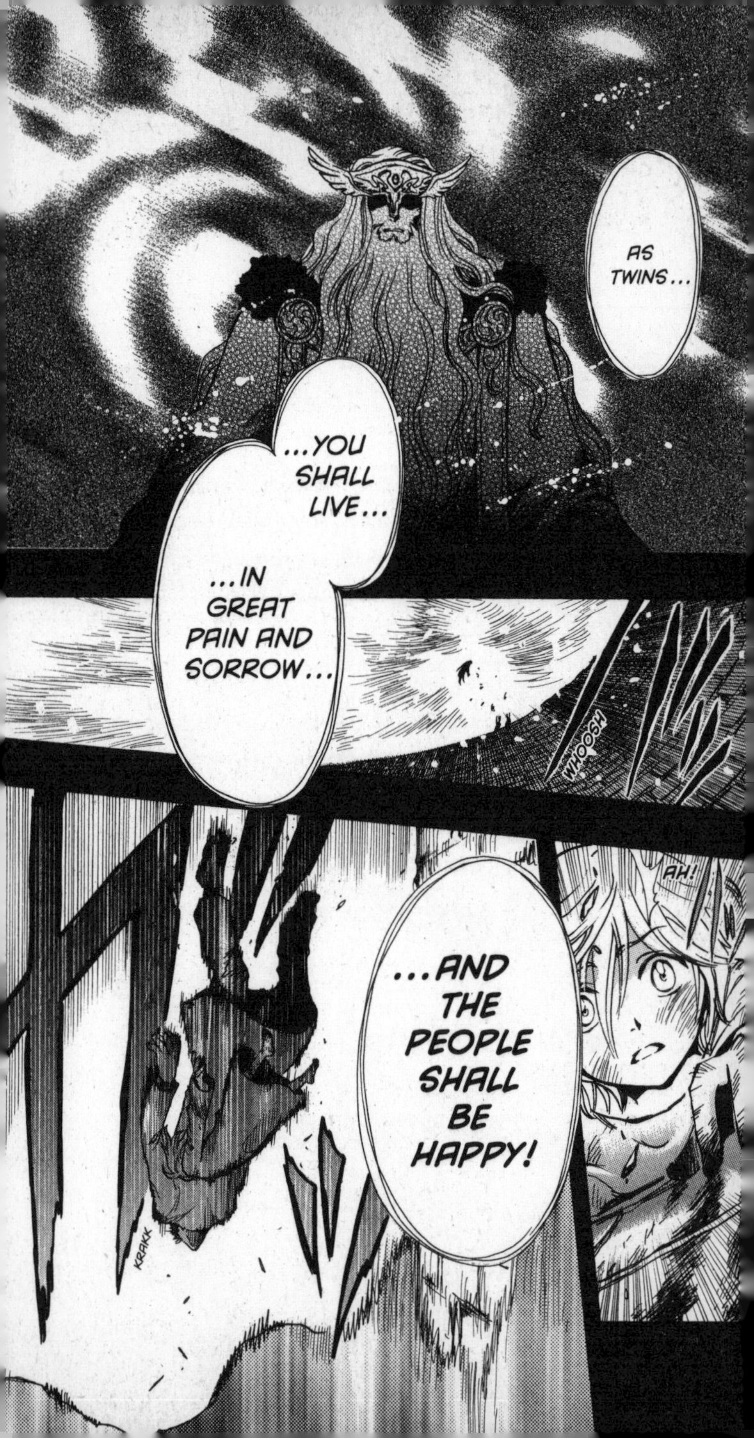
AS TWINS...
...YOU SHALL LIVE...
...IN GREAT PAIN AND SORROW...
WHOOSH
AH!
...AND THE PEOPLE SHALL BE HAPPY!
KRAKK

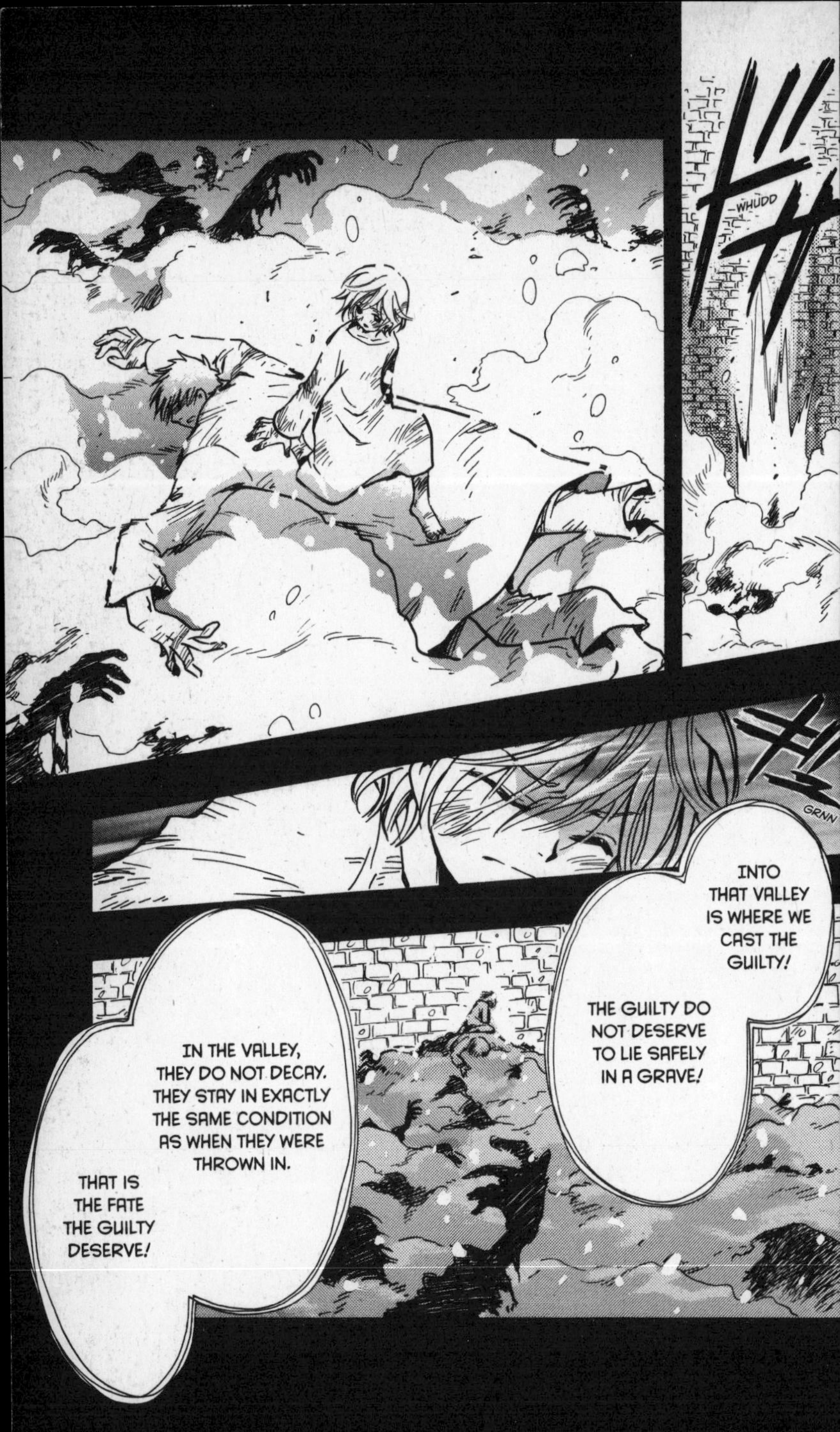
WHUDD
GRNN
INTO THAT VALLEY IS WHERE WE CAST THE GUILTY!
THE GUILTY DO NOT DESERVE TO LIE SAFELY IN A GRAVE!
IN THE VALLEY, THEY DO NOT DECAY. THEY STAY IN EXACTLY THE SAME CONDITION AS WHEN THEY WERE THROWN IN.
THAT IS THE FATE THE GUILTY DESERVE!

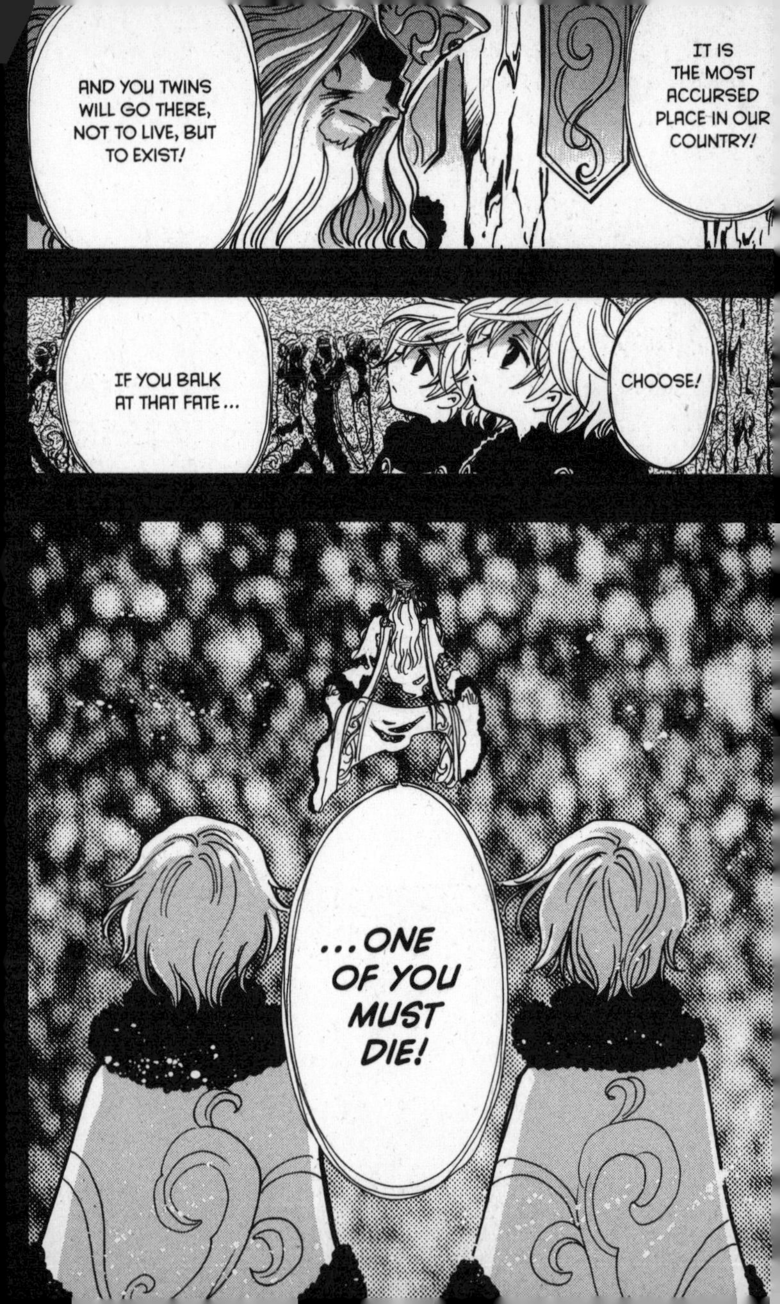
IT IS THE MOST ACCURSED PLACE IN OUR COUNTRY!
AND YOU TWINS WILL GO THERE, NOT TO LIVE, BUT TO EXIST!
CHOOSE!
IF YOU BALK AT THAT FATE...
...ONE OF YOU MUST DIE!

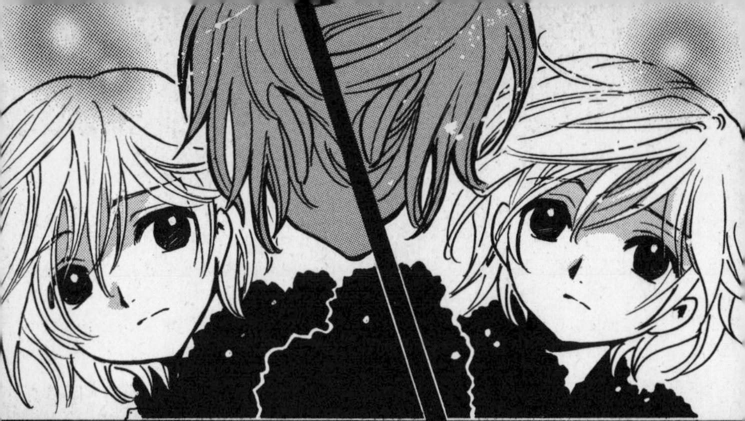
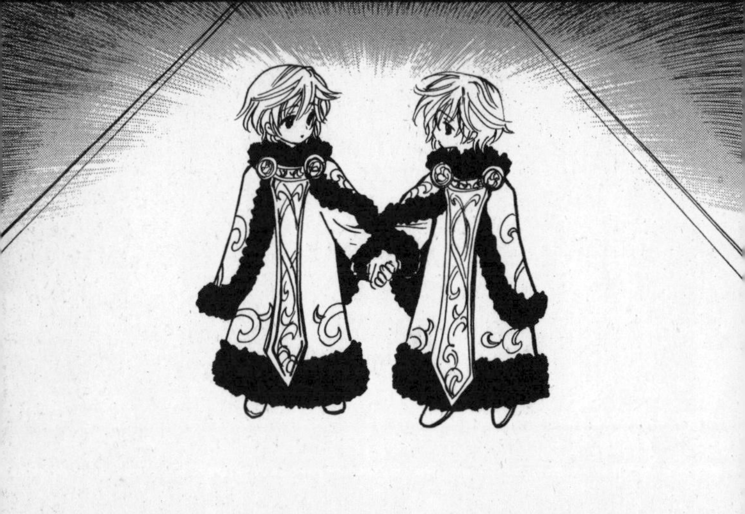
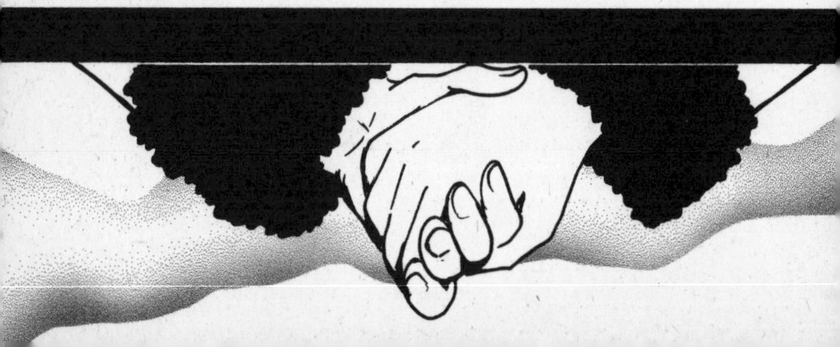

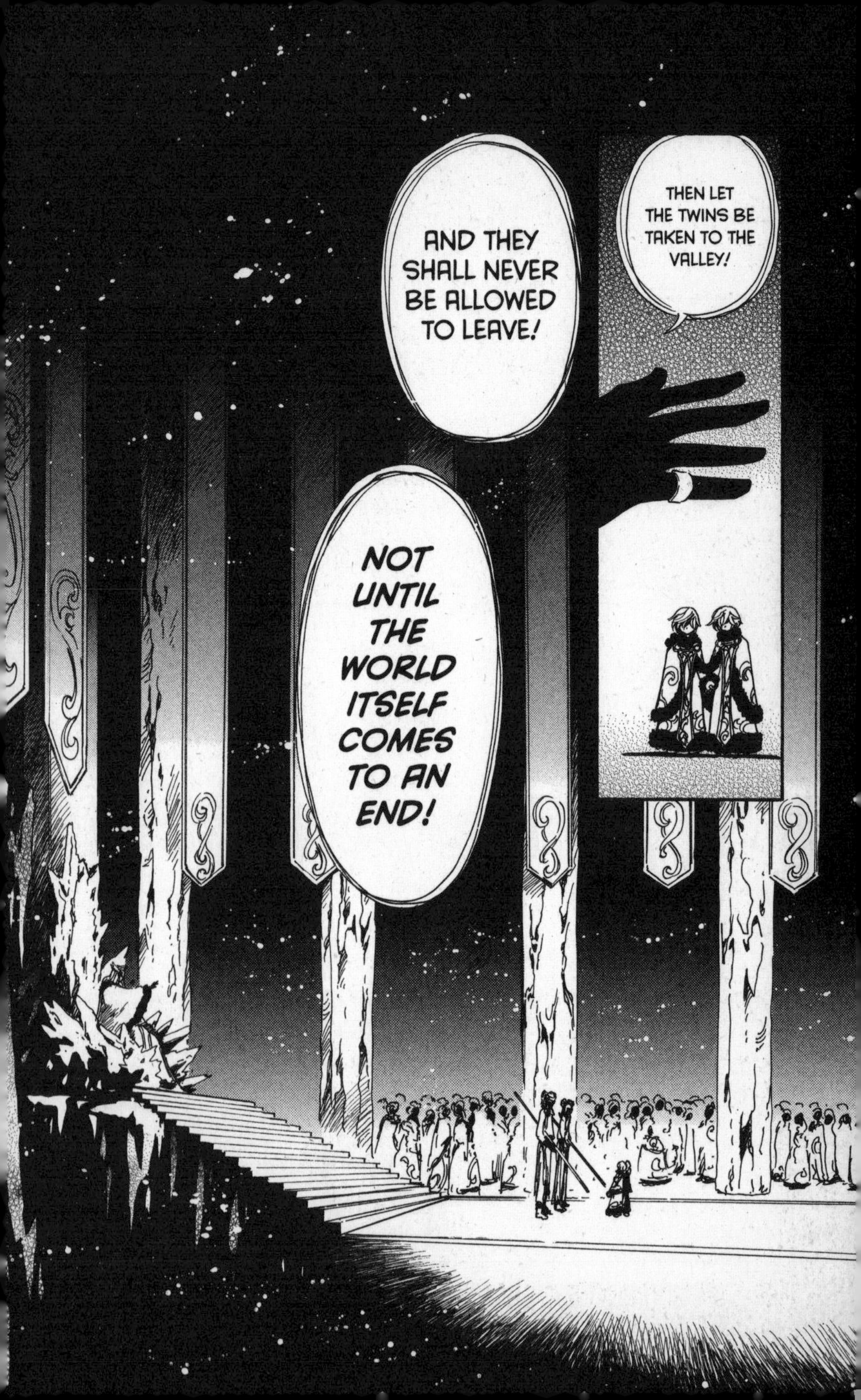
THEN LET THE TWINS BE TAKEN TO THE VALLEY!
AND THEY SHALL NEVER BE ALLOWED TO LEAVE!
NOT UNTIL THE WORLD ITSELF COMES TO AN END!

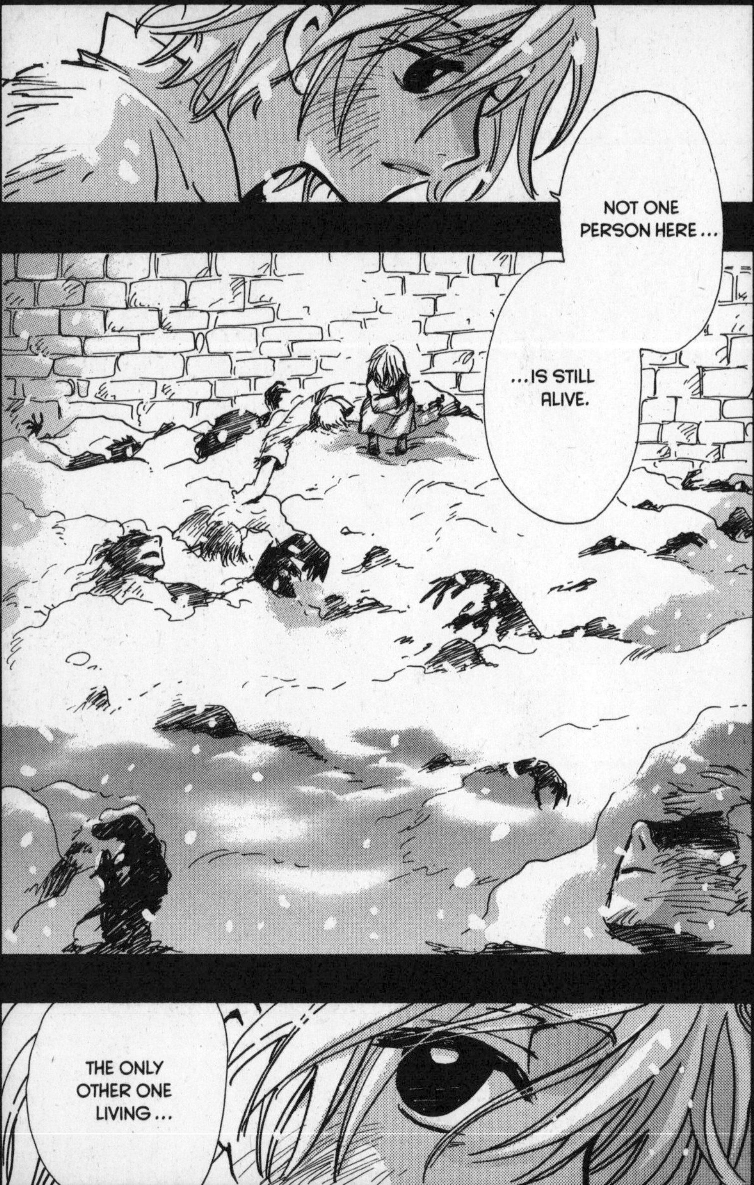
NOT ONE PERSON HERE...
...IS STILL ALIVE.
THE ONLY OTHER ONE LIVING...

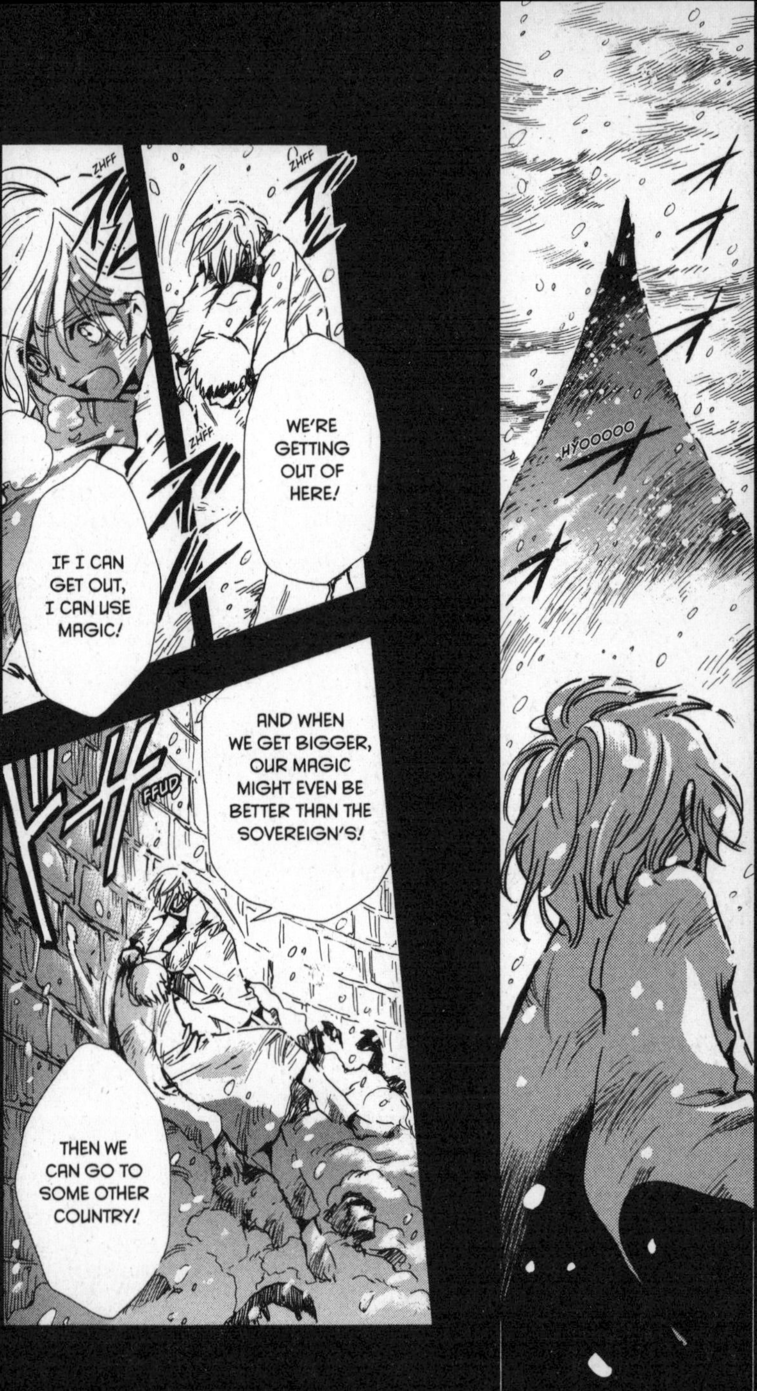
HYOOOOO
ZHFF
ZHFF
WE'RE GETTING OUT OF HERE!
ZHFF
IF I CAN GET OUT, I CAN USE MAGIC!
FFUD
AND WHEN WE GET BIGGER, OUR MAGIC MIGHT EVEN BE BETTER THAN THE SOVEREIGN'S!
THEN WE CAN GO TO SOME OTHER COUNTRY!

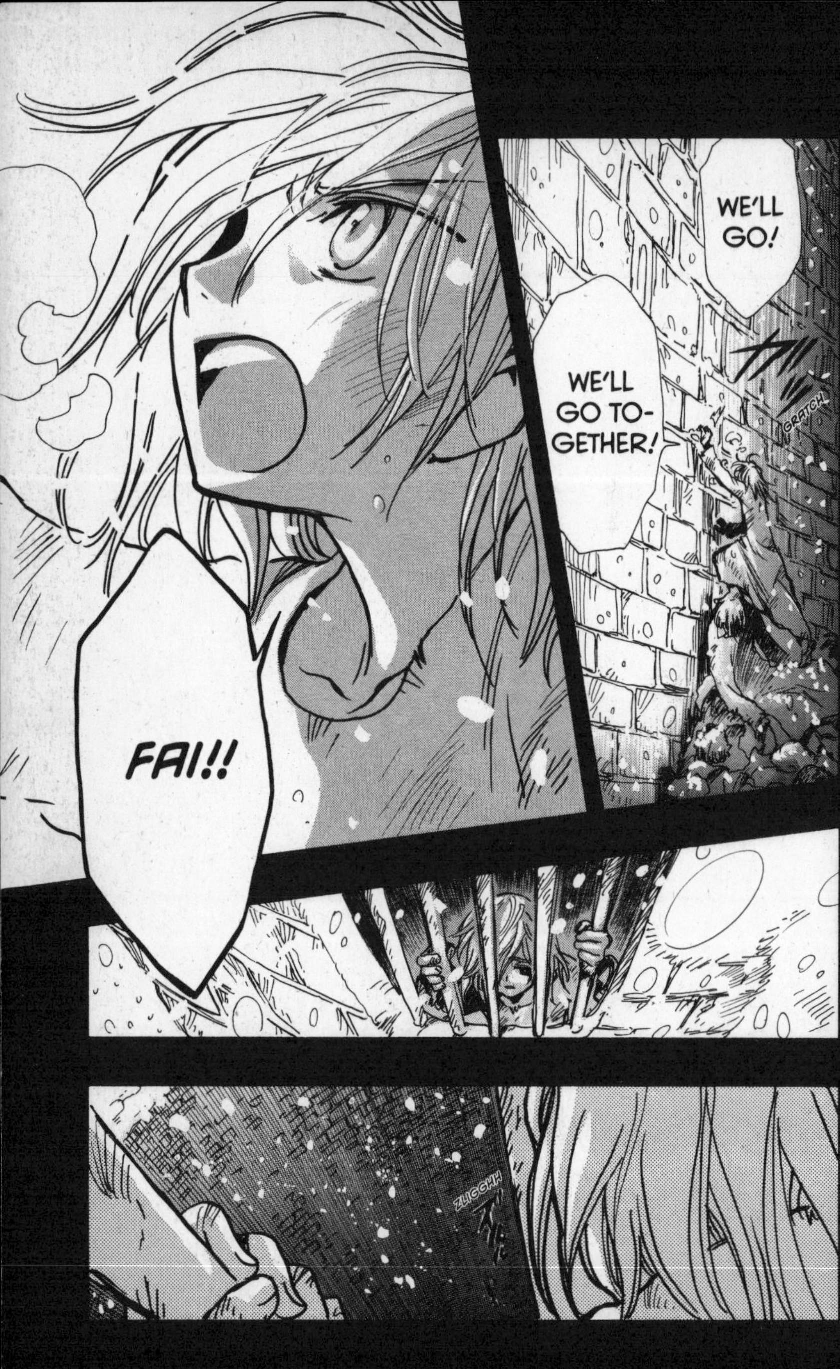
WE'LL GO!
WE'LL GO TO-GETHER!
GRATCH
FAI!!
ZLIGGHH

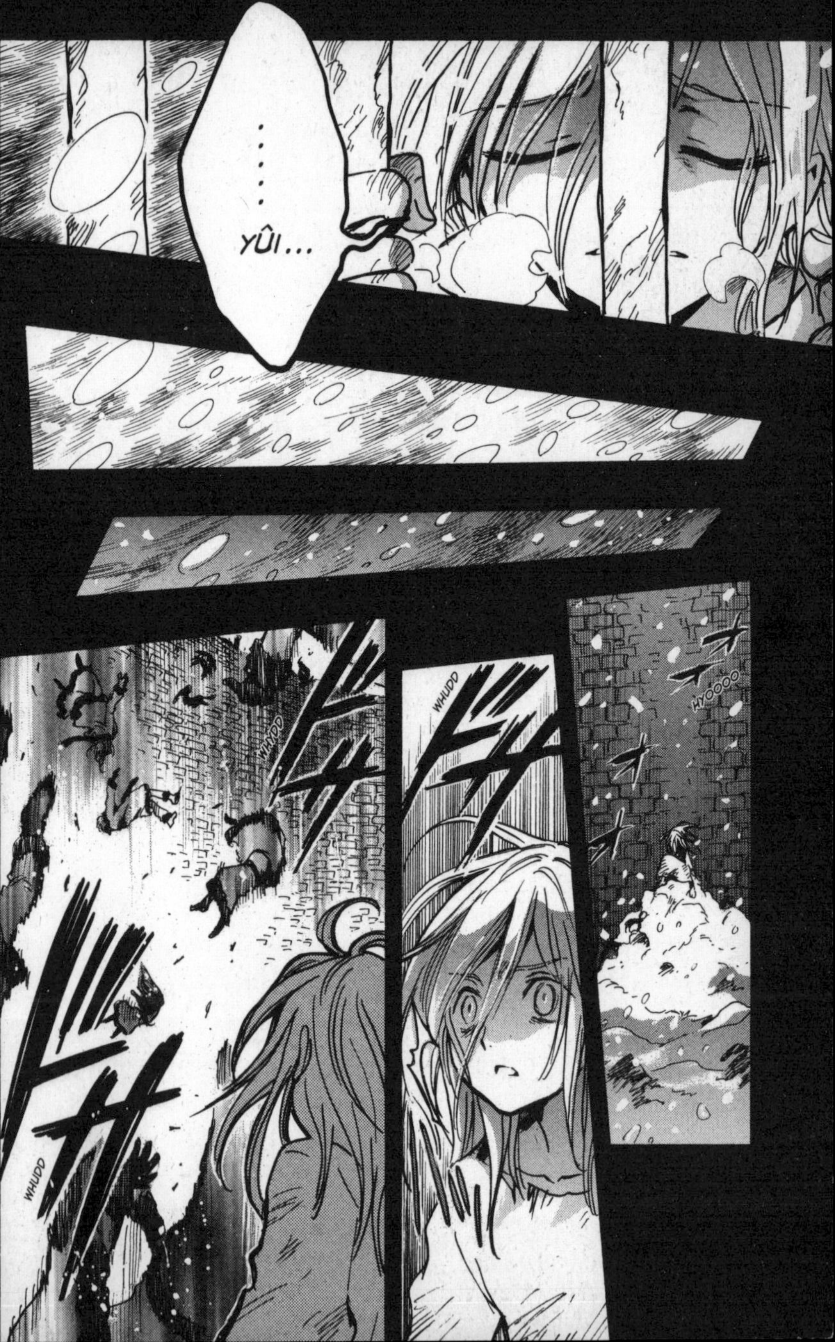
......
YÛI...
HYOOOO
WHUDD
WHUDD
WHUDD

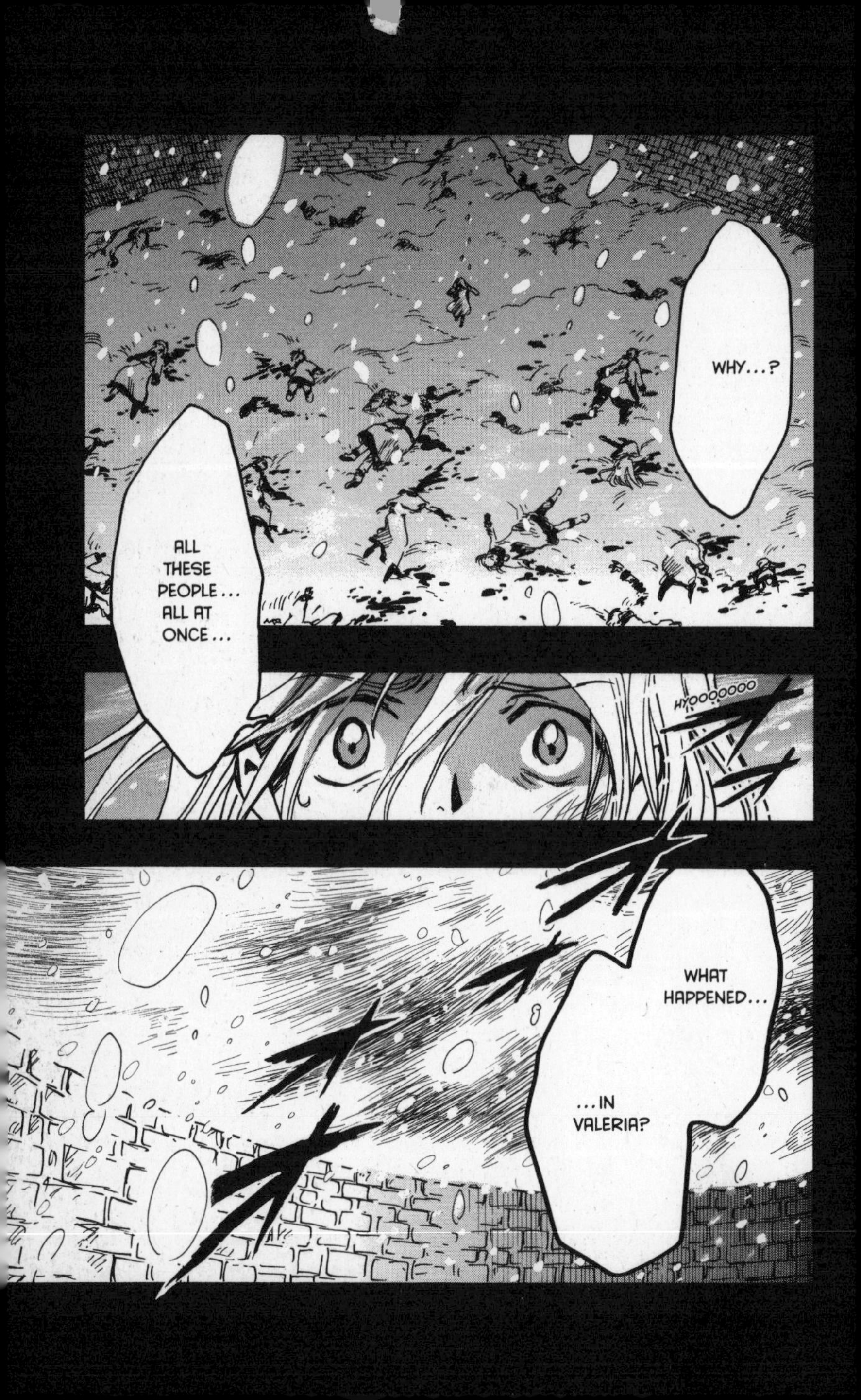
WHY...?
ALL THESE PEOPLE... ALL AT ONCE...
HYOOOOOOO
WHAT HAPPENED...
...IN VALERIA?

RESERVoir CHRoNiCLE

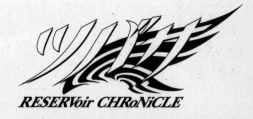

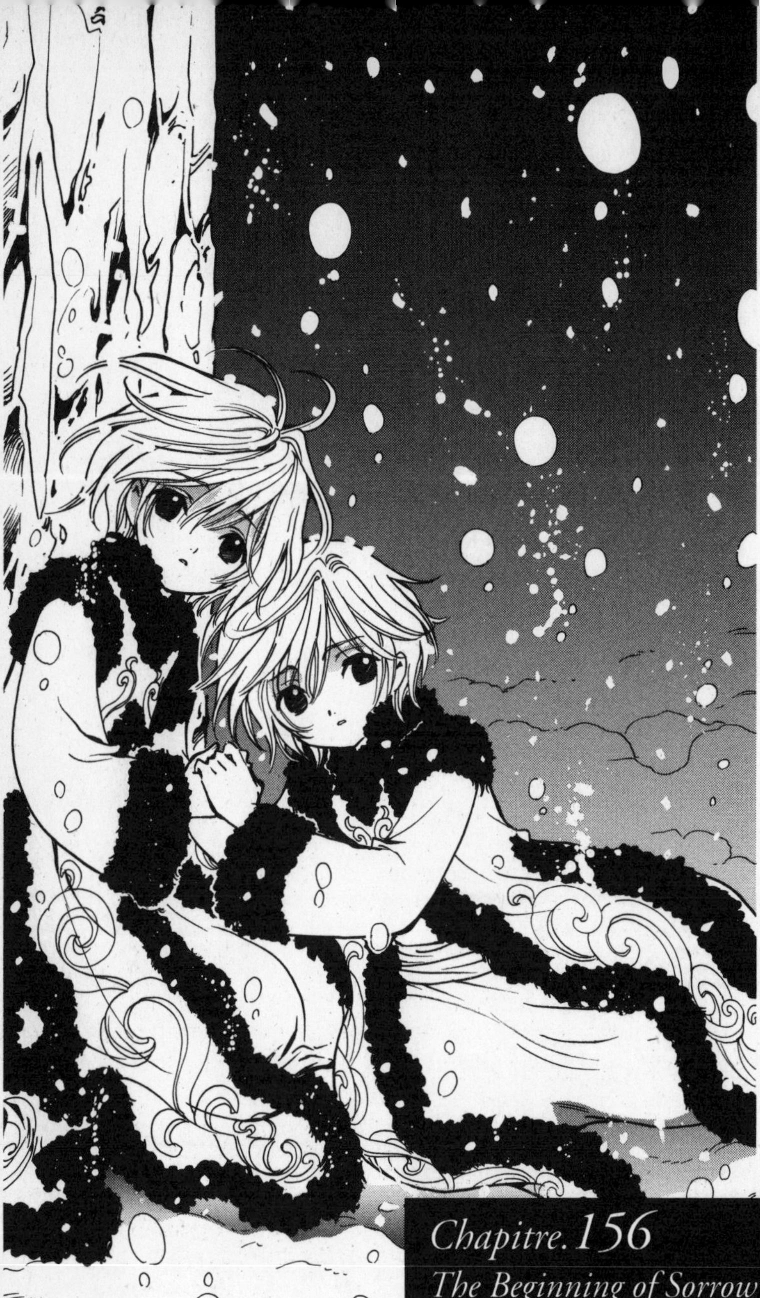

Chapitre. 156
The Beginning of Sorrow

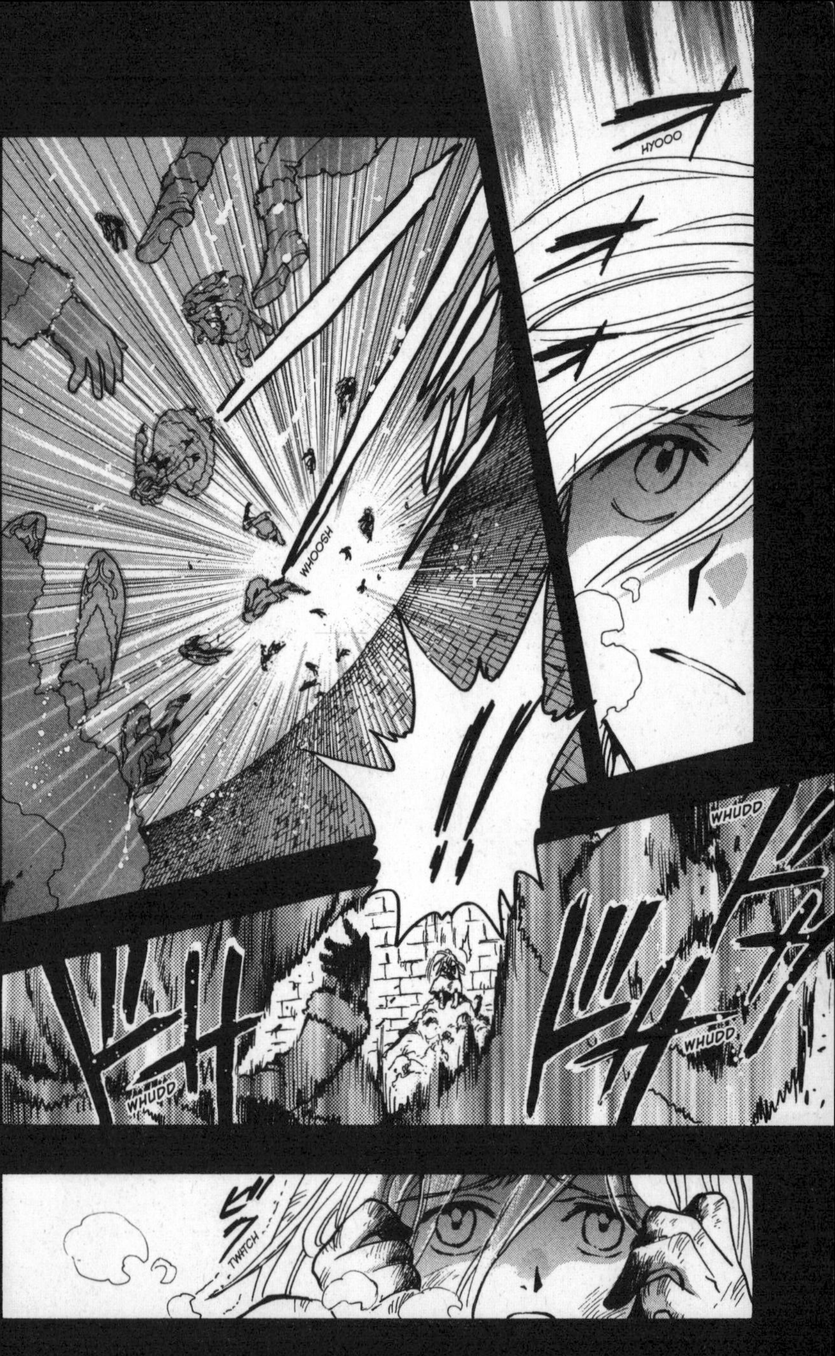
HYOOO
WHOOSH
WHUDD
WHUDD
WHUDD
TWATCH

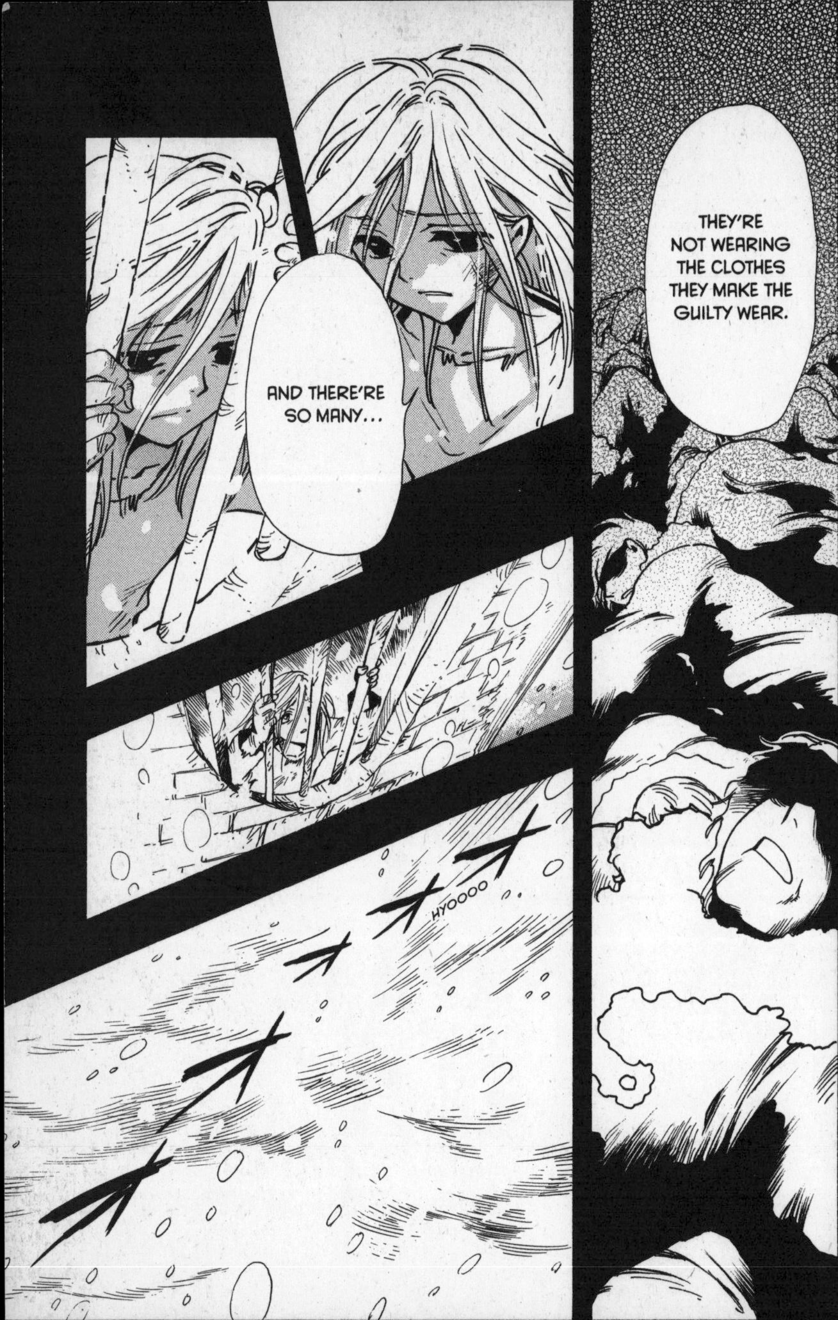
THEY'RE NOT WEARING THE CLOTHES THEY MAKE THE GUILTY WEAR.
AND THERE'RE SO MANY...
HYOOOO

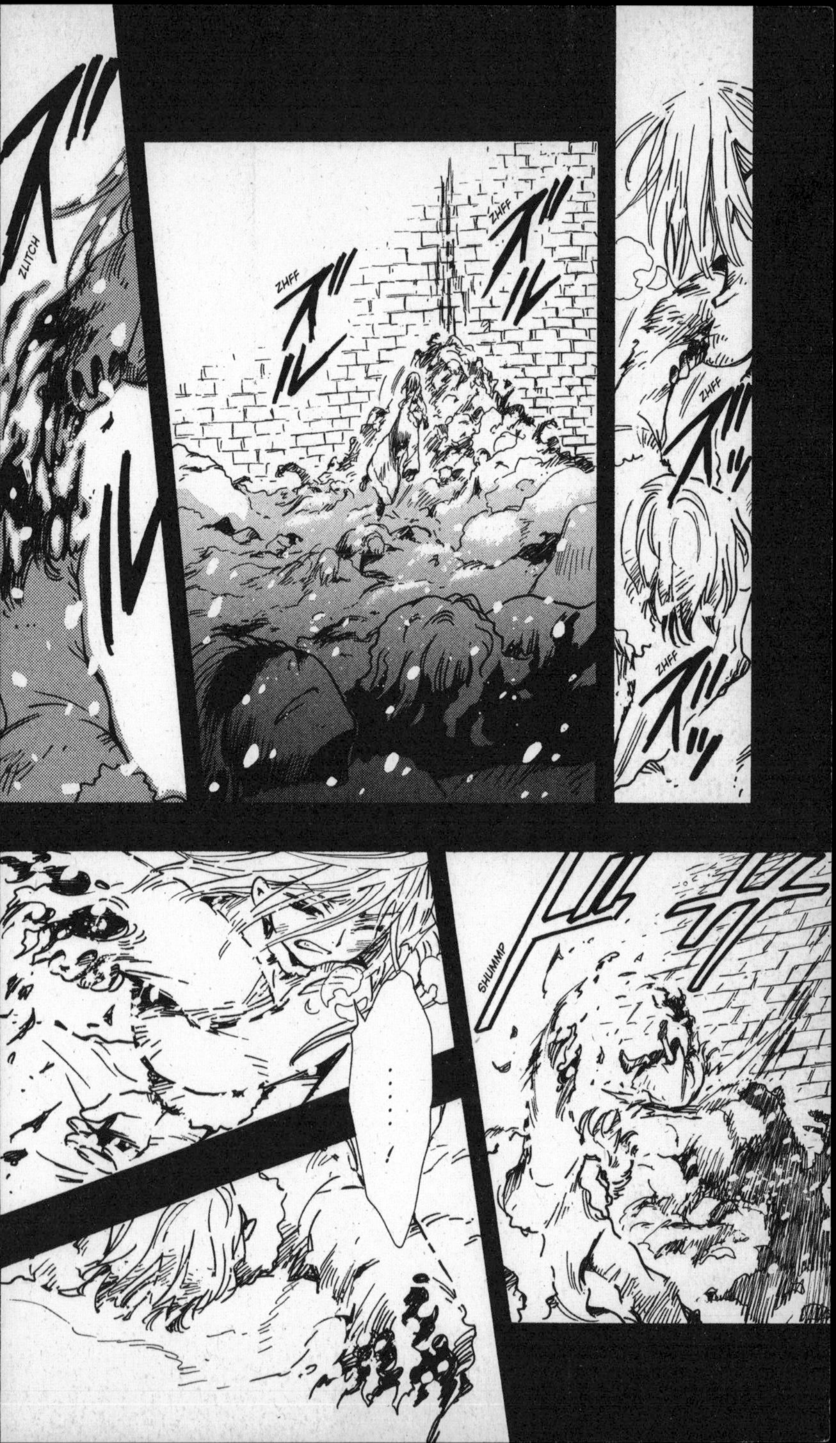
ZHFF
ZHFF
ZHFF
ZHFF
ZLITCH
SHUMMP
. . . . .

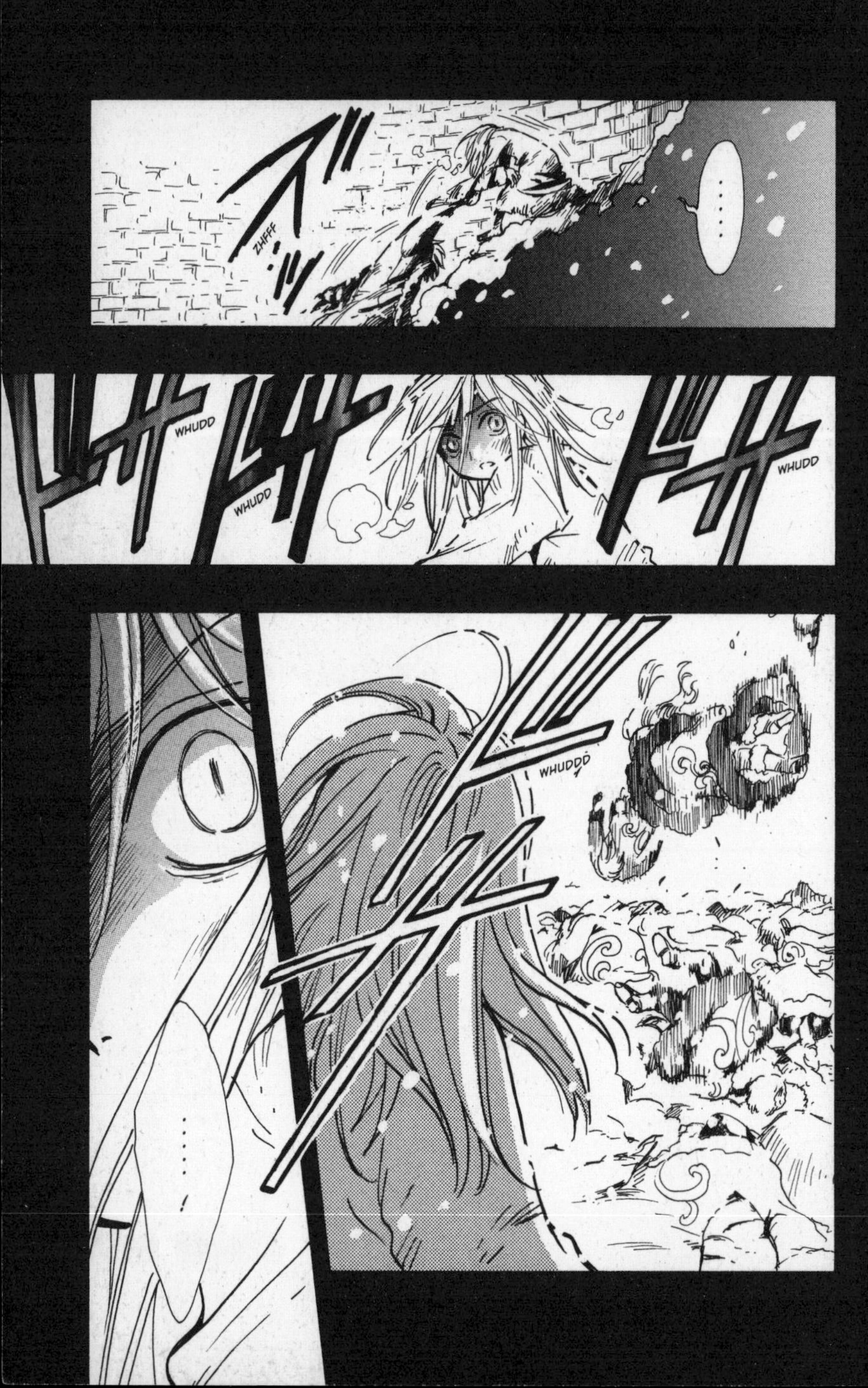
......
ZHFFF
WHUDD
WHUDD
WHUDD
WHUDDD
......

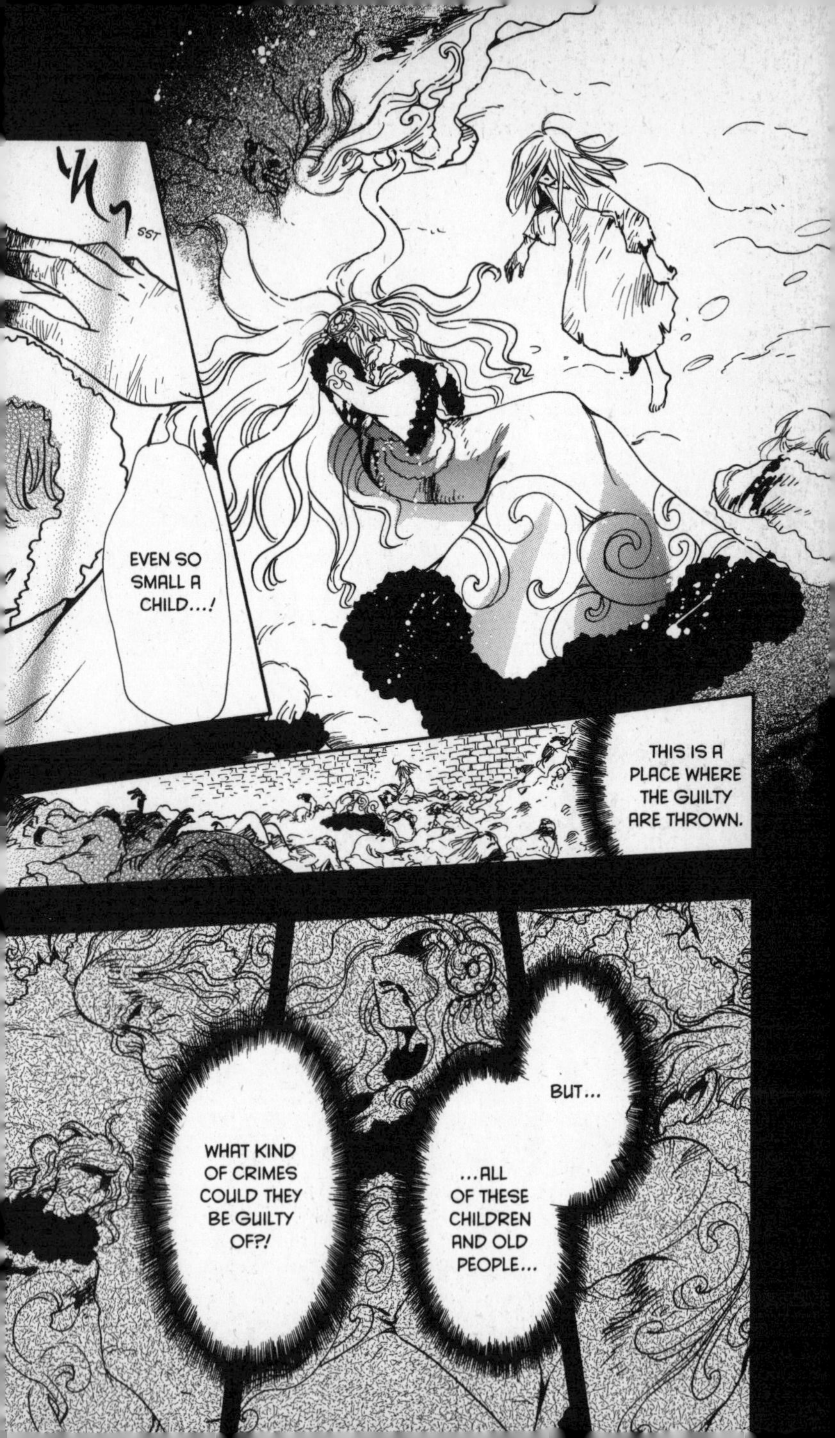
SST
EVEN SO SMALL A CHILD...!
THIS IS A PLACE WHERE THE GUILTY ARE THROWN.
BUT...
...ALL OF THESE CHILDREN AND OLD PEOPLE...
WHAT KIND OF CRIMES COULD THEY BE GUILTY OF?!

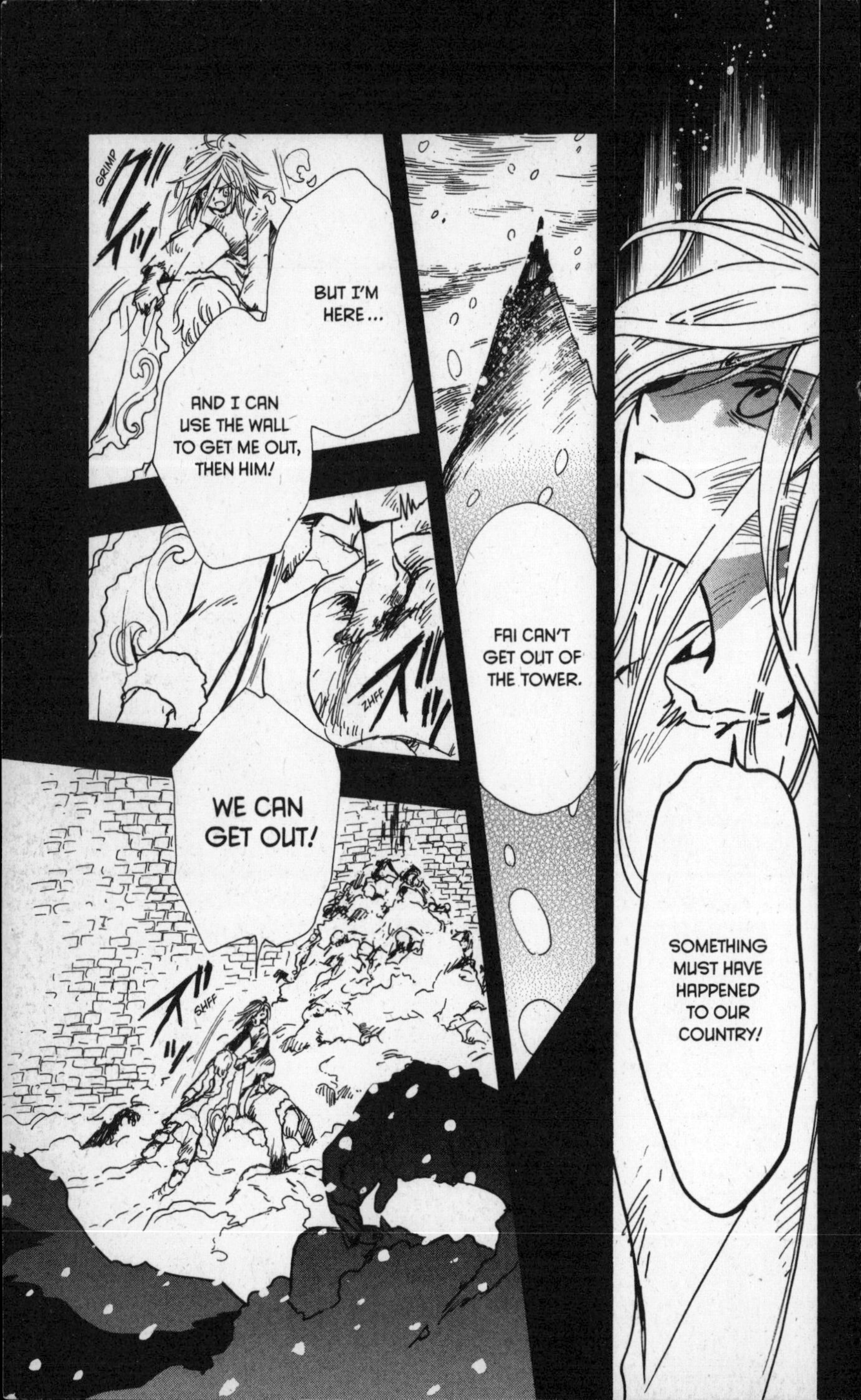
SOMETHING MUST HAVE HAPPENED TO OUR COUNTRY!
FAI CAN'T GET OUT OF THE TOWER.
GRIMP
BUT I'M HERE...
AND I CAN USE THE WALL TO GET ME OUT, THEN HIM!
ZHFF
WE CAN GET OUT!
SHFF

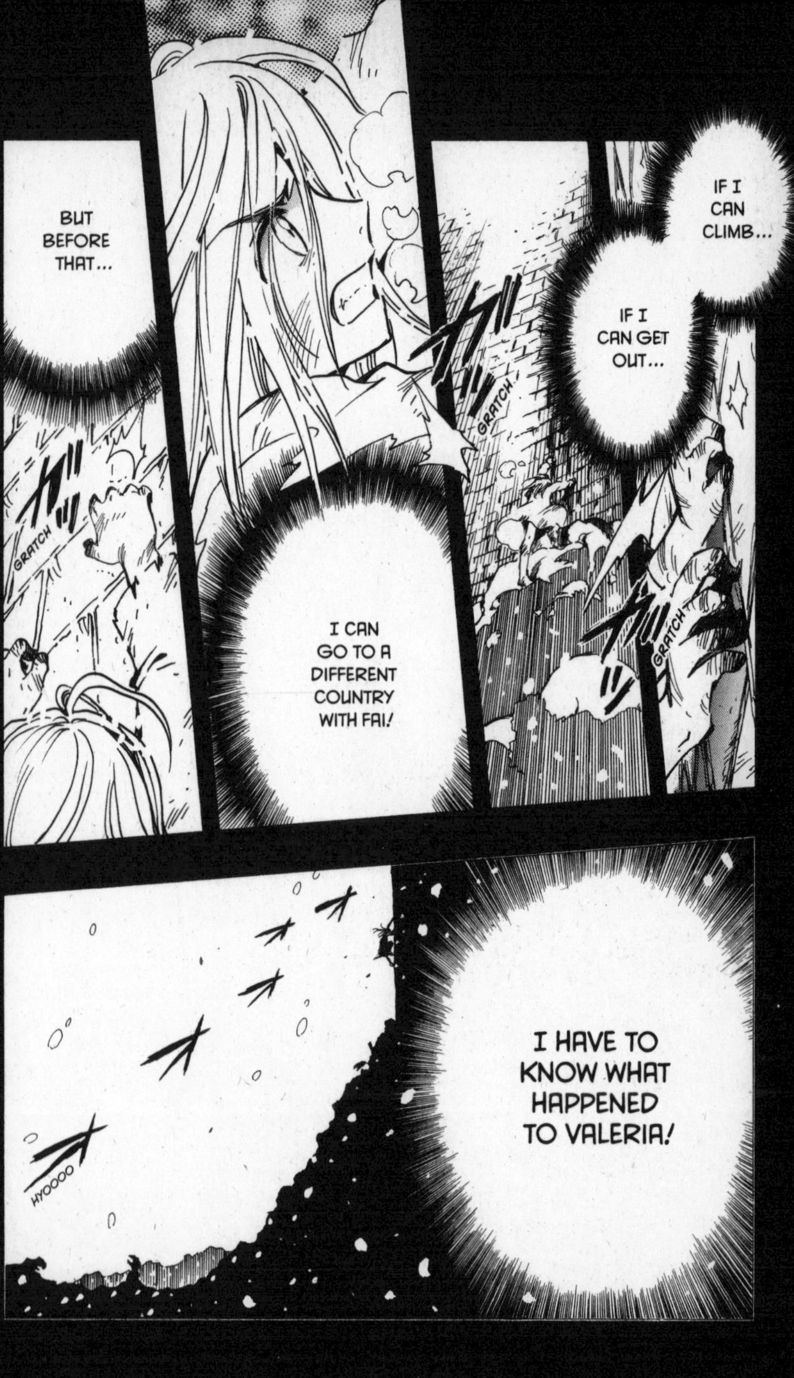
IF I CAN CLIMB...
IF I CAN GET OUT...
GRATCH
GRATCH
I CAN GO TO A DIFFERENT COUNTRY WITH FAI!
BUT BEFORE THAT...
GRATCH
I HAVE TO KNOW WHAT HAPPENED TO VALERIA!
HYOOOO

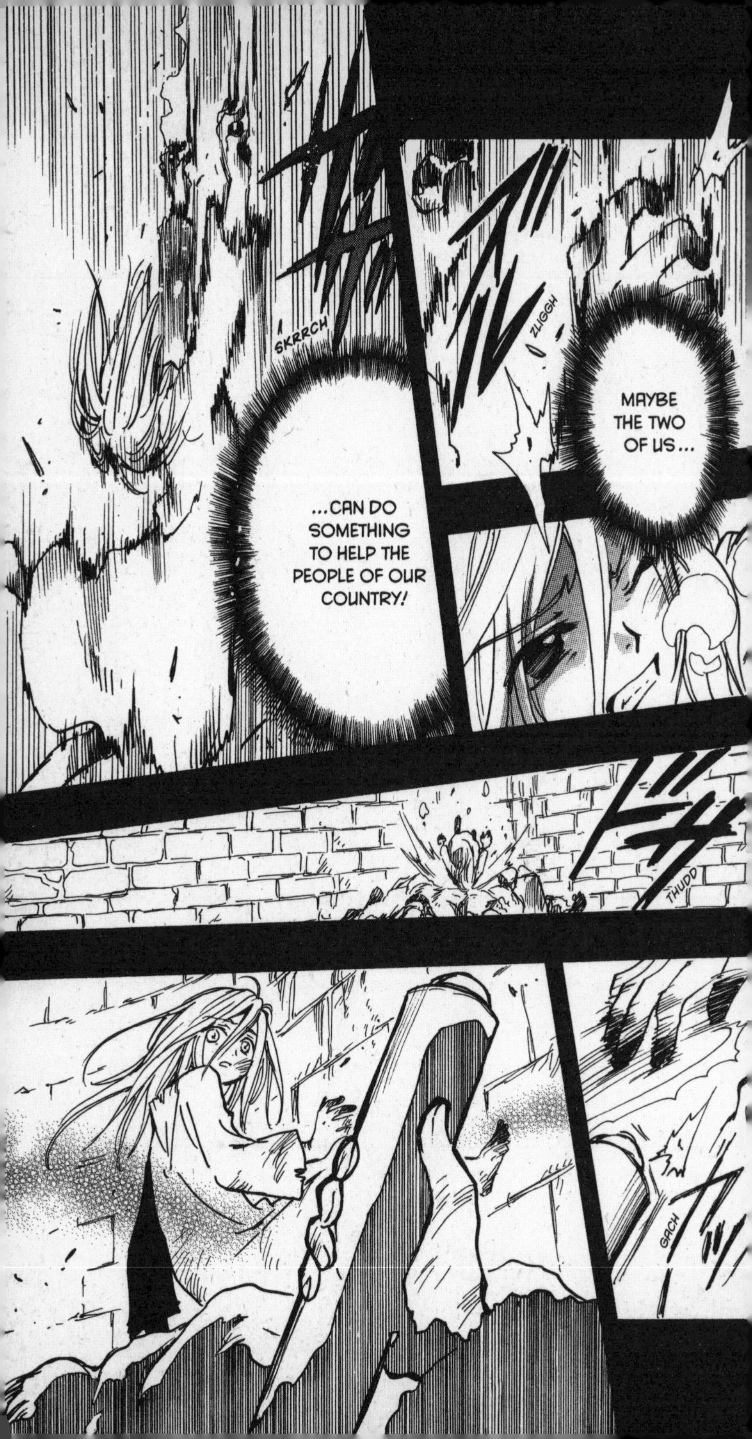
ZLIGGH
MAYBE THE TWO OF US...
SKRRCH
...CAN DO SOMETHING TO HELP THE PEOPLE OF OUR COUNTRY!
THUDD
GACH

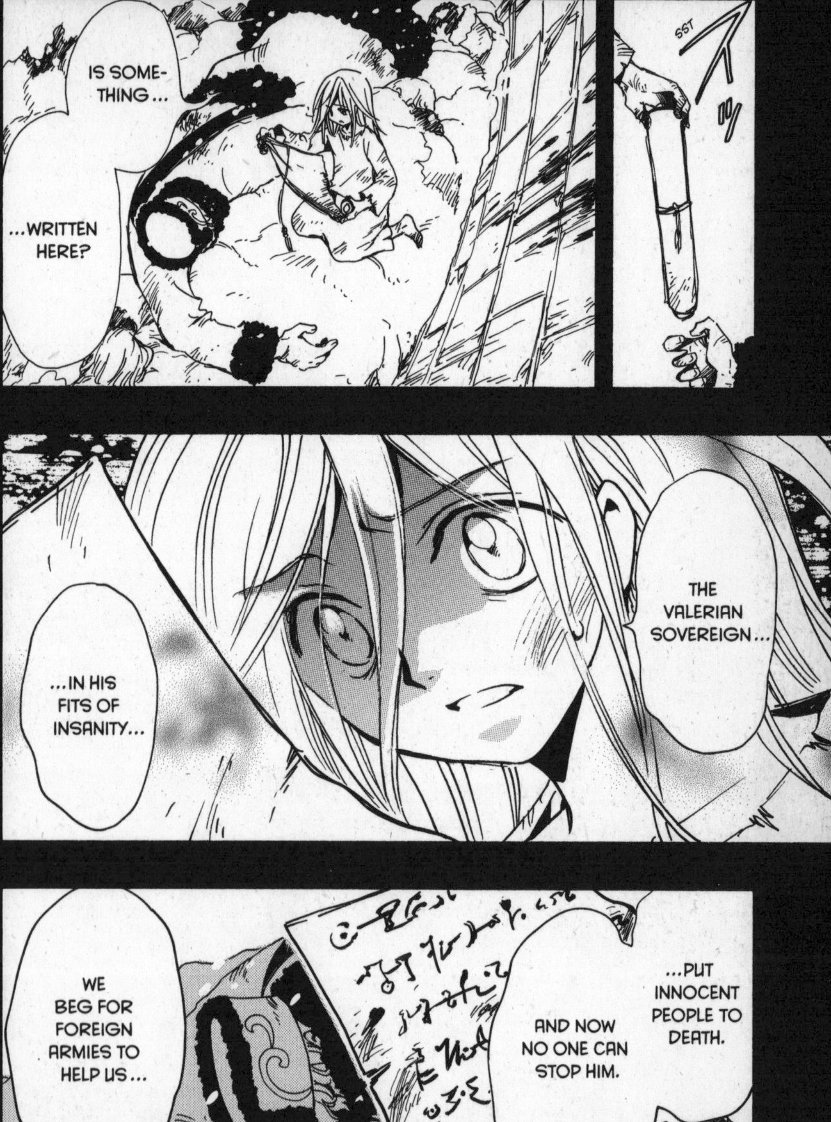
SST
IS SOME-THING ...
...WRITTEN HERE?
THE VALERIAN SOVEREIGN...
...IN HIS FITS OF INSANITY...
...PUT INNOCENT PEOPLE TO DEATH.
AND NOW NO ONE CAN STOP HIM.
WE BEG FOR FOREIGN ARMIES TO HELP US...

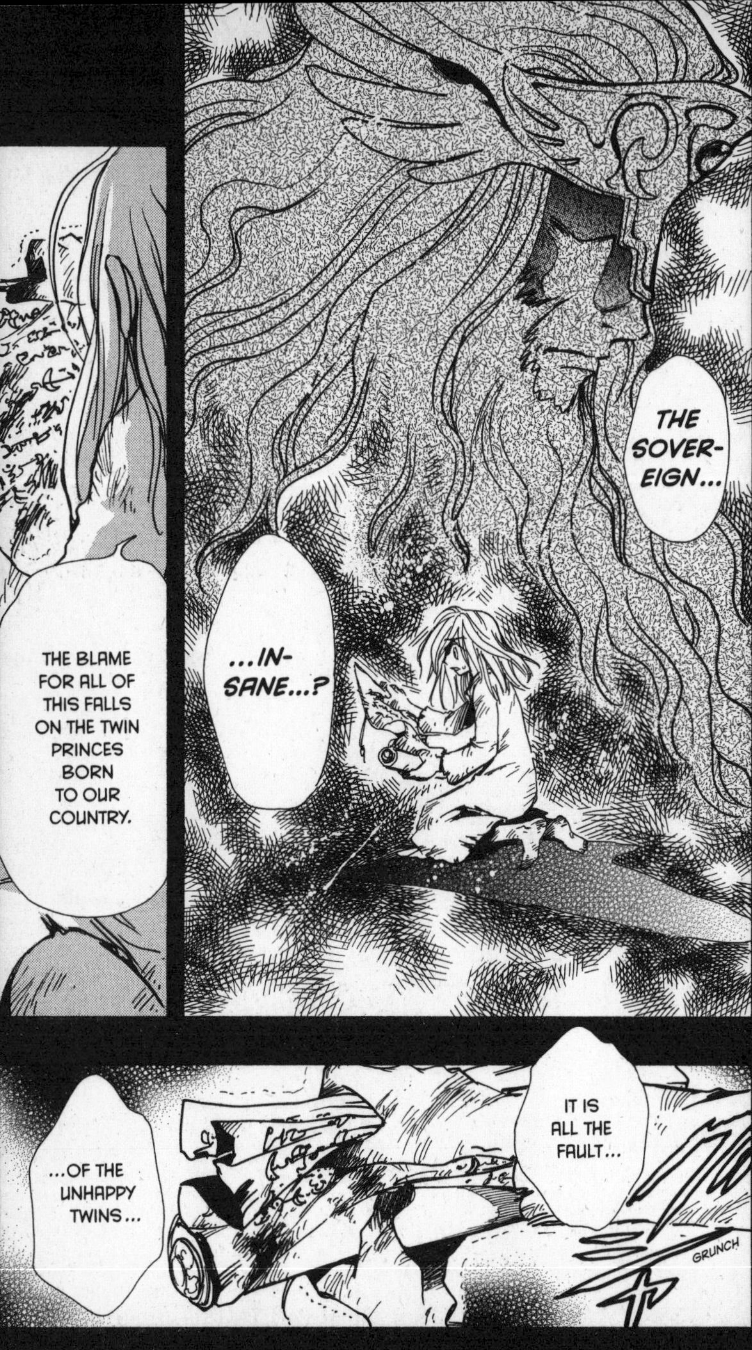
THE SOVEREIGN...
...INSANE...?
THE BLAME FOR ALL OF THIS FALLS ON THE TWIN PRINCES BORN TO OUR COUNTRY.
IT IS ALL THE FAULT...
...OF THE UNHAPPY TWINS...
GRUNCH

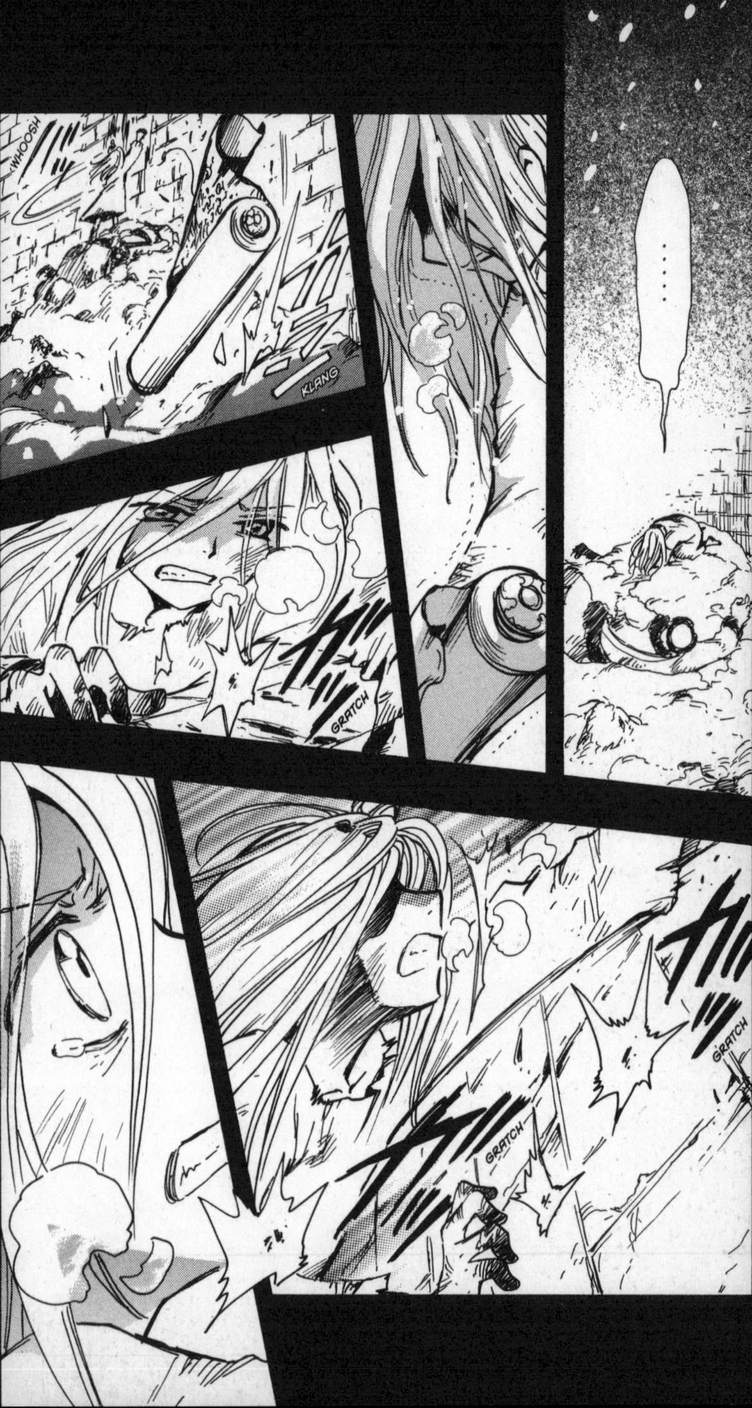
.....
WHOOSH
KLANG
GRATCH
GRATCH
GRATCH

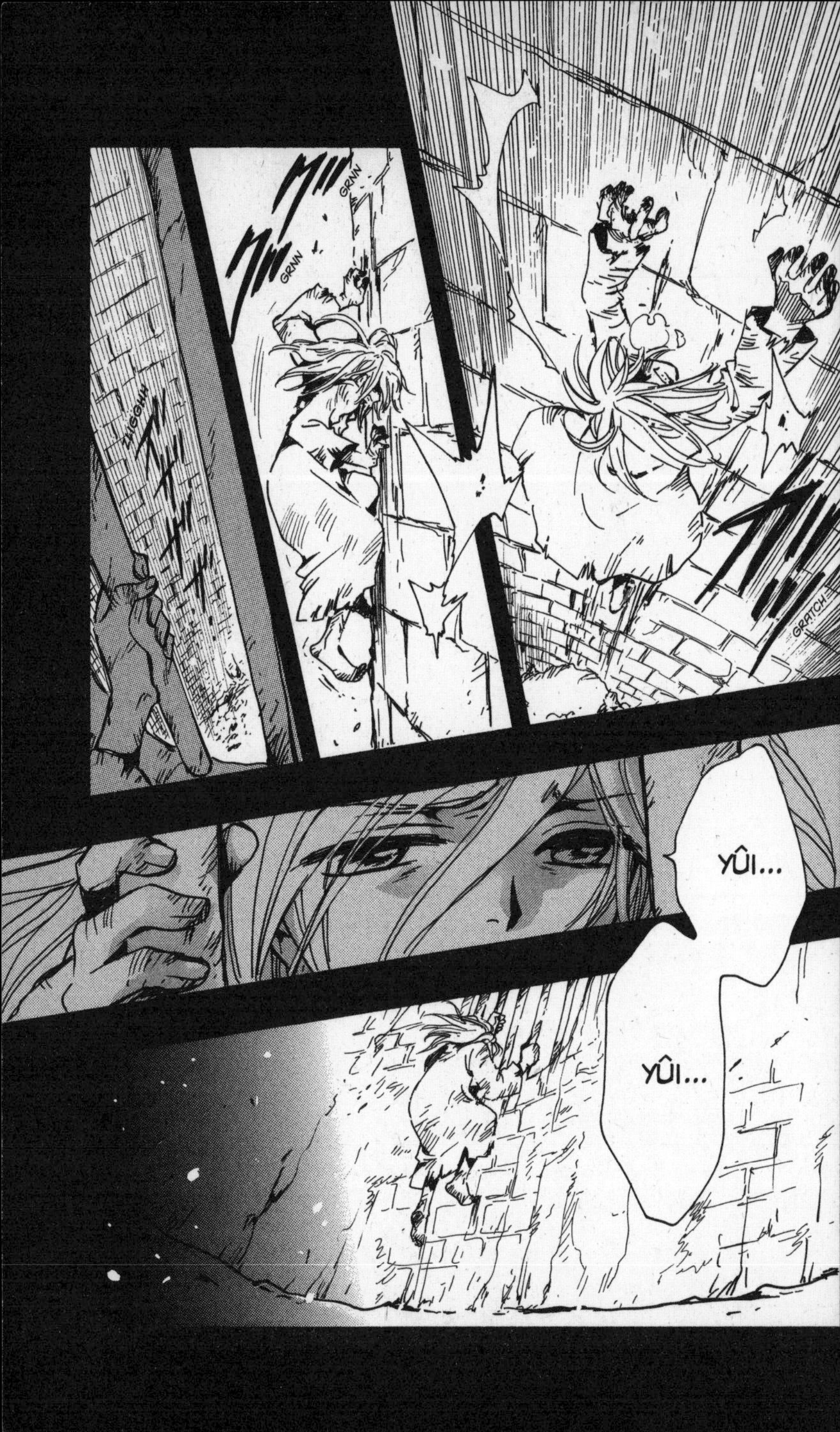
GRATCH
GRNN
GRNN
ZWIGGHH
YÛI...
YÛI...

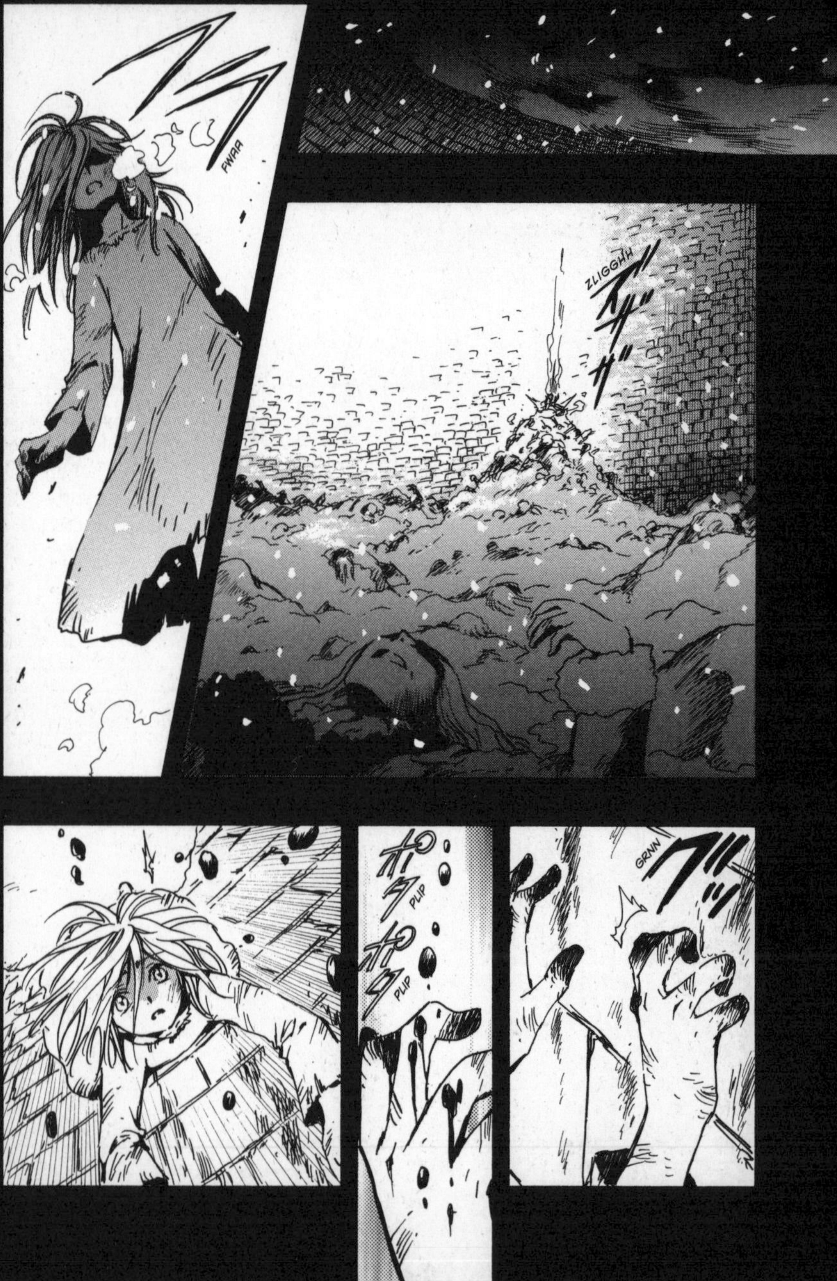
ZLIGGHH
FWAA
GRNN
PLIP
PLIP

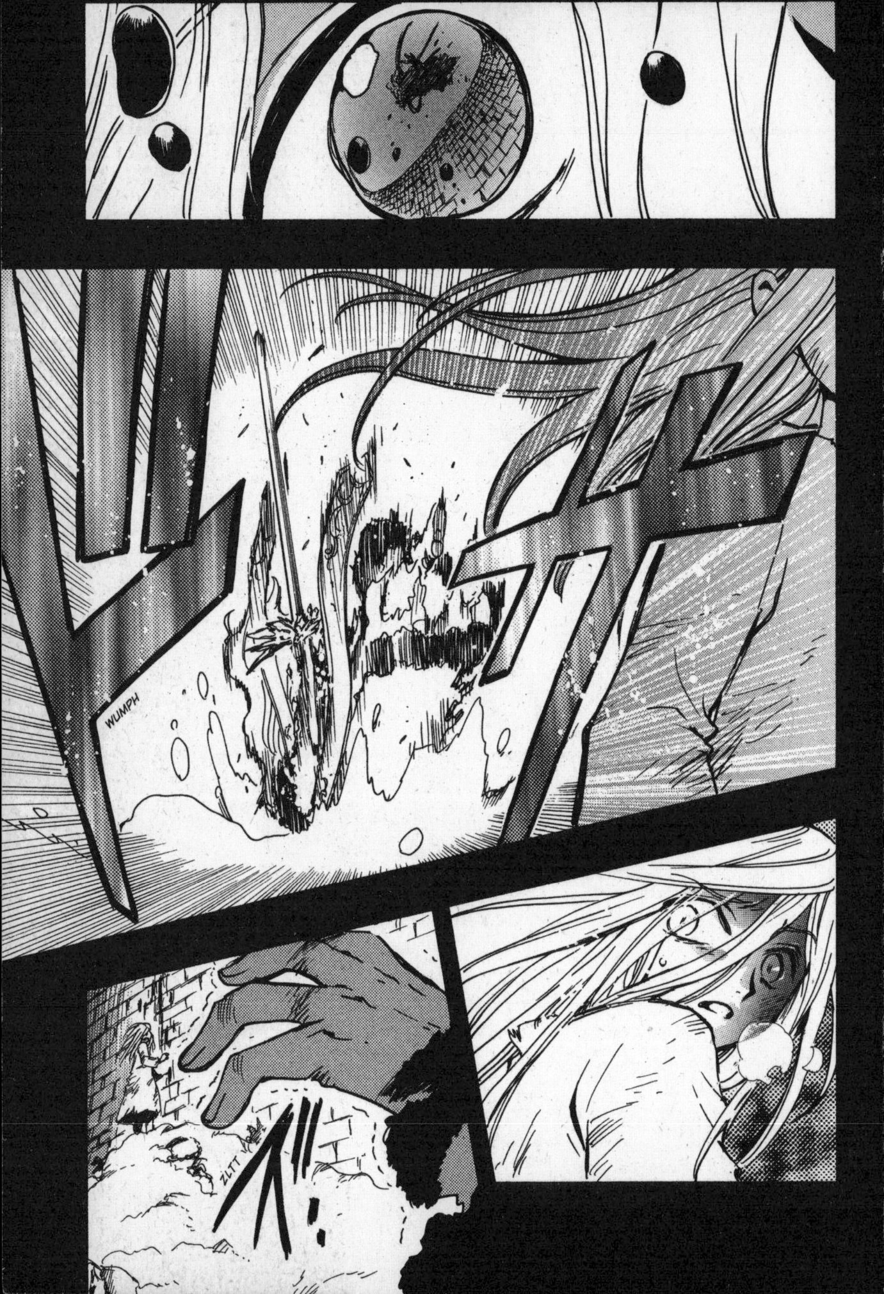
WUMPH
ZLTT

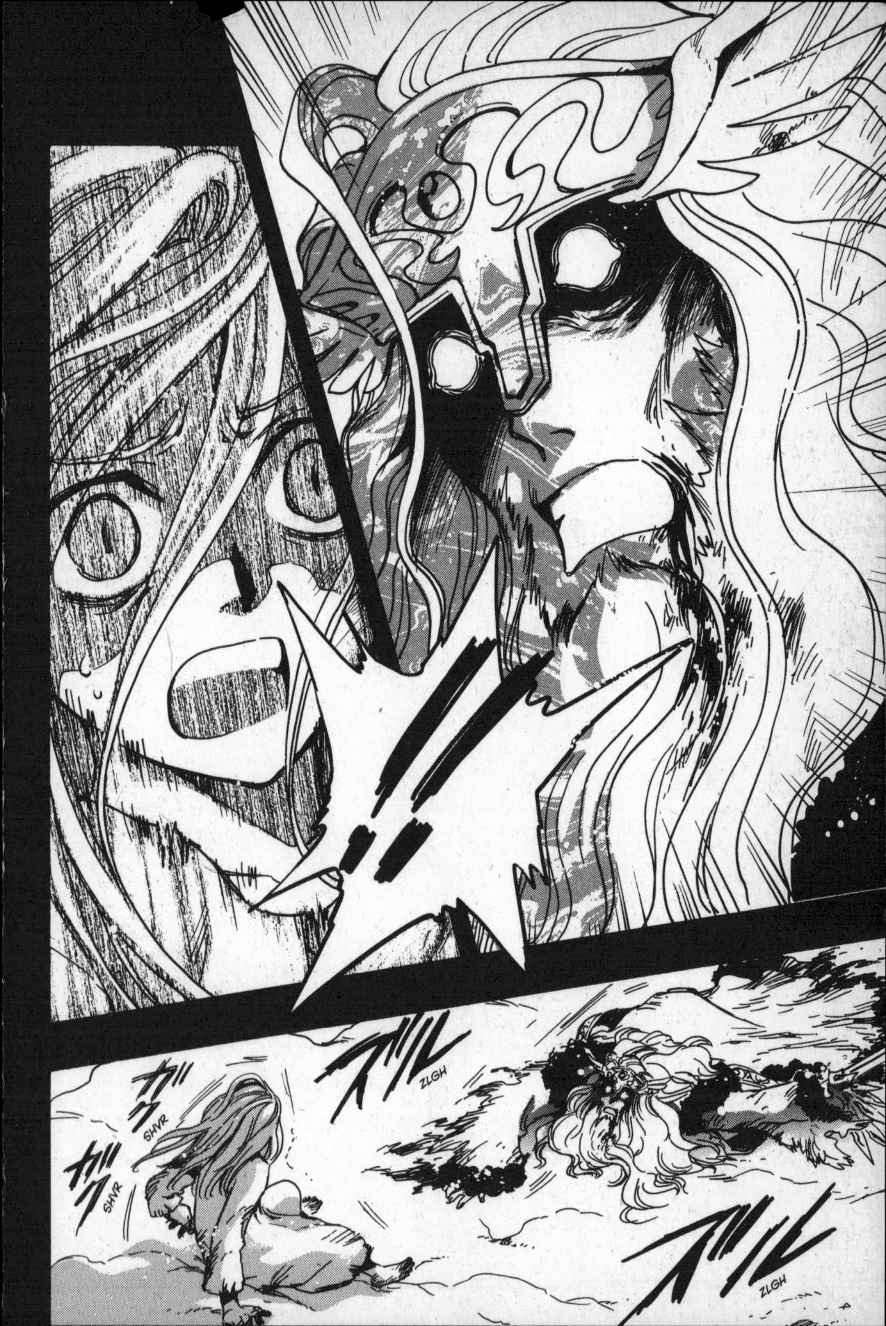
ZLGH
ZLGH
SHVR
SHVR

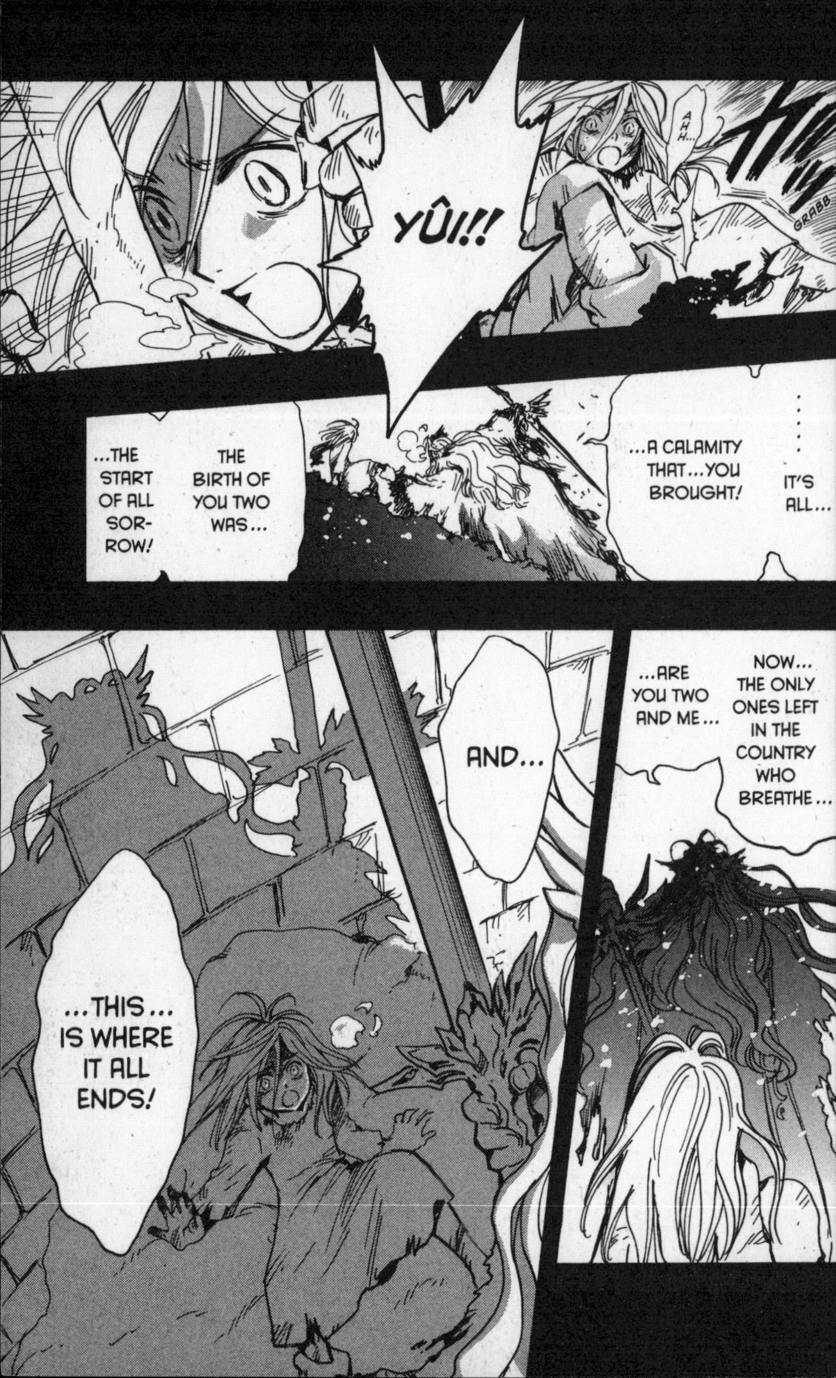
AHH...
GRABB
YÛI!!
IT'S ALL...
...A CALAMITY THAT...YOU BROUGHT!
THE BIRTH OF YOU TWO WAS...
...THE START OF ALL SOR-ROW!
NOW... THE ONLY ONES LEFT IN THE COUNTRY WHO BREATHE...
...ARE YOU TWO AND ME...
AND...
...THIS... IS WHERE IT ALL ENDS!

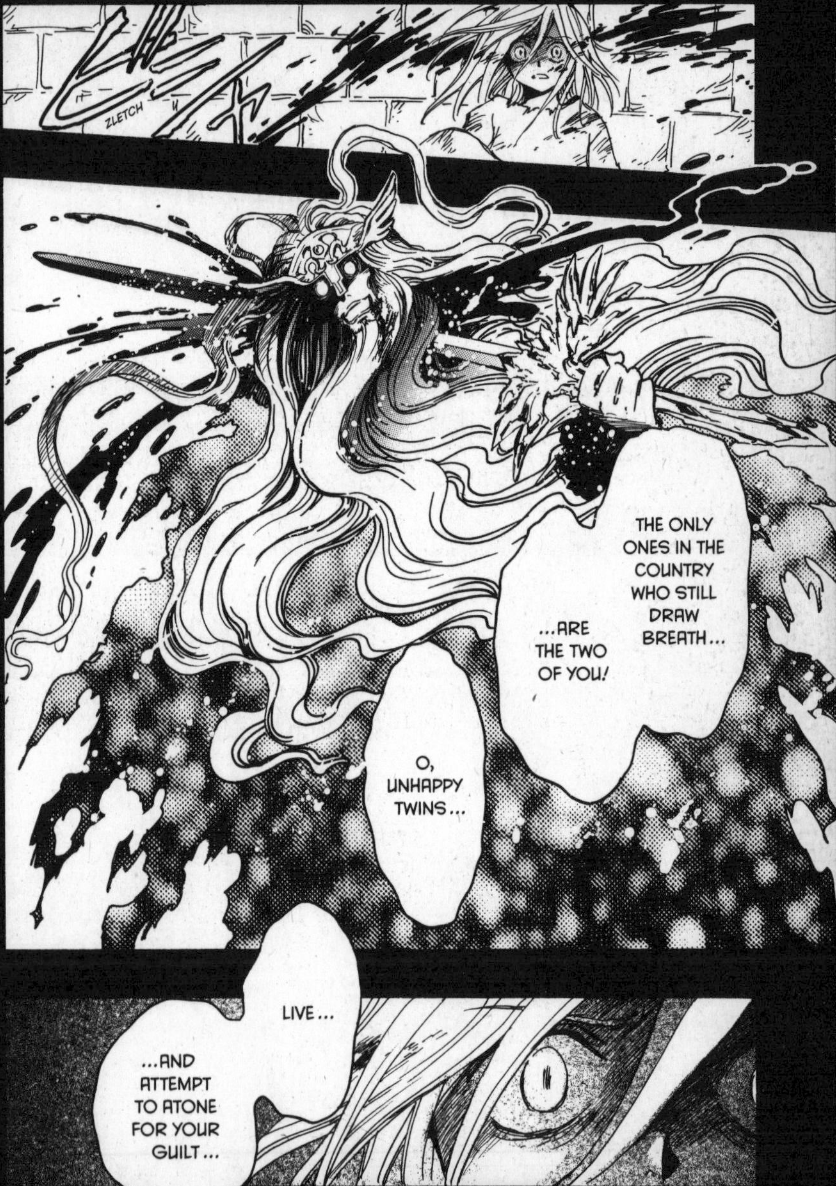
ZLETCH
THE ONLY ONES IN THE COUNTRY WHO STILL DRAW BREATH...
...ARE THE TWO OF YOU!
O, UNHAPPY TWINS...
LIVE...
...AND ATTEMPT TO ATONE FOR YOUR GUILT...

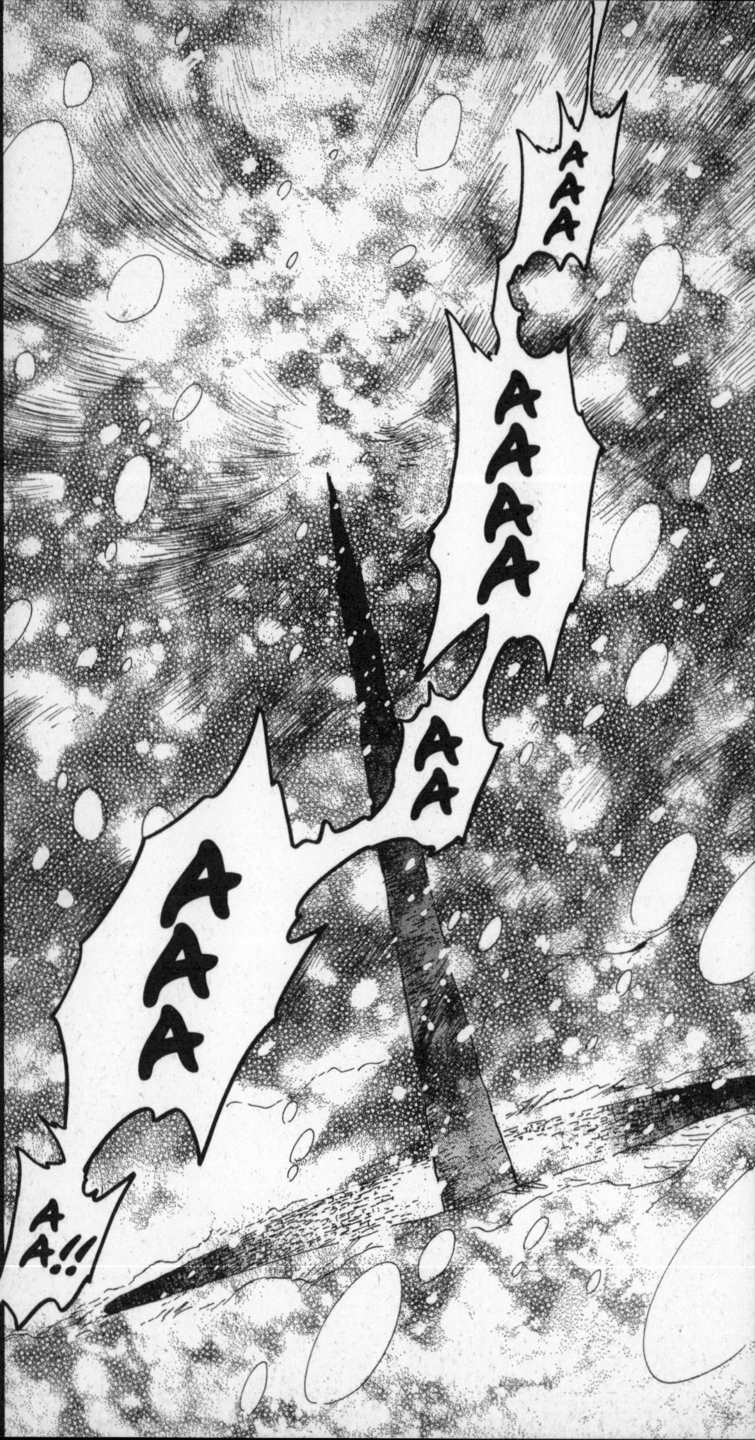
AAA
AAAAA
AA
AAA
AA!!

ツバサ
RESERVoir CHRoNiCLE

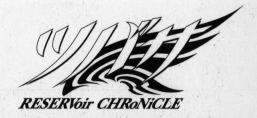

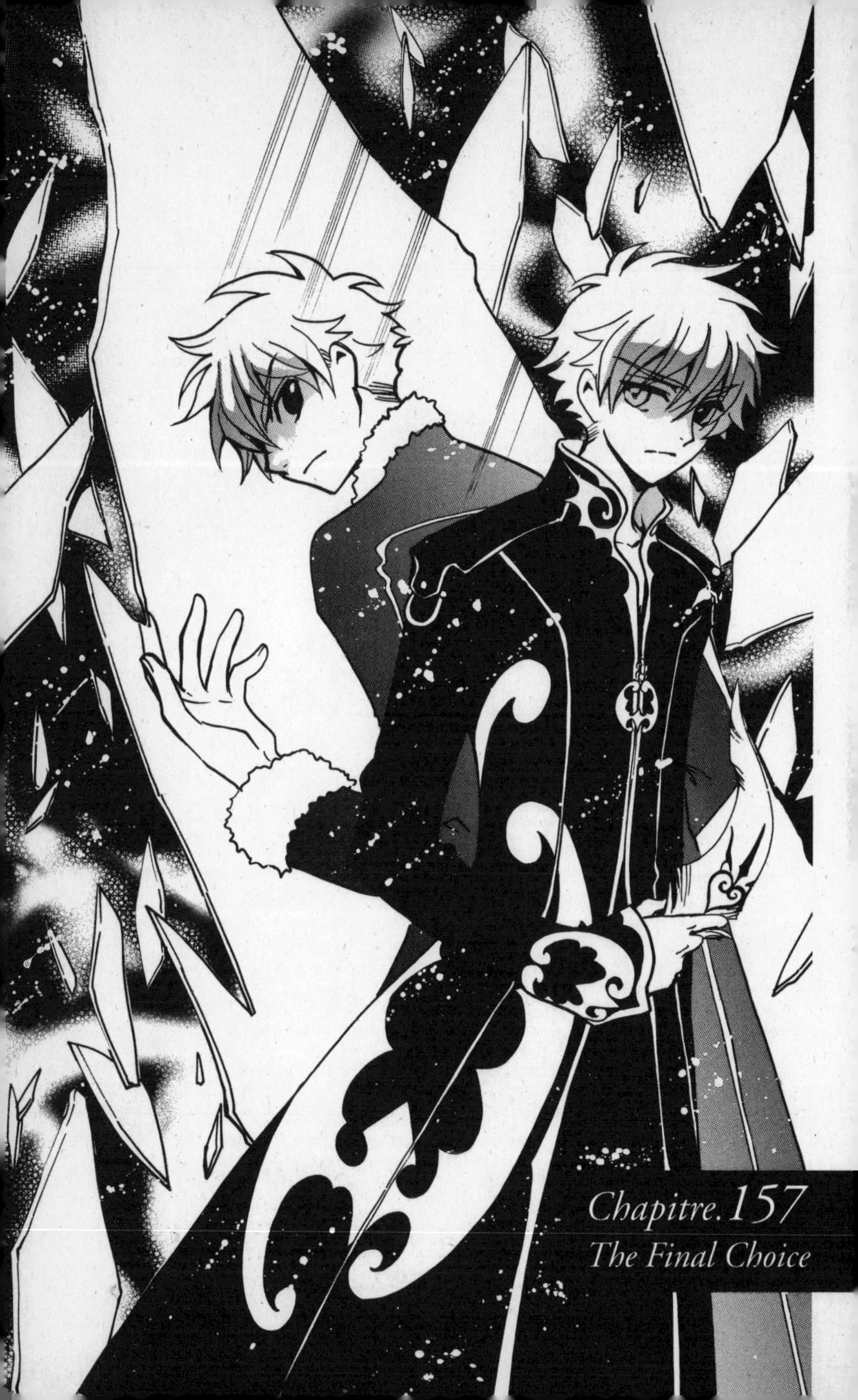
Chapitre. 157
The Final Choice

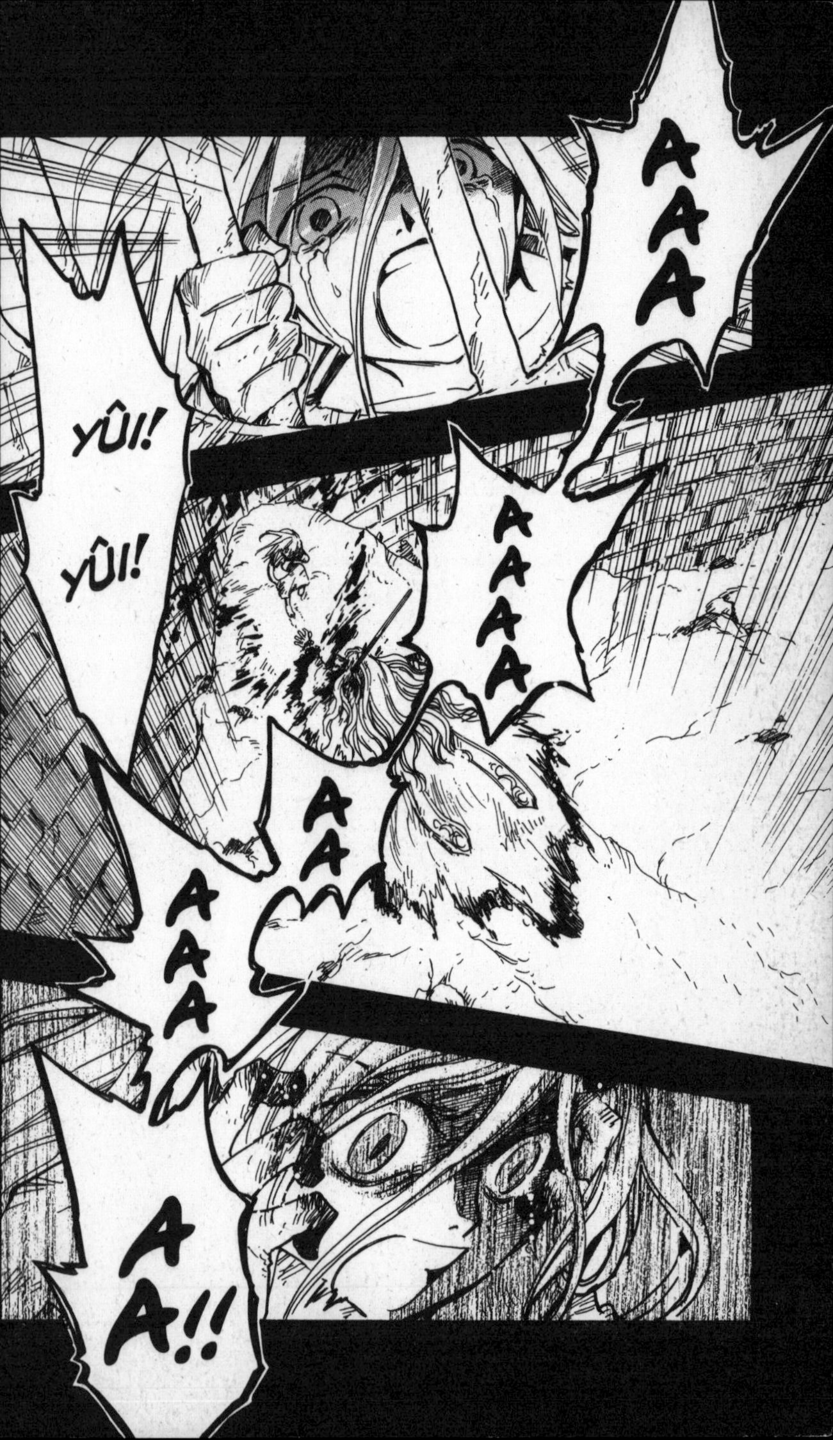
AAA
YÛI!
YÛI!
AAAA
AA
AAA
AA!!

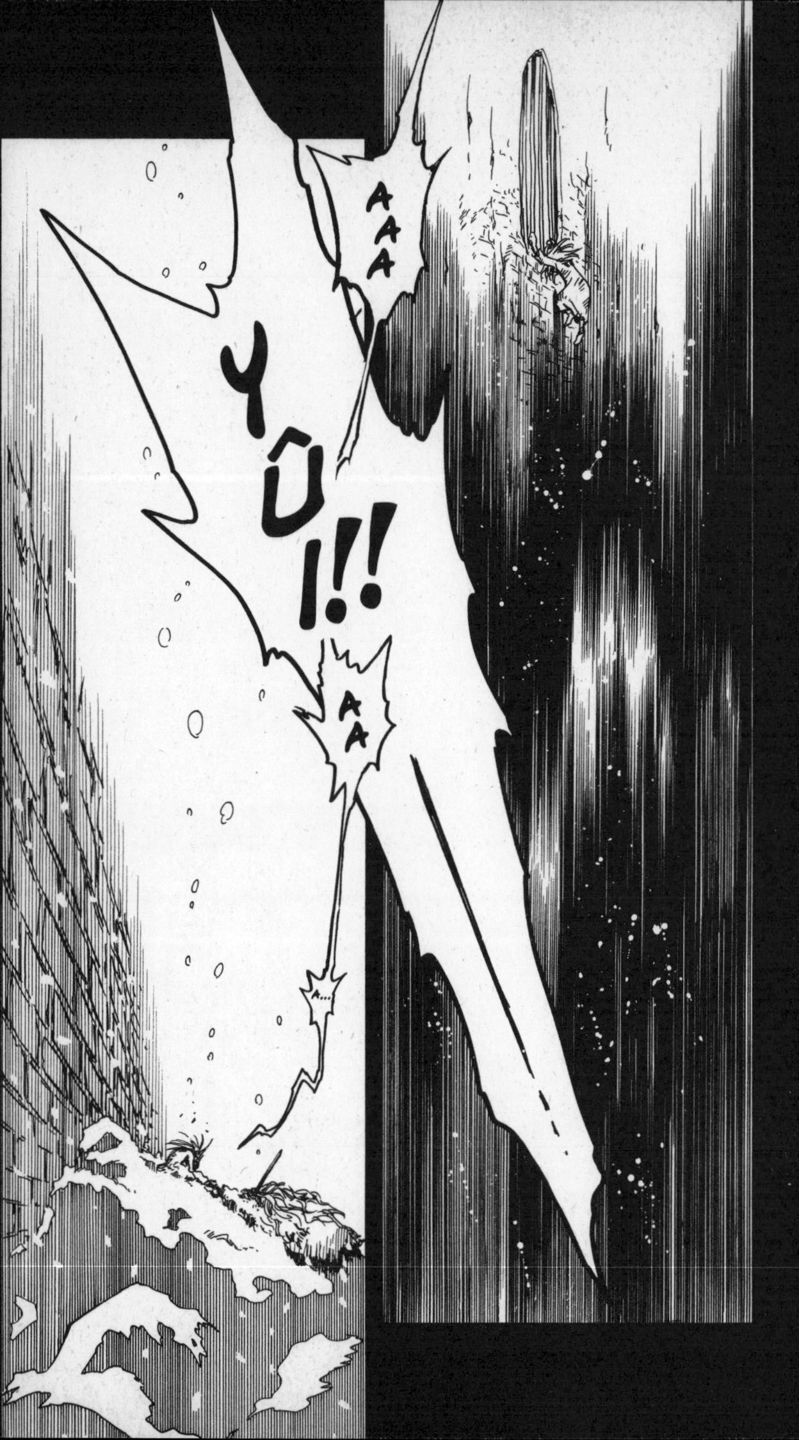
AAA YÛI!! AA
A...

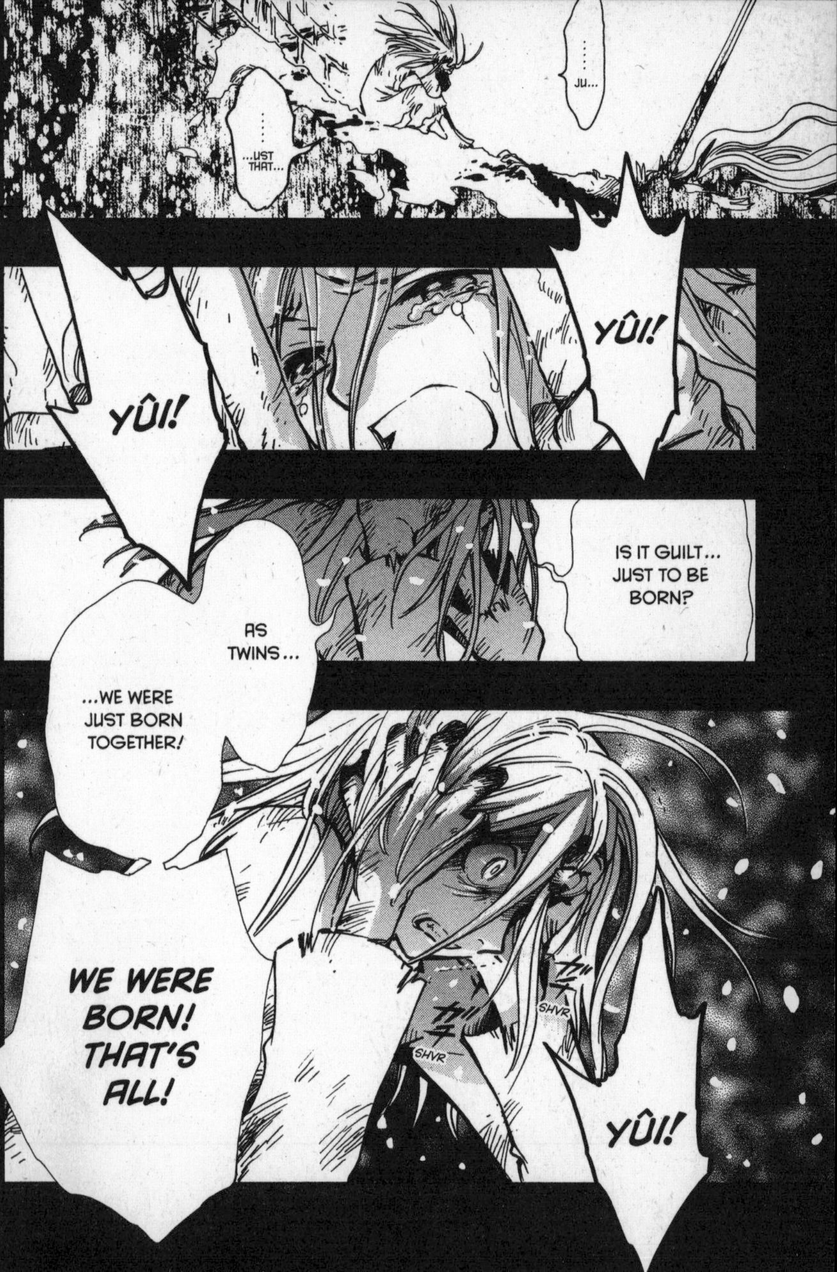
......
JU...
......
...UST THAT...
YÛI!
YÛI!
IS IT GUILT... JUST TO BE BORN?
AS TWINS...
...WE WERE JUST BORN TOGETHER!
SHVR
SHVR
YÛI!
WE WERE BORN! THAT'S ALL!

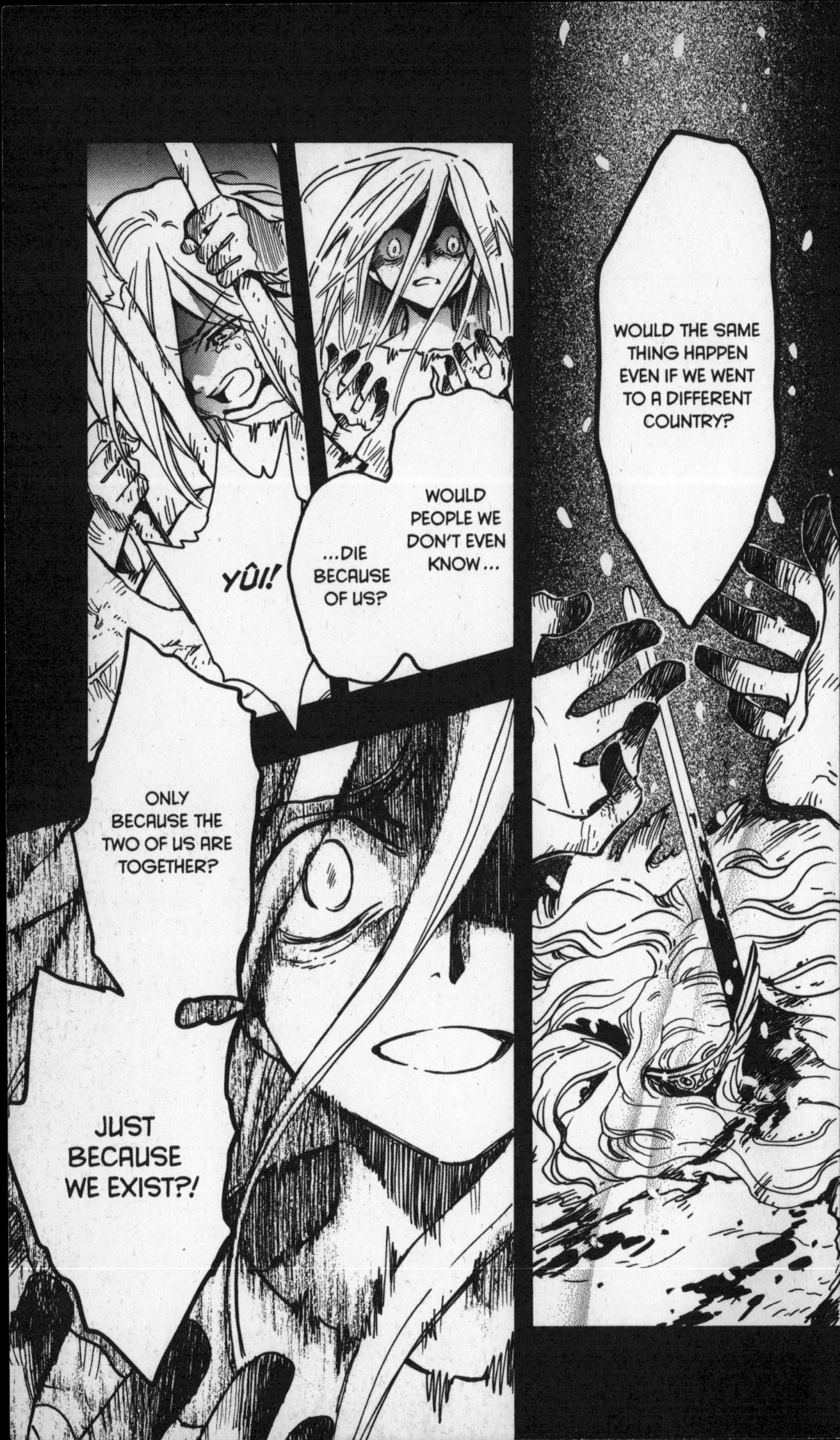
WOULD THE SAME THING HAPPEN EVEN IF WE WENT TO A DIFFERENT COUNTRY?
WOULD PEOPLE WE DON'T EVEN KNOW...
...DIE BECAUSE OF US?
YÛI!
ONLY BECAUSE THE TWO OF US ARE TOGETHER?
JUST BECAUSE WE EXIST?!

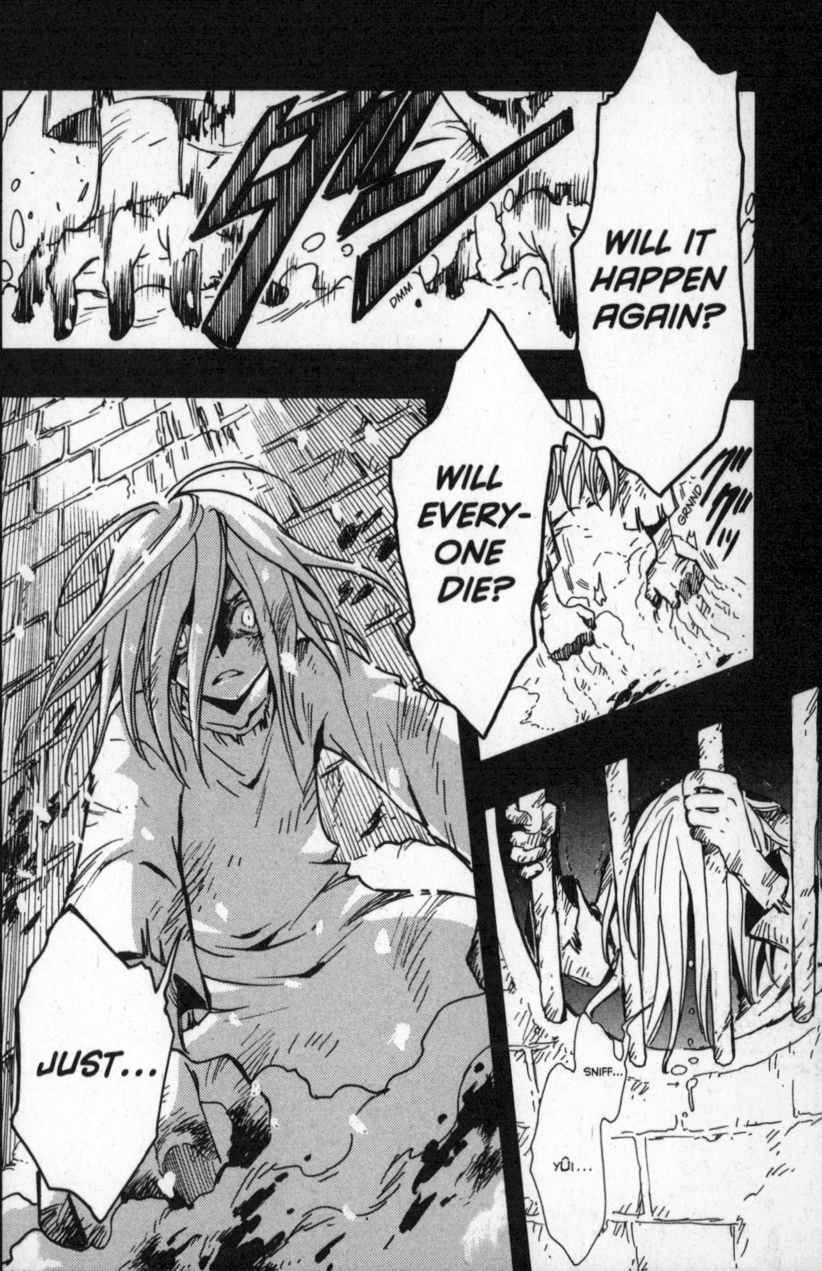
WILL IT HAPPEN AGAIN?
DMM
WILL EVERY-ONE DIE?
GRNND
SNIFF...
YÛI...
JUST...

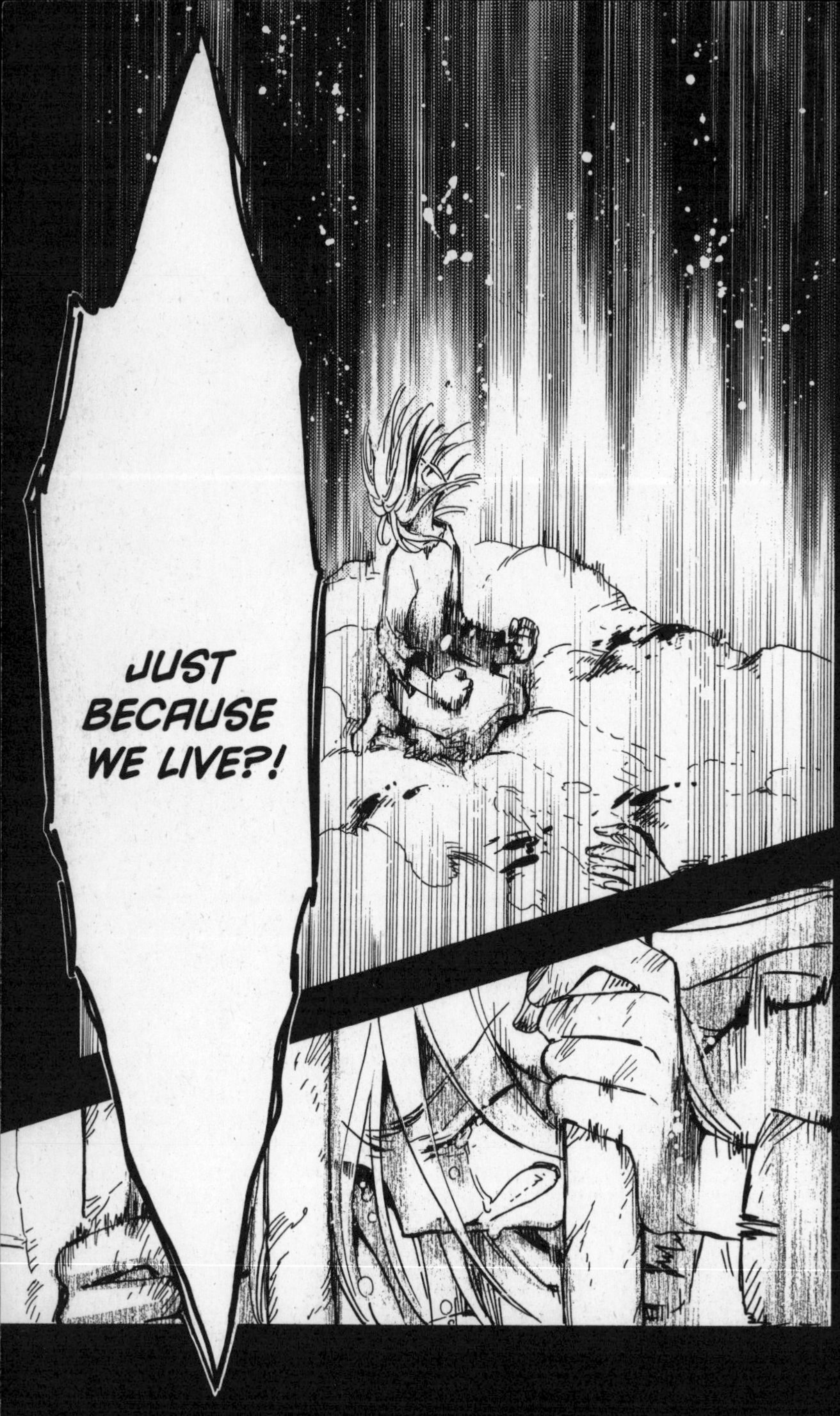
JUST BECAUSE WE LIVE?!

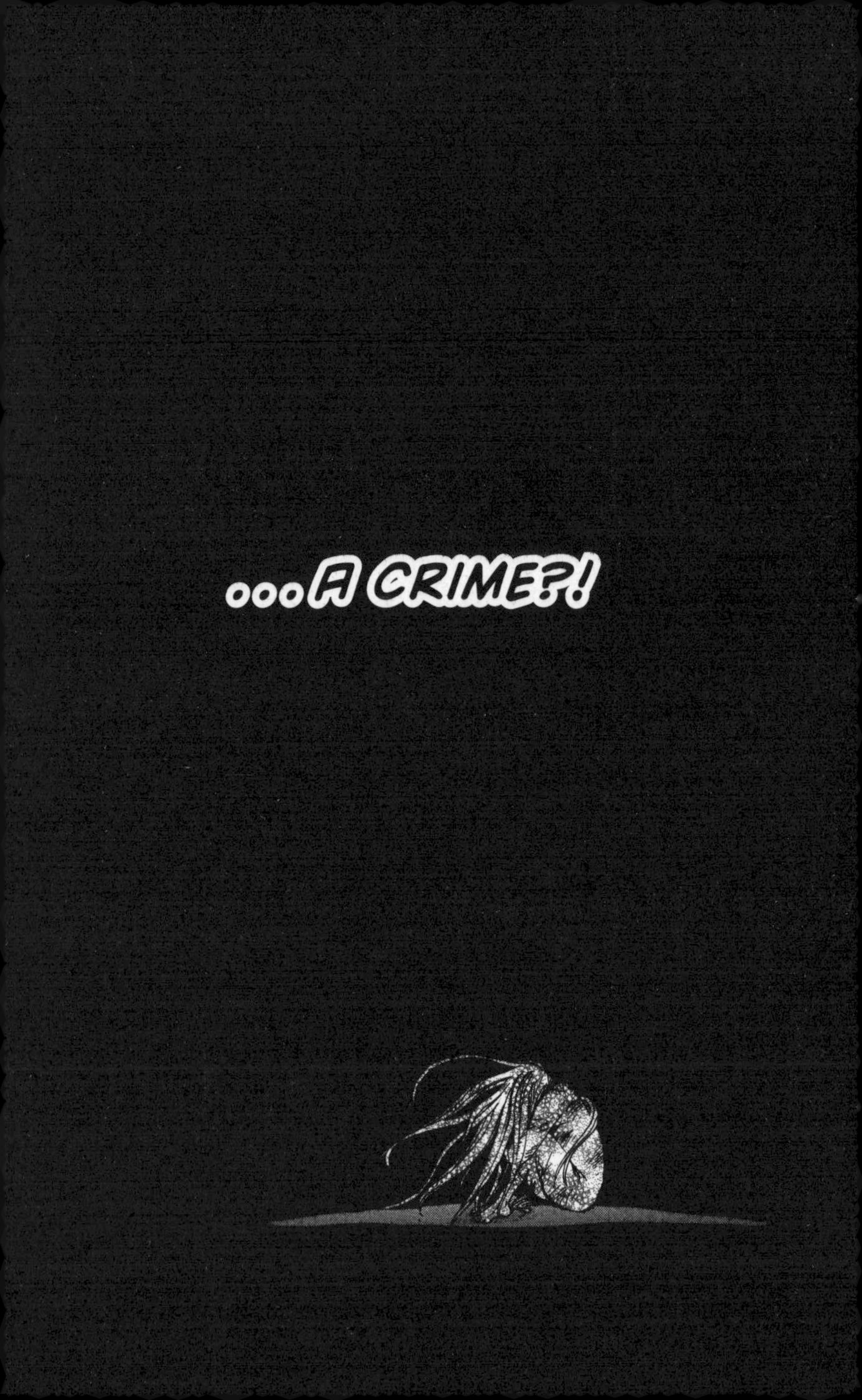
...A CRIME?!

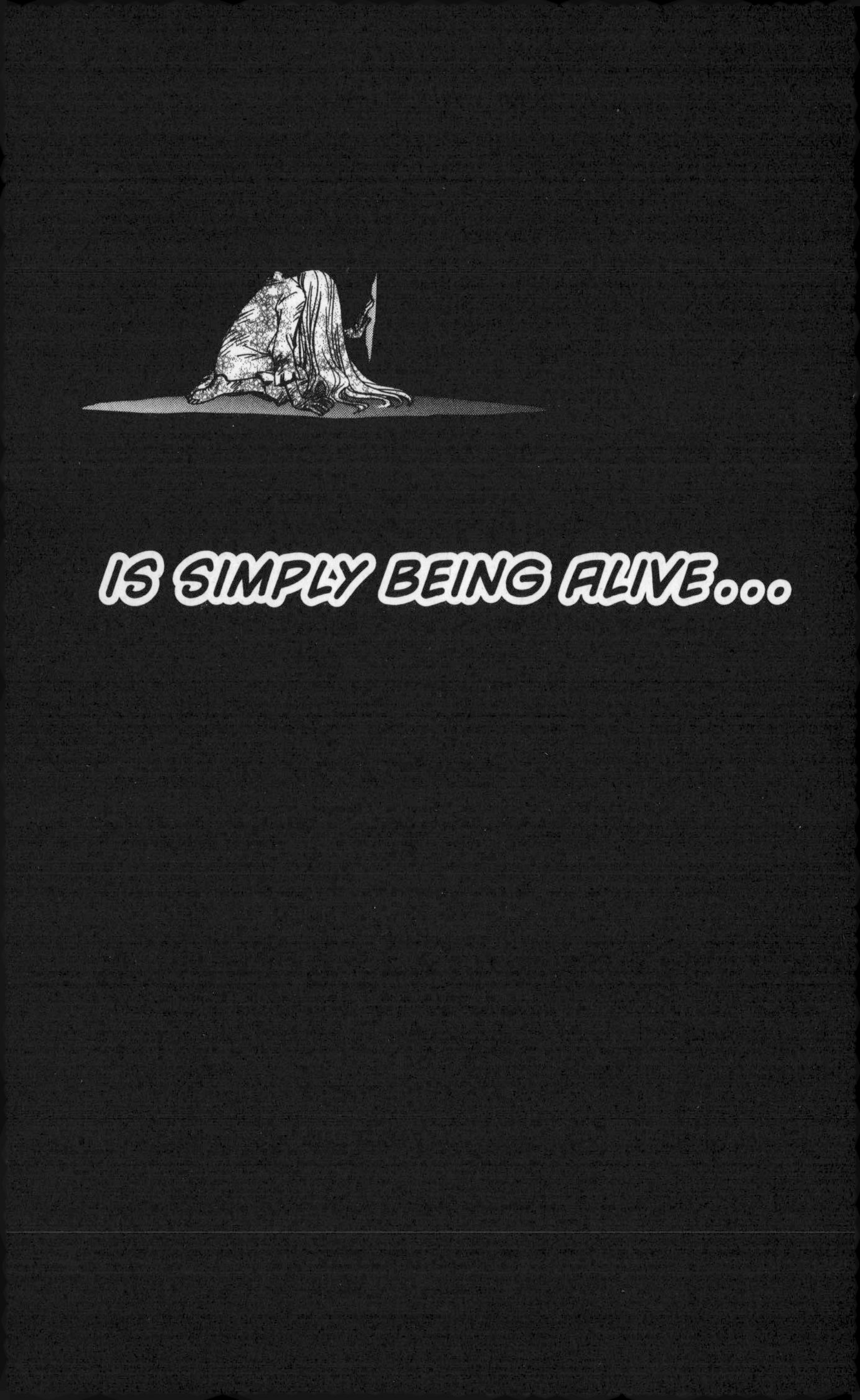
IS SIMPLY BEING ALIVE...

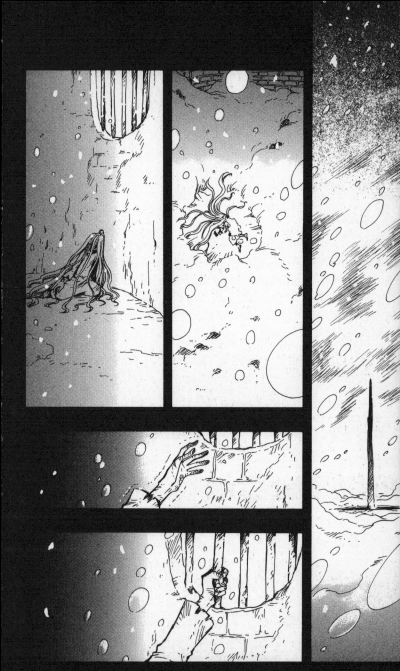

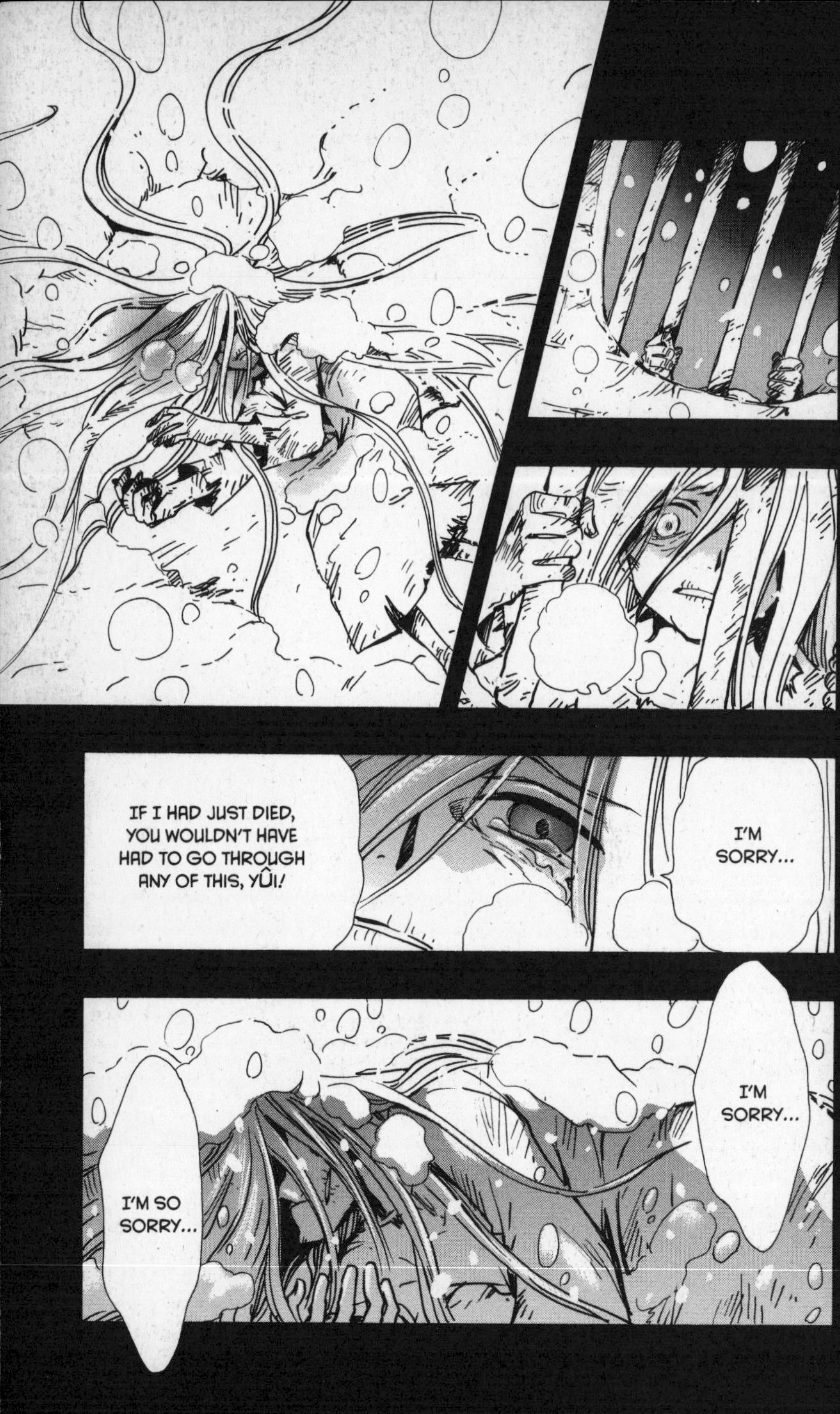
I'M SORRY...
IF I HAD JUST DIED, YOU WOULDN'T HAVE HAD TO GO THROUGH ANY OF THIS, YÛI!
I'M SORRY...
I'M SO SORRY...

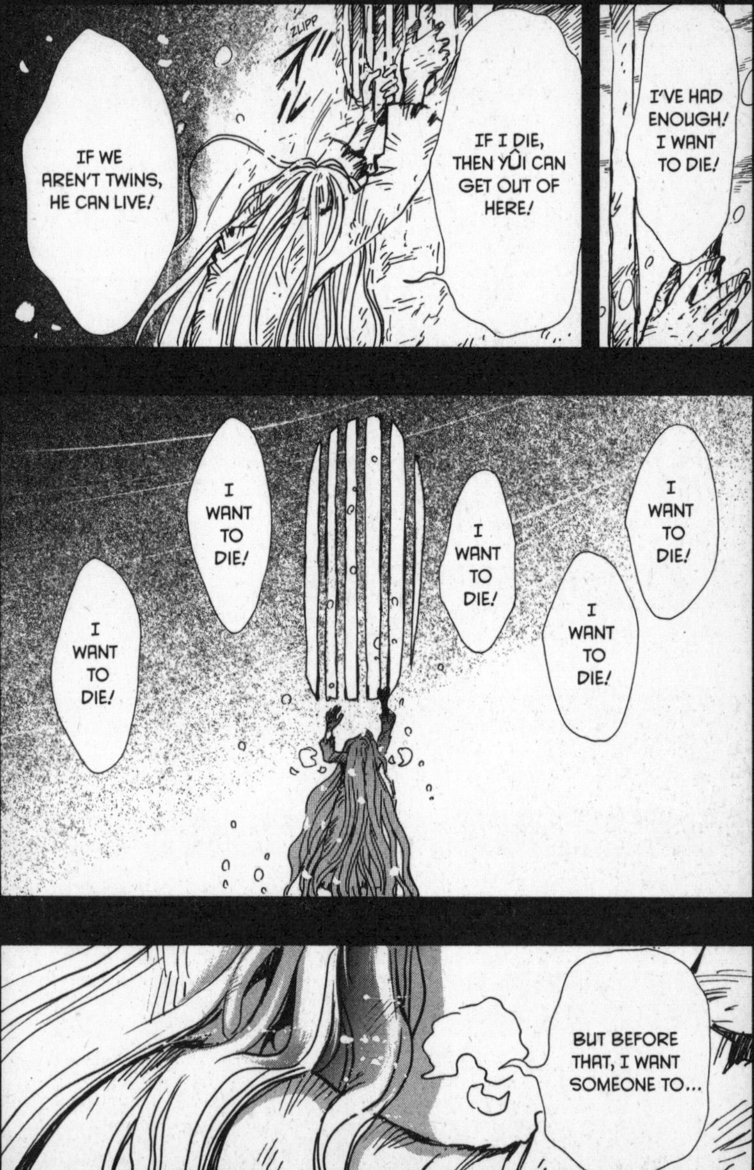
I'VE HAD ENOUGH! I WANT TO DIE!
IF I DIE, THEN YÛI CAN GET OUT OF HERE!
ZLIPP
IF WE AREN'T TWINS, HE CAN LIVE!
I WANT TO DIE!
I WANT TO DIE!
I WANT TO DIE!
I WANT TO DIE!
I WANT TO DIE!
BUT BEFORE THAT, I WANT SOMEONE TO...

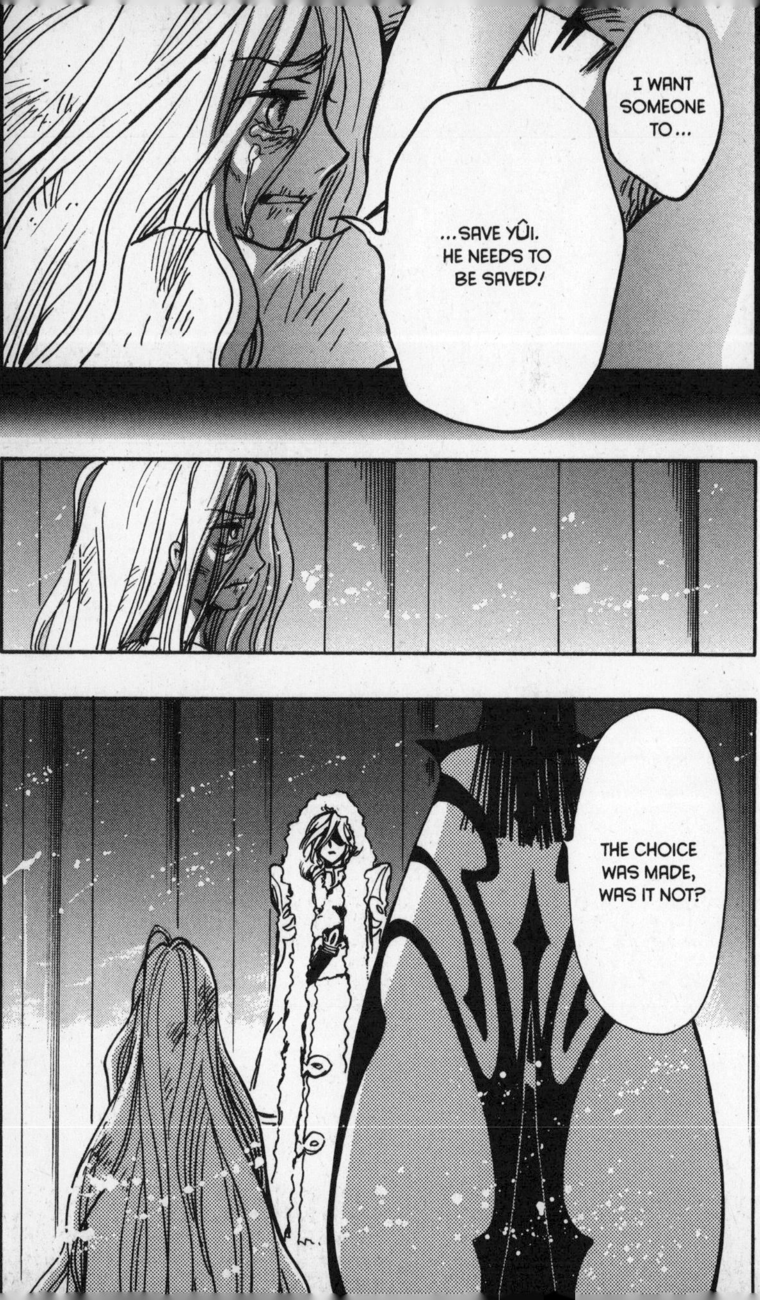
I WANT SOMEONE TO...
...SAVE YÛI. HE NEEDS TO BE SAVED!
THE CHOICE WAS MADE, WAS IT NOT?

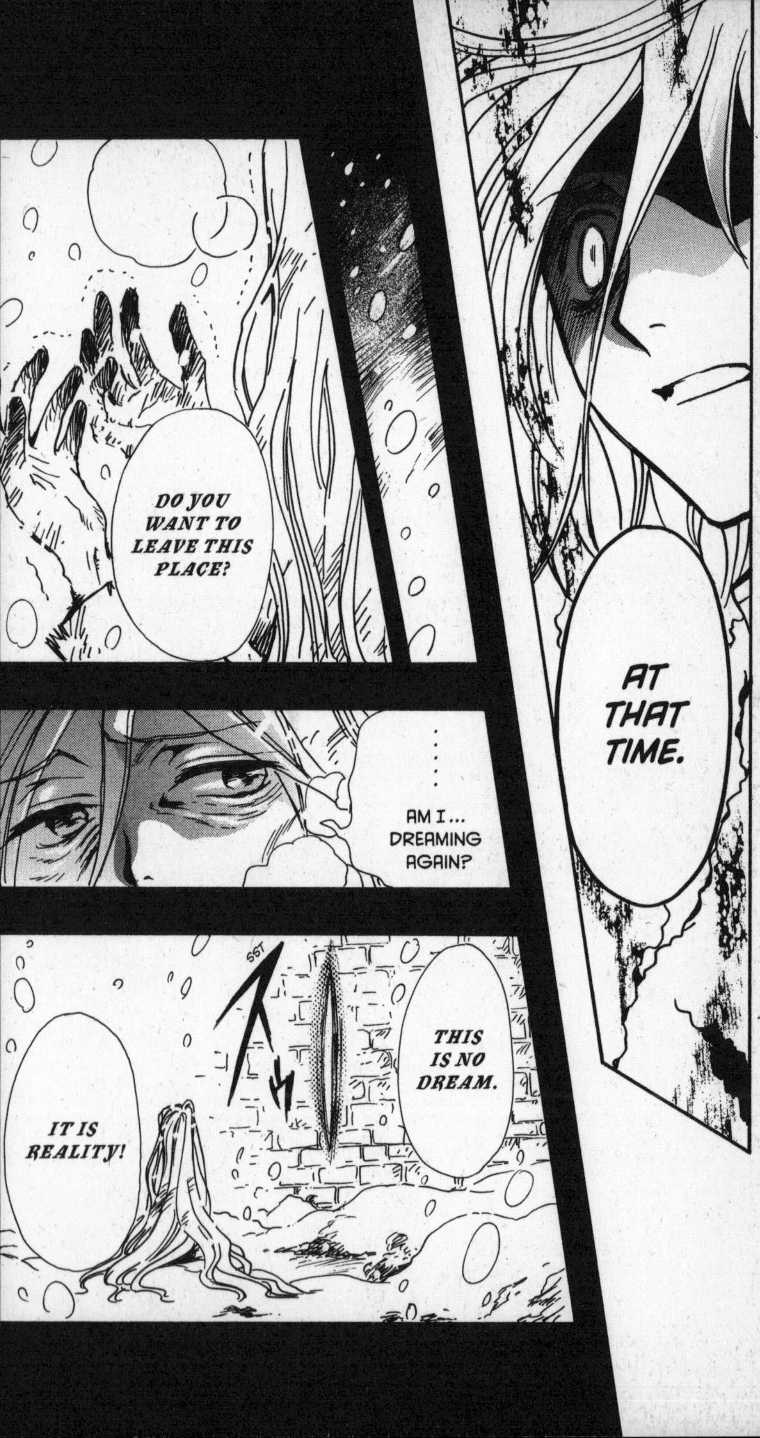
AT THAT TIME.
DO YOU WANT TO LEAVE THIS PLACE?
......
AM I... DREAMING AGAIN?
THIS IS NO DREAM.
SST
IT IS REALITY!

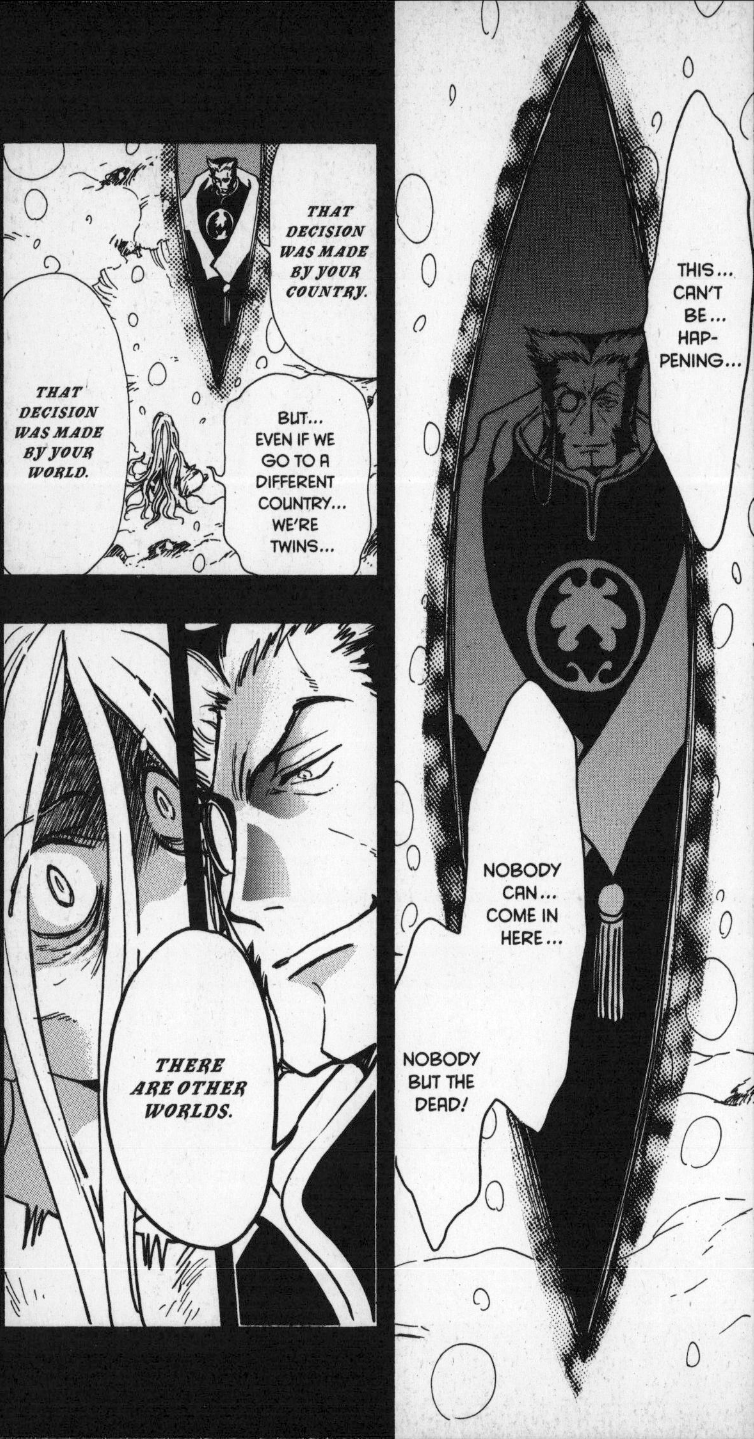
THIS... CAN'T BE... HAP-PENING...
NOBODY CAN... COME IN HERE...
NOBODY BUT THE DEAD!
THAT DECISION WAS MADE BY YOUR COUNTRY.
BUT... EVEN IF WE GO TO A DIFFERENT COUNTRY... WE'RE TWINS...
THAT DECISION WAS MADE BY YOUR WORLD.
THERE ARE OTHER WORLDS.

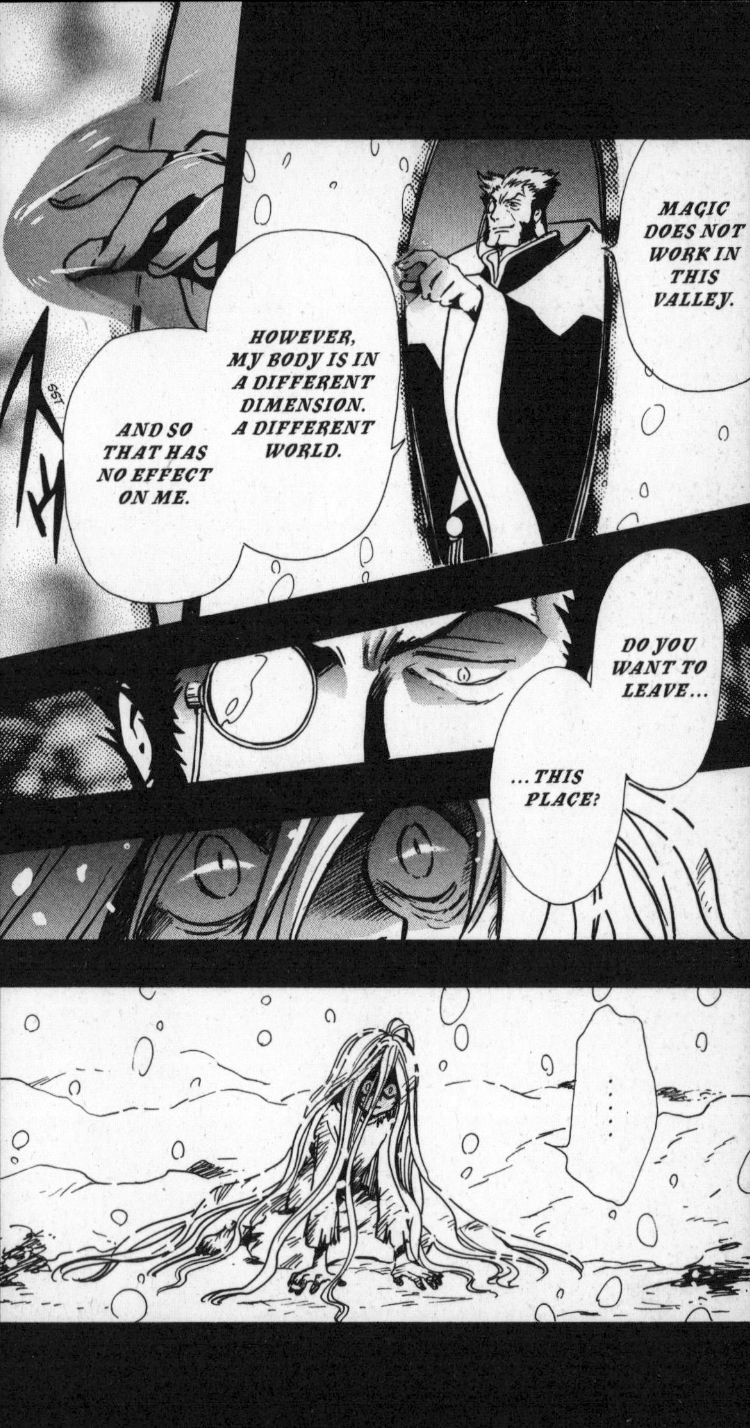
MAGIC DOES NOT WORK IN THIS VALLEY.
HOWEVER, MY BODY IS IN A DIFFERENT DIMENSION. A DIFFERENT WORLD.
AND SO THAT HAS NO EFFECT ON ME.
DO YOU WANT TO LEAVE...
...THIS PLACE?
......

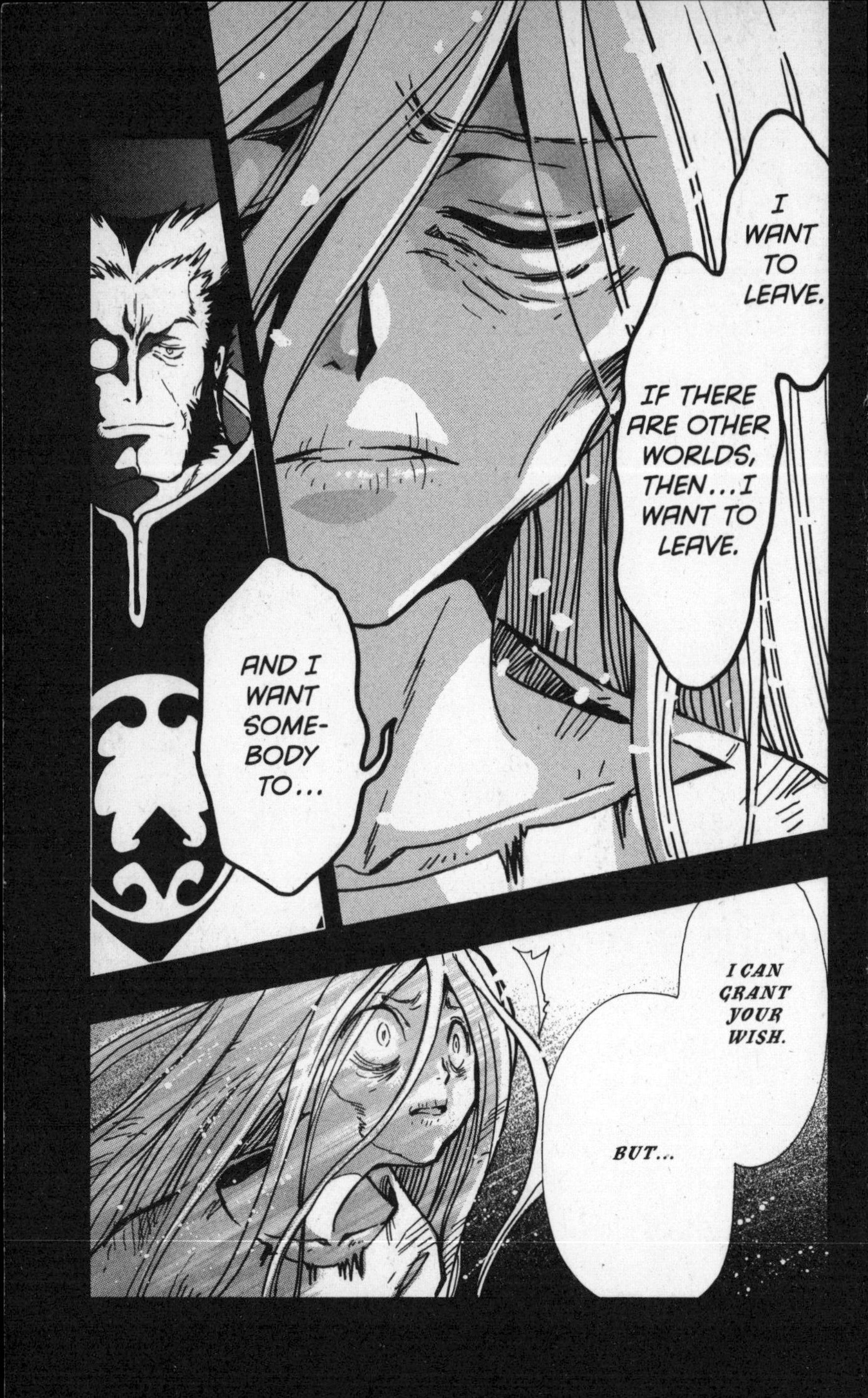
I WANT TO LEAVE.
IF THERE ARE OTHER WORLDS, THEN... I WANT TO LEAVE.
AND I WANT SOMEBODY TO...
I CAN GRANT YOUR WISH.
BUT...

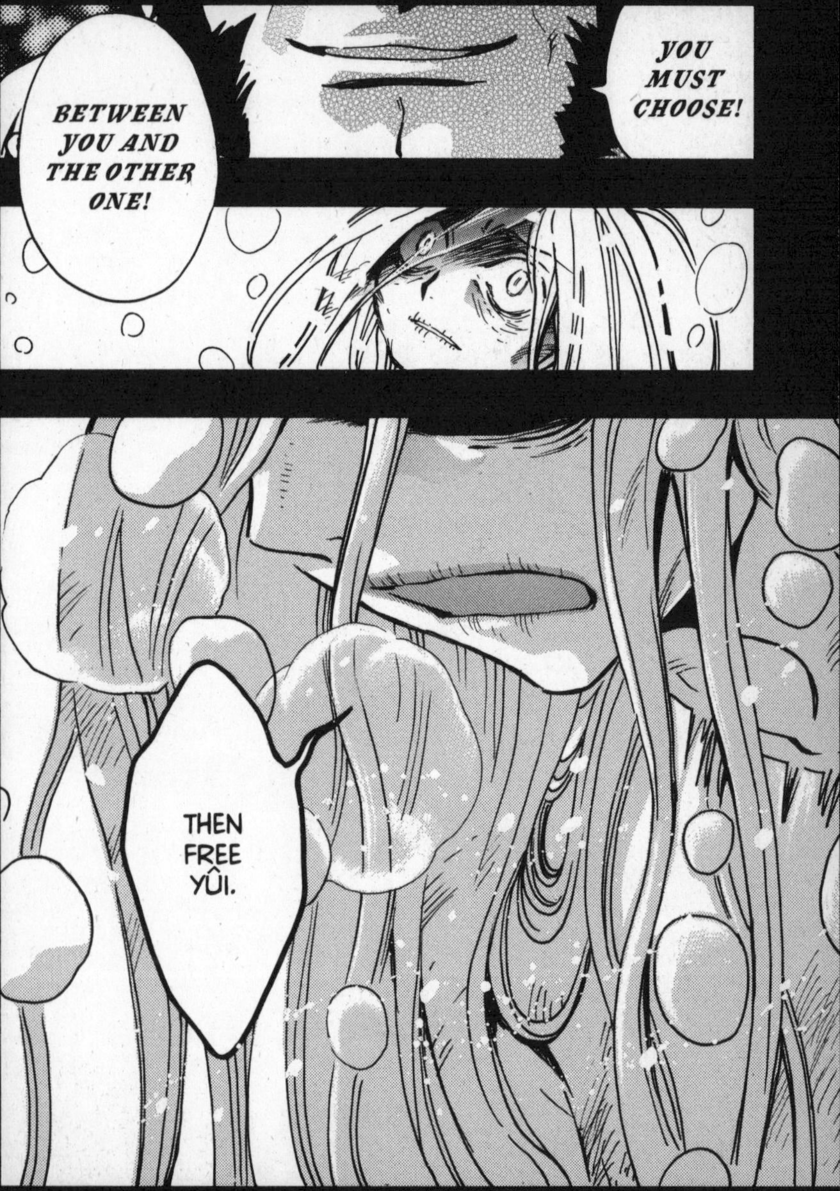
YOU MUST CHOOSE!
BETWEEN YOU AND THE OTHER ONE!
THEN FREE YÛI.

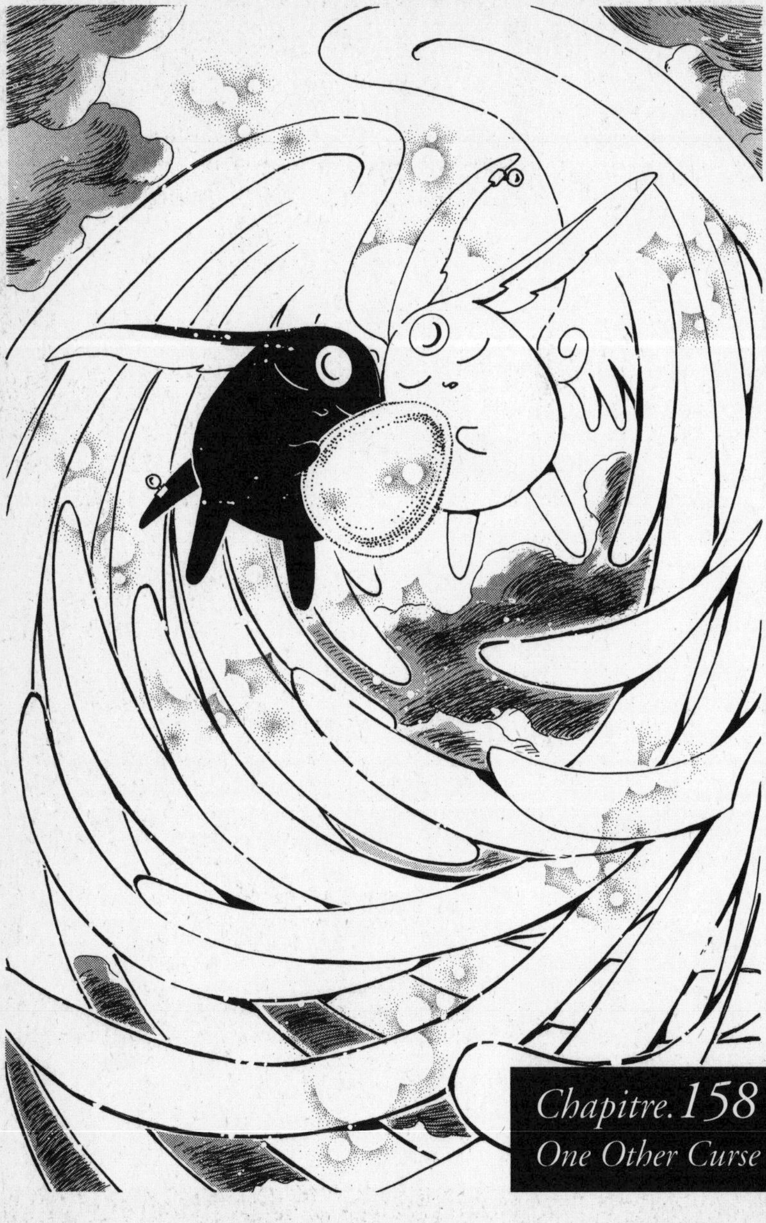

Chapitre. 158
One Other Curse

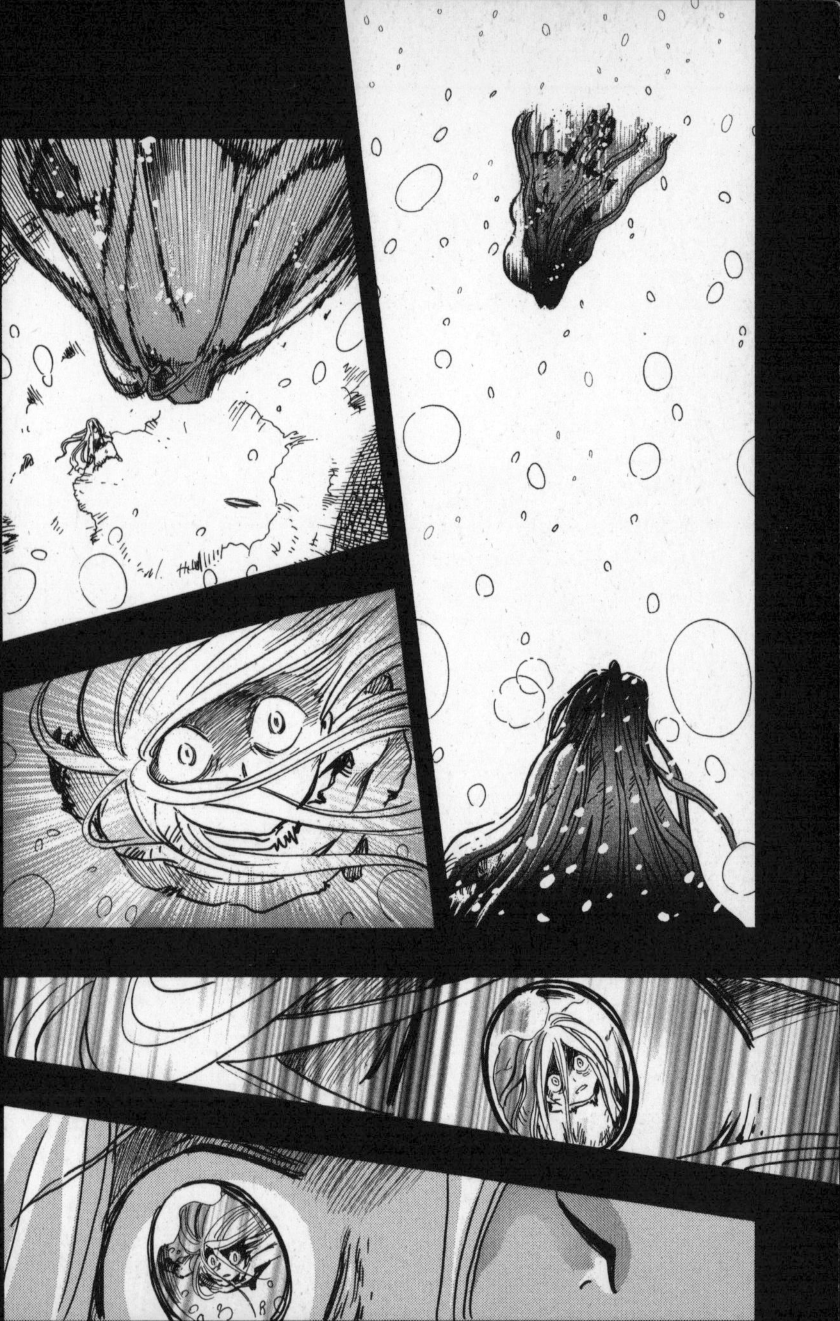

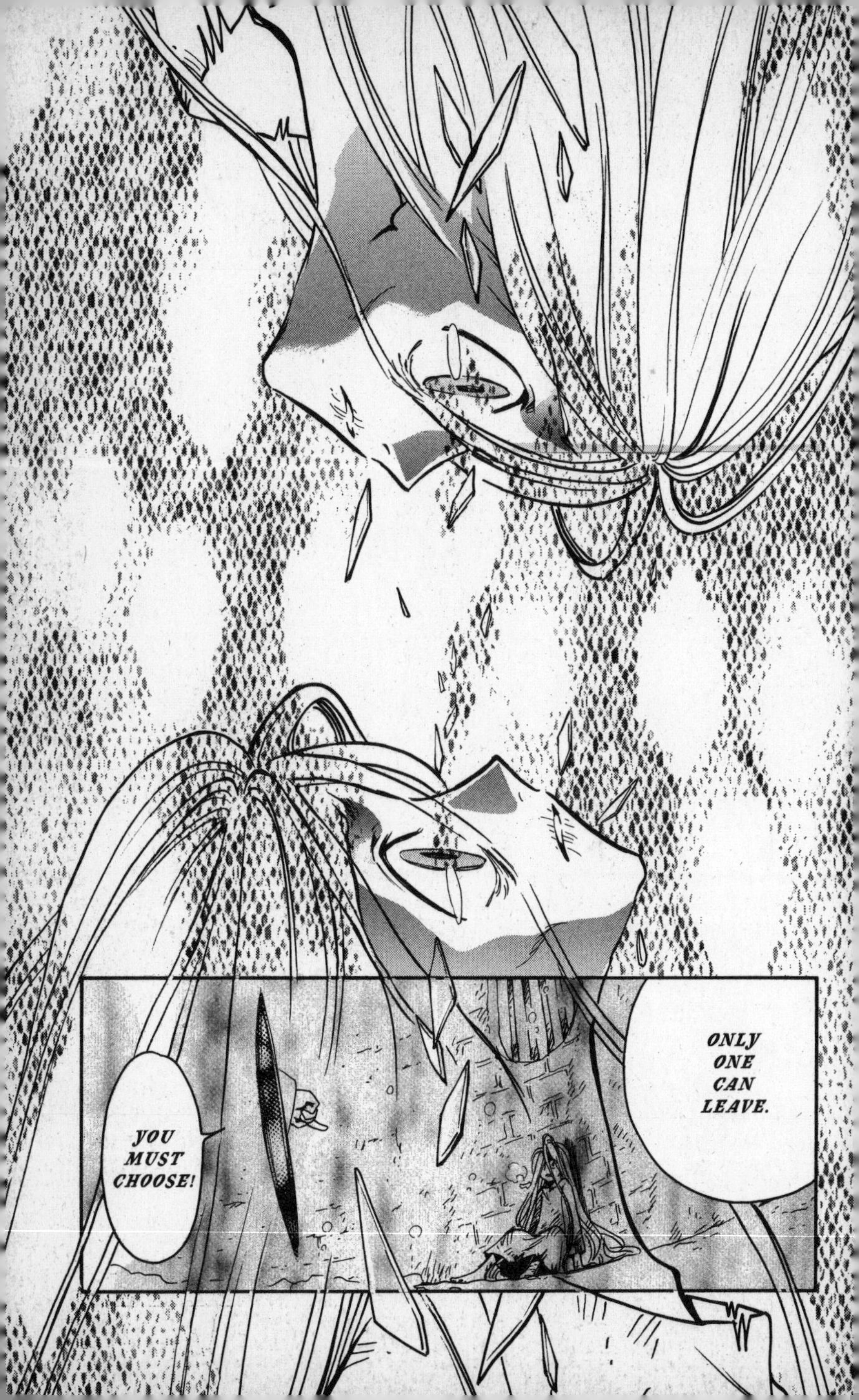
ONLY ONE CAN LEAVE.
YOU MUST CHOOSE!

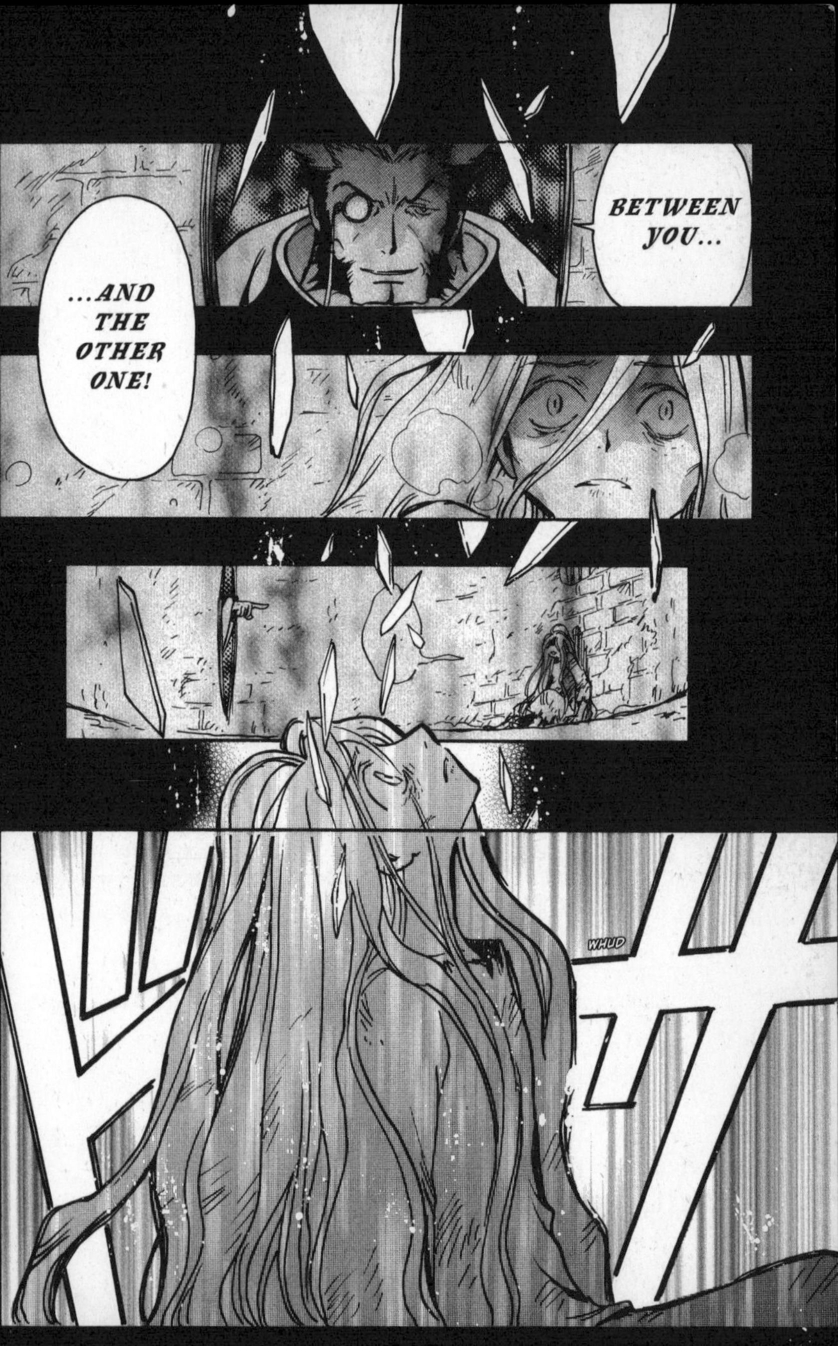
BETWEEN YOU...
...AND THE OTHER ONE!
WHUD

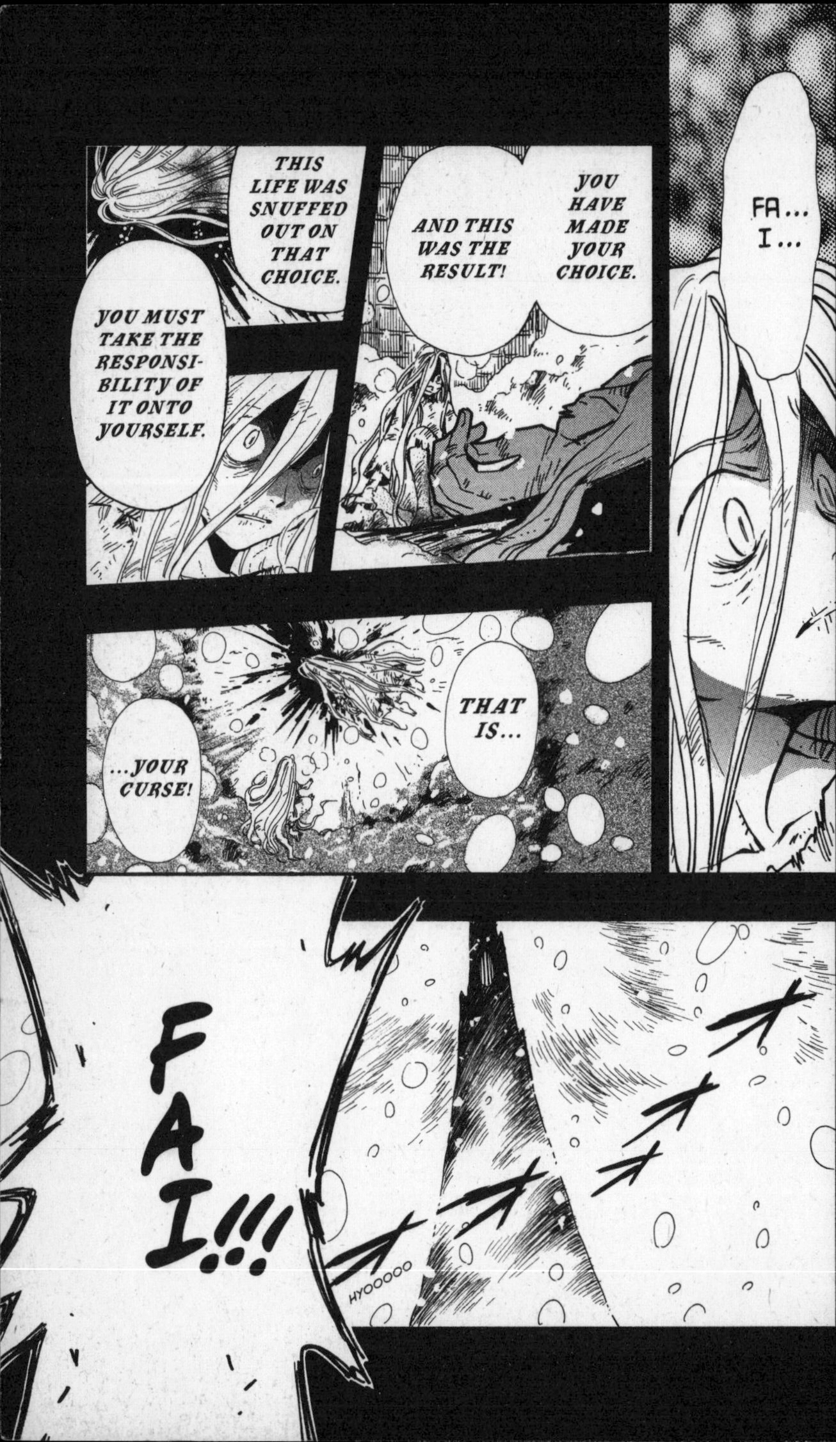
FA... I...
YOU HAVE MADE YOUR CHOICE.
AND THIS WAS THE RESULT!
THIS LIFE WAS SNUFFED OUT ON THAT CHOICE.
YOU MUST TAKE THE RESPONSI-BILITY OF IT ONTO YOURSELF.
THAT IS...
...YOUR CURSE!
FAI!!!
HYOOOOO

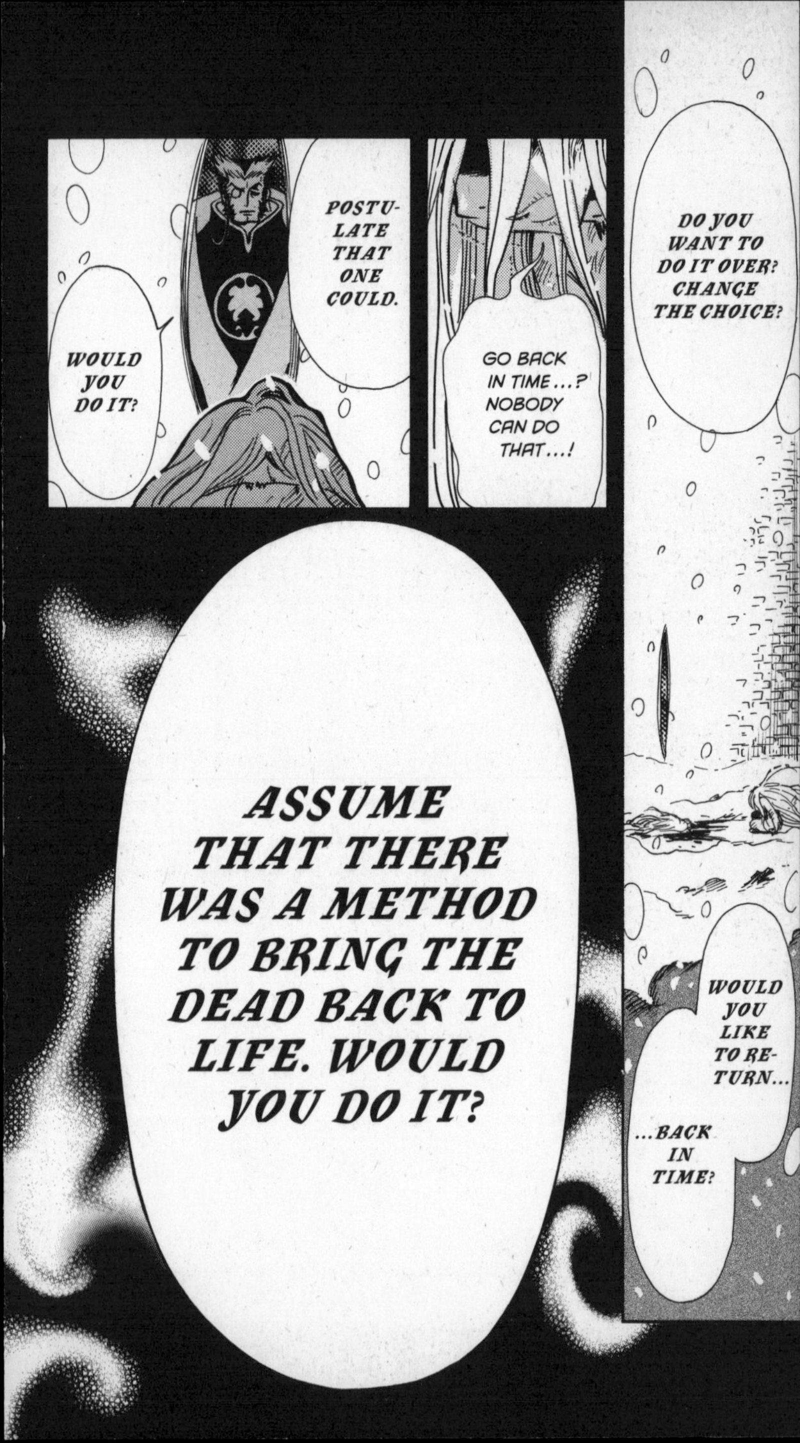
DO YOU WANT TO DO IT OVER? CHANGE THE CHOICE?
WOULD YOU LIKE TO RE-TURN...
...BACK IN TIME?
GO BACK IN TIME...? NOBODY CAN DO THAT...!
POSTU-LATE THAT ONE COULD.
WOULD YOU DO IT?
ASSUME THAT THERE WAS A METHOD TO BRING THE DEAD BACK TO LIFE. WOULD YOU DO IT?

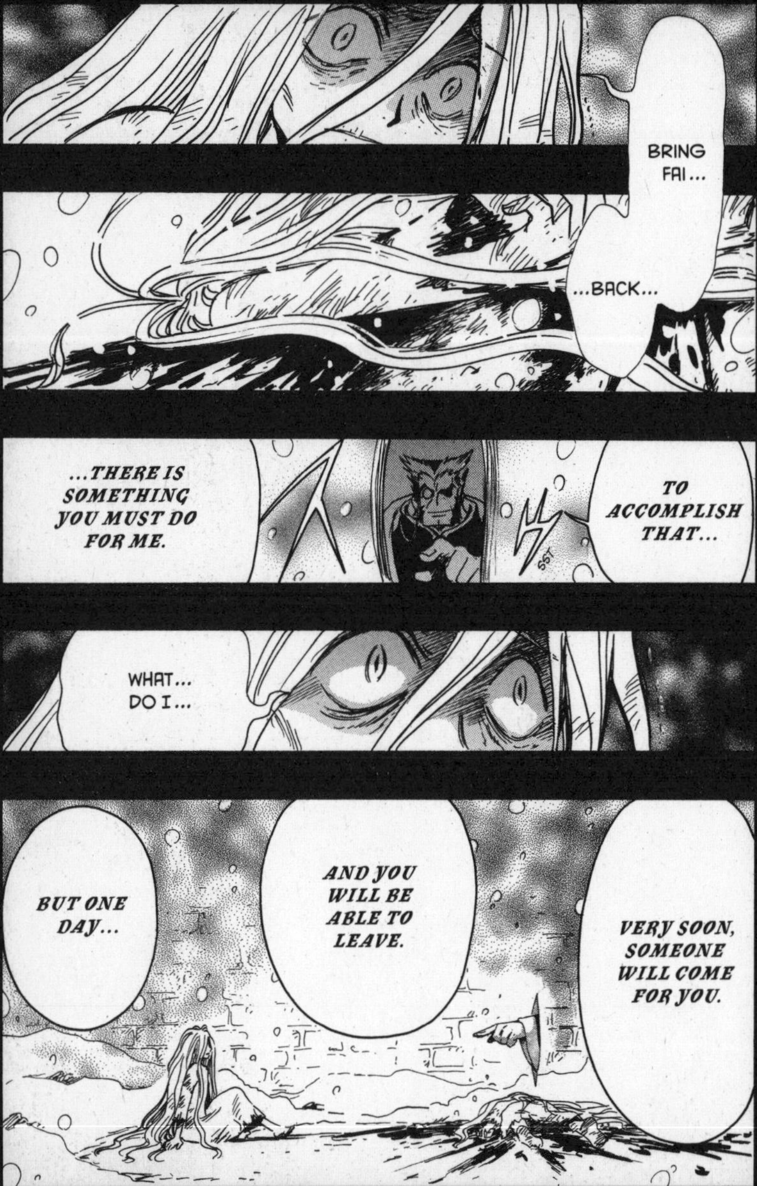
BRING FAI...
...BACK...
TO ACCOMPLISH THAT...
SST
...THERE IS SOMETHING YOU MUST DO FOR ME.
WHAT... DO I...
VERY SOON, SOMEONE WILL COME FOR YOU.
AND YOU WILL BE ABLE TO LEAVE.
BUT ONE DAY...

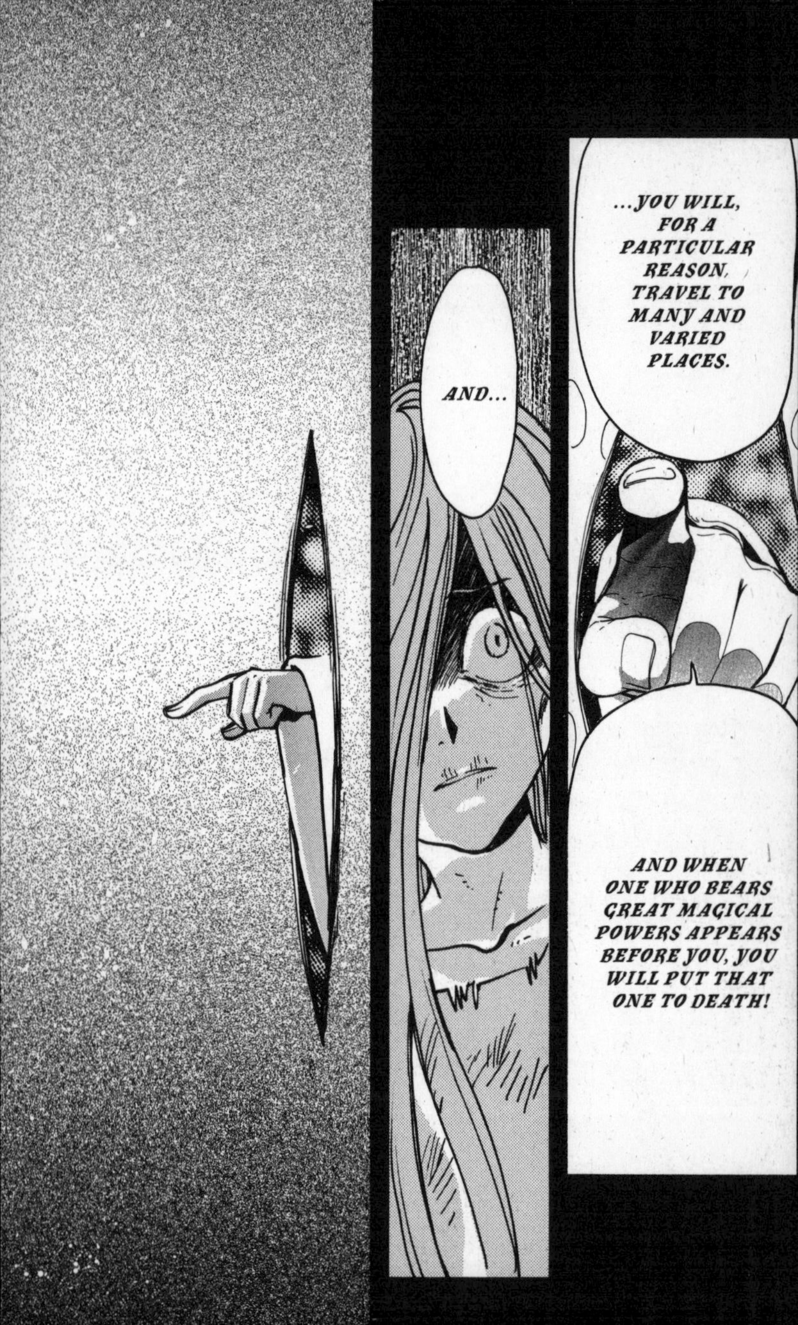
...YOU WILL, FOR A PARTICULAR REASON, TRAVEL TO MANY AND VARIED PLACES.
AND WHEN ONE WHO BEARS GREAT MAGICAL POWERS APPEARS BEFORE YOU, YOU WILL PUT THAT ONE TO DEATH!
AND...

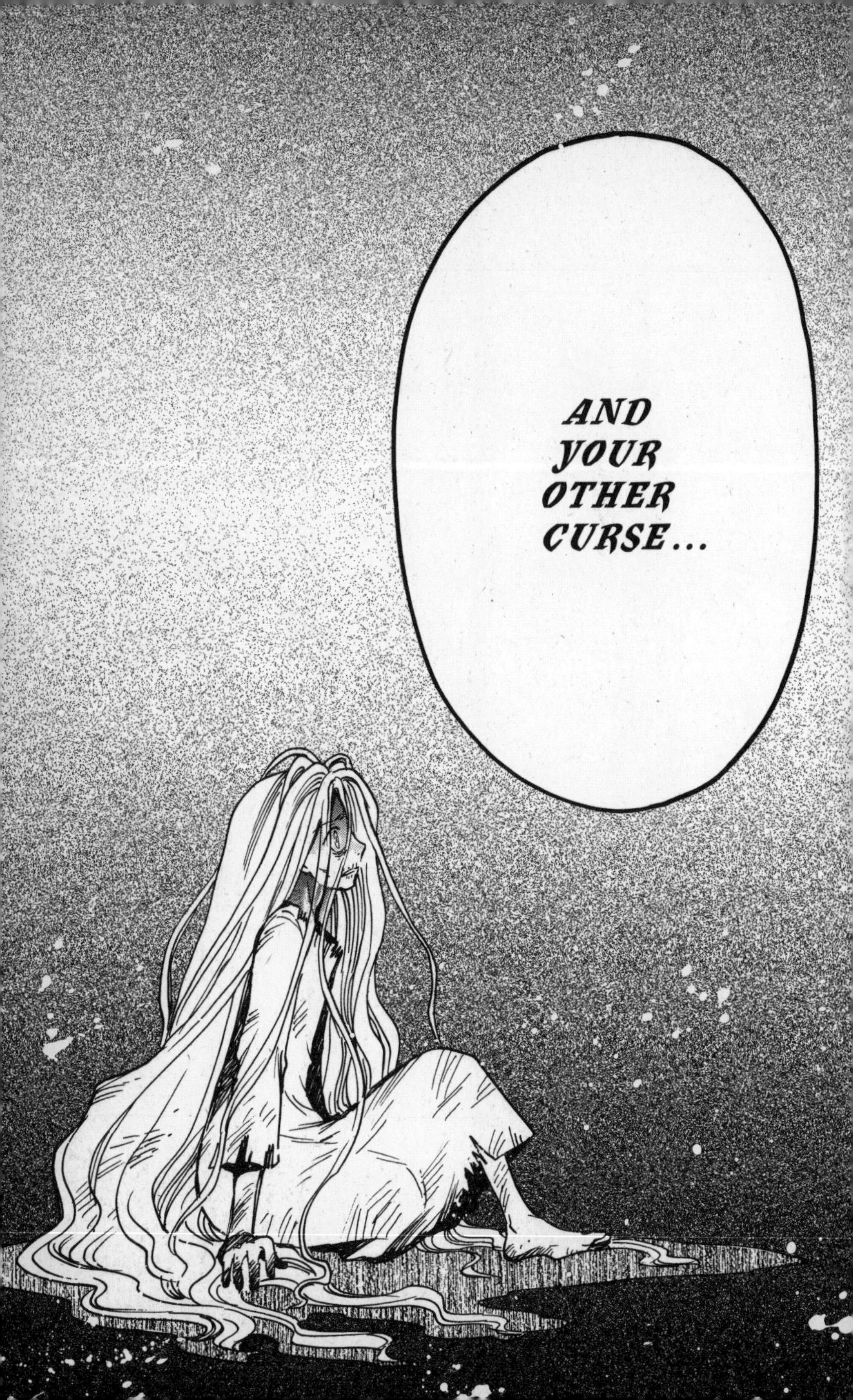
AND YOUR OTHER CURSE...

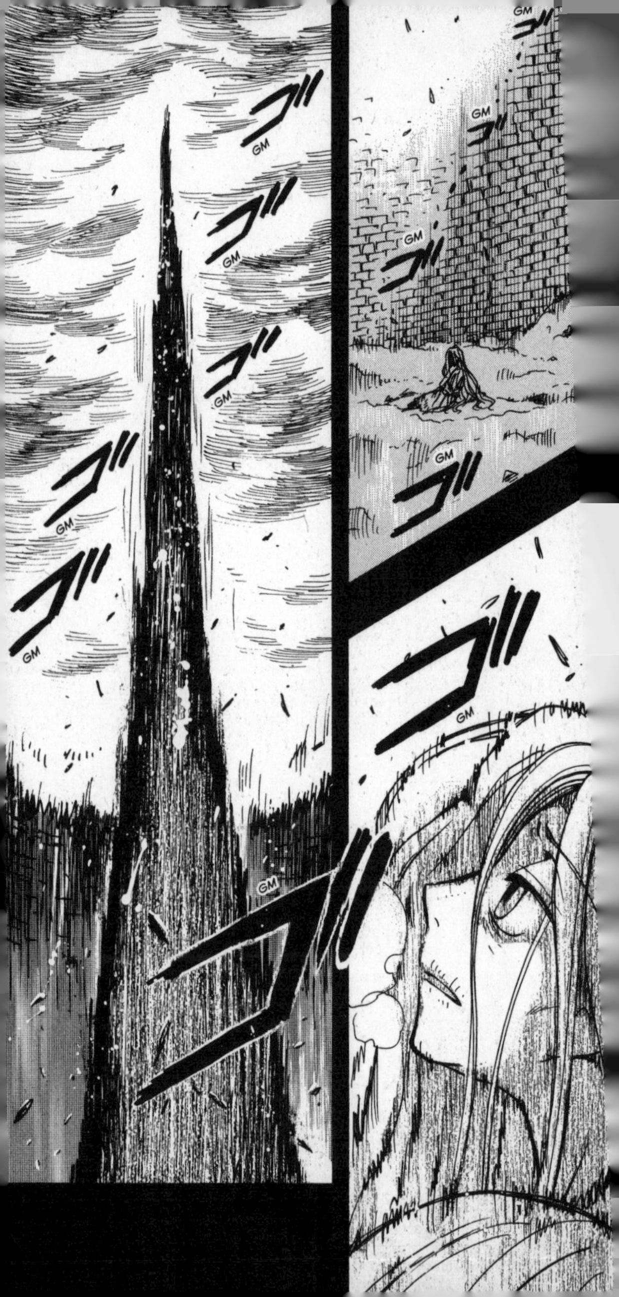

GM ゴ
GM ゴ
GM ゴ
GM ゴ
ゴ GM
ゴ GM
ゴ GM
ゴ GM
ゴ GM
ゴ GM
GM ゴ

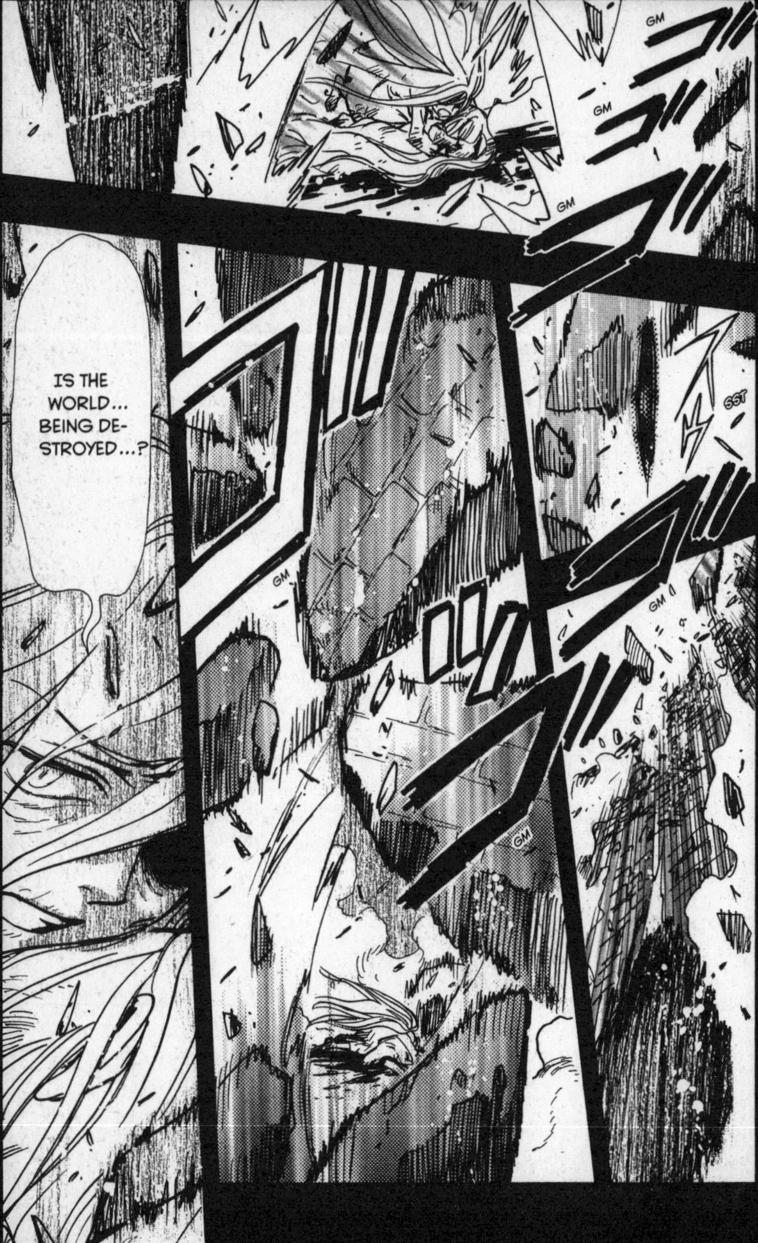
GM
GM
GM
SST
GM
GM
GM
IS THE WORLD... BEING DE-STROYED...?

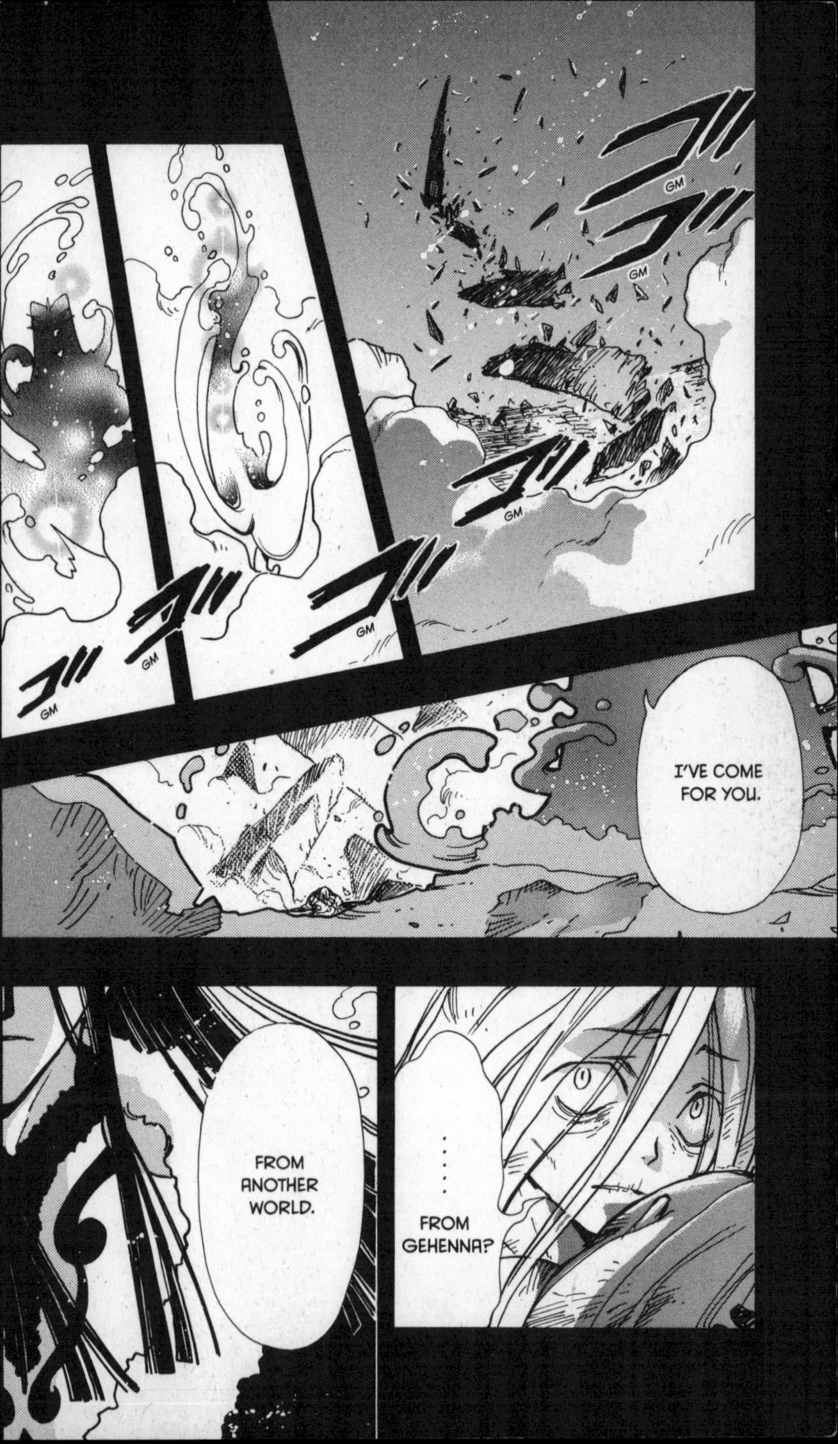

GM
GM
GM
GM
GM
GM
I'VE COME FOR YOU.
......
FROM GEHENNA?
FROM ANOTHER WORLD.

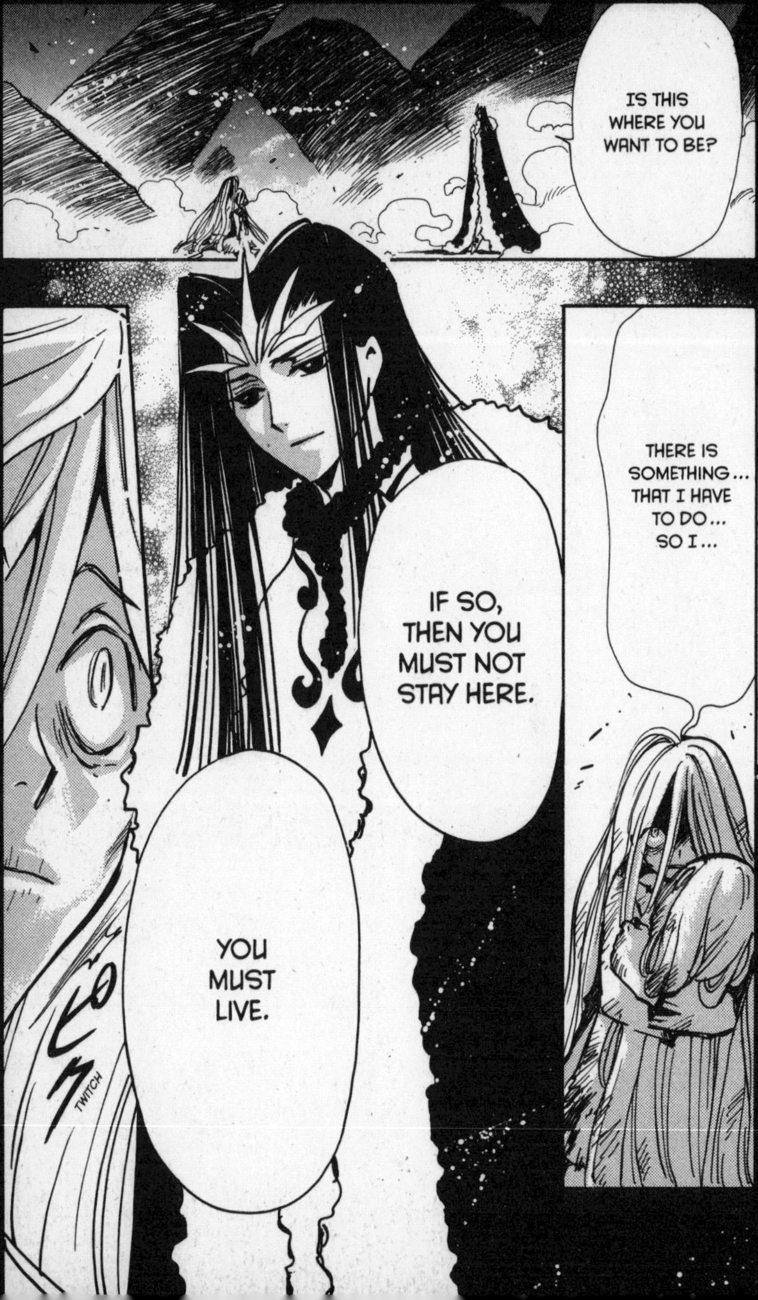
IS THIS WHERE YOU WANT TO BE?
THERE IS SOMETHING... THAT I HAVE TO DO... SO I...
IF SO, THEN YOU MUST NOT STAY HERE.
YOU MUST LIVE.
TWITCH

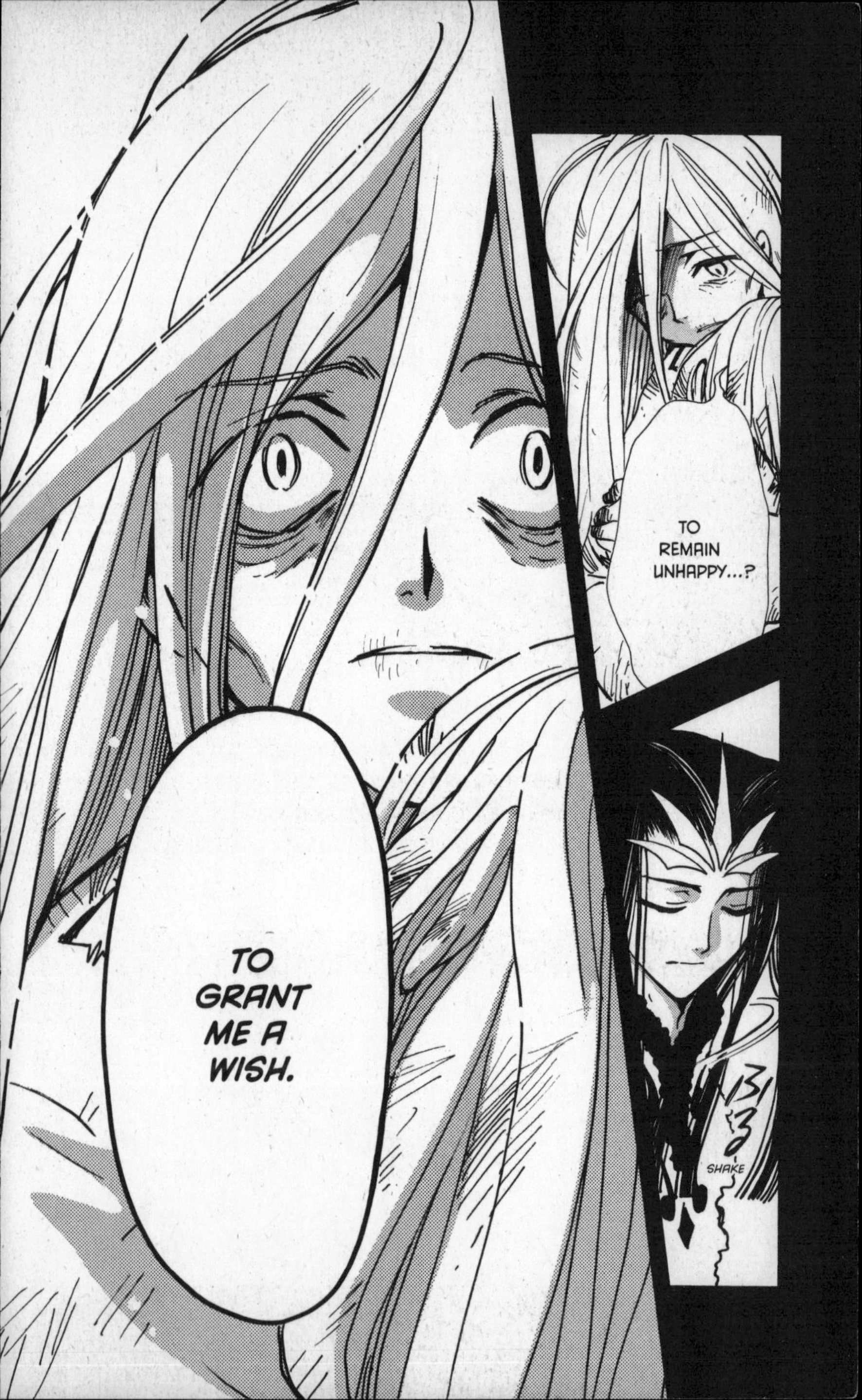
TO REMAIN UNHAPPY...?
SHAKE
TO GRANT ME A WISH.

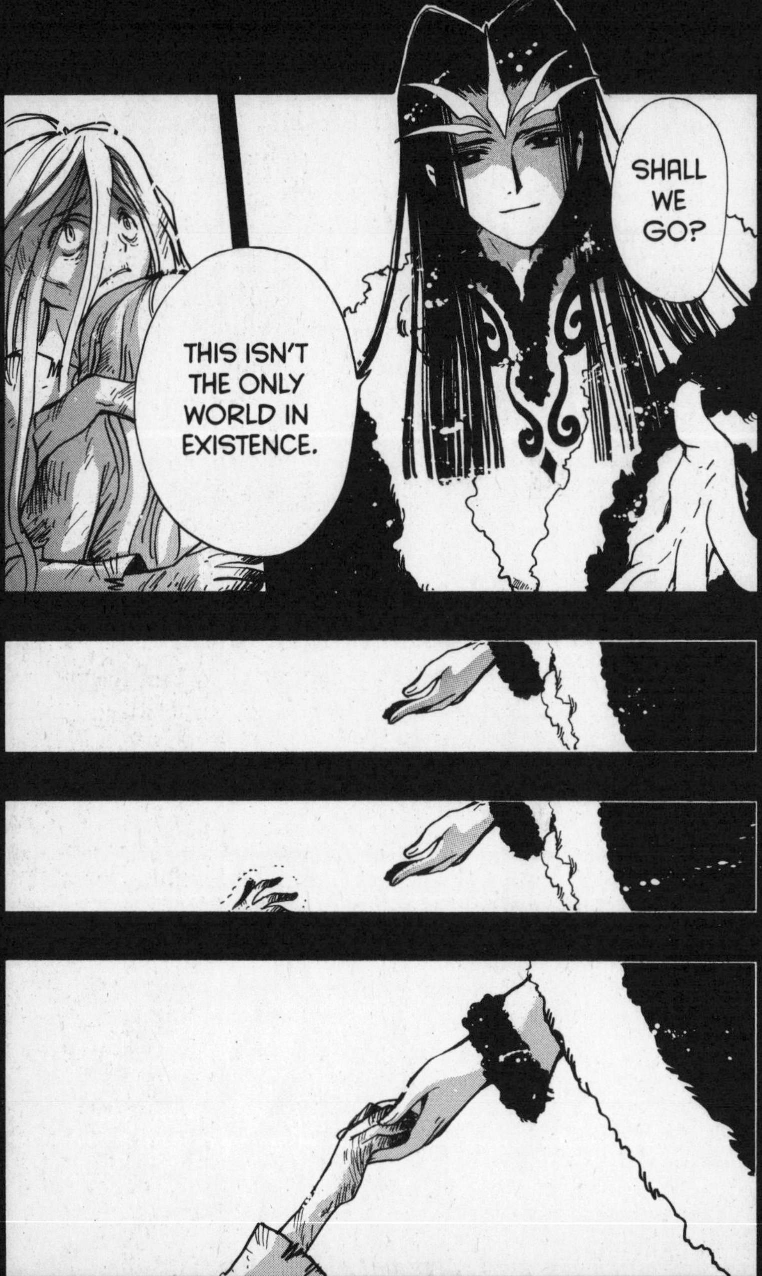
SHALL WE GO?
THIS ISN'T THE ONLY WORLD IN EXISTENCE.

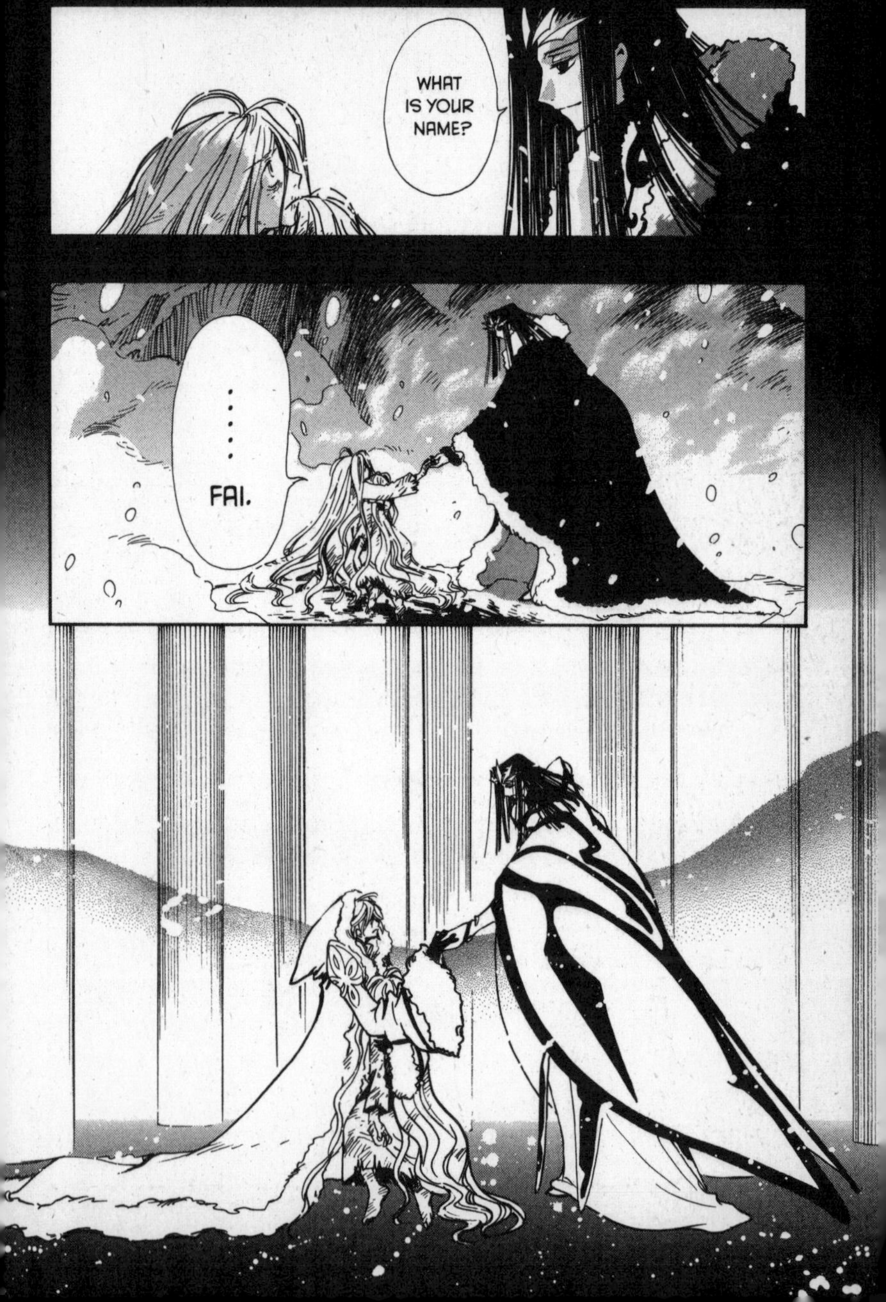
WHAT IS YOUR NAME?
.....
FAI.

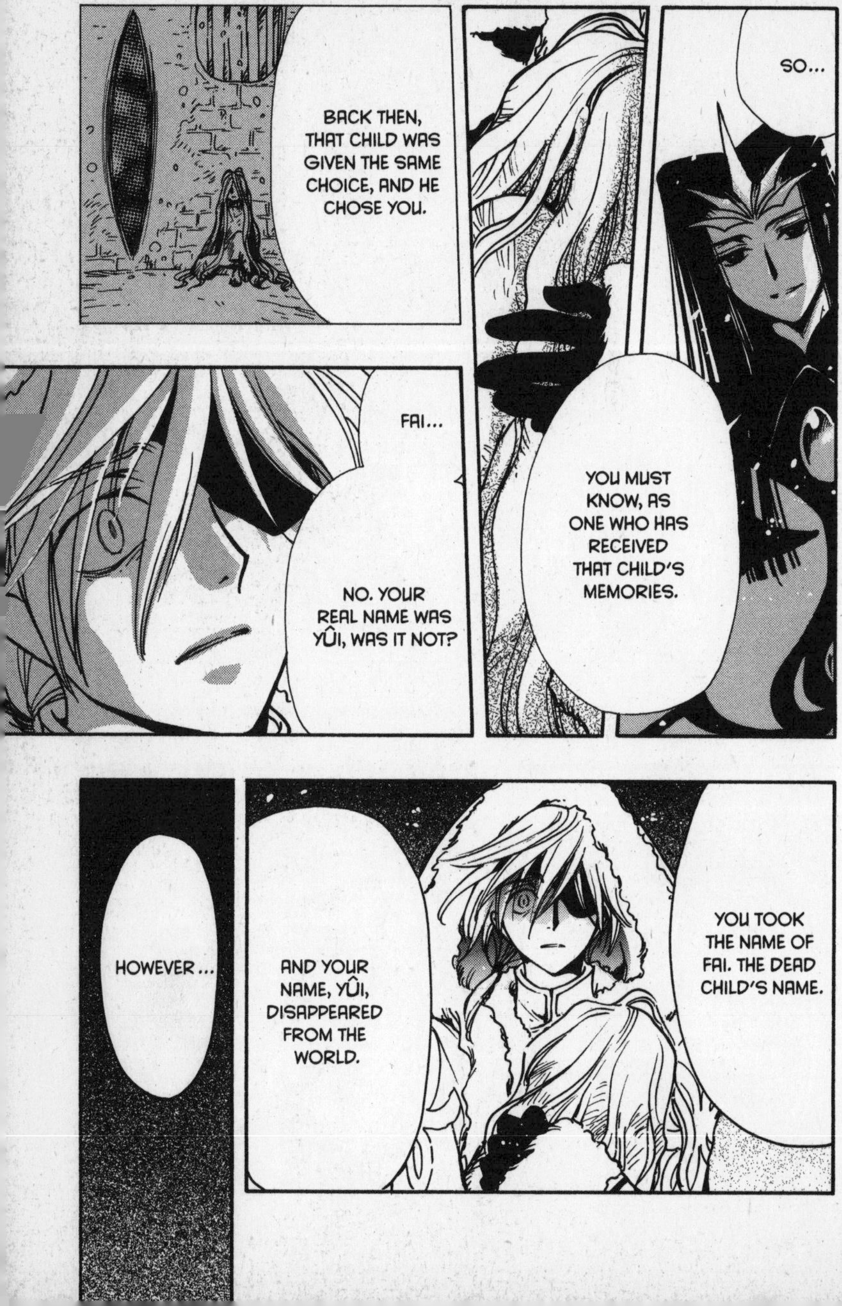
SO...
YOU MUST KNOW, AS ONE WHO HAS RECEIVED THAT CHILD'S MEMORIES.
BACK THEN, THAT CHILD WAS GIVEN THE SAME CHOICE, AND HE CHOSE YOU.
FAI...
NO. YOUR REAL NAME WAS YÛI, WAS IT NOT?
YOU TOOK THE NAME OF FAI. THE DEAD CHILD'S NAME.
AND YOUR NAME, YÛI, DISAPPEARED FROM THE WORLD.
HOWEVER...

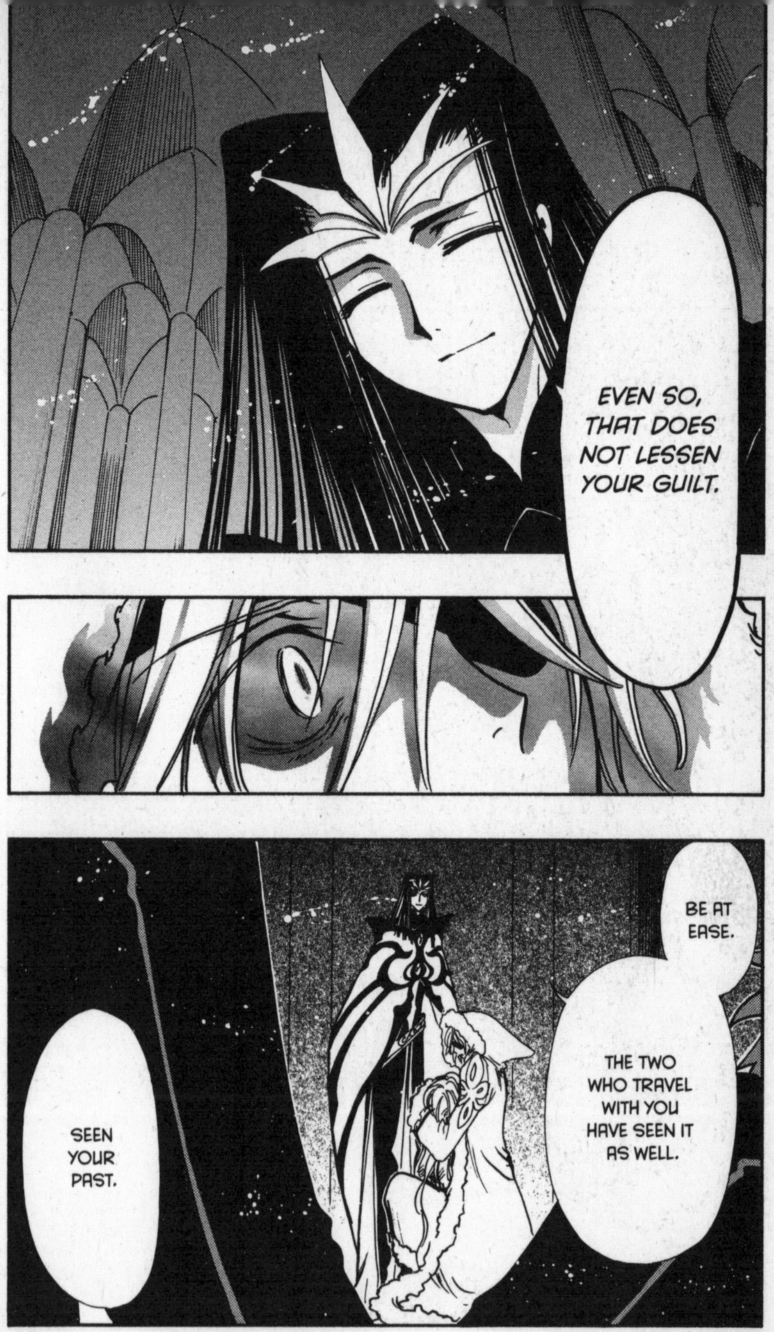
EVEN SO, THAT DOES NOT LESSEN YOUR GUILT.
BE AT EASE.
THE TWO WHO TRAVEL WITH YOU HAVE SEEN IT AS WELL.
SEEN YOUR PAST.

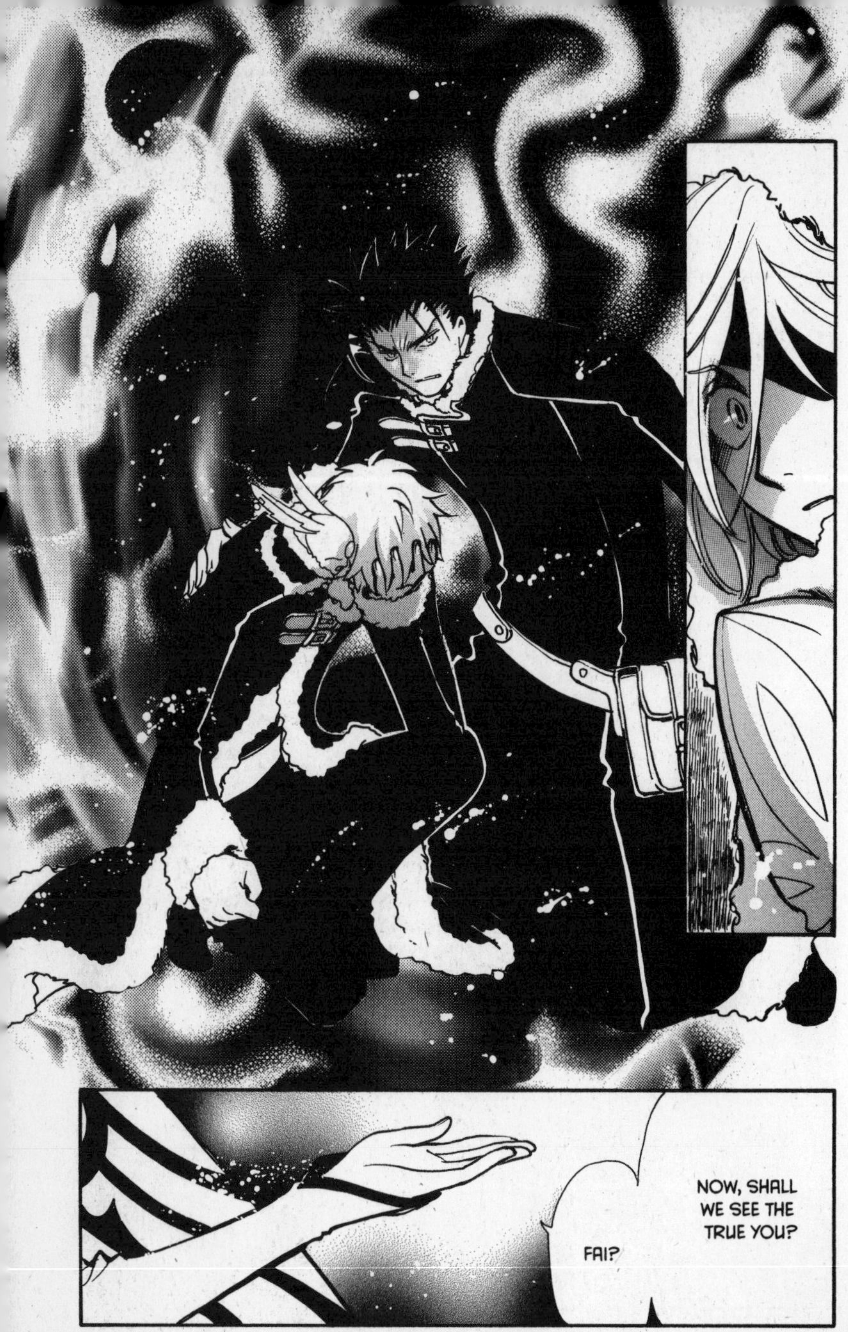
NOW, SHALL WE SEE THE TRUE YOU?
FAI?

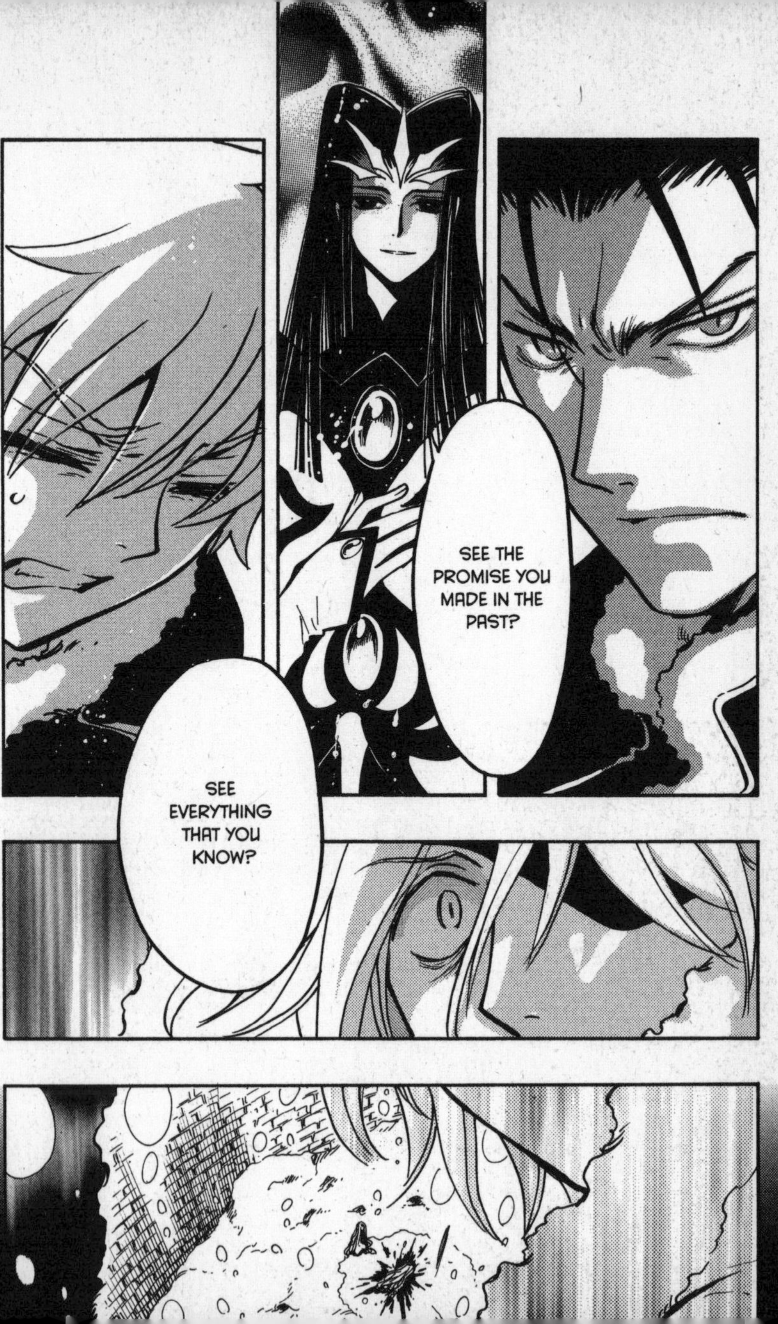
SEE THE PROMISE YOU MADE IN THE PAST?
SEE EVERYTHING THAT YOU KNOW?

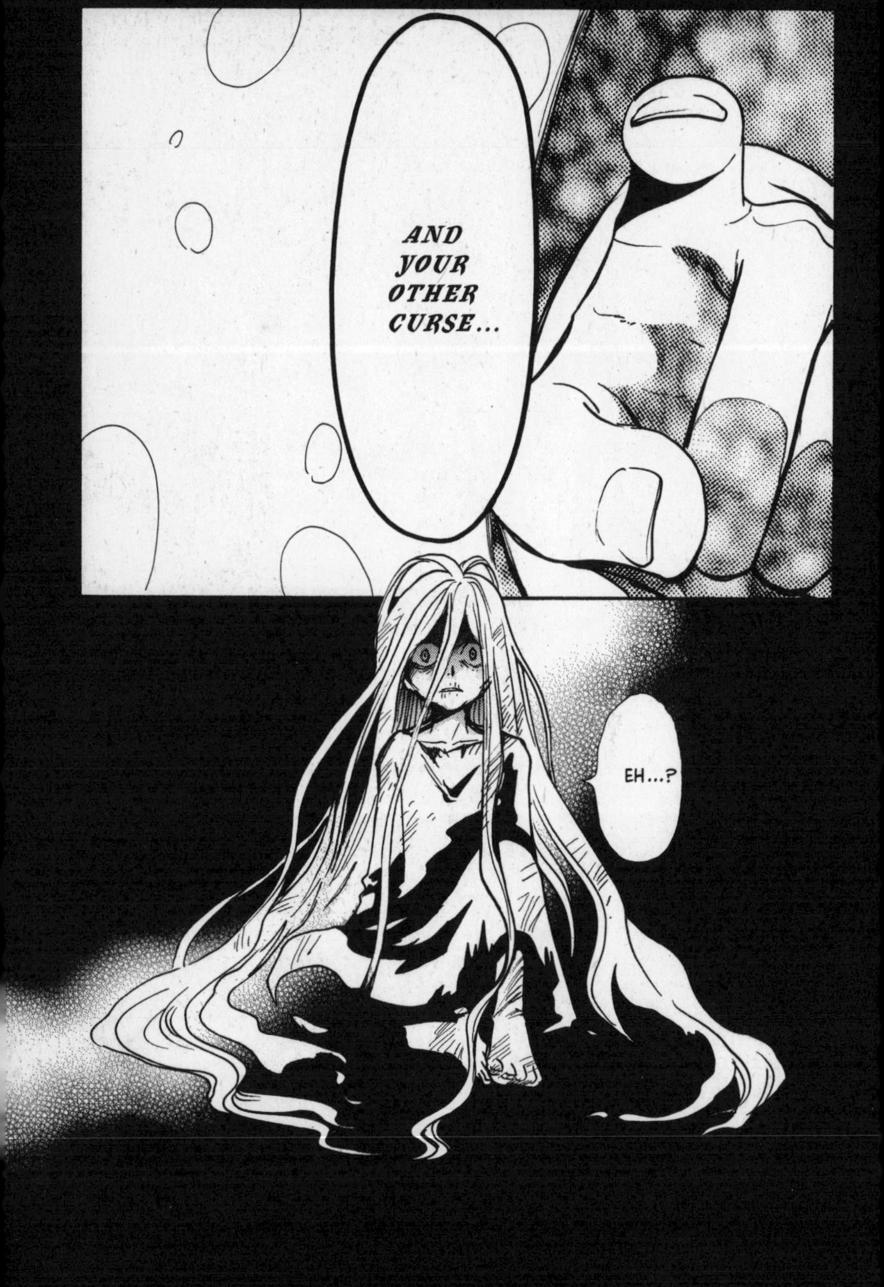
AND YOUR OTHER CURSE...
EH...?

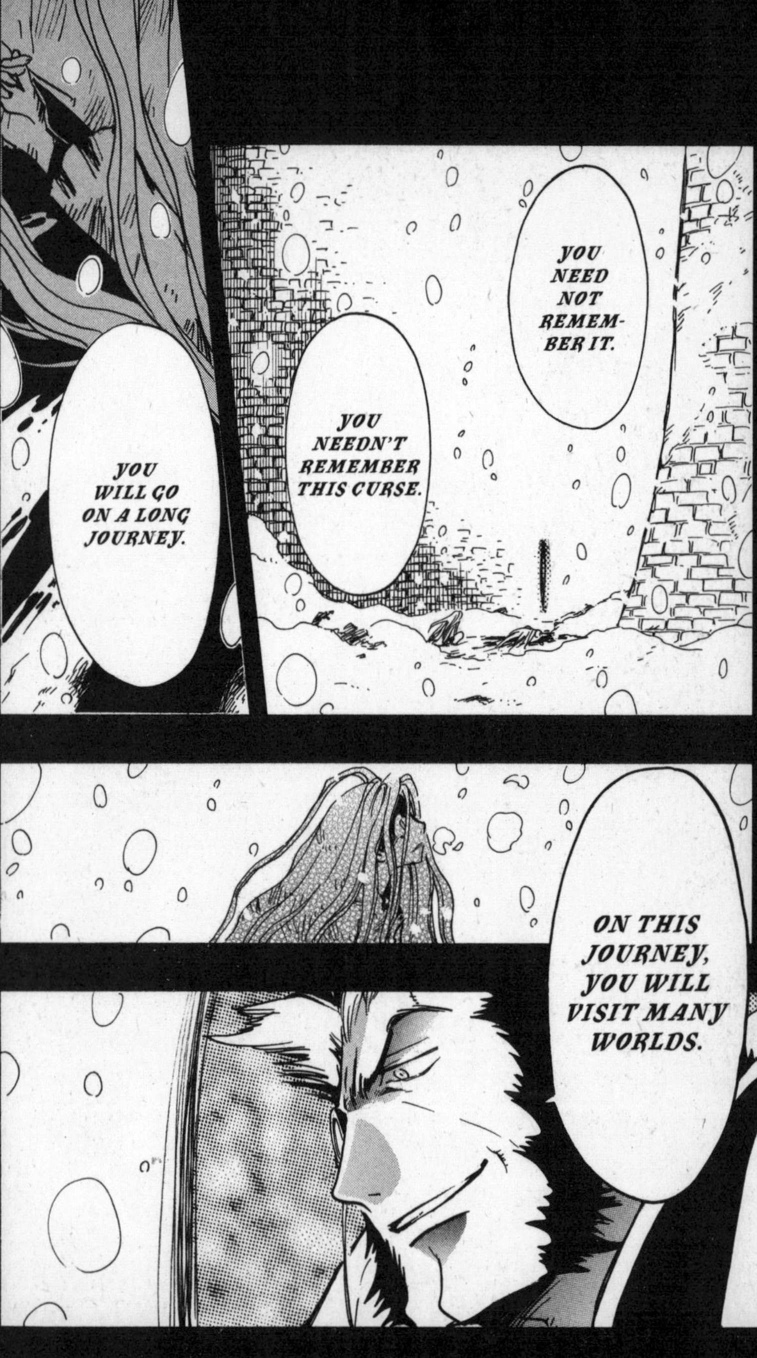
YOU NEED NOT REMEM-BER IT.
YOU NEEDN'T REMEMBER THIS CURSE.
YOU WILL GO ON A LONG JOURNEY.
ON THIS JOURNEY, YOU WILL VISIT MANY WORLDS.

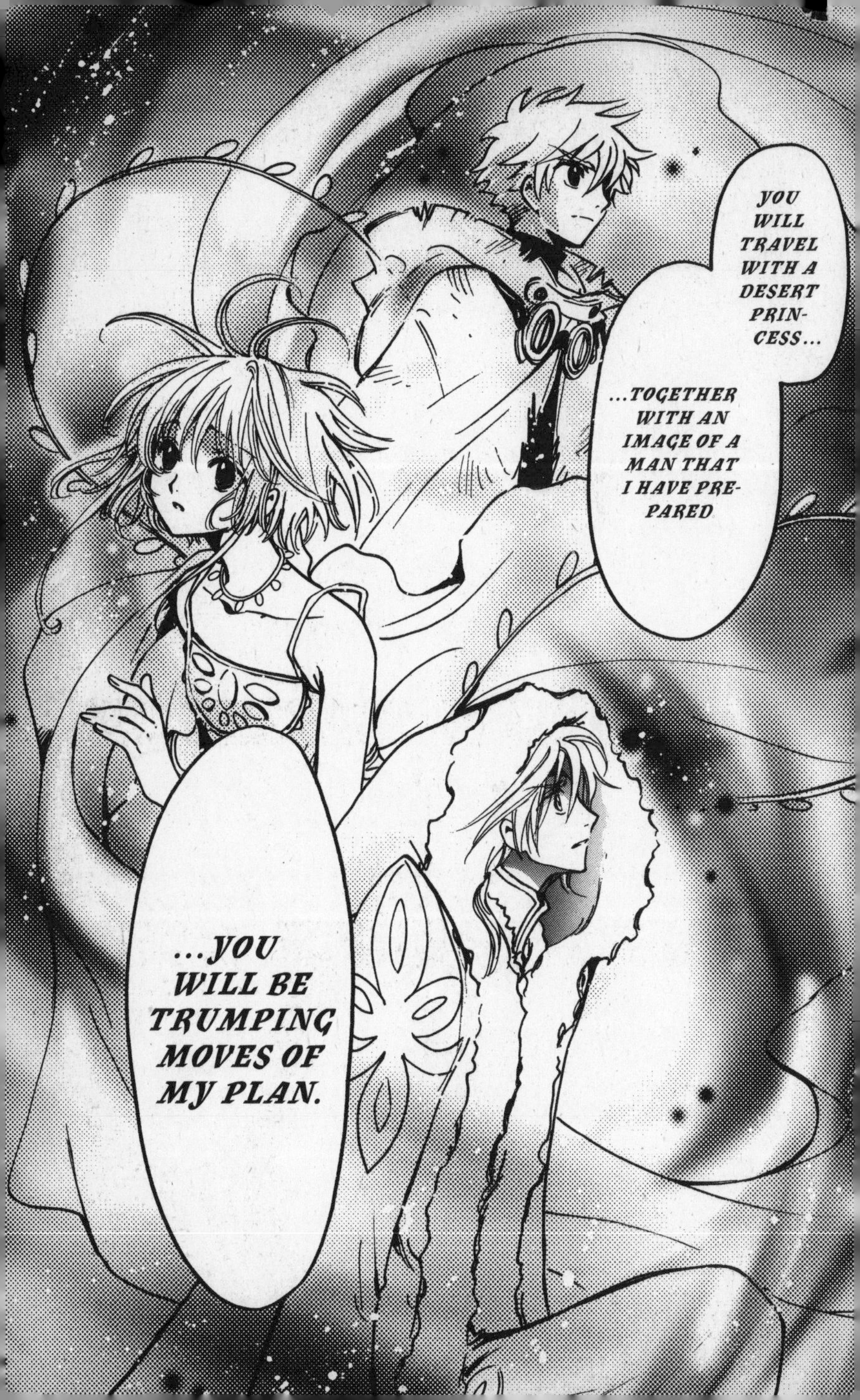
YOU WILL TRAVEL WITH A DESERT PRIN-CESS...
...TOGETHER WITH AN IMAGE OF A MAN THAT I HAVE PRE-PARED
...YOU WILL BE TRUMPING MOVES OF MY PLAN.

To Be Continued

About the Creators

CLAMP is a group of four women who have become the most popular manga artists in America—Nanase Ohkawa, Mokona, Satsuki Igarashi, and Tsubaki Nekoi. They started out as *doujinshi* (fan comics) creators, but their skill and craft brought them to the attention of publishers very quickly. Their first work from a major publisher was *RG Veda*, but their first mass success was with *Magic Knight Rayearth*. From there, they went on to write many series, including Cardcaptor Sakura and Chobits, two of the most popular manga in the United States. Like many Japanese manga artists, they prefer to avoid the spotlight, and little is known about them personally.

CLAMP is currently publishing three series in Japan: Tsubasa and xxxHOLiC with Kodansha and Gohou Drug with Kadokawa.

Translation Notes

Japanese is a tricky language for most Westerners, and translation is often more art than science. For your edification and reading pleasure, here are notes on some of the places where we could have gone in a different direction in our translation of the work, or where a Japanese cultural reference is used.

Luval, page 84

As mentioned before in these notes, we don't get any notice of how CLAMP intends to spell the names of characters and places until the spelling appears somewhere in the artwork or until the Character Guide comes out. Until then the best we can do is make a best guess as to the spelling. This name, Luval, could have been Ruvalle, Ruvar, Luvare, among many other spellings. Luval seemed close to the *katakana* spelling and sounded appropriate.

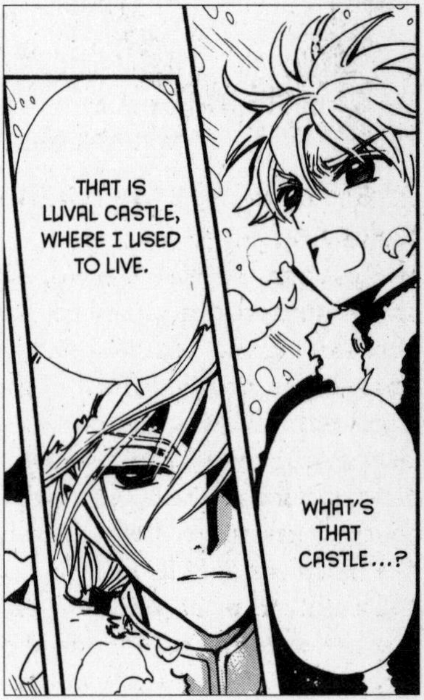
WHAT'S THAT CASTLE...?
THAT IS LUVAL CASTLE, WHERE I USED TO LIVE.

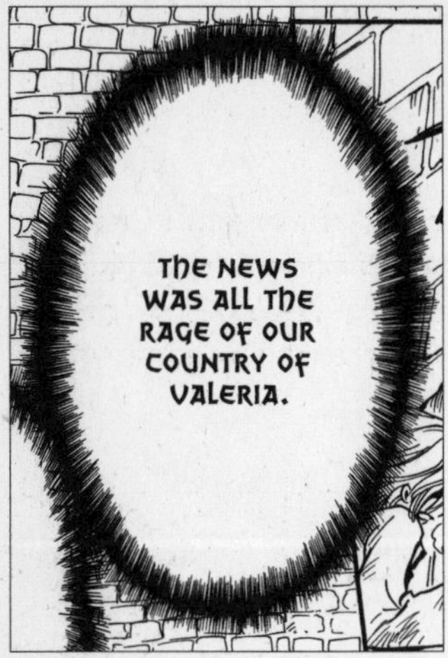
THE NEWS WAS ALL THE RAGE OF OUR COUNTRY OF VALERIA.

Valeria, page 102

As in the note for Luval on the previous page, we must make our best guess on this name and hope it matches with CLAMP's official spellings to come later. Again, for this name, any number of spellings were equally plausible, but Valeria seemed like a reasonable guess and quite close to the *katakana* spelling.

Elder Prince, Sovereign, Consort, page 102

In this case, the words are direct translations of the Japanese, but considering the wealth of names that English has for royalty, I thought some pattern other than king, queen, and crown prince would lend a slightly different atmosphere to the translation. It also solved a few problems with translating the Japanese since the word for Fai's mother, *Okisaki,* could indeed mean queen, but also means a woman who bears the king's children but has no political power of her own. And since Japanese has a word for queen, *joô,* "consort" seemed to fit the situation better.

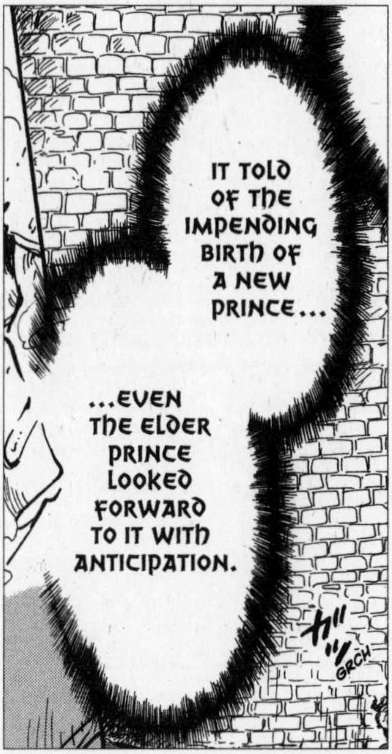
IT TOLD OF THE IMPENDING BIRTH OF A NEW PRINCE...
...EVEN THE ELDER PRINCE LOOKED FORWARD TO IT WITH ANTICIPATION.
GRCH

FROM ANOTHER WORLD.

: FROM GEHENNA?

Gehenna, page 168

Unlike the titles on page 183 such as "sovereign," the word Gehenna was not chosen by the translator but by CLAMP. In the Japanese version of this book, Gehenna, the name of Valeria's hell, was written out as *furigana* (the pronunciation guide for the *kanji* in the Japanese word balloon) next to the *kanji* compound meaning "hell."

BY YUKO OSADA

SEE THE WORLD WITH ME!

Kakashi is a small-town boy with a big dream: to travel around the world. He's so determined to leave his little island home behind that he stows away onboard a marvelous zeppelin—one that just happens to be loaded with treasure and a gang of ruthless criminals!

Special extras in each volume! Read them all!

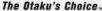

TOMARE!

[STOP!]

You're going the wrong way!

Manga is a completely different type of reading experience.

To start at the *beginning*,
go to the *end*!

That's right! Authentic manga is read the traditional Japanese way—from right to left. Exactly the *opposite* of how American books are read. It's easy to follow: Just go to the other end of the book, and read each page—and each panel—from right side to left side, starting at the top right. Now you're experiencing manga as it was meant to be!